MODERNISM AND AMERICAN MID-20TH CENTURY SACRED ARCHITECTURE

Mid-20th century sacred architecture in America sought to bridge modernism with religion by abstracting cultural and faith traditions and pushing the envelope in the design of houses of worship. Modern architects embraced the challenges of creating sacred spaces that incorporated liturgical changes, evolving congregations, modern architecture, and innovations in building technology.

The book describes the unique context and design aspects of the departure from historicism, and the renewal of heritage and traditions with ground-breaking structural features, deliberate optical effects and modern aesthetics. The contributions, from a pre-eminent group of scholars and practitioners from the US, Australia, and Europe are based on original archival research, historical documents, and field visits to the buildings discussed. Investigating how the authority of the divine was communicated through new forms of architectural design, these examinations map the materiality of liturgical change and communal worship during the mid-20th century.

Anat Geva, Ph.D., is a registered architect and a Professor of Architecture at Texas A&M University, where she teaches design, sacred architecture, history of building technology, and preservation. She has a long list of publications including a book, *Frank Lloyd Wright's Sacred Architecture: Faith, Form, and Building Technology*, published in 2012. She co-founded and co-edited the journal of the National Council of Preservation Education *Preservation Education & Research (PER)*, and was a co-editor of *ARRIS* (SESAH's Journal). She was one of the founders of the Forum on Architecture, Culture, and Spirituality (ACS) and served as a member on their executive committee. She is the past president of the Southeast Chapter of the Society of Architectural Historians (SESAH), and past secretary of the National Council for Preservation Education (NCPE).

"This book engages what may be considered the most innovative, challenging, and experimental period in the history of sacred architecture: mid-20th century America. In the span of a few decades, completely new and hitherto unimaginable examples of sacred buildings and art came into existence! Perusing the excellent case studies featured in the book makes us not only appreciate the amazing architectural, cultural, liturgical, and theological revolution underway but also understand its major forces, characters, stories, successes, and failures. The text is fascinating, accessible, clear, well organized, and nicely illustrated. The contributors are excellent scholars with high reputations. As a result, Dr. Anat Geva's book is a tour-de-force for any architecture practitioner, scholar, educator, or student interested in modern and contemporary sacred spaces."

— Julio Bermudez, Ph.D. Professor, Director Cultural Studies & Sacred Space
Graduate Concentration, The Catholic University of America

"In this significant volume, editor Anat Geva has widened our view of American sacred architecture in the mid-twentieth century with new scholarship that reappraises the promises and limits of modern architecture in our experience of the religious and spiritual. In case studies across 14 chapters, the authors grapple with the application of modernist form, materiality, and art to religious worship, revealing solutions that often bridged modernity and tradition and the local and universal. With new research on Mies van der Rohe, Johnson, Saarinen, Belluschi, Rudolph, and Mendelsohn as well as lesser-known architects, this book challenges us to think anew about how architecture sought to make God immanent to our modern world."

— Margaret M. Grubiak, Ph.D., Associate Professor, Architectural History,
Villanova University

"For too long, sacred architecture in modernism has been overlooked and underappreciated. Thanks to Professor Geva's work, that will no longer be the case. This groundbreaking collection raises major issues for continued discussion and exploration."

— Ben Heimsath, Principal, Heimsath Architects, Austin, Texas

MODERNISM AND AMERICAN MID-20TH CENTURY SACRED ARCHITECTURE

Edited by Anat Geva

Routledge
Taylor & Francis Group

LONDON AND NEW YORK

First edition published 2019
by Routledge
2 Park Square, Milton Park, Abingdon, Oxon, OX14 4RN

and by Routledge
711 Third Avenue, New York, NY 10017

Routledge is an imprint of the Taylor & Francis Group, an informa business

© 2019 Anat Geva

British Library Cataloguing-in-Publication Data
A catalogue record for this book is available from the British Library

Library of Congress Cataloging-in-Publication Data
A catalog record has been requested for this book

ISBN: 978-1-138-06280-1 (hbk)
ISBN: 978-1-138-06281-8 (pbk)
ISBN: 978-1-315-16143-3 (ebk)

Typeset in Bembo
by Swales & Willis Ltd, Exeter, Devon, UK

Religion is entitled to an architectural style of its own, expressing its searching for God.

Frank Lloyd Wright 1958/1992: 229

CONTENTS

FIGURES

CONTRIBUTORS

Ross Anderson, Ph.D., is a senior lecturer in architectural design, history and theory at the University of Sydney. Having completed his Ph.D. at the University of Cambridge with a thesis entitled "From the Bauhütte to the Bauhaus," his research on modern German and American architecture has been published in edited books and in journals including *AA Files*, *The Journal of Architecture* and *Art Bulletin*.

Ann Marie Borys, Ph.D., is an architect and Associate Professor at the University of Washington, where she teaches architectural design, history and theory, and professional practice. Her book, *Vincenzo Scamozzi and the Chorography of Early Modern Architecture*, was published in 2014.

Mary Reid Brunstrom is completing a Ph.D. in art history at Washington University in St. Louis, with a focus on modern sacred architecture in St. Louis. Recent publications include "Modern Architecture in St. Louis, 1928–1968: An Expanded View," a catalogue essay for the Saint Louis Art Museum's 2015 exhibition entitled *St. Louis Modern*. The publication received Missouri Preservation's 2017 Osmund Overby Award for documentation and interpretation of mid-century modern architecture.

Arthur J. Clement, AIA, is a registered architect, campus planner, construction manager, and architectural historian. He completed a campus heritage study for Tuskegee University who was awarded a grant from the Getty Foundation in Los Angeles, CA. He is currently writing a book on the campus development, architecture, public art and cultural landscapes of Georgia's ten black colleges and universities.

Lindsay Cook, Ph.D., was educated at Vassar College (B.A.) and Columbia University (M.A., M.Phil., Ph.D.) in New York. She is an art historian who specializes in medieval architecture and medievalism in modern and contemporary architecture. She recently completed her dissertation, "Architectural Citation of Notre-Dame of Paris in the Land of the Paris Cathedral Chapter."

Roderick D. Fluker, AIA, LEED AP, is a practicing architect and Associate Professor at Tuskegee University's Robert R. Taylor School of Architecture and Construction Science. He teaches environmental systems and technologies for buildings, design studio, and historic preservation. Fluker is a past recipient of the NCARB Award for creative integration of architectural issues central to practice within the academy. He received a B.Arch. from Tuskegee University and a M.Arch. from the University of Illinois at Chicago.

Anat Geva, Ph.D., is a registered architect and a Professor of Architecture at Texas A&M University, where she teaches design, sacred architecture, history of building technology, and preservation. She has a long list of publications including a book *Frank Lloyd Wright's Sacred Architecture: Faith, Form, and Building Technology* published in 2012. She co-founded and co-edited the journal of the National Council of Preservation Education *Preservation Education & Research (PER)*, and was a co-editor of *ARRIS* (SESAH's Journal). She was one of the founders of the Forum on Architecture, Culture, and Spirituality (ACS) and served as a member on their executive committee. She is the past president of the Southeast Chapter of the Society of Architectural Historians (SESAH), and past secretary of the National Council for Preservation Education (NCPE).

Michael J. Gibson is an independent scholar and cultural historian whose fields of interest include sacred architecture and landscapes and California architecture and urbanism. He holds degrees from USC School of Architecture, UCLA School of Law, and Loyola Marymount University. Currently a lawyer in private practice in Southern California, he is actively involved in several academic, governmental, and advocacy organizations linked to architectural history and heritage conservation.

Jason John Paul Haskins, AIA, LEED AP BD+C, holds a B.S. in Architectural Studies and an M.Arch. from the University of Texas with a research emphasis on the architecture of the nineteenth- and twentieth-century liturgical movements. He writes about liturgy, architecture, and history on the blog Locus Iste (http://locusiste.org). Jason currently practices with Bercy Chen Studio in Austin where he focuses on architect-led development of mixed-use affordable housing.

Jeremy Kargon is Associate Professor at Morgan State University's School of Architecture and Planning. Between 2014 and 2018, he served as the SA+P's Director for the Graduate Program in Architecture. Kargon's scholarship explores architecture's representation and its different manifestations. Current projects include studying the relationship between art and architecture, and documenting the impact of new environmental technologies upon architecture and planning.

Dean G. Lampros, Ph.D., completed his doctoral work in American and New England Studies at Boston University in 2013 and his BA in American History from the University of Pennsylvania in 1991. He is an independent scholar whose ongoing research focuses on intersections between the cultural landscape, material culture, consumer culture, ethnicity, and historic preservation. He divides his time between a home in Boston and a farm on Block Island.

Scott Murray is Associate Professor of Architecture at the University of Illinois at Urbana-Champaign. His research focuses on the cultural significance of architectural technology of the last hundred years, with an emphasis on innovative building-envelope design. He is the author of the books *Contemporary Curtain Wall Architecture* (2009) and *Translucent Building Skins* (2013). He received the M.Arch. degree from Harvard University's Graduate School of Design.

Gabriele Neri, Ph.D., is an architect, with a Ph.D. in History of Architecture and Urban Planning, is Adjunct Professor of History of Design and Architecture at the Polytechnic of Milan, Italy, since 2011. He is researcher and lecturer at the Mendrisio Academy of Architecture, Switzerland. He has published several essays and books about Pier Luigi Nervi, and has also edited an anthology of Nervi's writings and the reissue of his famous book *Scienza o arte del costruire?* (2014).

Milda B. Richardson, Ph.D., is Assistant Professor of Teaching in the Art + Design Department at Northeastern University. She received her graduate degrees from the History of Art and Architecture Department at Boston University. Her publications include "Iconoclasm and Resistance: Wayside Shrines in the Struggle for Lithuanian Independence," in *Architecture and Armed Conflict: The Politics of Destruction* (2014).

Heather Seneff, Director of the Visual Media Center, School of Art and Art History, University of Denver, has masters degrees in Art History and Library Science. She developed an interest in architecture while working in the School of Architecture at the University of Maryland College Park in the 1990s and the College of the Built Environments at the University of Washington in Seattle.

Joseph M. Siry, Ph.D., is Professor of Modern Architectural History at Wesleyan University. His books are *Carson Pirie Scott: Louis Sullivan and the Chicago Department Store* (1988), *Unity Temple: Frank Lloyd Wright and Architecture for Liberal Religion* (1996), *The Chicago Auditorium Building: Adler and Sullivan's Architecture and the City* (2002), which won the Society of Architectural Historians' Hitchcock Award, and *Beth Sholom Synagogue: Frank Lloyd Wright and Modern Religious Architecture* (2012).

Phillip James Tabb, Ph.D., is Professor Emeritus of Architecture at Texas A&M University, where he was department head 2001–05. He was the master-planner of the award-winning Serenbe Community located outside of Atlanta, Georgia. He received his B.S. from the University of Cincinnati, M.Arch. from the University of Colorado, and Ph.D. from the Architectural Association. He is a practicing urban designer, licensed architect, and author of five books, including *The Greening of Architecture: A Critical History and Survey of Contemporary Sustainable Architecture and Urban Design* (2013).

ACKNOWLEDGMENTS

Many contributed to this book and I would like to thank them all.

First, I thank all the authors who contributed to this manuscript. It was a pleasure working with each of them and to be engaged in revising the essays. Their scholarly work elevated the professional level of the book. I thank the reviewers for their constructive comments that strengthened the book.

I thank Texas A&M University's Glasscock Center for Humanities Research for awarding me the 2016 Glasscock Faculty Research Fellowship, which enabled me to prepare the proposal for this edited volume. I also thank the Department of Architecture, at Texas A&M University for supporting this Fellowship.

I thank Texas A&M University, its College of Architecture and Department of Architecture for awarding me a Development Leave in spring semester of 2018. This provided me the opportunity to complete this book.

I thank Trudy Varcianna, senior editorial assistant of architecture at Routledge for working with me on the initial phase of the publication; David Moore, the editorial assistant of built environment and architecture at Routledge who worked with me on the final phases of publishing this volume; the copy-editor Jeanne Brady from Cove Publishing Support Services, and the Routledge production team for their help to publish the book.

I thank my colleague Dr. Inbal Ben-Asher Gitler and my husband Dr. Nehemia Geva for their constructive comments; special thanks and love to Nehemia for his endless support of my work.

Finally, many thanks to my grownup children Uri and Roni, their spouses Gali and Rick, and my grandchildren, Maya, Ilan, Ella, and Adam who always proudly support my work.

INTRODUCTION

The sacred space

Anat Geva

The idea for this book developed while I organized a session entitled "Pushing the Envelope: American Mid-20th Century Sacred Architecture" for the 2016 annual conference of the Society of Architectural Historians. The call for papers for this session resulted in 21 proposals that demonstrated the large interest in the topic. Following the success of the session I approached the presenters and other potential authors with a request to contribute essays to an edited volume entitled *Modernism and American Mid-20th Century Sacred Architecture*. The resulting book consists of fourteen chapters written by stellar scholars from academia and architectural practice in the US, Europe, and Australia. This edited volume aimed to offer original material on various unique contextual and design aspects of mid-twentieth-century American modern sacred architecture, rather than attempt to produce a chronological/geographical analysis of the topic. As such, the book is organized along four major themes and an Epilogue that highlight different dimensions of sacred architecture and its relationship to modern aesthetics, liturgical changes, congregational developments, and innovation in building technology of that era.

Though the compilation of essays in the book presents a wide variety of topics, locations, and case studies, they all exhibit a common thread that constitutes the relationship of modernism and sacred architecture. The contributors analyze designs that departed from historicism, pushed the envelope of aesthetics and building technology, and bridged modernism with religion by abstracting cultural and faith traditions.

The interest in modern sacred architecture is growing[1] as part of the investigation of a fascinating experimental period in ecclesiastical architecture;[2] however, scholarship has only begun to explore this type of design. This unique book adds a new dimension to those studies of American sacred architecture. It launches a critical inquiry that represents a discourse within each section of the book and among all the volume's chapters to illustrate the inter-multi-disciplinary complexities of these buildings in America. These complexities represent the attempts of scholars and architects to investigate the sophisticated question of what constitutes a sacred space, especially in mid-twentieth-century modern America. The book illustrates the search for answers mainly in the context of the design of churches of various denominations, but also includes three examples of modern American synagogues. With that, this volume demonstrates that the phenomenon of modernism and the sacred crosses religions and locations in America.

This compilation also provides the contextual framework for the developments in modern sacred architecture in America. First, transformations in aesthetic took place with the emergence of the American modern architecture movement. These introduced simplicity and openness of form, the utility of innovative building technology, bold expressions of masses and materials, and abstraction of details and faith symbols.[3] Second, changes in liturgy were expressed in architecture and helped attract the next generation of Americans, who wanted to preserve their religion and create a nation closer to God.[4] And third, the establishment of post-WWII suburbs across America. With the move of congregations to the suburbs, their leaders, building committees, and architects had the opportunity to experiment with new design concepts and innovative building technologies in constructing new houses of worship.[5] These churches and synagogues reflected the congregation's religious and/or ethnic identity and their quest to belong to the new American era of modernism.[6]

To comprehend the scope and foci of the era's contextual changes and their impact on sacred architecture, one should consider the epistemology underlying the search for the solution of what makes a space sacred. One of the theological schools of thoughts that relates to this question and, as such, is pertinent to the understanding of this volume is theological aesthetic.[7] This approach perceives the sacred through the sensation, feeling, and imagination of beauty.[8] Philip Johnson stated, "A space where awe and reverence are the prime considerations, an inspiring challenge to the artist . . . the Jewish temple merely has to be beautiful. As simple as that."[9] Some accentuate a dialogue of the sacred with the arts and claim that original works of art and décor communicate the authority of the Divine.[10] Thus, it can be assumed that the commitment of the architect and artist in creating the sacred space is to evoke spirituality through beauty as an inspiring act of the poetic imagination.[11] Furthermore, in order to enhance the sensation of the divinity in the sacred place, it should be set apart from the profane[12] and create a journey that transposes believers into the spiritual realm.[13]

One of the examples that illustrate this theological aesthetic approach to modern sacred architecture is the Chapel of the *Convento de las Capuchinas Sacramentarias* in Tlalpan, Mexico City designed by Mexican architect Luis Barragán in 1955. He designed a distinct minimalistic modern chapel inside a convent that separates it from the outside world. The chapel exemplifies the modern aesthetic approach where the beauty of the space's architecture, that has minimal décor, defines the sacred. With pure geometry, simplicity, light, and color, Barragán created a serene and peaceful spiritual space, that evokes the sensation of divine presence for any faith, despite being a Catholic Chapel.[14]

Frank Lloyd Wright's religious architecture also demonstrates the modern aesthetic approach to designing sacred space.[15] He preached to depart from historicism and to design houses of worship that would reflect the era of modern America.[16] He expressed this modernity through the beauty of architecture itself, that was based on pure geometry, openness, light, architectural details, and abstracted symbols of faith. Furthermore, Wright used innovative building technology that often defined the building's aesthetics.[17] Modernist architects adopted these design concepts during the 1950s and 1960s, creating designs that departed from traditional religious buildings and embraced the new era.

In order to answer the question of what makes the space sacred, modern architects explored the sacred and expanded the modern rationalistic functional approach beyond the concept of "form follows function,"[18] exploring similar to Mies van der Rohe the idea of a transcendental technology.[19] They solved the functionality of the religious buildings with the design of complexes that catered to all programmatic requirements, and also looked at the beauty of the building as a vehicle for enhancing spirituality. This ideal of beauty in modernism reflected changes in theological aesthetic (form). Architects introduced bold, sleek, and dramatic designs that highlighted new materials, systems, and abstracted religious art.

The religious setting in the context of post-WWII America, and the reform changes in liturgy in the 1950s and 1960s, which culminated at the Second Vatican Council of the Catholic Church (1962–65), established the framework of accepting modern designs for houses of worship.[20] For example, during the 1960s, the Benedictines of St. John's Abbey Church in Minnesota were interested not just in the modern style, but mainly in the materials and methods that "could shape appropriate forms for a newly refined worship."[21] As such, form was influenced on the one hand by liberal changes in liturgy, and on the other hand, it possessed mutual relations with building technology.[22]

Usually, form called for the use of specific materials and systems.[23] However, availability and developments of new technologies often directly impacted form, leading to a new aesthetic that departed from traditional sacred architecture. Frank Lloyd Wright asserted that "[T]he forms were sculptured from materials according to the nature of construction and the life of the time."[24] Furthermore, materials, such as concrete, frequently defined the aesthetic characteristic of the building. In this respect, innovations in building technologies were and still are aligned with progress and modern architectural beauty.[25] Such was the case of exposed concrete, which was perceived by architect Marcel Breuer as a symbol of beauty that defines the St. John's Abbey's aesthetic expression.[26] Architects Roberto Chiotti and Michael Nicholas-Schmidt claim that in understanding the nature of materials and their "message," the designer has an opportunity to introduce the sacred through the relationship between his "creation and the Creator."[27] The emphasis on the potential of building materials to produce religious meanings demonstrates how modern architects justified their experimentation with new materials and technologies as part of their design of buildings that were predominantly associated with history and tradition.

In this book, authors examine modern materials such as concrete and glass to show how concrete enabled expressive flexible designs and free-flowing shapes, and glass introduced light into the sacred interior. The plasticity of concrete enhanced new systems like thin shell concrete roofs, parabolas, and larger-spans halls.[28] In religious architecture, concrete was considered as "God's gift to religion."[29] Indeed, most of the creative, sculptural applications of concrete are found in sacred architecture.[30] New finishes such as exposed bare concrete (Beton Brut) and bush hammered concrete (developed by architect Paul Rudolph)[31] were part of the new monumental aesthetics in the service of God.[32] In the interior of the sacred space, concrete provided a modern minimalistic background for art, which made the changes in liturgy tangible, especially in the Catholic Church.[33] Glass fenestration enhances the interior-exterior relationship, and enriches the spiritual experiences in the sacred space and its abstracted art.[34] It can be considered as the material most capable of transmitting Divine presence.[35] As such, light streaming through glass into the sanctuary guides worshipers' search for the divine.[36] Mies van der Rohe believed that "a sublime dematerialization of light, glass, and gleaming metal" enhances spirituality.[37] Indeed, details of glass and concrete, brick, or metal, create a play of light and shadows that reinforces spiritual experiences.

Other traditional materials such as brick, stone, and wood were also utilized to support the new forms, to simplify their construction, and to enhance sacredness. Brick is a material created by the sacred elements of earth and fire. Paul Rudolph used brick together with light to dramatize the spiritual space in his Tuskegee University Chapel.[38] Stone and wood are natural materials that express nature and locality. Stone as a long-lasting material is associated with the sacred element of earth.[39] It reveals the earth's grammar and as such represents permanence and human longing for eternity.[40] Wood as a warm material evokes a sense of home and safety.[41] Its humanly intimate touch is used in sacred architecture to enhance religious sentiments.[42]

Building systems such as light, acoustics, and thermal comfort were incorporated into the designs of these buildings and enriched the sacred ambiance and its interior spirituality. Some, like Frank Lloyd Wright's environmentally conscious designs, used passive systems to enhance natural light, acoustics, and thermal comfort.[43] Eero Saarinen used wavy forms of brick and other details in the interior of the MIT circular chapel, to achieve good acoustics, while integrating the mechanical systems for thermal comfort into the design, to blend them within the interior.[44]

As mentioned before, the religious aesthetic of the sacred interior is also enhanced by art and décor. Modernist architects believed in minimizing these elements, abstracting them, or avoiding them entirely in their designs of the religious facility.[45] This was part of their departure from the rich and complex decorations of historic houses of worship. As such, modern art and décor expressed changes in theological aesthetic.[46] While many congregations perceived this simplicity as representing modern America at that time,[47] the relinquishing of historicism in favor of a modern aesthetic was criticized by contemporary scholars such as Michael Rose and Steven J. Schroeder.[48] They argued that the aesthetic of modern sacred architecture "diminishes the individual worship experience by not sufficiently encouraging an encounter with the transcendent, with divine power."[49] Rabbi Yitz Greenberg and Rabbi J. J. Greenberg claimed that the minimalist approach, which implied simplicity of exposed concrete or whitewashed walls, deterred members of the congregations from participating more often in the synagogue's religious services.[50] Such notions raise the question of whether the modern style was too much for the congregations to digest.

Reactions against the austerity of modernism is illustrated in the construction of a new small chapel as an addition to the 1964 North Shore Congregation synagogue in Glencoe, Illinois. The chapel was designed by local architects Hammond, Beeby & Babka in 1979.[51] Minoru Yamasaki's original sanctuary that still serves as the focus of the congregation's complex was built as a modern representation of concrete and light. Amber glass separates concrete fan vault-shells and introduces skylights in the roof and slits of light in the walls. Transparent low windows bring the surrounding nature of Lake Michigan into the sanctuary and accompany the sacred effect of the colored glass.[52] Light and shadows became the core of the spiritual experience. The simplicity of whitewashed walls that reflect the light serves as the background for the only décor—the wooden Ark, the pulpit, the furniture on the Bimah, and the organ at the sanctuary's loft. When building the addition of a circular small chapel, the congregation turned away from Yamasaki's modernist approach and returned to historical precedents of European synagogues. The intimate space is based on rich décor and implements eclectic interior materials reminiscent of those traditions. The upper source of light follows historic faith dicta that restricted views of the surrounding landscape.[53] The architects of this chapel looked for sanctity that emphasizes the richness of traditional ornaments. As such, the congregation's experiment of the 1960s in constructing a modern building and their daring embrace of new aesthetics of the era, was replaced in the 1980s with a postmodern style that returned to the principles of historicism.

Two interesting design concepts can be observed throughout the book. The first appears as a common thread in all chapters. It is the expression of a hybrid design approach between modern design and religious "long standing legacy of classicism."[54] This complex relation between the congregations' cultural and religious heritage and modernism resulted in the abstraction of faith symbols and in the introduction of modern new shapes and art. It can be also seen as a hybridity between the congregation's identity and the modern call for the detachment from traditional values.[55] The second concept is the extent of attentiveness to environmental conditions. Most of these modern designs followed the universal modernist notion, which called for a departure not only from historicism, but also from the consideration of a specific place/environment. Still, this book shows some examples of regionalist architects such as Pietro Belluschi, Eugene Wukasch, and Charles Goodman who designed houses of worship with attention to specific site conditions.[56]

The case studies of the book are presented in fourteen chapters and an Epilogue organized in four parts, which focus on the phenomena described in this introduction. Changes in liturgy enabled modern architects to create those buildings as a place of God on the one hand, and as a community centre for educational and social activities on the other. The first stem out of theological aesthetics of modernism. While the latter grew organically out of modern culture and reflected the congregations' yearning to belong to new modern times and remain relevant to the next generation of congregants.[57]

The volume's Part I, entitled "Modernists and sacred architecture," includes three chapters that explore the design of sacred spaces by famous modernists such as Mies van der Rohe, Philip Johnson, and Paul Rudolph. These case studies focus on the legacy of these leading architects and their significant contributions to religious building of that era. It is interesting to note that all three projects are university chapels: the Illinois Institute of Technology Chapel, proposals for the Vassar College Chapel, and the Tuskegee University Chapel.[58] We can assume that the academy as a place of innovations and progress seemed a fit environment to express the new era of modernism. The architects created dramatic structures that expressed sleek and elegant modernity in their design concepts, aesthetic, and innovative use of materials and construction methods. The chapels by Mies van der Rohe and Paul Rudolph became icons of modern sacred architecture. The proposed chapel by Philip Johnson was never constructed in Vassar College, but was built as a synagogue in Port Chester, New York with minor adjustments. Its adaptation to a different religious building demonstrates that Johnson's design evoked sacredness and spirituality and not necessarily religiosity.

The analyses in this section illustrate that continuity of traditions served as inspiration for the introduction of the sacred, despite the attempts to depart from historic design styles.

In Chapter 1, "Minimal ritual: Mies van der Rohe's Chapel of St. Savior, 1952," Ross Anderson demonstrates how Mies van der Rohe, in his simple and minimalistic modern design of the Illinois Institute of Technology Interfaith chapel (Chapel of St. Savior) turned to classical geometry to enrich its proportions. Furthermore, Anderson shows that Mies based his approach to the sacred on Gothic building traditions, though he avoided the décor aesthetics of Gothic architecture.

In Chapter 2, "Religious freedom and architectural ambition at Vassar," Lindsay Cook examines three proposals for a new chapel in Vassar College (1951 and 1953). In her analysis of these proposals, Cook highlights different sacred design concepts: historicist, functionalist, and modernist. The interesting proposal that expressed religious freedom and modernism of the 1950s was designed by Philip Johnson, who combined functionality and spirituality. Building a new religious space was part of the college's belief that architecture can serve as a vehicle to increase students' participation in religious activities. Still, the college declined the three proposals and decided to restore its extant, historicist chapel. This raises the question of whether the modern proposal was too much for the college to accept, or was the decision merely based on budgetary considerations?

The third chapter of this section, "Tuskegee University's second chapel: a departure and a continuation" focuses on Paul Rudolph's chapel in a historically black university in Alabama. Art Clement and Rod Fluker explain that although the chapel was designed as a concrete modern building, eventually its innovative design was constructed from brick to continue the tradition of Tuskegee's campus architecture. Rudolph's collaboration with a local African American architectural firm – Fry & Welch – resulted in a special approach to the use of traditional material, where light became the innovative dramatic element of the structure.

Many other prominent modern architects could be added to this section, as well as additional types of houses of worship beyond university chapels. As such, it should be understood that this section with its case studies is illustrative of modern architects and the sacred, rather than comprehensive. The investigation of the three chapters of Part I opens a discourse on how leading modern architects of the era approached the question of how to design the sacred space.

Part II in the book, "The parabola, concrete and modern sacred architecture," includes four chapters that inquire how reinforced concrete played a role in determining the liturgical reformed houses of worship, i.e., "moving building forms from traditional into the realm of original and innovative."[59] These chapters address the utility of concrete, its aesthetics, and its applications (e.g. thin concrete shells and hyperbolic parabolas) in shaping modern sacred architecture. The case studies in this part demonstrate how concrete often became the aesthetics of the building, and how its direct influence on form and structural systems allowed experimentation with dramatic unique forms of religious buildings in America.

In Chapter 4, "Bold modern form: the parabola and St. Louis' sacred buildings," Mary Reid Brunstrom examines the iterations of parabolic form in three houses of worship. The projects are St. Louis's first modern synagogue, designed by Eric Mendelsohn, and two Catholic churches, one designed by Murphy and Mackey Architects, and the other by architect Gyo Obata of Hellmuth, Obata & Kassabaum. Brunstrom demonstrates that in the context of the archetypal Gateway Arch, thin-shell concrete construction enabled remarkable uses of parabolic form, both sacred and secular, in the region.

In Chapter 5, "The structural modeling and design of St. Mary's Cathedral, San Francisco, California, 1963–71," Gabriele Neri analyzes the concrete structure of the cathedral. It was built as the union of huge thin concrete hyperbolic paraboloids. This shape reflected experimentation with concrete and the freedom of expression in the 1960s, following the Second Vatican Council. Neri also focuses on the logistical challenges of the collaborations among American architect Pietro Belluschi, Italian engineer Pier Luigi Nervi, and the local architects of record, MSRL, in the design and construction of the cathedral during an era that preceded digital technology and digital communications.

In Chapter 6, "Charles Haertling's St. Stephen's Lutheran Church, Northglenn, Colorado, 1963–64," Heather Seneff describes the work of a local architect in a suburb of Denver, Colorado. Architect Haertling's Lutheran church of the 1960s is an example of the use of a concrete parabola roof that created a unique dramatic building. Thirty years later, the congregation built a new church in a traditional style near the modern original one. As such, Seneff raises the question if architect Haertling "pushed the envelope too far" in his modern church.

In the last chapter of this part on concrete (Chapter 7), "A monumental absence: Paul Rudolph's Christian Science Building, 1965 (demolished 1986)," Scott Murray examines Rudolph's building at the University of Illinois. He illustrates the decision-making processes in the design, construction, and demolition of this monument. The loss of this mid-twentieth century modern brutalist building raises again the question of whether Rudolph's legendary experiment with exposed concrete beyond materiality, may have been too much for the next generations/owners.

Part III, "Denominations, identity and modern sacred architecture," examines how congregations' identity, reformed liturgy, and religious denominations influenced the design of modern American sacred spaces, while catering to the changes of that time.

In Chapter 8, "Creating sacred spaces in the suburbs: Roman Catholic architecture in post-war Los Angeles, California," Michael Gibson illustrates the context of a tremendous growth in the Catholic population around the city and how they treated their faith in post World War II America. Gibson demonstrates the need for new Catholic churches in American suburbs and the influence of changes in liturgy, such as the Second Vatican Council on the design of those churches.

Chapter 9, "Critiquing modernism: the unorthodox Orthodox, 1950s–60s" by Dean Lampros, examines the Eastern Orthodox and Byzantine-rite churches in modern America. Lampros claims, "Modernist-Byzantine hybrids held a special affinity for second-generation Greek, Armenian, Arab, and Slavic Americans." These churches were designed in a modernist style that utilized modern materials and construction methods. However, they linked this modernity with bold traditional designs and art elements to reflect the congregations' ethnic roots and historic identity. Lampros demonstrates this hybridity with several church examples, highlighting Frank Lloyd Wright's Annunciation Greek Orthodox Church in Wauwatosa, Wisconsin (1961).

In Chapter 10, "J. Eugene Wukasch and mid-century Lutheran architecture in Texas, 1950–70," Jason John Paul Haskins analyzes the ecclesiastical design of Eugene Wukasch, a Lutheran architect "at the forefront of modern church architecture in Texas." In his innovative modern designs and use of modern materials and construction methods, Wukasch integrated traditions and history of the Lutheran Church to help construct a new American Lutheran identity. Moreover, Haskins demonstrates the environmentally conscious design of Wukasch's houses of worship in Texas.

In Chapter 11, "The nexus between Lithuanian vernacular and American modernism," Milda Richardson investigates the Lithuanian Catholic churches in America, designed and built by Lithuanian architects and artists who immigrated to the US after World War II. In this chapter, Richardson shows how these architects bridged Lithuanian vernacular forms with modernist vocabulary in their designs of places of worship for Lithuanian-American communities. These churches served and still serve as the symbol and identity of these congregations across the United States.

The final section, Part IV, "Modern interiors and liturgical fittings," examines the incorporation of abstracted faith symbols into modern functional religious architecture through art, architectural details, and light. The case studies discussed here illustrate again how architects attempted to define a unique modern realm for traditional faith rituals. The three chapters in this section investigate how sacred interiors enhanced the spiritual experience in modern American houses of worship by using abstract art, glass, light, and pure geometry.

Chapter 12, "Seeing, not knowing: symbolism, art, and 'opticalism' in mid-century American religious architecture" by Jeremy Kargon, suggests a unique design approach called 'opticalism.' The definition of this phenomenon is the use of "aggressive and large-scale visual effects" as part of the abstract art in religious interiors. This approach fits the quote by architect Luis Barragán who said "The Art of Seeing. It is essential to an architect to know how to see: I mean, to see in such a way that the vision is not overpowered by rational analysis."[60] Kargon analyzes optical effects in three houses of worship built in mid-twentieth-century Baltimore: Pietro Belluschi's Church of the Redeemer; Buckler, Fenhagen, Meyer, and Ayers, Architects' Har Sinai Synagogue, and Charles Stade's St. Paul's Evangelical Lutheran Church. Kargon concludes that "No longer merely situated within architecture, artwork instead determined the spatial precinct of the sacred experience."

Chapter 13, "The sanctuary wall: Unitarian rationalism illuminated," examines how new materials and structural explorations "transform the sanctuary wall into a diaphanous screen." In order to illustrate this transformation, Ann Marie Borys analyzes three Unitarian regional churches: the Unitarian Church of Arlington, Virginia; University Unitarian Church in Seattle, Washington, and St. John's Unitarian Church in Cincinnati, Ohio. Light simulations augment Borys' light analyses of these three examples. Her empirical study demonstrates that the structure and its light express not only the Unitarian faith, which embraces nature, but also reflect its spirituality that stems from the "interconnectedness of all things."[61]

Chapter 14 is entitled "Tradition and transcendence: Eero Saarinen's MIT Chapel and the nondenominational ideal." In this chapter, Joseph Siry investigates Eero Saarinen's non-denominational chapel at the Massachusetts Institute of Technology (MIT), in Cambridge, built in 1955. Siry discusses how the idea for such a chapel evolved as a reaction to the horrific events of World War II. He analyzes the building and highlights the modern characteristics of the circular chapel, as well as the intimate scale of the interior. The collaboration of Saarinen with artists to create a serene ambiance with minimal art and décor becomes the key to the transcendent experience in the building.

The final part of the book is the Epilogue, written by Phillip James Tabb. This chapter is a summary and conclusion, wherein Tabb highlights the challenges of modernism and sacred spaces. He compares Le Corbusier's Catholic Chapel of Notre Dame du Haut in Ronchamp, France (1954), with Philip Johnson's Rothko Chapel in Houston, Texas (1971). Tabb highlights the characteristics of modern sacred architecture, and each architect's distinct approach towards light. The Epilogue illustrates how this book's case studies presented architecture that was engaged in modern design and construction concepts in an attempt to answer the question of what makes the building sacred.

As a whole, the book's parts and their chapters describe the challenges that congregations and architects faced in mid-twentieth-century America when building their houses of worship. The richness of each of the volume's topics opens the door for further investigations of how mid-twentieth-century American sacred architecture expressed modernism in aesthetic and building technology, while catering to each specific faith. The integrity of the book is in its whole as the equilibrium of its parts. In summary, an edited volume is like the famous Indian fable of the blind men and the elephant, where six blind men try to describe their own version of an elephant by touching it. They all express different pictures of the animal. However, the argument among them is settled, as they understood that all their various pieces create the whole.[62]

Notes

1 Victoria Young, *Saint John's Abbey Church: Marcel Breuer and the Creation of A Modern Sacred Space* (Minneapolis, MN: University of Minnesota Press, 2014); Jay M. Price, *Temples for A Modern God: Religious Architecture in Post-war America* (New York, NY: Oxford University Press, 2013); Louis P. Nelson, *American Sanctuary: Understanding Sacred Spaces* (Bloomington, IN: Indiana University Press, 2006).
2 Peter Hammond, *Liturgy and Architecture* (New York, NY: Columbia University Press, 1961).
3 Price, *Temples for A Modern God,* 17.
4 Ibid., 173.
5 Gretchen Buggeln, *The Suburban Church* (Minneapolis, MN: University of Minnesota Press, 2015), xv.
6 Ibid., and Price, *Temples for A Modern God.*
7 Nelson, *American Sanctuary*, 3–4; Richard Kieckhefer, *Theology in Stone: Church Architecture from Byzantium to Berkeley* (New York, NY: Oxford University Press, 2004), 97–134.
8 Gesa Elsbeth Thiessen, ed. *Theological Aesthetics: A Reader* (Grand Rapid, MI: Wm. B. Eerdmans Publishing, 2004), 1.
9 Richard Meier. *Recent American Synagogue Architecture* (exhibition catalogue, New York, NY: The Jewish Museum, 1963), 22.
10 Walter Benjamin, in Nelson *American Sanctuary*, 4.
11 Citation from the Pritzker Jury on Barragán's award (1980): https://web.archive.org/web/2007 1029012341/http://www.pritzkerprize.com/barragan.htm.
12 "And the captain of the LORD's host said unto Joshua, Loose thy shoe from off thy foot; for the place where on thou standest is holy. And Joshua did so" (Joshua 5:15): Mircea Eliade, *The Sacred and the Profane: The Nature of Religion* (New York, NY: Harcourt, Brace, 1959).
13 Anat Geva, *Frank Lloyd Wright's Sacred Architecture: Faith, Form, and Building Technology* (London: Routledge, 2012), 24–28; Tom Barrie, *Spiritual Path, Sacred Place: Myth, Ritual, and Meaning in Architecture* (Boston, MA: Shambhala, 1996).
14 The author's visit to the chapel (December, 2013).
15 Geva, *Frank Lloyd Wright's Sacred Architecture.*
16 Ibid.
17 Ibid.
18 On modernism see Kenneth Frampton, *A Genealogy of Modern Architecture*, edited by Ashley Simone (Zurich, Switzerland: Lars Muller Publishers and Kenneth Frampton, 2015); Young, *Saint John's Abbey*, 32.
19 Framton, *A Genealogy of Modern Architecture*, 11.
20 Young, *Saint John's Abbey Church*, 18; and Chapter 8 in this book.
21 Young, *Saint John's Abbey Church*, 32.
22 See a conceptual model in Geva, *Frank Lloyd Wright's Sacred Architecture*, 13.
23 Ibid.
24 Frank Lloyd Wright, *Genius and the Mobocracy* (New York, NY: Duell, Sloan and Pearce, 1949). Reprinted in Bruce Pfeiffer, ed. *Frank Lloyd Wright Collected Writings* (New York, NY: Rizzoli International Publication, 1994), vol. 4, 336.
25 Hamilton Smith, in Victoria Young, "Sacred Connections through Concrete," *Faith & Form* XLI, no. 1 (2018): 11–15; Young, *Saint John's Abbey Church*, 40.
26 Young, "Sacred Connections through Concrete," 12.
27 Roberto Chiotti and Michael Nicholas-Schmidt, "Shared Universe, Sacred Story," *Faith & Form* XLI, no. 1 (2018): 25–27.
28 Adrian Forty, *Concrete and Culture*, (London: Reaktion Books LTD, 2012), 14; Young, *Saint John's Abbey Church*; Part II in this book.
29 A quote of Bishop of Brentwood in Forty, *Concrete and Culture*, 169.
30 Forty, *Concrete and Culture*, 169.

31 See for example, Chapters 3 and 7 in this book.
32 Young, "Sacred Connections through Concrete," 12.
33 Young, *Saint John's Abbey Church*, xvii.
34 See Part IV in this book.
35 James Hadley, "A Type of Transmuted Divinity", *Faith & Form* XLI, no. 1 (2018): 16–17.
36 Ibid.
37 Frampton, *A Genealogy of Modern Architecture*, 1.1.
38 Chapter 3 in this book.
39 Geva, *Frank Lloyd Wright's Sacred Architecture*, 38.
40 Caroline Humphrey and Piers Vitebsky, *Sacred Architecture* (New York, NY: Barnes & Noble Books (reprinted from 1997 Little Brown), 2005).
41 Chiotti and Schmidt, "Shared Universe."
42 Ibid.
43 Geva, *Frank Lloyd Wright's Sacred Architecture*, 216–254.
44 Chapter 14 in this book.
45 Henry Russell Hitchcock, *The International Style*, revised edn. (New York, NY: W. W. Norton & Company, 1997).
46 Chapter 14 in this book.
47 Price, *Temples for A Modern God*.
48 Jeanne Halgren Kilde, *Sacred Power, Sacred Space: An Introduction to Christian Architecture and Worship* (New York, NY: Oxford University Press, 2008), Chapter 7, note 1.
49 Ibid., 161.
50 Jack Wertheimer, "The American Synagogue: Recent Issues and Trends," *American Jewish Year Book* (2005): 3–83.
51 Samuel D. Gruber, *American Synagogues: A Century of Architecture and Jewish Community* (New York, NY: Rizzoli, 2003), 140–145; the author's visit to the synagogue (April 2016).
52 The author's visit to the synagogue (April 2016).
53 Ibid.; Shalom Dov Steinberg, *The Format of the First Jerusalem Temple* (in Hebrew) (Jerusalem: Vagshel, 1994); Shalom Dov Steinberg, *The Format of the Second Jerusalem Temple* (in Hebrew) (Jerusalem: Vagshel, 1993).
54 Frampton, *A Genealogy of Modern Architecture*.
55 Chapters 9 and 11 in this book.
56 Chapters 10 and 13 in this book.
57 Buggeln, *The Suburban Church*, xv.
58 In the book, there is a discussion about two additional university chapels: Paul Rudolph's Christian Science Building at the University of Illinois is introduced in Chapter 7, and Eero Saarinen's MIT Chapel in Chapter 14.
59 Young, *Saint John's Abbey Church*, 34.
60 Barragán's acceptance speech of the Pritzker Prize (1980). See Note 11.
61 Christ-Janer, Albert and Mary Mix Foley. *Modern Church Architecture: A Guide to the Form and Spirit of 20th Century Religious Buildings* (New York, NY: McGraw-Hill, 1962), 272.
62 "The Blind Men and The Elephant" http://www.jainworld.com/literature/story25.htm.

References

Barrie, Tom. *Spiritual Path, Sacred Place: Myth, Ritual, and Meaning in Architecture* (Boston, MA: Shambhala, 1996).
Buggeln, Gretchen. *The Suburban Church* (Minneapolis, MN: University of Minnesota Press, 2015).
Chiotti, Roberto and Nicholas-Schmidt, Michael. "Shared Universe, Sacred Story," *Faith & Form* XLI, no. 1 (2018): 25–27.
Christ-Janer, Albert and Mix Foley, Mary. *Modern Church Architecture: A Guide to the Form and Spirit of 20th Century Religious Buildings* (New York, NY: McGraw-Hill, 1962).
Eliade, Mircea. *The Sacred and the Profane: The Nature of Religion* (New York, NY: Harcourt, Brace, 1959).
Forty, Adrian. *Concrete and Culture* (London: Reaktion Books Ltd, 2012).

Frampton, Kenneth. *A Genealogy of Modern Architecture*, edited by Ashley Simone (Zurich, Switzerland: Lars Muller Publishers and Kenneth Frampton, 2015).

Geva, Anat. *Frank Lloyd Wright's Sacred Architecture: Faith, Form, and Building Technology* (London: Routledge, 2012).

Gruber, Samuel D. *American Synagogues: A Century of Architecture and Jewish Community* (New York, NY: Rizzoli, 2003), 140–145.

Hadley, James. "A Type of Transmuted Divinity," *Faith & Form* XLI, no. 1 (2018): 16–17.

Hammond, Peter. *Liturgy and Architecture* (New York, NY: Columbia University Press, 1961).

Hitchcock, Henry Russell. *The International Style*, revised edn. (New York, NY: W. W. Norton & Company, 1997).

Humphrey, Caroline and Vitebsky, Piers. *Sacred Architecture* (New York, NY: Barnes & Noble Books (reprinted from 1997, Little Brown), 2005).

Kieckhefer, Richard. *Theology in Stone: Church Architecture from Byzantium to Berkeley* (New York: Oxford University Press, 2004).

Kilde, Jeanne Halgren. *Sacred Power, Sacred Space: An Introduction to Christian Architecture and Worship* (New York: Oxford University Press, 2008).

Meier, Richard. *Recent American Synagogue Architecture* (exhibition catalogue) (New York, NY: The Jewish Museum, 1963).

Nelson, Louis P. *American Sanctuary: Understanding Sacred Spaces* (Bloomington, IN: Indiana University Press, 2006).

Price, Jay M. *Temples for A Modern God: Religious Architecture in Post-war America* (New York, NY: Oxford University Press, 2013).

Steinberg, Shalom Dov. *The Format of the First Jerusalem Temple* (in Hebrew) (Jerusalem: Vagshel, 1994).

———. *The Format of the Second Jerusalem Temple* (in Hebrew) (Jerusalem: Vagshel, 1993).

Thiessen, Gesa Elsbeth, ed. *Theological Aesthetics: A Reader* (Grand Rapids, MI: Wm. B. Eerdmans Publishing, 2004), 1.

Wertheimer, Jack. "The American Synagogue: Recent Issues and Trends," *American Jewish Year Book* (2005): 3–83.

Wright, Frank Lloyd. *Genius and the Mobocracy* (New York, NY: Duell, Sloan and Pearce, 1949). Reprinted in Bruce Pfeiffer, ed. *Frank Lloyd Wright Collected Writings* (New York, NY: Rizzoli International Publication, 1994), vol. 4, 336.

Young, Victoria. "Sacred Connections through Concrete," *Faith & Form* XLI, no. 1 (2018): 11–15.

———. *Saint John's Abbey Church: Marcel Breuer and the Creation of A Modern Sacred Space* (Minneapolis, MN: University of Minnesota Press, 2014).

PART I

Modernists and sacred architecture

1

MINIMAL RITUAL

Mies van der Rohe's Chapel of St. Savior, 1952

Ross Anderson

> I chose an intensive rather than an extensive form to express my conception, simply and honestly, of what a sacred building should be . . . The chapel will not grow old. It is of noble character, constructed of good materials, and has beautiful proportions . . . It was meant to be simple; and, in fact, it is simple. But in its simplicity it is not primitive, but noble, and in its smallness it is great—in fact, monumental.
>
> *Mies van der Rohe*[1]

The Robert F. Carr Memorial Chapel of St. Savior at Illinois Institute of Technology in Chicago is Mies van der Rohe's single ecclesiastical building, and as such it commands a unique place in his vast rationalist œuvre. Completed in October 1952, the diminutive brick chapel was first revealed to the public in an article that was carefully composed for an issue of the journal *Arts and Architecture* (Fig. 1.1). The compact double-page portrait entitled "A Chapel" comprises one large signature photograph, three small vignettes, one plan drawing, a short project description and four brief, awkwardly phrased statements by the architect, including the one above. The article serves as a compact record of Mies' aspirations for the chapel and his own estimation of the results. But it also tellingly reveals his difficulty in articulating his comprehension of the duty of religious architecture in the modern period, a time in which, to use Friedrich Schiller's pithy statement of recognition, "the temples remain sacred to the eye, when the Gods have long become ridiculous."[2] It will be seen that the unique challenge of the design of a sacred building elicited an architectural response from Mies that sets the modest chapel apart from all of his other work in subtle yet significant ways.

The spare rectangular chapel sits aloof on the vast lawned IIT campus in Chicago's Near South Side that spreads itself over an area equal to eight city blocks. The long north and south façades are made from buff-colored bricks set in English bond. Resolutely windowless, they turn through ninety degrees at their ends to frame the corners like square brackets. The short east and west façades comprise five equally sized full-height panels. The outermost are the returns of the long brick walls and the central three are glass, framed by impeccably detailed black steel frames. The façades are identical, except that the entry is fully transparent, while

FIGURE 1.1 Mies van der Rohe, "A Chapel" (Chicago, Illinois), *Arts and Architecture* 70, no. 1 (January 1953): 18–19.

the rear is translucent. The chapel tends to be photographed so as to appear as a lantern—fully exposing the column-free interior focused on the solid travertine altar. The black extruded steel roof beams are entirely exposed to view, as are the pre-cast concrete ceiling panels that they support. Regularly spaced spotlights concealed within the depth of the beams are directed towards the long uninterrupted brick walls, and towards the lustrous deeply pleated altar curtain that divides the congregation from the cloistered chambers behind. The only furnishings are two low oak-veneer benches, and a gleaming stainless-steel altar rail and cross. The interior possesses the puritan spirit of a Shaker meeting-room, and the governing beatitude evidently concerns the meek of the earth. The overall appearance is one of bare, taut, ascetic precision.

Unsurprisingly for the taciturn architect to whom the statement "build, don't talk"[3] is attributed, the real arena for his struggle was architecture as an embodied practice—on the drawing board, and with an eye to the construction site—rather than the discourses surrounding building, where he was ill at ease. The following close analysis and interpretation of the chapel is based principally upon scrutiny of his architectural drawings and on the written correspondence and archival photographs that have been archived along with them.[4] It also takes into account material held at libraries and archives in Chicago, writings by the architect himself, secondary literature by others and direct observations made at the chapel itself.[5] The drawings and diagrams below are not simply illustrations of the critical analysis—indeed, they are the medium in which it was conducted. There was all the time a "to and fro" between operating with the computer technology now available for carrying out drawings, and reflection on the tools that were originally at the architect's disposal—principally, the drawing board, T-square, dividers and other manual drawing implements.[6]

The design of the chapel

Mies received the brief for the chapel on 18 March 1949 and the groundbreaking ceremony took place on 1 June 1951. Between these dates, his office produced a very extensive suite of drawings for the chapel, ranging from evocative charcoal sketches, through multiple iterations of the plan, to meticulously delineated and annotated details to be handed to builders. The original brief actually called for two buildings.[7] In addition to the sanctuary, the chapel's plan included a free-standing parish hall and living quarters for a chaplain, which would be built first and would serve as a community hall and a temporary chapel. A number of possible configurations of the two buildings were trialed on the drawing board between early June 1949 and the end of July 1950.[8] Although the orientation of the two buildings relative to each other, and to the site, varied in each configuration, the walls were always made to align with the cardinal directions and were spaced as multiples of the 24-foot grid that Mies had disposed with relentless conviction across the entire campus.[9] The detached parish hall was eventually pared from the project, leaving only the chapel. It had an exposed steel structure centered on intersections of the underlying 24-foot grid, delivering a rectangular plan measuring 48 by 72 feet. By early October 1950, this version of the chapel had been fully worked-up in a complete suite of detailed working drawings and specifications that were sent out to tender.[10] The estimates that were returned were evidently either much higher than anticipated, or the budget situation had worsened, since it was decided that the cost would need to be significantly reduced.[11] This necessitated a rethink of the size, method of construction and finishes of the chapel.

An excerpt from a letter that Wallace E. Conkling, the bishop of the Episcopal diocese of Chicago and the sponsor of the project, sent to Mies on 19 January 1951 serves to illuminate the situation at that time. He wrote:

> I deeply appreciate that you were so graciously willing to reconsider the plans for the Chapel, on much less expensive lines . . . it is urgently necessary that we should get the building down in cost as much as we can, for I am now endeavoring to build up my reserves at least to the minimum figure.[12]

By 21 April 1951, Mies was able to present fully resolved plans for the chapel that would be more economical to build.[13] It will be shown to be a much richer and more enigmatic architectural proposition than the first version, and one that distinguishes the chapel from the other buildings on the campus. He seems to have acknowledged that it was in fact the apparently banal question of expenses that stimulated his architectural imagination, concluding his *Arts and Architecture* article with the statement: "I would not have built the chapel differently if I had a million dollars to do it."[14]

The geometry of the chapel

Mies deployed the adroit sequence of geometric operations demonstrated in Figure 1.2 to deliver the final disposition of the plan of the chapel. Needing to reduce the dimensions of the proposed chapel from the version that had been sent out to tender, Mies condensed the width of the nave by half a module—from 48 to 36 feet. He did the same thing in the perpendicular direction, delineating a square. The next, and absolutely decisive move was to deploy the "golden mean."[15] He cast a quarter circle centered on the midpoint of the square through the corner diagonally opposite, and then, at the point where the arc met the vertical, drafting across a horizontal line to meet an extension of the edge of the square, resulting in a golden rectangle.[16] Once established, the geometrical armature was made to pervade the plan. For example, a second golden rectangle that was nested inside the smaller portion of the first in order was used to locate the non-loadbearing interior walls.

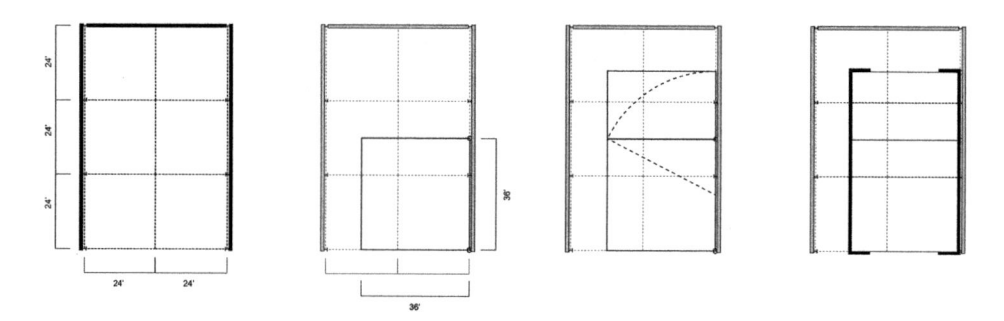

FIGURE 1.2 The sequence of geometric operations that Mies used to derive the form and dimensions of the final load-bearing brick plan of the chapel out of the earlier structural steel and brick-infill version.

Drawings by the author, May 2017.

Throughout history, the "golden mean" has been thought of as beautiful—even "divine."[17] Luca Pacioli summarized the alleged grounds for its special significance in the Christian context in five short statements published in his 1509 book *On the Divine Proportion*. In the first he noted that it is one only and not more; in the second that the definition of the golden mean involves precisely three lengths, analogous to the trinity; and in the third that the mathematical irrationality of the golden mean parallels the incomprehensibility of God:

> Just like God cannot be properly defined, nor can be understood through words, likewise our proportion cannot be ever designated by intelligible numbers, nor can it be expressed by any rational quantity, but always remains concealed and secret, and is called irrational by the mathematicians.[18]

Amongst some modern architects there was an attempt to recuperate the significance of geometry and proportion for architecture by coupling ancient teachings, including the "secrets" of medieval masons, with their own powers of invention.[19] Mies would have been introduced to such thinking while working with Peter Behrens in Berlin, and also through his close study of books such as Hendrik Petrus Berlage's *The Foundations and Development of Architecture*,[20] which was one of the small number of books that he was able to take with him to America from Germany in 1938. Berlage provides a lengthy account of the use of geometry and proportion through history together with bold declarations on how they should be deployed in modern times. Towards the end he states three conclusions based on his preceding studies, which should determine "the path that we must set out on, the path that will be worthwhile for the future, and that shall lead us to a new art."[21] They are: "(1) An architectonic composition should be founded on a geometric schema; (2) The characteristic forms of earlier styles should not be used; (3) The architectonic forms should develop along functional lines."[22] The architecture of Mies' chapel accords to these directives.

The golden rectangle has greatest tangible presence in the ground plane. The area for the congregation is delineated by the 36-foot square, and the remainder of the rectangle, which has an irrational dimension, takes in the altar, choir and sacristy. The symbolic associations are self-evident—the lay area given over to the earthly is bound by the "grounded" figure of the square, while the area allied to the sacred is "immeasurable." The threshold between the two is orchestrated by the most minimal of means as the floor of the nave rises up as a single very low step. It reads rather as a wrinkle in the earth than an act of building. The altar is the focus of the ascension, and it is where the very substantial chthonic content of the chapel is founded (Fig. 1.3). Interestingly, the client shared, and perhaps even exceeded Mies' estimation of the importance of the altar to the chapel. Bishop Conkling penned the following lines in a letter in late 1951, "My dear Mies . . . Even though our funds be so limited, we *must*, do the Altar right, above all else, for that is the thing for which we are building the Chapel."[23] This kind of sentiment—fixated on one emblematic and immovable fragment of an architectural setting—is symptomatic of a broader phenomenon in modern architecture. As Peter Carl has stated: "In the absence of an explicit and shared transcendence susceptible to the sort of sustained mediation one sees in such works as Gothic cathedrals . . . one is left only with the appeal to the transcendence of the chthonic."[24] The Swiss stage designer Adolphe Appia is an important reference in this discussion since he previewed and consolidated themes that came to be developed in the architecture of Mies and others.[25] The austere atmospheric drawing that Appia made in 1926 for the second act of Christoph Gluck's *Iphegenia in Tauris*

FIGURE 1.3   The solid travertine altar that measures 8' wide × 2'8" deep × 3'3" high and weighs
7½ tons.

Photograph by the author, July 13, 2013.

FIGURE 1.4   Adolphe Appia, Stage setting for Christoph Gluck's *Iphegenia in Tauris. Act Two:
Interior of the Artemis Temple*, 1926. Charcoal, graphite pencil and white pastel on
grey *Canson & Montgolfier* paper (1'7" × 2'1").

Swiss Archive of the Performing Arts, Bern (Inv. No. 20b).

particularly resonates with the architecture of the chapel. It takes in a view towards the altar
in the temple of Artemis, seen from the side through a profoundly expectant ambient gloom
(Fig. 1.4). The drawing marries primitive embodied experiences of spatiality and orientation
with removed perspectival clarity and precision, much like the chapel.

The materiality of the chapel

At the time that the golden rectangle was introduced, the primary structure for the proposed
chapel was converted from exposed steel to load-bearing brick.[26] The significance of this second pivotal decision goes well beyond questions of construction. Importance was transferred

FIGURE 1.5   Current view of the chapel showing the glazed entry façade and the long windowless load-bearing walls in buff-colored brick.

Photograph by the author, July 13, 2013.

from the precisely measured and finely wrought steel structure, emblematic of technology, to the raw matter of the bricks that were sourced directly from "the earth." The bricks were no longer going to be infill—they were going to be doing the "work" of the building (Fig. 1.5).

In a 1977 interview, Philip Johnson recalled that Mies had a particular affection for the North German *Backsteingotik*, which might provide a clue to the symbolic significance of load-bearing brick for him within the context of religious architecture.[27] According to Johnson, it was in the tall *Hallenkirchen* where Mies "felt most at home,"[28] and they were "his favorite buildings."[29] Coupling the recognition that the chapel is the single building on the IIT campus that is load-bearing brick with the fact that it is Mies' only religious building, the allusion to the *Backsteingotik* tradition was likely intentional. Further, it should be noted that Mies had a religious upbringing, and that his father was a stonemason. In an interview late in his life, Mies recounted a tense discussion that had taken place many years back in Aachen, Germany between his brother Ewald and their father Michael. Ewald had apparently suggested that some masonry details high up on a building might be simplified since they would never be seen up close, to which Michael responded:

> You're none of you stonemasons anymore! You know the finial at the top of the spire of the cathedral at Cologne? Well, you can't crawl up there and get a good look at it, but it is carved as if you could. It was made for God.[30]

There is good evidence that Mies' appreciation of the Gothic extended well beyond the anecdotal and might more accurately be described as unexpectedly studious. A surprisingly large number of the 150 books in his personal library that have been identified as being most important to him are on Gothic architecture.[31] Religious writings, including primary theological texts by St. Augustine and St. Thomas Aquinas, are also amongst the select group. There is direct archival evidence that some of these books were consulted during the design of the chapel and that they nourished discussions between the client and architect. The campus chaplain J. Ralph Deppen wrote a letter to Mies that began:

> First, I want to thank you for sending me the books. I have been trying to work with them, in spite of the "rust" on my German. With the aid of a pocket dictionary, I am making some progress. I found also, that I have Guardini's "Spirit of the Liturgy" in English. That I have now finished, and the reading was most rewarding.[32]

Deppen went on to convey to Mies that at a dinner earlier in the week with Bishop Conkling, the two of them had "spoken of you and the new drawings at great length", adding: "I really believe that his 'Gothic soul' begins to sense some kinship in your work."[33]

In addition to the architectonic significance of the conversion of the proposed column and beam steel structure to load-bearing brick at the time that the golden rectangle was introduced, there were consequences for the architectural composition, which Mies exploited creatively. The original steel I-beam columns would have been obliged to accord with the severe 24-foot campus grid. And as can be seen in the superimposed plans in Figure 1.6, it would have been very apparent that the smaller version of the chapel was not a clean multiple of the module. As it is, the long brick walls are uninterrupted along their entire length internally and they do not register as being "irrationally" dimensioned. Although there is no immediate discernible trace of the original 24-foot module in the final building, the overlaid plans reveal that the exposed roof beams that span the nave mark it. One of

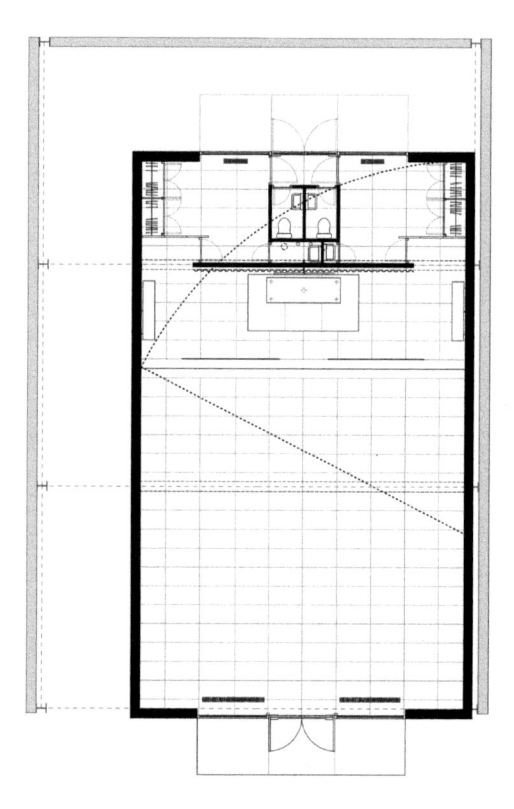

FIGURE 1.6 Plan of the chapel based upon the final plans, sections, elevations and detail drawings that Mies issued on April 21, 1951.

Drawing by Sean Bryen, May 2017; geometric analysis by the author.

these beams situates the altar wall and the other divides the distance between this wall and the entry in two. The module and the original design for the chapel therefore maintain what might be termed an absent-presence in the building. What is most impressive is the way that the disposition and dimensioning of the simple plan possesses a self-evident quality, which has been delivered by the golden rectangle, and its derivatives, in concert with the 24-foot module out of which it was drawn.

The modern architectural background of the chapel

The twin orientation to primitive "earth" and to sophisticated geometry and technology in the chapel, and in modern architecture more generally, was prefigured by Denis Diderot and Jean le Rond d'Alembert's immense Enlightenment undertaking—the *Encyclopédie*.[34] It presented an early move to reify local typicalities of artisanry, transfiguring the working practices and their settings that had been deeply embedded in the often-messy life of the city into spacious, well-lit empty rooms that, as Roland Barthes asserted, mobilized an "aesthetic of nudity" (Fig. 1.7).[35] The treatment of religious decorum in the minimal chapel is akin to the treatment of artisanry in the *Encyclopédie*. In the medieval situation, a church or chapel was an often-elaborate architecturally embodied measure of the mediation between humanity and their God. However, in Mies' architecture, the situation is abstracted into a relation between viewer and object, as the altar and the gleaming stainless-steel cross in a bright empty room carry the representational burden.

Mies' understanding of the duty of contemporary church building, and its relationship to the architecture of the past, was in part conditioned by his admiration for the architecture and writings of the German architect Rudolf Schwarz. He evidently read Schwarz's 1938 book *Vom Bau der Kirche* [On Church Building] avidly, and was closely involved in its translation into English as *The Church Incarnate: The Sacred Function of Christian Architecture*.[36] He also wrote a glowing foreword to the book, acclaiming the way that it "throws light for the first time on the question of church building, and illuminates the whole question of architecture

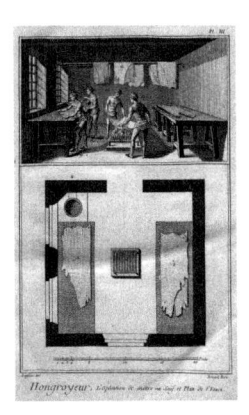

FIGURE 1.7   "Tanner of Hungarian Leather, Plate III: Tallowing Operation and Plan of the Drying Room," in Denis Diderot and Jean le Rond d'Alembert, eds., *Encyclopédie*, vol. 7 (Paris, 1769).

Courtesy of the ARTFL Encyclopédie Project, University of Chicago.

FIGURE 1.8 Detail of the entry façade of the chapel.

Photograph by the author, July 13, 2017.

itself . . . I have read it over and over again."[37] *The Church Incarnate* presents an account of the architecture of various historical times in order to proclaim a supra-historical essence of "the sacred" that might be embodied by the contemporary *Zeitgeist*. Schwarz wrote:

> It would of course be possible to copy the deep doorways . . . or the pointed arches of the Gothic. But it would not be true. For us the wall is no longer heavy masonry but rather a taut membrane, we know the great tensile strength of steel and with it we have conquered the vault.[38]

The text is accompanied by a number of highly abstracted diagrams that purport to account for the essential features of buildings from different periods, such as the Gothic cathedral. Mies' chapel accords with the sentiment of Schwarz's text and diagrams.

The composition of the "west" entry to the chapel certainly alludes to the deep Gothic tradition of triple triumphal arch portals framed by paired towers.[39] However, the original "thickness" of the architecture and ornament that mediated between the sacred interior and the profane city outside, and that took in deep archivolts, jamb figures, tympanum, elaborate stonework, sculpture and tracery has been "flattened." To use Schwarz's words, it has become a "taut membrane" (Fig. 1.8). K. Michael Hays has written about this condition in Mies' architecture more generally, noting that it "moves toward a non-identity that is visibly marked by the strain to maintain itself"[40] and that it is "internally torn and conflicted by all that foreign matter it cannot really hope to exorcise but nevertheless seeks to partially redeem."[41] This confliction that is embodied in the architecture itself can also be witnessed in historical photographs of the chapel.

Photographic representations of the chapel

Since its first outing in Mies' article that was discussed at the outset of this chapter, the photograph of the chapel by the renowned Chicago photographers Hedrich Blessing has come to "stand for" the building in a remarkably exclusive way. Almost every author who has written on the building in the decades that have followed that publication has felt compelled to accompany his or her text with it.[42] Rather fortuitously, alongside the print of the photograph that has been continuously published, two other versions from its negative have been archived at the Museum of Modern Art (MOMA) alongside the drawings for the chapel.[43] Comparing the prints closely, it is possible to discern a host of painterly darkroom techniques such as dodging, burning, masking and cropping that have been used to a greater or lesser degree in each print. The intended effect of these procedures is overstated in one of them, which must have been a test. While the interior of the chapel is perfectly exposed, the exterior treatment is sketch-like. The building is fringed by an artificial halo that is the result of masking and dodging. According to a freehand note written directly on the print, a bothersome electricity wire in the top left foreground needs to be cropped out. The burning-in that was intended to efface a historical building in the background has been taken too far, sinking the entire left-hand edge of the image into shadow. These excesses were corrected in the final print. Through very careful manipulation in the darkroom, it succeeded in its ambition to present the chapel as an isolated modern moment of enchantment, aloof from the reality of its context.

The other much more tightly cropped exterior photograph in the *Arts and Architecture* spread possesses its own intriguing history.[44] Taken by Joseph J. Lucas Jr. on October 26, 1952, it witnesses the moment that the small assembly shuffles aside to permit the religious procession concluded by Bishop Conkling to enter the chapel for his dedicatory sermon. The photograph's dual role in the article is plainly to depict the chapel's dedication as a worthy historical event, and to demonstrate the "use value" of the architecture. Thereby, it served as a corrective to the demeanor of the larger photograph. A chance discovery of the uncropped photograph in a low-circulation campus bulletin from December 1952 has revealed the full expanse of the scene (Fig. 1.9).[45] It records the presence of a darkly imposing double-story Victorian building with a gambrel roof that looms behind the chapel and leers over it to the religious procession below. A second building presences itself as a large mysterious phantom reflection on the

FIGURE 1.9 Photograph of the chapel that accompanies the article "Mies van der Rohe's Philosophy of Architecture is Outlined," *Armour Research Foundation News* 4, no. 12 (December 1952), 3. Ryerson and Burnham Archives, The Art Institute of Chicago.

glazed entry façade. The excision of the historical buildings from the version of the photograph that was published in the *Arts and Architecture* spread supports Hays' claim that "so-called universal space carries within it—as a trace, one is tempted to say, in its *unconscious*, as part of its very self-definition—the everyday actions, quotidian distraction, and materialist vulgarities that it is supposed to have suppressed."[46]

The chapel in conclusion

This chapter has revealed through close scrutiny of the archival evidence that Mies van der Rohe embraced the commission for the Robert F. Carr Memorial Chapel of St. Savior as a singular opportunity to deeply engage with architectural themes that are not present in his secular buildings. He drew upon his extensive knowledge and interest in Gothic architecture, and designed the diminutive chapel as a building that is both modern and historically mindful. Unlike every other building on the IIT campus, the chapel is built of load-bearing brick. This construction method is an undoubted allusion to the *Backsteingotik* tradition of church building that Mies particularly admired. This chapter has also revealed the less obvious way that he arrived at the final plan of the chapel via a dexterous series of geometric operations involving the 24-foot governing module and the ratio of the "golden mean." His attempt to retrieve the potential significance of proportion and geometry for architecture by coupling the secretive ethos of medieval masons with modern abstraction aligned with the thinking of his immediate predecessors Hendrik Petrus Berlage and Rudolf Schwarz.[47]

Mies' vigilance in regards to the determination of the geometrical relationships that strictly governed the design of the chapel was matched by his control over the way the building was portrayed after it was built.[48] Although apparently offering an invitation to a world both profound and stable, the empty lantern-like nonsectarian chapel appears not to require actual worshippers. It reveals the problematic nature of religious architecture in the modern period, a time that aspires towards universal meanings that are to be paradoxically achieved by the individual creative architect. By way of contrast, the building tradition of the Gothic was the result of successive and largely anonymous contributions made by generations of builders. Nevertheless, as has been shown, Mies' deft appropriation of Gothic architecture and "sacred geometry" warranted the confidence of his assertion that the small modern chapel is an expression "simply and honestly, of what a sacred building should be."[49]

Acknowledgments

I would like to thank the American Philosophical Society for their award of a Franklin Research Grant that enabled me to travel to New York and Chicago in July 2013 to conduct the primary research for this chapter.

Notes

1 Mies van der Rohe, "A Chapel," *Arts and Architecture* 70, no. 1 (January 1953): 19.
2 Friedrich Schiller, *On the Aesthetic Education of Man*, trans. Keith Tribe (London: Penguin, 2016), 30.
3 Franz Schulze, *Mies van der Rohe: A Critical Biography* (Chicago, IL: University of Chicago Press, 1985), 120.
4 The full suite of original drawings for the chapel are held in the *Ludwig Mies van der Rohe Archive* at the Museum of Modern Art (MOMA). Many of the drawings and two photographs of the chapel have

been reproduced in Arthur Drexler, ed., *Robert F. Carr Memorial Chapel of Saint Savior, S.R. Crown Hall, and Other Buildings and Projects*, vol. 5 of *The Mies van der Rohe Archive: Illustrated Catalogue of the Mies van der Rohe Drawings in the Museum of Modern Art* (New York, NY: Garland Publishing, 1986–92). I would like to thank Paul Galloway, the Architecture and Design Study Center Supervisor, for his generous expert assistance in navigating the collection. In addition to retrieving the drawings he made available rare original photographs and a large amount of written correspondence.

5 I visited the chapel on 13 July 2013 together with Elisabeth Dunbar and T. Gunny Harboe. Dunbar is the Director of the Mies van der Rohe Society in Chicago and Harboe is the architect responsible for the continuing preservation and restoration of the building that began in 2008. He was awarded the 2016 Crombie Taylor Citation of Merit by the American Institute of Architects for his work on the chapel. I would like to thank them both for providing access to the building and for sharing their knowledge and insights into its original design and construction.

6 This empathy for the original production, which can be approached and progressively understood yet remains proximately distant, would be termed a "fusion of horizons" in the language of contemporary hermeneutics. See for example Hans-Georg Gadamer, "The Hermeneutic Significance of Temporal Distance," in *Truth and Method*, 2nd edn. (London: Continuum, 2004), 290–300.

7 The architectural brief called for the provision of: "<u>A</u>: Parish hall (community center) and living quarters for resident; <u>B</u>: Church to seat 150 people." Robert F. Carr Memorial Chapel of St. Savior architectural brief, page 1 of 5, 18 March 1949.

8 *Plot Plan* (Archive 4903.136); *Plot Plan* (Archive 4903.137); *Plot Plan* (Archive 4903.148); and *Plot Plan* (Archive 4903.147)

9 According to Peter Carter: "Since most of the Institute's departments shared the same general requirements for classrooms, laboratories, drafting rooms, workshops and lecture auditoria, Mies van der Rohe decided to plan the campus on the basis of a three-dimensional structural grid derived from the requirements of a typical classroom—its multiplication providing accommodation for the other functions. The unit chosen was 24 feet square by 12 feet high. By covering the whole site with a grid based on this module, columns could be located at the intersections and, because the site was relatively flat, floor heights would be consistent." Carter, *Mies van der Rohe at Work* (New York, NY: Praeger, 1974), 115.

10 *Plot Plan* (Archive 4903.68); *Foundation and Floor Plans* (Archive 4903.69); *Roof Plan and Detail* (Archive 4903.70); *Elevation and Stair Details, Details of Basement Entrance* (Archive 4903.71); *West Wall Louver Details* (Archive 4903.72); *East Wall Details* (Archive 4903.73); *West Wall Details* (Archive 4903.74); *North and South Wall Details* (Archive 4903.75); *Interior Wood Details* (Archive 4903.76); *Foundations* (Archive 4903.77); *Foundation Details* (Archive 4903.78); *Plan, Sections and Elevations* (Archive 4903.79); and Steel Details (Archive 4903.76).

11 Mies met with the general contractor H. G. Armstrong on 31 October 1950 to discuss, in Armstrong's words, "the possibilities of effecting a saving through the use of alternate methods, materials, systems and detailing in connection with the proposed new chapel at the Illinois Institute of Technology". H. G. Armstrong to Mies van der Rohe, November 1, 1950.

12 Wallace E. Conkling to Mies van der Rohe, January 19, 1951.

13 The final construction cost was $70,000.

14 Mies van der Rohe, "A Chapel," 19.

15 "A straight line is said to be cut in extreme and mean ratio when, as the whole line is to the greater segment, so is the greater to the less." Thomas L. Heath, trans. *Euclid. The Thirteen Books of the Elements*, vol. 2 (New York, NY: Dover, 1956), 188. If the length of the greater segment is 1 then the length of the whole line is approximately 1.618.

16 Note that while the golden rectangle has previously been recognized in the chapel by others, its derivation from the original proposal for the building has not. Two texts that mention the presence of the golden rectangle in the building are: Jun-ichi Sano, "On the Golden Ratio in the Plan of Mies' IIT Chapel," *Summaries of Technical Papers of Annual Meeting Architectural Institute of Japan 1990* (1990): 1029–30; and Kimberly Elam, *Geometry of Design* (Princeton, NJ: Princeton Architectural Press, 2001).

17 For a summary account of the discovery of the golden mean, and the various meanings that have been attributed to it through history, see Mario Livio, *The Golden Ratio* (New York, NY: Broadway Books, 2002).

18 Luca Pacioli, *Divina proportione* [On The Divine Proportion] (Venice, Italy: Paganini, 1509), vol. 1, chap. 5.

19 For a discussion of this proclivity amongst modern architects, with particular reference to Peter Behrens, see my essay "The Medieval Masons' Lodge as Paradigm for Peter Behrens's Dombauhütte in Munich, 1922," *The Art Bulletin* 90 (September 2008): 442–466.

20 Hendrik Petrus Berlage, *Grundlagen und Entwicklung der Architektur* [The Foundations and Development of Architecture] (Berlin, Germany: Julius Bard, 1908). Philip Johnson commented in a 1977 conversation with Ludwig Glaeser: "the only man he [Mies] ever mentioned was Berlage. He never mentioned Behrens," to which Glaeser replied "Berlage was probably safest because, although he knew him well personally, the relationship was not too direct." Published in Philip C. Johnson, *Mies van der Rohe*, 3rd edn. (New York, NY: Museum of Modern Art, 1978), 208.

21 Berlage, *Grundlagen und Entwicklung der Architektur*, 100.

22 ibid., 100. Translation by the author.

23 Wallace E. Conkling to Mies van der Rohe, 22 December 1951. The word 'must' is underlined in the original letter.

24 Peter Carl, "Architecture and Time: A Prolegomena, Part 1," *AA Files* 22 (Autumn 1991), 60.

25 Ross Anderson, "The Appian Way," *AA Files* 75 (Winter 2017): 163–182; Lutz Robbers, "1912-Hellerau as Spielraum," in *Participation in Art and Architecture*, eds. Martino Stierli and Mechtild Widrich (London: I.B. Tauris, 2015), 197–226.

26 The conversion of the structure from steel-frame to loadbearing brick occurred between 6 October 1950 and 21 April 1951. This is evidenced by two identically composed versions of the plan, and one wall section, issued on those dates. The relevant drawings for the structural steel and brick infill version of 6 October 1950 are: *Foundation and Floor Plans* (Archive 4903.69); and *North and South Wall Details* (Archive 4903.75). And the relevant versions for the load bearing brick version of 21 April 1951 that was built are: *Foundation and Floor Plans* (Archive 4903.59); and *North and South Wall Details* (Archive: 4903.65).

27 Johnson, *Mies van der Rohe*, 3rd edn., 206.

28 Ibid.

29 Ibid.

30 Conversation between Mies van der Rohe and Dirk Lohan in 1968, published in Schulze, *Mies van der Rohe*, 13.

31 Mies' personal library of around six hundred books is now held at the University of Illinois at Chicago Library. In 1975, Werner Blaeser met with members of Mies' family and one of his close friends and identified the 150 titles that were most important to Mies: Alexander von Gleichen-Russwurm, *Die gotische Welt: Sitten und Gebräuche im späten Mittelalter* [The Gothic World: Customs and Conventions in the Late Middle Ages] (Stuttgart, Germany: Julius Hoffmann, 1919); Jahn Healey, trans. *Saint Augustine, The City of God* (London: J.M. Dent & Sons, 1934); Anton Charles Pegis, trans. and ed. Thomas Aquinas, *The Basic Writings of Thomas Aquinas* (New York, NY: Random House, 1945); Erwin Panofsky, *Gothic Architecture and Scholasticism* (Latrobe, PA: The Archabbey Press, 1951); John Fitchem, *The Construction of Gothic Cathedrals* (Oxford, UK: Clarendon Press, 1961); Otto von Simson, *The Gothic Cathedral: Origins of Gothic Architecture and the Medieval Concept of Order* (New York, NY: Pantheon, 1965); and François Cali, *Das Gesetz der Gotik: eine Studie über gotische Architektur* [The Law of the Gothic: A Study on Gothic Architecture] (Munich, Germany: Prestel, 1963). For the full selection, see Werner Blaeser, *Mies van der Rohe: The Art of Structure*, trans. D. Q. Stephenson (Basel, Switzerland: Birkhäuser, 1993), 228–231.

32 J. Ralph Deppen to Mies van der Rohe, 18 January 1951.

33 Ibid.

34 Denis Diderot and Jean le Rond d'Alembert, eds., *Encyclopédie, ou dictionnaire raisonné des sciences, des arts et des métiers* [Encyclopedia, or Classified Dictionary of Sciences, Arts, and Trades], 35 vols. (Paris, France: André le Breton, Michel-Antoine David, Laurent Durand and Antoine-Claude Briasson: 1751–72). The architectural content in the *Encyclopédie* is dispersed under the entries "Architect, Architecture, Decoration (Architecture)" and "School (Architecture)".

35 Roland Barthes, "The Plates of the Encyclopedia," in *A Barthes Reader*, ed. Susan Sontag (New York, NY: Hill and Wang, 1986), 221.

36 "Mies helped very much with the translation—that is, he helped Cynthia Harris to understand Schwarz's ideas." Blaeser, *Mies van der Rohe*, 231.

37 Mies van der Rohe, unpaginated foreword to *The Church Incarnate: The Sacred Function of Christian Architecture* by Rudolf Schwarz, trans. Cynthia Harris (Chicago, IL: Henry Regnery, 1958).

38 Schwarz, *The Church Incarnate*, 9.

39 Curiously, it turns out that the chapel is in fact oriented completely contrary to convention. The altar end of the building that is implicitly equated with both liturgical and magnetic east actually faces due west, a fact that is not immediately disclosed in the plan drawings. Mies' plans assent to the medieval practice of "orienting" a drawing by pointing the part of the plan that has the highest ontological import "up." At that time, the altar that was always in the east was therefore always situated at the top of the page, and the main west entry was at the base. However, in Mies' chapel, liturgical east is magnetic west.

40 K. Michael Hays, "The Mies Effect," in *Mies in America*, ed. Phyllis Lambert (Montréal, Canada: Canadian Centre for Architecture, 2001), 698.

41 Ibid., 701.

42 Significant publications in which the photograph appears include Philip C. Johnson, *Mies van der Rohe*, 2nd edn. (New York, NY: Museum of Modern Art, 1953); Ludwig Hilbersheimer, *Mies van der Rohe* (Chicago, IL: Paul Thebald, 1956); Arthur Drexler, *Ludwig Mies van der Rohe* (New York, NY: George Braziller, 1960); Franz Schulze, *Mies van der Rohe: A Critical Biography* (Chicago, IL: University of Chicago Press, 1985); Fritz Neumeyer, *The Artless Word: Mies van der Rohe on the Building Art* (Cambridge, MA: MIT Press, 1991); and Adrian Forty, *Words and Buildings: A Vocabulary of Modern Architecture* (London: Thames & Hudson, 2000).

43 The three photographic prints were all made from Hedrich-Blessing Negative Number 15691-D, and do not have their own individual accession numbers. They are held in the *Ludwig Mies van der Rohe Archive* at the *Museum of Modern Art*.

44 Mies van der Rohe, "A Chapel," 18.

45 The small halftone reproduction of the full photograph was reproduced in unattributed, "Mies van der Rohe's Philosophy of Architecture is Outlined," *Armour Research Foundation News* 4, no. 12 (December 1952): 3. A copy is held in the Ludwig Mies van der Rohe Collection held at the Ryerson & Burnham Libraries at the Art Institute of Chicago.

46 Hays, "The Mies Effect," 699; original emphasis.

47 Berlage, *Grundlagen und Entwicklung der Architektur*; Schwarz, *The Church Incarnate*.

48 Mies judiciously chose the time of day and angle of view for the signature photograph of the chapel taken in October 1952, and he oversaw its cropping and manipulation in the darkroom.

49 Mies van der Rohe, "A Chapel," 19.

References

Anderson, Ross. "The Appian Way." *AA Files* 75 (Winter 2017): 163–182.

———. "The Medieval Masons' Lodge as Paradigm for Peter Behrens's Dombauhütte in Munich, 1922." *The Art Bulletin* 90 (September 2008): 442–466.

Aquinas, Thomas. *The Basic Writings of Thomas Aquinas*. Translated and edited by Anton Charles Pegis (New York, NY: Random House, 1945).

Barthes, Roland. "The Plates of the Encyclopedia." In Susan Sontag, ed. *A Barthes Reader*, 218–235 (New York, NY: Hill and Wang, 1986).

Berlage, Hendrik Petrus. *Grundlagen und Entwicklung der Architektur* (Berlin, Germany: Julius Bard, 1908).

Blaeser, Werner. *Mies van der Rohe: The Art of Structure*. Translated by D. Q. Stephenson (Basel, Switzerland: Birkhäuser, 1993).

Cali, François. *Das Gesetz der Gotik: eine Studie über gotische Architektur* (Munich, Germany: Prestel, 1963).

Carl, Peter. "Architecture and Time: A Prolegomena, Part 1." *AA Files* 22 (Autumn 1991): 48–65.

Carter, Peter. *Mies van der Rohe at Work* (New York, NY: Praeger, 1974).

Diderot, Denis and Jean le Rond d'Alembert, eds. *Encyclopédie, ou dictionnaire raisonné des sciences, des arts et des métiers*. 35 vols (Paris, France: André le Breton, Michel-Antoine David, Laurent Durand and Antoine-Claude Briasson, 1751–72).

Drexler, Arthur. *Ludwig Mies van der Rohe*. (New York, NY: George Braziller, 1960).

———, ed. *Robert F. Carr Memorial Chapel of Saint Savior, S.R. Crown Hall, and Other Buildings and Projects*, vol. 5 of *The Mies van der Rohe Archive: Illustrated Catalogue of the Mies van der Rohe Drawings in the Museum of Modern Art* (New York, NY: Garland Publishing, 1986–92).

Elam, Kimberly. *Geometry of Design* (Princeton, NJ: Princeton Architectural Press, 2001).

Fitchem, John. *The Construction of Gothic Cathedrals* (Oxford, UK: Clarendon Press, 1961).

Forty, Adrian. *Words and Buildings: A Vocabulary of Modern Architecture* (London: Thames & Hudson, 2000).

Gadamer, Hans-Georg. "The Hermeneutic Significance of Temporal Distance." In *idem. Truth and Method*. 2nd edn., 290–300 (London: Continuum, 2004).

Gleichen-Russwurm, Alexander von. *Die gotische Welt: Sitten und Gebräuche im späten Mittelalter* [The Gothic World: Customs and Conventions in the Late Middle Ages] (Stuttgart, Germany: Julius Hoffmann, 1919).

Hays, K. Michael. "The Mies Effect." In *Mies in America*, edited by Phyllis Lambert, 692–705 (Montréal, Canada: Canadian Centre for Architecture, 2001).

Healey, Jahn. trans. *Saint Augustine, The City of God* (London: J.M. Dent & Sons, 1934).

Heath, Thomas L., trans. *Euclid. The Thirteen Books of the Elements* (New York, NY: Dover, 1956).

Hilbersheimer, Ludwig. *Mies van der Rohe* (Chicago, IL: Paul Thebald, 1956).

Johnson, Philip C. *Mies van der Rohe*. 3rd edn. (New York, NY: Museum of Modern Art, 1978 (2nd edn., 1953)).

Livio, Mario. *The Golden Ratio* (New York, NY: Broadway Books, 2002).

"Mies van der Rohe's Philosophy of Architecture is Outlined." *Armour Research Foundation News* 4, no. 12 (December 1952): 3.

Neumeyer, Fritz. *The Artless Word: Mies van der Rohe on the Building Art* (Cambridge, MA: MIT Press, 1991).

Pacioli, Luca, *Divina proportione* [On The Divine Proportion] (Venice, Italy: Paganini, 1509).

Panofsky, Erwin. *Gothic Architecture and Scholasticism* (Latrobe, PA: The Archabbey Press, 1951).

Robbers, Lutz. "1912-Hellerau as Spielraum." In *Participation in Art and Architecture*, edited by Martino Stierli and Mechtild Widrich (London: I.B. Tauris, 2015), 197–226.

Rohe, Mies van der. "A Chapel." *Arts and Architecture* 70, no. 1 (January 1953): 18–19.

Sano, Jun-ichi. "On the Golden Ratio in the Plan of Mies' IIT Chapel." *Summaries of Technical Papers of Annual Meeting Architectural Institute of Japan 1990* (1990): 1029–1030.

Schiller, Friedrich. *On the Aesthetic Education of Man*. Translated by Keith Tribe (London: Penguin, 2016).

Schulze, Franz. *Mies van der Rohe: A Critical Biography* (Chicago, IL: University of Chicago Press, 1985).

Schwarz, Rudolf. *The Church Incarnate: The Sacred Function of Christian Architecture*. Translated by Cynthia Harris (Chicago, IL: Henry Regnery, 1958).

Simson, Otto von. *The Gothic Cathedral: Origins of Gothic Architecture and the Medieval Concept of Order* (New York, NY: Pantheon, 1965).

2

RELIGIOUS FREEDOM AND ARCHITECTURAL AMBITION AT VASSAR COLLEGE, 1945–54

Lindsay Cook

Le Corbusier motored up to Vassar College during his 1935 lecture tour of the United States. He provided a colorful description of the architecture and student body he encountered at the women's liberal arts college in his travelogue *When the Cathedrals Were White*:

> We arrive at the college "within a budding grove."[1] The buildings are scattered over lawns in a splendid park. Before my speech, I go to see the theater where I am to talk. A dozen girls are taking down the sets of a play put on the evening before. They designed and executed the sets themselves: framework, plywood panels, saws, nails, hammers, and pliers, jars of color and brushes. They are in overalls or in bathing suits. I enjoy looking at these beautiful bodies, made healthy and trim by physical training. The buildings have the atmosphere of luxurious clubs. The girls are in a convent for four years. A joyous convent.[2]

Notwithstanding the tongue-in-cheek tone of this account, in the architect's imagination, the students he encountered at Vassar were akin to sexually frustrated nuns. Belying this naïve impression was the fact that in her spare time, the average student preferred attending lectures and cocktail parties over going to church.[3] On an architectural level, however, the polemical architect could hardly be blamed for drawing an analogy to monasticism. Indeed, while Vassar did not actually function as a convent, in many respects it did look like one, with its medieval revival library, chapel, and arts buildings. And yet, at the time of Le Corbusier's visit, student religious engagement on campus was undergoing a change. Over the course of the next two decades, Vassar's administrators would reflect upon the role religion should play in student life. They would eventually look to architecture as a potential vehicle for bolstering spiritual engagement, as this chapter will show. Three overall visions for sacred architecture competed at Vassar during the post-war era: the historicist as shown in the standing chapel (Fig. 2.1), the functionalist as proposed by the College's consulting architect Waldron Faulkner (Figs. 2.2, 2.3), and the modernist as exemplified by Philip Johnson's alternative project (Fig. 2.4). This chapter explores the institutional and

FIGURE 2.1 Vassar College Chapel, Poughkeepsie, New York; Shepley, Rutan and Coolidge; 1904.

Photograph by the author.

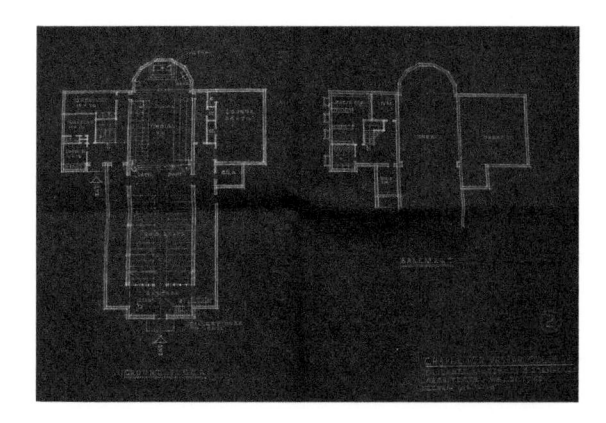

FIGURE 2.2 Vassar College Chapel project; Faulkner, Kingsbury & Stenhouse; Scheme B, 1952.

© Archives & Special Collections, Vassar College.

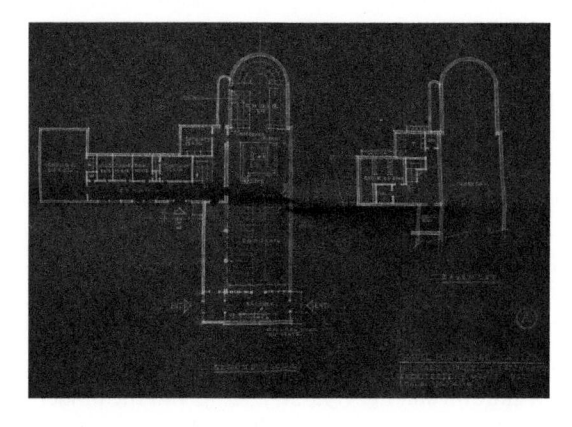

FIGURE 2.3 Vassar College Chapel project; Faulkner, Kingsbury & Stenhouse; Scheme A, 1952.

© Archives & Special Collections, Vassar College.

FIGURE 2.4 Vassar College Chapel project; Philip Johnson; exterior, c. 1953.
© Avery Architectural & Fine Arts Library, Columbia University.

architectural contexts of the three proposals submitted between 1951 and 1953 for a new sacred space on campus. It demonstrates that all three were intended to reverse the decades-long trend of waning religious practice at Vassar.[4]

Background: the "joyous convent" and its critics

Students, faculty, administrators, benefactors, and alumnae came together on October 4, 1902, for a ceremony to lay the cornerstone of the first free-standing Vassar College Chapel, designed by the Boston firm Shepley, Rutan and Coolidge (Fig. 2.1).[5] According to a *New York Times* report, the students

> marched to the site by classes in a long line suggestive of class day and there witnessed the short but impressive service conducted by College President [James Monroe] Taylor. As the stone was lowered into place the students sang "Our Alma Mater."[6]

This romantic portrait exemplified the community that the College hoped would result from the construction of a new, separate chapel. The entire student body assembled in the chapel on a regular basis. The building was an emblem of the campus community. And yet, the fact that the institution required attendance at daily religious services raises questions about the ties of faith among the students who streamed out of the chapel's granite and sandstone portals. The strength of this community was tested in 1926 when student protests resulted in the elimination of mandatory chapel and attendance dropped dramatically.[7]

The institution of voluntary chapel asserted the right of the individual to choose her own path in the name of academic freedom, which extended to religious matters. Reflecting on the change many years later, College President Henry MacCracken framed it in a positive light.[8] In his view, the religious program had become more "earnest and sincere" since the institution of voluntary chapel.[9] The shift also had the negative consequence of dislocating the campus community.[10] Major events such as World War II brought students together naturally, but these bonds loosened at war's end, leaving a void that the College hoped a voluntary, corporate religious program would fill.[11] Faced with diminishing chapel attendance, the institution felt it had to find other ways to make campus spiritual life more appealing. It sought to create an environment in which students would choose to spend their time. This desire for community was the primary impetus for the plan to build a new, significantly smaller chapel at Vassar in the 1950s.[12]

General social and religious trends in post-war America informed life at Vassar, and the College was not immune to the anxious tensions of the nuclear age and mounting Cold War. Elite universities became subject to scrutiny in the struggle between "godly" America and "godless" Communism. In 1951, conservative social commentator William F. Buckley, Jr. published *God and Man at Yale*, a work railing against the liberal intelligentsia for allegedly smothering dissenting opinion in the name of academic freedom.[13] In the book, Buckley discussed his experiences as an undergraduate at Yale, where he found the spiritual education profoundly disappointing.[14] He viewed the need for better instruction at college as a major concern for "those parents and alumni who deem active Christian faith a powerful force for good and for personal happiness," and for society as a whole.[15]

Buckley also implicated Vassar in his apologia. He alleged that from matriculation to Commencement, Vassar students moved "from the conservative to the 'liberal,' from God and man to nature and the state."[16] As evidence, Buckley cited the *Holiday* magazine article "The Vassar Girl," written by critic, novelist, and Vassar alumna Mary McCarthy.[17] It is somewhat surprising that Buckley did not find McCarthy's piece reassuring, as it depicted the majority of current students as politically and religiously conservative. McCarthy argued that the aims of founder Matthew Vassar continued to be central to the College's values, including his conviction that ongoing religious practice at college was essential because "the mothers of a country mold the characters of its citizens, determine its institutions, and shape its destiny."[18] In other words, the founding credo of Vassar College advanced the idea that its students should have a religious education so that they were equipped to exert a positive moral influence on American society by rearing its next generation. While McCarthy painted a conservative portrait of the average Vassar woman of the 1950s, she herself was a prominent exception to the rule.[19] It was in this polarized political climate that plans for a new Vassar Chapel took shape. The project was, in part, a material rejoinder to the complaints lodged by McCarthy and Buckley. But while this dispute was the most public evidence for the College's spiritual reckoning, campus administrators and spiritual leaders were already attuned to these matters.

Communities of faith

Almost immediately after the elimination of mandatory daily prayer in the chapel, the College created the Vassar Community Church. It was not confined to a bricks-and-mortar building but was conceived as a community of faith. The group aimed to provide a platform for pluralistic religious investigation.[20] The College also appointed its first full-time chaplain, Charles McCormick, in 1945.[21] He served as the advisor to the Community Church and attempted to revitalize student interest in the organization. McCormick envisioned the Community Church as a microcosm of the College.[22] It was "a means of self-discovery, learning new skills in human relations, constructive service, and religious growth. In a sense, it is a laboratory in which the individual may come to know herself, her neighbor, and her God."[23] Many students found the Community Church valuable, as it aimed to put students in charge of the religious life of the College.[24] As one student wrote in an editorial in the campus newspaper, "Only a community church gives everyone on campus a chance to express her convictions if she so desires. Community Church is you and me."[25] Another student specified that the value of the organization lay in its "encouraging us to appreciate and understand the religions of others, and to worship together."[26] Professor of English Helen Lockwood related the group's purpose to contemporary existential anxieties: "What the world needs to survive right now is a deepened realization among all people of their common ground." She continued, pointedly, arguing that in the nuclear age, "Christians, Jews, humanists know that they must move toward brotherhood or perish."[27]

At the outset of the 1949–50 academic year, after much debate among Vassar trustees, administrators, faculty, and students, a new religious organization, the Community Religious Association (CRA) replaced Community Church.[28] Whereas the Community Church had assembled students of various faiths in collective, non-denominational spiritual gatherings, CRA was an administrative envelope containing several discrete sectarian entities.[29] In a series of articles in the campus newspaper, many students weighed in on the change. One expressed her opinion that, while the creation of CRA was necessary, she lamented that the event marked "a regression rather than an advance in the religious life of the College."[30] The student went on to flesh out the differences between the two programs, wishing Vassar's needs were more in line with the old organization:

> The Community Church stressed the value of group worship, in which the students were aware that each individual in the group was worshipping in the manner which best fulfilled her religious needs. On the other hand, the students now feel the need of group worship in which the individual realizes that the majority of the group holds the same religious tenets as her own. The Community Religious Association is the first backward step toward religious solidarity rather than religious independence.[31]

Despite some misgivings about CRA, Vassar maintained the new group, and it became the primary religious organization on campus.[32] An article in the 1952 yearbook described the intended role of CRA, providing at once a practical and ideological definition of the group:

> CRA: Vassar Community Religious Association: (derived from the Vassar Community Church) coordinating factor for diverse faiths and manifold interests; legislated by CRA Council, administered by the Worship Committee—and representative of ALL. . . . See also Hillel, Newman Club, the Quaker Group, and the Christian Science Organization: affiliated groups provided for the expression of specific beliefs and relating these to the wide scope of community—and world—living.[33]

The organization intended to forge a community of faith at Vassar so that alumnae might follow its example after graduation.[34] Between 1951 and 1953, Vassar considered expressing its pluralistic religious stance through architecture. Two architects proposed a total of three projects intended to meet this need. All three expressed new design concepts. Two were predominantly functionalist, and the third was decidedly modernist. Ultimately, the College retrofitted the existing historicist chapel to provide for the modern campus religious community.

Visions for a functionalist new chapel

Vassar President Sarah Gibson Blanding wrote to John D. Rockefeller III in January 1952 to thank him and his wife, Blanchette Hooker Rockefeller, for a gift they had recently made to Vassar.[35] Blanding indicated that $5,000 from their gift would go toward addressing the "condition of the chapel," which had "been a major concern."[36] The fundraising campaign centered on the renovation of the original building.[37] Deferred maintenance had left it looking "disgraceful."[38] To justify the undertaking, Blanding cited the chapel's leaky roof and outdated interior, as well as her wish to "block off a part of the building so that the students and faculty who attend our daily chapel service feel the community of worship."[39] She believed the chapel to be "so essential in lifting people out of themselves."[40] Blanding's anxiety that personal freedom, if left unchecked, might give way to individual isolation or even self-absorption is palpable in her remarks, as is her optimism that architecture could prevent such negative outcomes.[41] Chaplain William Kirkland was the other driving force behind the development of plans for a new, free-standing religious center on campus.[42] His specifications for the building, which he hoped would increase spiritual engagement among the student body, addressed function above all:

> A more suitable and appropriate place for holding daily chapel is greatly needed. There are good reasons for believing that a small chapel would greatly strengthen the daily worship life of the students . . . By providing an adequate and appropriate physical setting for not only worship but the entire program of religious activities, an official status and backing for the religious concern would be made for which there is no effective substitute. It will do much toward getting religion off the edge and into the center of the campus.[43]

Kirkland's ideas were consistent with broader trends in religious thought on campuses and in residential areas throughout the United States, where the social functions of religion were becoming increasingly important.[44] The post-war American religious revival came with a material manifestation, in the form of thousands of new sacred buildings.[45] Architects and building planners published a flurry of books in the post-war period geared toward communities planning to construct new religious edifices.[46] For the most part, these studies encouraged inexpensive, unremarkable, simple buildings, but they almost always addressed the need for new social spaces, like religious schools, social halls, and offices, intended to perfect these structures as epicenters of belonging.[47] Architectural periodicals likewise attest to the religious building boom, with ongoing typological coverage of religious commissions. For example, buildings for mainline Protestant, Jewish, and Catholic congregations, as well as the occasional interfaith group, filled the pages of *Architectural Record* for over a decade beginning in 1947. The magazine articles capture the discourse surrounding the theoretical and practical problems designers of sacred architecture then faced, such as how to design modern American synagogues, how to convey "churchliness" through architecture rather than symbolic ornament, and how to maneuver around aesthetically conservative members of church committees.[48]

The post-war religious revival in the United States touched the microcosm of the Vassar community unevenly. It reached administrators, spiritual leaders, and trustees, but the student body proved largely resistant to its lure.[49] Kirkland entertained the idea that modernist architecture, in particular, might be the magnet required to attract students to the campus religious program. Sharing his vision for the new chapel, Kirkland wrote:

> It would seem appropriate to have the building embody a classical form of Christian architecture, but with a modern adaptation or expression. This would combine the values of the depth and length of the historical tradition of the Christian Faith, but it would also give emphasis to its contemporary relevance . . . Any form too easily suggesting that religion is an anachronism—a relic held over from the past—would be unfortunate. Likewise, any extreme modern form would be ill-advised, for it would sacrifice the depth and authority of the great historical tradition.[50]

Kirkland echoed many of the stylistic and symbolic concerns surrounding sacred buildings among contemporaries working in the fields of theology and architecture.[51] However, he departed from CRA's stated interfaith ambitions by articulating a concept for the new chapel that amounted to a modern mask for a traditional Christian church.[52]

The architect Waldron Faulkner submitted schemes for a new campus sacred building in May 1952.[53] By that date, the scope of the project had increased from an addition to the 1904 chapel to a design for a new free-standing religious center.[54] In a letter to the chaplain, Faulkner shared two possible plans for the new building. The blueprint labeled "Scheme B" adhered to the chaplain's functional and formal specifications (Fig. 2.2).[55] But the architect preferred the design variation suggestively labeled "Scheme A" (Fig. 2.3).[56] Both plans feature seating at ground and gallery levels for 250 people and room for 80 in the choir. Whereas Scheme B has a single, central entrance to the main vessel, Scheme A features two lateral points of entry, one on either side of the narthex. The altar is situated behind the choir and at the end of the apse in Scheme B. Scheme A establishes the altar closer to the assembly by placing it in front of the choir.[57] The pulpit in Scheme A is placed marginally closer to the congregation relative to Scheme B. Scheme B maintains a cruciform plan, which, while perceptible from the exterior, would have dissolved once inside, with the arms of the transept divided up into several auxiliary rooms. Favoring this plan, the chaplain signaled his attachment to traditional Christian forms. Scheme A, on the other hand, wholly diverges from this conventional layout, opting instead for a T-shaped interpenetration of worship and social spaces.[58] Both arrangements have an additional entrance that feeds directly into the rooms for social gatherings. Contemporary building manuals and journal articles indicate that architects commonly united spiritual and congregational spaces under one roof.

Faulkner's two plans feature identical functional components and similar liturgical furnishings, all of which adhered to the chaplain's specifications. Faulkner apparently solidified his position as an institutional architect who was willing to take direction by following the chaplain's orders. As Vassar's consulting architect, Faulkner was well acquainted with the practical concerns of his clients, and he often drew up plans for buildings that he knew would never see the light of day. This case was no exception. It is clear from the report of the Buildings and Grounds Committee that the construction of the small chapel hinged on finding a private donor "interested in giving such a chapel to the College."[59]

At this stage, the influential Vassar alumna and trustee Blanchette Rockefeller intervened. She did not bankroll Faulkner's proposal. Instead, she commissioned Philip Johnson to submit an alternative design to compete with Faulkner's schemes.[60] Mrs. Rockefeller and her husband knew Johnson from his tenure at the Museum of Modern Art, and they were among his first architectural clients. A comprehensive list of Johnson's built works and unrealized projects confirms that the Rockefellers ordered the modernist renderings produced for the Vassar Chapel project in 1953.[61] Mrs. Rockefeller was at that point the Chairman of the Buildings and Grounds Committee and thus at the forefront of molding Vassar's architectural ambitions.[62] Thus, when President Blanding wrote to Mr. Rockefeller to inform him of the project for a new chapel, she was formally communicating plans developed with the deep involvement of Mrs. Rockefeller.[63]

Philip Johnson's proposal

Among Johnson's architectural drawings in Avery Architectural & Fine Arts Library at Columbia University is a pair of large (27" × 36") charcoal and pencil sketches on board associated with the Vassar Chapel project.[64] While the draftsman is unknown, we can safely assume that Johnson directed their execution, but did not actually draw them himself.[65] Until now, both renderings have been associated with the Vassar project. However, reconciling the original drawings with the photographic record of additional documents securely connected to the Vassar project in the Special Collections at the Getty Research Institute leads to a different conclusion. The exterior rendering conveys a sense of the building's massing (Fig. 2.4). The main vessel is a cube with rounded edges. Projecting from this windowless box is the primary entrance, which takes the form of an elliptical cylinder. In the drawing, four pairs of co-eds stream toward the chapel, dotting the pine-specked landscape, and a solo young woman casts a long shadow on the great portal, dramatizing her arrival at the threshold. The presence of these youthful female figures in the rendering corroborates the assumption that this drawing was, indeed, created for the Vassar Chapel project, even though it was not labeled as such.

Details of the other Avery drawing contradict the interpretation that it is the pendant to the exterior rendering discussed above. The presence of an adult woman and young child are inconsistent with the collegiate setting, and neither the frontal seating arrangement nor the conspicuous cross on the altar are in line with the chaplain's specifications for a centralized, liturgically flexible building. These inconsistencies are not evidence that the architect was unaware or disrespectful of his client's wishes, but proof, rather, that institutional memory within Johnson's office was short. By the time the drawings were inventoried for donation to Avery, the staff assigned to identify projects from decades earlier erroneously associated this drawing with the Vassar project, rather than recognizing it as a detail of his contemporary project for St. Michael's Catholic Church in Houston, Texas, never built. The interior Johnson actually envisioned for the Vassar Chapel was far more radical. Although the original plan, section, and interior elevation drawings are no longer extant, the cardboard-mounted photographic versions of these views survive among Johnson's papers at the Getty (Figs. 2.5, 2.6, 2.7). Johnson submitted them in 1953 and ostensibly received them back from the client.

FIGURE 2.5 Vassar College Chapel project; Philip Johnson (Helmut Jacoby, draftsman); interior, 1953.

© Getty Research Institute, Los Angeles (980060).

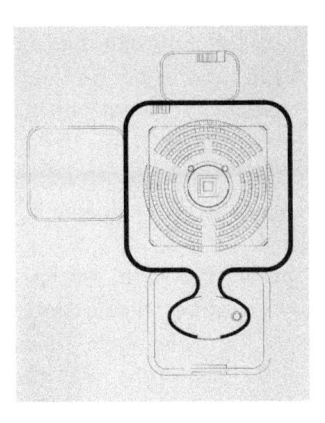

FIGURE 2.6 Vassar College Chapel project; Philip Johnson; plan, c. 1953.

© Getty Research Institute, Los Angeles (980060).

The Vassar renderings are, in all likelihood, some of the earliest Helmut Jacoby produced in Johnson's office after graduating from the Harvard Graduate School of Design.[66] At the very least, Jacoby produced one of the drawings for the Vassar project, as the interior rendering bears his signature.[67] His name appears below an androgynous figure. It is tempting

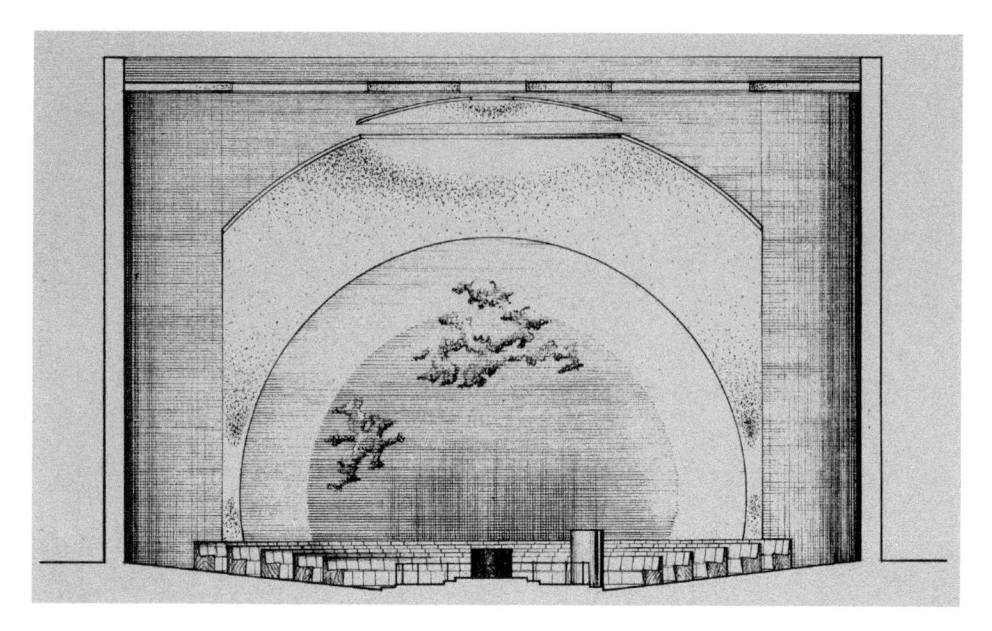

FIGURE 2.7 Vassar College Chapel project; Philip Johnson; section, c. 1953.
© Getty Research Institute, Los Angeles (980060).

to interpret this figure as a young woman appropriating the "Ivy look," a trend in collegiate menswear.[68] However, Jacoby shared a memory from his tenure in Johnson's office that suggests an alternative interpretation:

> I remember once drawing a college for [Johnson], and putting in a whole lot of boys. When Johnson saw it, he asked me whether he had not mentioned that it was a girls' college! But he still left everything just the way I had drawn it.[69]

Jacoby did not name the college, and while he would have been referring to the Sarah Lawrence campus plan, the anecdote provides a glimpse of the laissez-faire working procedures in Johnson's office in that era.

Like Faulkner before him, Johnson drew from a deep well of historical sources for his Vassar project. However, the latter's resulting scheme departed drastically from those models when taken as a whole. For the plan of the vestibule, Johnson may have considered prototypes such as St. Peter's Square or the plan of the presbytery of Santa Maria della Salute in Venice.[70] For the centrally planned sanctuary, he united eclectic elements freely. The nonstructural ciborium overhead evokes the crossing of a Gothic church. Johnson's reverence for Chartres Cathedral is palpable in his contemporary lectures, and while this element is by no means an exact translation of a Chartrain vault, it is likely that the building influenced him during his first foray into sacred architectural design.[71] Johnson held up Chartres and, to a lesser extent, other French cathedrals as paragons of what was possible architecturally when space took priority over economy and function. Conversely, as he said in a 1953 address delivered in a symposium at Smith College on the topic of "The Relation of Art and Morals," by privileging function and economy over spatial effects, "you'll never get any church, you'll never get any religion."[72] In the variant of this speech that Johnson gave at the Minneapolis Institute of Arts in 1954, he added:

> [Economy] seems to me particularly tragic in church architecture, where ad maiorem gloriam Dei is apt to get mixed-up with costs per pew and end up with cinder block structures in the midst of the richest civilization in the history of the world.[73]

Johnson's soaring interior likewise recalls the vaulted and domed spaces of John Soane's existing and demolished works in London, in vogue in 1952 thanks to John Summerson's monograph, which contains numerous plates featuring this signature spatial device.[74] Claude-Nicolas Ledoux's scheme for a spherical dwelling is yet another important source for the chapel project.[75] Unlike many examples of Ledoux's "speaking architecture," the abstract nature of the spherical design particularly attracted modern architects, Johnson included.[76] In addition to these historical sources, Johnson's design relates formally and conceptually to the schemes published in *Vom Bau der Kirche*, the 1938 book on the archetypes of church architecture by the German architect and urban planner Rudolf Schwarz.[77] Johnson read German and may have perused the book itself, but it is equally plausible that he absorbed Schwarz's ideas from either the illustrated summary in the June 1948 issue of *Architectural Record* or the one in the October 1952 issue of *The Architectural Review*.[78] Both images introduced Schwarz's ideas to Anglophone professionals and illustrated his "sacred inwardness" plan, which can be traced in Johnson's Vassar Chapel plan.

Moreover, the proposed site for the new chapel may have provided inspiration to the architect. The religious center was to sit "in the pines in front of the Aula," on the outer edge of the Athletic Circle, a student recreational hub.[79] By contrast to Faulkner's angular design, the rounded corners would have fit into the existing landscape, and the functional spaces would have been cleverly tucked away underground and in the pine-forested area behind the building, leaving the main approach unobstructed. Jacoby clearly took this location into account in his stylish exterior rendering. Overall, while it appears that most of Johnson's sources belonged to a Christian milieu, the resulting design was emphatically non-sectarian. He aimed to create a transcendent sacred space for the multiple faith communities that would worship in it.

Vassar's President Blanding unveiled the plan for a new, smaller chapel in October 1953, more than a year after the College had received the Faulkner renderings, and almost certainly after Johnson had submitted his schemes for the chapel.[80] The minutes from a meeting of the Vassar Board of Trustees referenced "two models in contemporary design for a small chapel."[81] Neither model is known to survive, but it is likely that Faulkner and Johnson submitted one apiece.[82] An article in the student newspaper furnished the justification for and practical details about this proposal:

> More stimulation would be received when people worship closely together. Another reason is that visiting ministers are often given the wrong impression when they see few people scattered in the large chapel, and therefore believe that people here have little regard for spiritual life. Alumnae receive the same impression, especially when recalling scenes of students streaming across the campus to attend chapel.[83]

This small sacred space was, therefore, meant to play two important roles: to enhance the spiritual life of the student body, encouraging a feeling of the community of faith, and to help

Vassar quiet alumnae and outside critics who thought that a conspicuous reduction in chapel attendance signified a lack of spirituality among the student body.[84]

Criticism of Johnson's proposal

In the first article about the proposed religious center in the student newspaper, President Blanding endeavored to shape popular opinion about the importance of the project.[85] She described spiritual life as an important part of a "well-rounded individual." She continued:

> It is discouraging to see so few people in chapel: we seem to be turning away from the values which all religions represent and towards a materialistic philosophy. It is hoped that a new chapel will help end this tendency by encouraging more people to participate in the spiritual life of the campus.[86]

The irony that Blanding's cure for materialism required costly building materials was not lost on some outspoken student critics.[87] The editorial board of the student newspaper seized upon this point:

> If the administration is worried about the fact that we seem to be turning away from the values which all religions represent and towards a materialistic philosophy (and we also find this discouraging), it is hard to see how it is a step away from materialism to offer as a solution the building of a new chapel.[88]

According to the editors, the institution's proposal to build a superfluous sacred building only confirmed suspicions of its materialism.[89]

Chaplain Kirkland responded to this line of criticism by reiterating the need for a religious center to educate the "whole person," providing "resources and facilities that educate and challenge the spirit as well as the mind."[90] Kirkland also doubted the original chapel's efficacy in providing a sense of community among students in the age of voluntary chapel: "It is very difficult for a group of 100 to achieve the real sense of unity and community so vital to corporate worship in a vast building that has a 1500 seating capacity."[91] In valuing the material investment in a new space, he advanced the thesis that French philosopher Jacques Maritain elaborated in 1945 regarding the fable of American materialism. Maritain viewed the perceptions of materialism in America as one result of "an old prejudice, confusing spirituality with an aristocratic contempt for any improvement in material life."[92] As religious scholar Martin Marty later framed the matter, although "pure" materialism implied the neglect of spiritual matters and "pure" spirituality implied the neglect of material or worldly interest, "the American situation has allowed for few pure separations of the two sets of impulses."[93] Particularly in the wake of World War II, the administration identified the construction of a chapel as the most potentially effective strategy for cultivating a community of faith.[94] But Kirkland's vision for a new chapel never came to fruition. He left the chaplaincy in 1954, the same year in which Waldron Faulkner requested to be released from his contract as Vassar's consulting architect.[95]

The chapel project raised issues about the mechanics of creating places for communities to blossom that remained on the College's mind for many years.[96] When Kirkland's successor, Robert Bonthius, wrote his first chaplain's report to President Blanding in 1955, he reiterated the need for a "smaller place of worship . . . for regular chapel and special religious services."[97] Still in line with Kirkland's project, Bonthius saw a need for a smaller place suitable for Jewish, Catholic, and Protestant services to attract worshippers of these faiths. Unlike his predecessor, Bonthius believed that adding a side chapel onto the existing building would suffice to achieve these goals.[98] In 1954, the vigorous plans for a small, independent religious center faded. Neither Faulkner's nor Johnson's proposal was built.

The legacy of Johnson's Vassar Chapel proposal

The legacy of Johnson's 1953 project for the Vassar Chapel can be traced in a version of his synagogue design for Congregation Kneses Tifereth Israel (KTI) in Port Chester, New York (1954). Johnson maintained the domed, elliptical cylindrical entrance vestibule, first envisioned for the Vassar project, in the final design of the synagogue (Fig. 2.8). He modified the interior originally designed for Vassar only slightly in his initial proposal for the KTI synagogue interior. The changes made in the preliminary drawing transformed the interfaith chapel into a purpose-built modern synagogue. He added a bimah (elevated platform), ark (container for the Torah scrolls), ner tamid (hanging lamp), and two seven-branch standing menorahs and rearranged the seats to form rows facing the ark (Fig. 2.9). Johnson submitted the initial presentation drawing before the location of KTI's new sacred

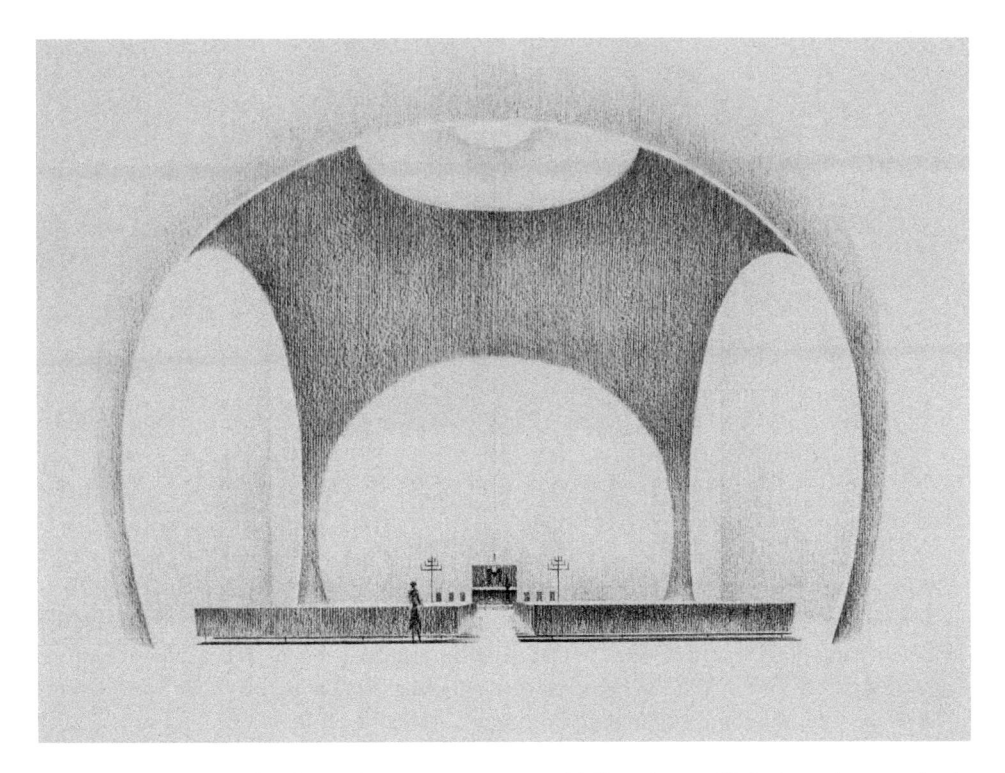

FIGURE 2.8 Kneses Tifereth Israel Synagogue project; Philip Johnson (E. J. Cyr, photographer); interior, c. 1953.

FIGURE 2.9 Kneses Tifereth Israel Synagogue; Philip Johnson; exterior, 1953–55.
Photograph by the author.

FIGURE 2.10 Kneses Tifereth Israel Synagogue; Philip Johnson; interior, 1953–55.
© Archives, Congregation Kneses Tifereth Israel.

space had been determined. For this reason, the drawing is labeled "Greenwich Synagogue," even though the final site was in Port Chester. Dated working drawings in Avery show that the first version of the sanctuary featured a single canopy designed around a sphere. Johnson abandoned this design in 1953 in favor of a rectangular plan containing seven bays. As built in 1954, the steel structure, concrete infill, plaster "vaults," wood cladding, and stained-glass slit windows came together to form a "monumental jewel box" (Fig. 2.10).[99]

Johnson's initial proposals for sacred spaces in Poughkeepsie and Port Chester likewise relate visually to the contemporary design for St. Michael's Church in Houston.[100] Their similarities led Johnson's own staff and future archivists to correlate some drawings with the wrong project. Henry-Russell Hitchcock added to the confusion by illustrating his introductory essay to Johnson's early architectural production with an illustration of the plan of the Vassar Chapel, referring to it as an "un-built Greenwich church," unwittingly conflating the Vassar interfaith chapel, the synagogue, and the Houston Catholic church.[101] The mistake suggests that the plan looked convincingly to Hitchcock like a Christian church, despite its unusual centralized seating arrangement. Hitchcock's assumption will seem like less of an intellectual leap if we bear in mind the plan's formal connections to the first church type schematized in Schwarz's treatise, devoted explicitly to Christian church architecture.[102] Nevertheless, the fact that one of the leading architectural historians of the day (and close personal associate of Johnson) confused the three projects only a decade after their creation is a testament to the commonalities among Johnson's various expressions of the sacred.

Conclusion

At Vassar, the historicist vision for sacred architecture prevailed over the functionalist and the modernist. Instead of building a new chapel by Faulkner or Johnson, the original 1904 chapel was refurbished and remained in use. Ideological and demographic shifts largely prompted this outcome. The student body's desire to participate in organized religion on campus diminished just as its confessional diversity increased.[103] And yet, the College did not, as a rule, oppose modernism. In fact, the construction of Marcel Breuer's Ferry House (completed 1951), a vehicle for cooperative living, and Eero Saarinen's Noyes House (completed 1958), a futuristic dormitory, bookended the chapel project chronologically. As overall enrollment swelled, modernist residential architecture proliferated, but it lacked a sacred architectural corollary. In the 1950s, the Vassar Girl's "joyous convent" gained not a sacred building, but rather the plush, colorful sunken ring at the heart of the Noyes lounge known as the "Passion Pit."[104]

Acknowledgments

The author is grateful to the following people for their assistance in the preparation of this chapter: Nicholas Adams, Barry Bergdoll, Monica Blank, Suli Fassler, Dorothy Friedman, Shelley Hayreh, Alison Hinchman, Cammie McAtee, Margot Metzger, Janet Parks, Dean Rogers, Joan Rosenbaum, Rita Unger, and Evans Woollen.

Notes

1 Le Corbusier alluded to *À l'ombre des jeunes filles en fleurs*, the second volume of Marcel Proust's magnum opus *À la recherche du temps perdu* (Paris: Gallimard, 1919). Several of Le Corbusier's observations about Vassar students mirror Proust's narrator's description of the girls he admired as they walked along the coast of Balbec.

2 Le Corbusier, *When the Cathedrals Were White, A Journey to the Country of the Timid People* (New York, NY: Reynal & Hitchcock, 1947), 136–137. Mardges Bacon presents a detailed account of the architect's American tour in *Le Corbusier in America: Travels in the Land of the Timid* (Cambridge, MA: MIT Press, 2001).

3 Le Corbusier estimated that 600 students (i.e. roughly half of the student population) attended his lecture.

4 By the 1951–52 academic year, an average of 55 people attended daily chapel. William Kirkland, "Report to the President from the Chaplain: 1951–52," folder "Annual Reports to the President," Office of Religious and Spiritual Life, box 1, Vassar College Archives & Special Collections.

5 "Vassar Cornerstone Laying," *New York Times*, October 5, 1902.

6 Ibid.

7 "The College Girl Starts a Revolution: She Demands Individual Training, Rejects Cloistered Seclusion and Wants to be a Doer in the Work of the World Today," *New York Times*, May 13, 1928. See also Barbara Miller Solomon, *In the Company of Educated Women* (New Haven, CT: Yale University Press, 1985), 47–50.

8 "Asserts Students Are Alive to Crisis: MacCracken Assures Interfaith Conference They Recognize Need of the Spiritual," *New York Times*, November 30, 1940.

9 Ibid.

10 Solomon, *In the Company of Educated Women*, 91–93.

11 "V.C. Chaplains," folder 7.32, Vassar College Subject File, Vassar College Archives & Special Collections.

12 Kirkland, "Report to the President from the Chaplain: 1951–52"; Kirkland, "Report to the President from the Chaplain: 1952–1953," folder "Annual Reports to the President," Office of Religious and Spiritual Life, box 1, Vassar College Archives & Special Collections.

13 William F. Buckley, Jr., *God and Man at Yale: The Superstitions of "Academic Freedom"* (Chicago, IL: Regnery, 1951), 9.

14 Ibid.

15 Ibid., 4.

16 Ibid., 195.

17 Mary McCarthy, "The Vassar Girl" (1951), in *On the Contrary* (New York, NY: Farrar, Straus and Cudahy, 1961), 193–214.

18 Ibid., 194 (quoting Matthew Vassar).

19 Ibid., 202–203.

20 "Founders Envisage 'Community Church' as Flexible Channel," *Vassar Miscellany News* (Poughkeepsie, NY), December 1, 1948.

21 "V.C. Chaplains."

22 Charles G. McCormick, "Role of a Community Church on a College Campus," December 9, 1948, folder 8.70, Vassar College Subject File, Vassar College Archives & Special Collections, 5.

23 McCormick, "Role of a Community Church," 6.

24 "Free Inquiry," *Vassar Miscellany News*, December 1, 1948.

25 Aspasia Courtessis, "Students Find Many Positive Values in Community Church; Seek Clarification of Position of Organization on Campus," *Vassar Miscellany News*, December 1, 1948.

26 Ebba Joe Tate, "Students Find Many Positive Values in Community Church; Seek Clarification of Position of Organization on Campus," *Vassar Miscellany News*, December 1, 1948.

27 Helen Lockwood, "Faculty Members Consider Place of Religion in Vassar Community," *Vassar Miscellany News*, December 1, 1948.

28 "V.C. Community Church," folder 8.70, Vassar College Subject File, Vassar College Archives & Special Collections.

29 "S. Cruikshank, A. Mackay, P. Moran Weigh Relative Merits of V.C. Community Church and College Religious Association," *Vassar Miscellany News*, November 16, 1949.

30 Ibid.

31 Ibid.

32 "V.C. Community Religious Associations," Folder 8.72, Vassar College Subject Files, Vassar College Archives & Special Collections.

33 *Vassarion* (Poughkeepsie: Vassar College, 1952), 45.

34 Charles G. McCormick, "Role of a Community Church on a College Campus," December 9, 1948, folder 8.70, Vassar College Subject File, Vassar College Archives & Special Collections.

35 Vassar College Board of Trustees, February 1952 Meeting Minutes, binder "Trustees Minutes: 1949–50 through 1952–53," Vassar College Archives & Special Collections.

36 Ibid.

37 Ibid.

38 Ibid.

39 Sarah Gibson Blanding to John D. Rockefeller III (JDR 3), January 15, 1952, folder 886, box 119, series "Educational Interests," RG III2G, Rockefeller Foundation Archives, Rockefeller Archive Center (RAC).

40 Ibid.

41 Ibid.

42 Kirkland, "Report to the President from the Chaplain: 1951–52."

43 Ibid.

44 Patrick Allitt, *Religion in America Since 1945: A History* (New York, NY: Columbia University Press, 2003). The chapter "Religion and Materialism" provides an overview of socio-economic conditions in the post-war period and a concise summary of church building in the 1940s and 1950s.

45 Ibid., 33.

46 Richard Kieckhefer, *Theology in Stone: Church Architecture from Byzantium to Berkeley* (New York, NY: Oxford University Press, 2004), 265–292.

47 Ibid.

48 See the "Religious Buildings" series in *Architectural Record*, particularly the issues dated September 1947, June 1948, December 1949, August 1951, and December 1953.

49 For a discussion of weak attendance figures, see Kirkland, "Report to the President from the Chaplain: 1951–52."

50 Ibid.

51 Ibid.

52 This approach is echoed in contemporary guides about church building, and it is conceivable that he picked up one such manual.

53 A partner in the Washington, D.C.-based architectural firm Faulkner, Kingsbury & Stenhouse, Faulkner had previously designed the Vassar infirmary (1940). See "Architect Waldron Faulkner Dies," *Washington Post*, May 14, 1979.

54 Ibid.

55 Kirkland, "Report to the President from the Chaplain: 1951–52." Kirkland signaled seven rooms he wanted the religious center to have, each with a designated function: a robing room for the choir, small office for the choir director, small room for choir music library, small kitchen, chaplain's office, and an office for the CRA president. Faulkner incorporated into his proposal all of these spaces except for the kitchen.

56 Ibid.

57 Kieckhefer, *Theology in Stone*, 275, 279.

58 Ibid., 267.

59 Report of Buildings and Grounds Committee Meeting, October 16, 1953, folder "Committee on Buildings and Grounds, 1950–54," box 1, President's Office Transfer, Sarah Gibson Blanding Papers, Vassar College Archives & Special Collections.

60 Johnson billed the College three times between December 1952 and February 1953—initially through Mrs. Rockefeller's secretary and then directly—and was paid using the $1,000 donation Mrs. Rockefeller had earmarked for this purpose. Folder "Chapel (Proposed-Small) (Not Built)," box 6, Buildings and Grounds Department Files, Vassar College Archives & Special Collections.

61 Philip Johnson Papers, 1908–2002, bulk 1925–98, Getty Research Institute, Research Library, Accession no. 980060, Series III, box 19, folder 1. The chapel is listed as "Vassar (Rockefeller) Poughkeepsie, NY" next to the date of the project, 1953.

62 "Committee on Buildings and Grounds, 1950–54," box 1, President's Office Transfer, Sarah Gibson Blanding Papers, Vassar College Archives & Special Collections.

63 Ibid.

64 Avery Drawings & Archives, NYDA.1974.003.00033 (exterior) and NYDA.1974.003.00034 (interior).

65 Thanks to Evans Woollen, an architect who worked in Johnson's New Canaan office from 1953–54, for this clarification.

66 See Thomas Mellins, "Helmut Jacoby's Architectural Renderings: The Drawing as Analogue," in *Helmut Jacoby: Master of Architectural Drawing* (Tübingen: Wasmuth, 2001), 28.

67 Philip Johnson Papers, 1908–2002, bulk 1925–98, Getty Research Institute, Research Library, Accession no. 980060, Series III, box 19, folder 11. According to this list, Helmut Jacoby drew the exterior rendering in Avery Architectural & Fine Arts Library, as well as the interior formerly associated with the Vassar Chapel project but actually belonging to the contemporary project for St. Michael's Catholic Church, Houston (NYDA 1974.003.00034).

68 Rebecca C. Tuite, "Fashioning the 1950s 'Vassar Girl': Vassar Student Identity and Campus Dress, 1947–60," *Fashion Theory* 17, no. 3 (2013): 299–320.

69 Interview with Helmut Jacoby, in *Helmut Jacoby*, 50.

70 "Religious Buildings," *Architectural Record* 103 (June 1948): 119. See also Kieckhefer, *Theology in Stone*, 236.

71 See, for instance, Franz Schulze, *Philip Johnson: Life and Work* (New York, NY: Alfred A. Knopf, 1994), 188.

72 The art historian and Jewish émigré Edgar Wind organized the symposium. See Karen Michels, "The Emigration of Iconology," in *Jewish Identity in Modern Art History* (Berkeley: University of California Press, 1999), 173.

73 Philip Johnson Papers, 1908–2002, bulk 1925–98, Getty Research Institute, Research Library, Accession no. 980060, Series VII, box 36, folder 9, draft of speech to be delivered at the Minneapolis Institute of Arts in 1954, p. 12.

74 John Summerson, *Sir John Soane* (London: Art and Technics, 1952); Oliver Bradbury, *Sir John Soane's Influence on Architecture from 1791: A Continuing Legacy* (Farnham, UK and Burlington, VT: Ashgate, 2015), 383–424.

75 Philip Johnson, "House at New Canaan, Connecticut," *The Architectural Review* 108, no. 645 (September 1950): 154.

76 Anthony Vidler, introduction to Claude-Nicolas Ledoux, *L'Architecture* (Princeton, NJ: Princeton Architectural Press, 1983), x.

77 Rudolf Schwarz, *Vom Bau der Kirche* (Würzburg: Werkbund-Verlag, 1938).

78 *Architectural Record* 103 (June 1948): 117–119; Gerhard Rosenberg, "The Seven Lamps of Rudolf Schwarz," *The Architectural Review* 112 (October 1952): 261–262.

79 Vassar College Board of Trustees, May 1953 Meeting Minutes, binder "Trustees Minutes: 1949–50 through 1952–53, Vassar College Archives & Special Collections.

80 Kirkland, "Report to the President from the Chaplain: 1951–52"; "Blanding Considers Plan for New, Smaller Chapel."

81 Vassar College Board of Trustees, May 1953 Meeting Minutes.

82 In a letter of January 21, 1953, Keene (of the Buildings and Grounds Committee) instructed Faulkner to send his model to Mrs. Rockefeller for review in New York before sharing it with the rest of the Buildings and Grounds Committee. Folder "Chapel (Proposed-Small) (Not Built)," box 6, Buildings and Grounds Department Files, Vassar College Archives & Special Collections.

83 "Blanding Considers Plan for New, Smaller Chapel," *Vassar Miscellany News*, October 7, 1953.

84 Sarah Gibson Blanding, letter to Rev. James A. Pike of Christ Church Rectory in Poughkeepsie regarding a recent visit by Rev. Bryan Green, November 25, 1948, folder 8.70, Vassar College Subject File, Vassar College Archives & Special Collections.

85 Sarah Blanding, quoted in "Blanding Considers Plan for New, Smaller Chapel."

86 Ibid.

87 "First Things First . . .," *Vassar Miscellany News*, October 14, 1953.

88 Ibid.

89 Ibid.

90 William Kirkland, "Kirkland Writes . . .," *Vassar Miscellany News*, October 21, 1953.

91 Ibid.

92 Jacques Maritain, quoted in Martin E. Marty, "Materialism and Spirituality in American Religion," in Robert Wuthnow, ed., *Rethinking Materialism: Perspectives on the Spiritual Dimension of Economic Behavior* (Grand Rapids, MI: Eerdmans, 1995), 237.

93 Martin E. Marty, "Materialism and Spirituality in American Religion," 247.

94 "Blanding Considers Plan for New, Smaller Chapel."

95 Vassar College Board of Trustees, "Consulting Architect," May 1954 Meeting Minutes, binder "Trustees Minutes: 1953–54 through 1957–58," Vassar College Archives & Special Collections.

96 In fact, this idea was being fleshed out concurrently at Marcel Breuer's Ferry House, a cooperative dormitory built at Vassar in 1951. This building was another expression of the college-for-living model that emerged after World War II. Breuer's building was a contemporary secular response to Vassar's longing for community.

97 Robert H. Bonthius, "Report on the Chaplaincy for the Year 1954–1955," folder "Annual Reports to the President," Office of Religious and Spiritual Life, box 1, Vassar College Special Collections.

98 Bonthius, "Report on the Chaplaincy for the Year 1954–1955."

99 Avram Kampf, *Contemporary Synagogue Art: Developments in the United States, 1945–1965* (New York, NY: Union of American Hebrew Congregations, 1966), 37. For a full description of the sanctuary and the role of the design in Philip Johnson's reckoning with his past anti-Semitism, see Anat Geva, "An Architect Asks for Forgiveness: Philip Johnson's Port Chester Synagogue," (2014), www.acsforum.org/symposium2014/papers/GEVA.pdf.

100 Frank D. Welch, *Philip Johnson & Texas* (Austin: University of Texas Press, 2000), 57.
101 Henry-Russell Hitchcock, introduction, in *Philip Johnson: Architecture 1949–1965* (New York, NY: Holt, Rinehart and Winston, 1966), 10.
102 Schwarz, *Vom Bau der Kirche*.
103 Vassar's first gestures toward racial and ethnic inclusivity coincided with the shift in its religious demographics. See McCarthy, "The Vassar Girl," 212.
104 The Passion Pit is the circular depression containing a multicolored sofa and large cocktail table in the Noyes Hall lounge. See the March 4, 1959, issue of the *Yale Daily News* for related coverage.

References

Allitt, Patrick. *Religion in America Since 1945: A History* (New York, NY: Columbia University Press, 2003).

"Architect Waldron Faulkner Dies," *Washington Post*, May 14, 1979.

"Asserts Students Are Alive to Crisis: MacCracken Assures Interfaith Conference They Recognize Need of the Spiritual," *New York Times*, November 30, 1940.

Bacon, Mardges. *Le Corbusier in America: Travels in the Land of the Timid* (Cambridge, MA: MIT Press, 2001).

"Blanding Considers Plan for New, Smaller Chapel," *Vassar Miscellany News*, October 7, 1953.

Bofinger, Helge, and Wolfgang Voigt, eds. *Helmut Jacoby: Master of Architectural Drawing* (Tübingen: Wasmuth, 2001).

Bradbury, Oliver. *Sir John Soane's Influence on Architecture from 1791: A Continuing Legacy* (Farnham, UK and Burlington, VT: Ashgate, 2015).

Buckley, Jr., William F. *God and Man at Yale: The Superstitions of "Academic Freedom"* (Chicago, IL: Regnery, 1951).

"The College Girl Starts a Revolution: She Demands Individual Training, Rejects Cloistered Seclusion and Wants to be a Doer in the Work of the World Today," *New York Times*, May 13, 1928.

Courtessis, Aspasia. "Students Find Many Positive Values in Community Church; Seek Clarification of Position of Organization on Campus," *Vassar Miscellany News*, December 1, 1948.

"First Things First . . .," *Vassar Miscellany News*, October 14, 1953.

"Founders Envisage 'Community Church' as Flexible Channel," *Vassar Miscellany News* (Poughkeepsie, NY), December 1, 1948.

"Free Inquiry," *Vassar Miscellany News*, December 1, 1948.

Geva, Anat. "An Architect Asks for Forgiveness: Philip Johnson's Port Chester Synagogue," 2014, www.acsforum.org/symposium2014/papers/GEVA.pdf. Accessed January 2018.

Hitchcock, Henry-Russell. Introduction, in Philip Johnson, *Philip Johnson: Architecture 1949–1965* (New York, NY: Holt, Rinehart and Winston, 1966).

Johnson, Philip. "House at New Canaan, Connecticut," *The Architectural Review* 108, no. 645 (September 1950): 152–159.

Kampf, Avram. *Contemporary Synagogue Art: Developments in the United States, 1945–1965* (New York, NY: Union of American Hebrew Congregations, 1966).

Kieckhefer, Richard. *Theology in Stone: Church Architecture from Byzantium to Berkeley* (New York, NY: Oxford University Press, 2004).

Kirkland, William. "Kirkland Writes . . .," *Vassar Miscellany News*, October 21, 1953.

Le Corbusier. *When the Cathedrals Were White, A Journey to the Country of the Timid People* (New York, NY: Reynal & Hitchcock, 1947).

Ledoux, Claude Nicolas. *Architecture de C.N. Ledoux* (Princeton, NJ: Princeton Architectural Press, in association with the Avery Architectural and Fine Arts Library of Columbia University, 1983).

Lockwood, Helen. "Faculty Members Consider Place of Religion in Vassar Community," *Vassar Miscellany News*, December 1, 1948.

Marty, Martin E. "Materialism and Spirituality in American Religion." In Robert Wuthnow, ed. *Rethinking Materialism: Perspectives on the Spiritual Dimension of Economic Behavior*, 237–253 (Grand Rapids, MI: Eerdmans, 1995).

McCarthy, Mary. "The Vassar Girl." In *idem*, *On the Contrary*, 193–214 (New York, NY: Farrar, Straus and Cudahy, 1961; first published May 1951 in *Holiday*).

Mellins, Thomas. "Helmut Jacoby's Architectural Renderings: The Drawing as Analogue." In H. Bofinger and W. Voigt, eds. *Helmut Jacoby: Master of Architectural Drawing* (Tübingen: Wasmuth, 2001).

Michels, Karen. "The Emigration of Iconology." In Catherine Sousloff, ed. *Jewish Identity in Modern Art History* (Berkeley, CA: University of California Press, 1999).

"Religious Buildings," *Architectural Record* 103 (June 1948).

Rosenberg, Gerhard. "The Seven Lamps of Rudolf Schwarz," *The Architectural Review* 112 (October 1952): 261–262.

"S. Cruikshank, A. Mackay, P. Moran Weigh Relative Merits of V.C. Community Church and College Religious Association," *Vassar Miscellany News*, November 16, 1949.

Schulze, Franz. *Philip Johnson: Life and Work* (New York, NY: Alfred A. Knopf, 1994).

Schwarz, Rudolf. *The Church Incarnate*. Translated by Cynthia Harris (Chicago, IL: Regnery, 1958).

———. *Vom Bau der Kirche* (Würzburg: Werkbund-Verlag, 1938).

Solomon, Barbara Miller. *In the Company of Educated Women* (New Haven, CT: Yale University Press, 1985).

Soussloff, Catherine M., ed. *Jewish Identity in Modern Art History* (Berkeley: University of California Press, 1999).

Summerson, John. *Sir John Soane* (London: Art and Technics, 1952).

Tate, Ebba Joe. "Students Find Many Positive Values in Community Church; Seek Clarification of Position of Organization on Campus," *Vassar Miscellany News*, December 1, 1948.

Tuite, Rebecca. "Fashioning the 1950s 'Vassar Girl': Vassar Student Identity and Campus Dress, 1947–60," *Fashion Theory* 17, no. 3 (2013): 299–320.

"Vassar Cornerstone Laying," *New York Times*, October 5, 1902.

Vidler, Anthony. Introduction to Claude-Nicolas Ledoux, *L'Architecture* (Princeton, NJ: Princeton Architectural Press, 1983).

Welch, Frank D. *Philip Johnson & Texas*. (Austin, TX: University of Texas Press, 2000).

Wuthnow, Robert, ed. *Rethinking Materialism: Perspectives on the Spiritual Dimension of Economic Behavior* (Grand Rapids, MI: Eerdmans, 1995).

3

TUSKEGEE UNIVERSITY'S SECOND CHAPEL

A departure and a continuation

Arthur J. Clement and Roderick D. Fluker

Paul Rudolph's expressive design for Tuskegee University's second chapel is universally admired and acknowledged as an important commission in his body of work.[1] The Alabama Architectural Foundation gave the Distinguished Building Award in 2009 to Tuskegee Chapel for structures over 25 years old which are still considered exemplary and significant in the state. However, the planning, architecture, and construction of the chapel has not been studied in depth.[2] This chapter explores four questions regarding this chapel. First, how did such a dramatic religious structure emerge on a historically black college campus in Alabama during the divisive Civil Rights struggles of the 1960s? Second, Rudolph's original design was envisioned as "a sanctuary of sculptured concrete." But, the completed chapel is a brick structure. What caused the shift in material selection and how was the design concept affected? Third, does the chapel exhibit important characteristic found in Rudolph's other works from the 1960s when he was known as the "crew-cut maverick of modernism."[3] Fourth, what was the role and contribution of Fry & Welch, an African

FIGURE 3.1   Front elevation of the Tuskegee Chapel, Tuskegee, Alabama, 2011.

Courtesy of the Tuskegee University Archives.

American architectural firm, in the design and construction of the chapel? The chapter will describe the collaboration between Tuskegee, Paul Rudolph, and Fry & Welch that produced a masterful religious building during the mid-twentieth century (Fig. 3.1).

An age of new optimism: the 1950s

Tuskegee University's first chapel, erected in 1898 as a brick masonry and heavy timber structure with a large auditorium capable of seating more than 2,000 persons, was destroyed by fire on January 23, 1957. Designed by the pioneering, African American architect, Robert R. Taylor, the "symbolic and historic chapel" was a significant loss for the Tuskegee community.[4] Taylor, who graduated from then Boston Tech (now MIT) in 1892, was hired by Booker T. Washington, the first Principal of the Tuskegee Normal School in Macon County, to design and supervise construction of Neo-Classical brick buildings.[5] Taylor's forty-year career ended in 1932, and included supervising the planning and erection of the Booker T. Washington Monument located adjacent to the first chapel in 1922.[6]

Following the chapel's fire, Dr. Luther. H. Foster, Jr., then president of Tuskegee, issued a public statement, which said, "We are making plans to rebuild the Chapel as nearly like the original as this can possibly be done."[7] Dr. Foster's desire for a replacement chapel and his vision for modernizing Tuskegee soon merged. Born in 1913, Foster received his bachelor degrees from Virginia State and Hampton Universities, and earned a M.B.A. from Harvard University before arriving in 1941 as Tuskegee's new business manager.[8] Prior to becoming Tuskegee's president in 1953, Foster completed his M.A. and Ph.D. degrees from the University of Chicago.[9] The following year, the US Supreme Court made its landmark, school desegregation decision in *Brown* vs. *Board of Education of Topeka*. Additionally, the Montgomery, Alabama bus boycott begun in 1955 and, led by the Rev. Dr. Martin Luther King, Jr., succeeded in achieving its goal of an integrated bus service throughout Montgomery in December 1956.[10] Buoyed by these recent civil rights victories, Dr. Foster optimistically described in his 1956–57 Annual Report to the Trustees a new vision for re-organizing Tuskegee into a modern-day university with a new Cultural Arts Center and Chapel.[11]

Planning the new chapel: 1957–60

Around the country, many colleges and universities were re-assessing the form and function of their campus chapels.[12] Frank Lloyd Wright designed what many consider one of the early, modernist college chapels at Florida Southern College in Lakeland, Florida (1941). He was a major influence on Paul Rudolph's early career.[13] Eero Saarinen designed a windowless, circular chapel with indirect lighting for the MIT campus in Cambridge, Massachusetts (1955).[14] Skidmore Owings & Merrill created a cathedral-like structure with soaring aluminum and glass tetrahedrons for the Air Force Academy's Cadet Chapel (1962).[15] Equally influential was the hilltop, pilgrimage Chapel of Notre-Dame du Haut near the parish of Ronchamp in France, which opened in 1955.[16] Designed by Le Corbusier, the boldly shaped chapel has rough cast, concrete walls painted white. The non-traditional, religious structure has a bellowing, upswept roof and expressive spatial qualities both inside and outside. Rudolph later acknowledged that Le Corbusier's Ronchamp Chapel influenced his imaginative design for the Tuskegee Chapel.[17]

Dr. Foster initially engaged Fry & Welch, an African American architectural firm, to prepare preliminary plans for a replacement chapel.[18]At that time, the firm was designing a new group of dormitory buildings near the center of campus.[19] Both Fry & Welch had deep ties to Tuskegee. Louis E. Fry, Sr. was born in Bastrop, Texas in 1903.[20] He finished his architectural studies at Kansas State University in 1930. Fry headed the Architectural Department at Tuskegee Institute from 1935 to 1940. He later taught at Howard University's Department of Architecture from 1947 to 1972.[21] John A. Welch was born in Tuskegee, Alabama in 1906.[22] He received a high school diploma from Tuskegee, and later an architectural degree from Howard University in 1930.[23] He briefly served as head of Tuskegee's Architecture Department before being drafted in 1941 to serve in World War II.[24] After the war, Welch completed his architectural education at Catholic University in Washington, DC while working in Fry's architectural office.[25] In 1954, Welch became a full partner, and the firm was re-named Fry & Welch. Three years later, Welch returned to Tuskegee to serve as Dean of the School of Mechanical Industries, a position once held by Robert Taylor.[26]

Fry & Welch presented their preliminary plans for a new chapel to the trustee board on April 13, 1957 which were approved with minor changes.[27] Dr. Foster reported to the trustee board he expected to reach a settlement of approximately $400,000 from the insurance companies for the loss of the original chapel.[28] During the spring 1958 board meeting, John A. Welch presented schematic drawings for a new chapel.[29] Dr. Foster requested and received approval from the board to appoint a Program Development Committee to further study the proposed Cultural Center and Chapel.[30] Dr. Foster later appointed the Rev. Dr. Daniel W. Wynn, Institute Chaplain, Dr. Relford Patterson, head of the Music Department and director of the choir, and Dean John A. Welch, to develop a program of requirements for the new chapel.[31] In addition to holding religious services, the new chapel would serves as a concert hall for Tuskegee's famed Golden Voices Choir.[32]

At the fall 1958 board meeting, Chairman O'Connor spoke about the formation of an Advisory Committee, responsible to the Building Construction Committee of the Board, and about Moreland G. Smith, a new trustee who recently become chairman of the Buildings and Ground Committee.[33] Mr. Smith reported the committee had considered the president's vision for Tuskegee but placed it within the context of a new campus master plan.[34] Smith's report of the Buildings and Grounds Committee, dated October 14, 1958, included approval of the idea of a modern structure for the replacement chapel per the sketches presented by John A. Welch of Fry & Welch Architects, the previous April.[35]

Moreland G. Smith, a white architect from Montgomery, Alabama, was befriended by Dr. Foster and asked to join the Tuskegee Board of Trustees in 1957.[36]. Both men were "churchmen," active Episcopalians in their respective cities, and were both involved with the shifting civil rights landscape in Alabama.[37] Smith was a founder and principal of Sherlock, Smith and Adams, a large engineering and architecture firm in Montgomery.[38] Although Smith's term on Tuskegee's Board of Trustees ended in 1960, his involvement with the chapel project continued as an architectural consultant to Dr. Foster.[39] From 1960 through 1965, Smith served as Chairman of the Alabama Advisory Committee to the US Commission on Civil Rights.[40] Smith's pro-civil rights activities caused Governor George Wallace of Alabama, a staunch segregationist, to retaliate by refusing to award new state contracts to Smith's firm.[41] Despite simmering racial tensions in other cities across Alabama, Tuskegee Institute benefited from the interracial cooperation between Luther Foster and Moreland Smith, and between John A. Welch and Paul Rudolph on the new chapel project.

During the spring 1959 trustee meeting, Smith introduced Paul Rudolph, then Dean of Yale's Department of Architecture to the board of trustees.[42] Rudolph presented the guiding principles of his future master plan for Tuskegee and reported that the campus center will incorporate both the new chapel and the Booker T. Washington Monument. Campus traffic would be restricted to the periphery, resulting in a pedestrian-oriented center campus. Tuskegee's tradition of low-height, brick building placed on the ridges, rather than the valleys, should be continued.[43]

Also present for the spring meeting were three members of the newly formed Master Plan Advisory Committee, who were donating their services to Tuskegee.[44] The committee consisting of:

- Douglas Haskell, editor of the magazine, *Architectural Forum*, New York City;
- David A. Williston, a retired, African American landscape architect (a former Tuskegee faculty member and designer of the 1948 Tuskegee Master Plan), Washington, DC;
- Minoru Yamasaki, a Japanese American architect and principal in the firm Yamasaki, Leinweber and Associates, Birmingham, Michigan, and
- Moreland Smith, Tuskegee trustee, who served as chair of the Advisory Committee.[45]

At the fall 1959 board meeting, Paul Rudolph presented to the Advisory Committee and to the board of trustees his initial concept of a mall plan for the center of campus. Rudolph's plan and rendering included a new chapel connected by covered walkways along the edge of the open space, a large campanile, and the proposed Cultural Arts Center located at the northern end of the open lawn. The Advisory Committee and the trustee board approved in principal Rudolph's plan and Fry & Welch's previous chapel design was set aside. Welch remained actively involved with the project playing a dual role of in-house project coordinator, and as Fry & Welch's local representative. Prior to the board meeting, Welch sent a letter to Paul Rudolph summarizing the program of requirements for the chapel and cultural center. In his letter,[46] Welch wrote, "This building [the chapel] must, by its architecture, express the highest spiritual qualities that our civilization can conceive. Such expression must be evident to all who see or enter it."[47] Rudolph's mall plan for the center campus, including the covered walkways and campanile, was not built.

In 1965, the Department of the Interior and the National Park Service designated Tuskegee Institute a "registered National Historic Landmark under the provisions of the Historic Sites Act of August 21, 1935."[48] In 1972, Tuskegee submitted a major proposal to the National Park Service for designation as a National Historic Park.[49] During the review process, Tuskegee learned that federal officials objected to the placement of the new administration building designed by Rudolph within the proposed boundaries of the new historic district.[50] Despite Rudolph's objections, Tuskegee later moved the location for the new administration building west of the campus center and the proposed historic district.[51] In 1974, a portion of the Tuskegee's original campus became a National Historic Site (NHS) operated by the National Park Service.[52] The boundaries of the historic district, which encompassed the NHS, excluded Tuskegee's modernist chapel[53] (Fig. 3.2). Thus, Rudolph's mall plan for the campus center was derailed by Tuskegee's successful designation as a NHS. Rudolph continued to serve as Tuskegee's master campus planner working closely with Dr. Foster on a 1978 campus plan update.[54] Rudolph's final Tuskegee project was the General Chappie James Center for Aerospace Engineering and Health Education that opened in 1986.

1. Chapel
2. Administration Building (re-sited)
3. Site Envisioned for Cultural Arts Center
4. Site Envisioned for Central Mall
5. Campus Historic District
6. Washington Monument

FIGURE 3.2 Aerial image of the center of campus, the chapel, and a portion of the boundary of Tuskegee's National Historic District, 2007.

Image annotated by the author.

Presentation of a sculptured concrete design for the chapel

During the spring 1960 trustee meeting, three years after the chapel fire, Paul Rudolph presented his now iconic, sculptural concrete design for the chapel as part of an updated plan for the campus center in a new rendering[55] (Fig. 3.3). Rudolph's remarks were summarized in the meeting minutes:

> The proposed Chapel should and will be a building of singular significant to the Institute. The Chapel should thus be a building distinguished by the character and assurance of its design. The particular form of the proposed Chapel derives from considerations of light, acoustics, material, and site.[56]

Rudolph's pen-and-ink renderings for the Tuskegee Chapel were later published in *Architectural Forum* in September of 1960 under the title, "Sanctuary of Sculptured Concrete."[57] The floor

1. Chapel
2. Administration Building
3. Cultural Arts Center
4. Covered Walkways
5. Central Mall

FIGURE 3.3 Rudolph's 1960 rendering of the Tuskegee Institute Campus Precinct Plan.
Courtesy of the Tuskegee University Archives.

plans, elevations, an interior rendering of the chapel's sanctuary, and a bird's-eye rendering of the rear of the chapel looking across the proposed mall captured the attention and imagination of the architectural community searching for modernist expressions of Christian worship in the United States. For Tuskegee, Rudolph's concrete chapel expressed an aesthetic departure from the surrounding historic brick buildings on campus.

Paul M. Rudolph's projects: the 1950s–1970s

Paul Marvin Rudolph was born in Elkton, Kentucky in 1918.[58] His father was an United Methodist minister and educator. His mother was an amateur artist, who encouraged the artistic and musical skills of her only son.[59] Rudolph graduated from the Alabama Polytechnic Institute, now Auburn University, in 1940.[60] After serving in the Navy during World War II, Rudolph finished his studies at the Harvard University's Graduate School of Design, earning a Master's degree in 1947.[61] He was then awarded the Wheelwright Traveling Fellowship which permitted a year of travel through Europe in 1948–49.[62] Rudolph launched his career designing modernist residences and schools in Florida during the early 1950s.

During his most fertile period of the late 1950s and 1960s, Rudolph completed his best-known works, including Yale's Art and Architecture Building (1958–63), the New Haven Parking Deck (1958–62), the Tuskegee Institute Chapel (1959–69), the Endo

Laboratories Building, Garden City, Long Island, NY (1960–64), the Southern Massachusetts Technological Institute campus, now UMass-Dartmouth (1962–73), the Colgate University Arts & Humanities Building, Hamilton, NY (1963–64), the Orange County Government Center, Goshen, NY (1963–71) and the Boston Government Service Center (1962–71). By the 1970s, Rudolph's popularity had faded, and his brutalist concrete designs lost favor. Architectural historians now place Rudolph in the group of late modernist architects who developed an expressive architectural vocabulary during the mid-twentieth century.[63]

Rudolph designed ten religious buildings during his prolific career. His most prominent houses of worship are three chapels, which are most anomalous to his other works.[64] The Tuskegee Chapel in Tuskegee, Alabama which is the largest of the chapels, represents the pinnacle of Rudolph's ecclesiastical architecture. The Erich Lindeman Mental Health Center, which is part of the Boston Government Service Center (BGSC) in Boston, Massachusetts (1962–71) has a small meditation chapel located in one of the upper turrets. The oval-shaped, chapel interior has Rudolph's signature of a corrugated concrete finish within an intimate setting.[65] The third religious structure is Cannon Chapel at Emory University, Atlanta, Georgia (1975–81).[66] The chapel is a cast-in-place concrete structure, located near Emory's main quadrangle. Nonetheless, the three chapels demonstrate Rudolph's "affinity for emotionally charged interiors of [his] religious buildings."[67]

Completion of the construction documents and building the chapel: 1965–69

During their October 1960 meeting, the trustee board authorized President Foster to enter into a separate contract with Fry & Welch Architects to prepare the construction drawings and specifications for the new chapel in accordance with Rudolph's chapel design.[68] Fry & Welch's role evolved into serving as the local architect of record for the project.

John A. Welch, of Fry & Welch, was involved in the Tuskegee Chapel project, from beginning to end. Welch presented the initial plans for a new chapel to the board of trustees in 1957 and 1958, prior to the engagement of Paul Rudolph.[69] Welch advocated for a modern design of the chapel.[70] When he joined the faculty in 1957 as Dean of Mechanical Industries, Welch continued a tradition at Tuskegee of supervising the design and construction of new buildings on campus.[71] He coordinated the development of the program requirements for the chapel and Cultural Arts Center. His roots as a Tuskegee native, as a graduate of Tuskegee, and as Administrative Dean meant he was part of the cultural fabric of the Tuskegee community. Welch had known President Foster since the 1940s. He was active during the construction phase of the new chapel, functioning as the Owner's Representative, approving change orders to the contractor's contract, and meeting with Rudolph when he toured the site.[72] Welch undoubtedly knew Cady Metcalf, and probably recruited him to become the lead brick mason for the chapel. When the project was completed, Welch was asked by a reporter to express his thoughts about the chapel. He replied:

> It is a masterpiece. It is so firmly anchored to the ground and the setting, and yet at the same time it gives the appearance of being so light. It has a vitality to it. It's not like so many buildings, just plunked there on the ground; it belongs there.[73]

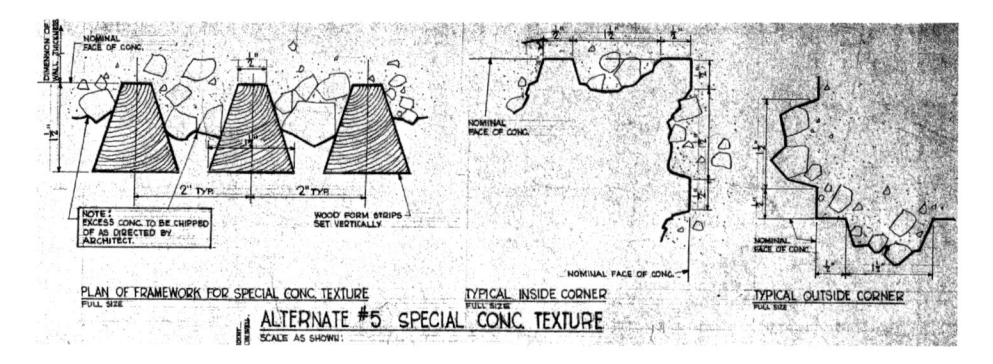

FIGURE 3.4   Detail of special concrete texture for Tuskegee Chapel from the Concrete Scheme Construction Documents, dated January 22, 1965.

Fry & Welch completed the construction documents (CDs) and bid documents for a cast-in-place, concrete structure in January 1965.[74] The CDs included a construction detail for a "corrugated concrete" finish similar to that used on the Yale University School of Art and Architecture Building (Fig. 3.4). The detail called for removing the formwork and chipping by hand, or using a bush hammer, to create a rough-textured finish that ran vertically along the surface of the concrete wall.[75] When the bids were received from general contractors, the quotes far exceeded Tuskegee's construction budget.[76] Tuskegee was unsuccessful in finding a contractor willing to quote a stipulated sum for the concrete structure as designed.[77]

During a pivotal meeting in Washington, DC on February 5, 1966, Tuskegee made the decision to switch from concrete to brick with a steel frame for the new chapel.[78] Tuskegee's familiarity with brick buildings was a key factor as Rudolph observed in his initial presentation to the trustee board in 1959.[79] In addition, the complexity of the concrete design made re-bidding the project difficult without drastically altering Rudolph's design, which Dr. Foster insisted upon keeping.[80] Fry & Welch became more involved with orchestrating the construction detailing used in the masonry scheme.[81] Rudolph continued to exercise artistic control over the overall design and the coordination of the color palette of materials.[82] A third factor was an evolution in Rudolph's search for a more cost-effective, but decorative exterior finish. In 1963, Rudolph experimented with a "fluted block and split-ribbed block" as a less expensive finish to the costly formwork and bush-hammering required for a corrugated concrete finish.[83] Rudolph use a fluted block on Crawford Manor, a high-rise housing structure in New Haven, Connecticut (1962–66). He then used a brown split-ribbed block on the exterior and interior of the Dana Creative Center at Colgate University, in Hamilton, New York (1963–66).[84] Thus, Tuskegee's decision in 1966 to use brick on the chapel project in lieu of a concrete finish also coincided with a material shift in Rudolph's other designs.

Fry & Welch finished the construction documents for the "brick scheme" in July 1966. The sculptural quality of Rudolph's design was not easily translated into brick masonry according to Major Holland, FAIA, who worked on the chapel project early in his career.[85] A native of Tuskegee, Holland finished Howard University's architecture program in 1964.[86] He joined Fry & Welch in 1966 just as they completed the brick CDs. Once construction started the following year, Holland was sent to Tuskegee to serve as the project representative and "to coordinate with Paul Rudolph on aesthetic matters."[87]

The chapel project was re-bid. Unfortunately, the brick scheme was nearly as expensive as the concrete scheme.[88] Eager to move forward, Tuskegee officials negotiated a cost–plus a fixed fee with a guaranteed maximum price with F. N. Thompson, Inc. of Charlotte, North Carolina, who partnered with Street Construction in Atlanta, Georgia. The final construction cost, which included numerous change orders and delays, was nearly $2 million according to Holland.[89]

The groundbreaking ceremony for the new chapel was held on March 18, 1967, ten years after the burning of the original chapel.[90] Holland recalled the structural steel fabrication and erection proved challenging.[91] The roof design had not changed much from the concrete scheme to the brick scheme. The floor plan, shaped like a pinwheel, also did not change. The steel fabricator had difficulty closing the angles of the steel frame around the unusual floor layout.[92] Moreover, the columns in the sanctuary were of varying, vertical lengths since the floor of the sanctuary sloped downward. Because of the geometry of the sanctuary and the sloping roof, no two joists were parallel.[93] The roof joists each angled at different slants to form a warped or sloping plane. Temporary shoring and bracing were installed until the permanent, custom-fabricated and field-measured bridging were welded into place.[94] Once the structural steel was erected and the concrete floors were poured, the next step in the construction process was the brick masonry work (Fig. 3.5).

A succession of masonry contractors arrived on site, reviewed the plans and field conditions of the project which had multiple angular, sloping walls, no 90-degree intersections, many sloping floors, and sheer walls as high as 35–40 feet. Unable to get it together after several frustrating days, they simply gave up and walked off the job site.[95] A few of the "Tuskegee-trained masons" became aware of the situation, including Cady Metcalf, Charlie Rhone, William Carter, and others. They took on the project and produced outstanding brickwork.[96]

While the design concept was largely unchanged, the building took on a new dimension in brick. Sloping parapets, irregular corners, tapering walls, cantilevers handled by corbeling the brick, and slanted buttress walls all required cut brick.[97] Thus, the wall sections and detailing for formed concrete were revised not just in material description, but wholly re-detailed

FIGURE 3.5 Structural steel erection and brick masonry wall construction, c. 1968.

Courtesy of Major L. Holland, FAIA, retired.

FIGURE 3.6 View of the brick masonry wall in the sanctuary, 2014.

Photograph by the author.

using brick construction.[98] Brick corbels and overlapped joints added a dynamic aesthetic expressed in the balcony and sidewall skylights. Other details were added, including elegantly stepped, canted walls along the interior walls of the sanctuary, to more effectively distribute the conditioned air (Fig. 3.6).

Rudolph desired a "monolithic" appearance for the chapel and selected a smooth, consistently toned brick with matching mortar.[99] Once erected, the russet-orange brick walls resembled the glow surrounding an evening sunset. The interior finish selections for the carpet, the pew stain, and the copper cladding on the entry doors into the sanctuary closely matched the brick color.[100] Surprisingly, the monochromatic interior provided a certain warmth that enriched the spatial quality of the sanctuary.

Architectural tour of the new chapel

Rudolph sited the new chapel approximately 100 feet northwest of the footprint of the first chapel to capture more of the sloping terrain and accommodate the two floor levels beneath the main sanctuary floor. The new location also permitted a larger entrance and covered porch into the front of the chapel. The floor plan inside the sanctuary has three rows of pews facing an elevated pulpit and chancel. At the corners of the floor plan are stairwells leading up and down the four floor levels (Fig. 3.7). On the exterior, the cascading stairs on either side of the chapel terrace down the ridge to the lower grade. No elevator was installed. The multi-leveled building is a challenge for persons with disabilities.

The main entry and elevation of the chapel faces east with a massive roof overhang that connects to a canted, brick wall that rises upward to a large, precast concrete cross. The chapel is approached on foot from either side. Masonry walls with varying heights and vertical planes create an abstract composition of solids and shadows. The exterior, outer corners have interlacing brick units that overlap one another. Just under the main roof overhang is an outdoor pulpit in the same russet-orange brick as the chapel walls. The two sets of entry doors are recessed, and the glass panels in each door leaf are covered with circular beads in the shape of a cross in relief. The transom above the doors consists of bronze panels with figures in relief created by Edward L. Pryce, Tuskegee's former Superintendent of Buildings and Grounds. Pryce also painted a figurative mural with Christian themes on the walls in the lounge on the lower level.

The rear elevation features another vertical plane of sheer brick walls that rise to a high point of 70 feet. The base of the structure extends to terraced, brick retaining walls. The ground level is framed by large window openings and sloping masonry piers that angle outward.

The narthex is an elongated, dimly lit space with a low ceiling. The ceiling extends into the sanctuary below the balcony, creating a dramatic effect as the high volume of the sanctuary slowly emerges (Fig. 3.8). The narthex is filled with pictures of former deans of the chapel, former choir directors, some artwork, and a replica of the Tuskegee "Singing Windows."[101] These stained-glass windows contain three panels filled with images of Negro spirituals, and recall the original windows installed in the first chapel. Also encased in one of the narthex walls is a "Memorial Brick" taken from Washington's birth home in Virginia.

Inside the sanctuary, the windowless, asymmetrical room is bathed in natural light from skylights in the roof along both perimeter walls. Angled, masonry sheer walls on either side

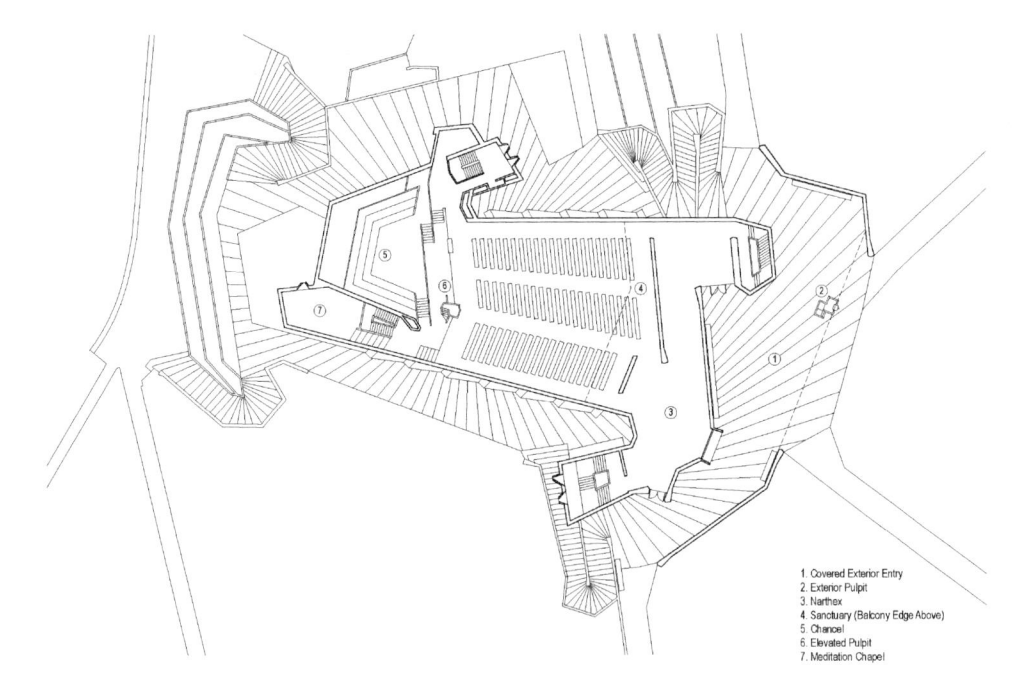

1. Covered Exterior Entry
2. Exterior Pulpit
3. Narthex
4. Sanctuary (Balcony Edge Above)
5. Chancel
6. Elevated Pulpit
7. Meditation Chapel

FIGURE 3.7 Floor plan of the sanctuary level of the chapel.

Redrawn by the author from the Brick Scheme Construction Documents, dated July 22, 1966.

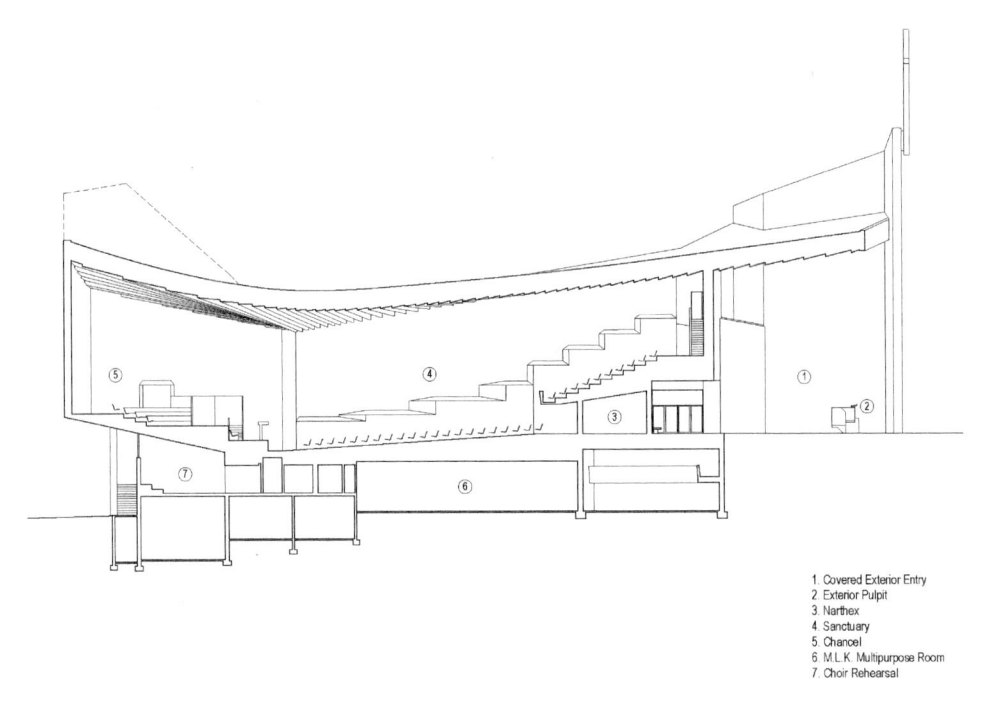

1. Covered Exterior Entry
2. Exterior Pulpit
3. Narthex
4. Sanctuary
5. Chancel
6. M.L.K. Multipurpose Room
7. Choir Rehearsal

FIGURE 3.8 Building section of the chapel structure, showing four levels.

Redrawn by the author from the Brick Scheme Construction Documents, dated July 22, 1966.

of the room narrow toward a raised pulpit that projects forward with an elevated canopy. On the north side of the chancel is pew seating for the famed Tuskegee Golden Voices Choir. Mounted on the chancel wall are sound drapes and a large university logo. Natural light enters the sanctuary from skylights just under the roof along the perimeter walls (Fig. 3.9). The angled walls and undulant ceiling beneath the sloping roof help with the acoustics. The main ceiling slopes downward to the front, and curves to either side of the room. The sanctuary has seating for approximately 1,200 persons, including balcony seating above.

In his other buildings from the 1960s with large interior spaces, Rudolph used brightly colored carpet and upholstery fabric to contrast with the grey, rough-textured concrete walls. Inside the Tuskegee Chapel, the interplay of the multi-colored light filtering down from the skylights above onto the uneven surfaces of brick walls creates an interior space unlike any of Rudolph's other religious buildings. A small meditation chapel is tucked behind the main chancel. A slanted skylight at the roof, and several rows of colored, glazed skylights angled in the masonry wall illuminate the small chapel below, echoing Ronchamp Chapel.[102] The angled skylights are hues of blue, red, and pink. The light descends downward and creates another example of Rudolph's movement through space and light (Fig. 3.10).

A Japanese architectural magazine published a detailed analysis of the interior space of the Tuskegee Chapel, and beautifully described the sanctuary in words and color photographs as a paradox of texture, color, and void.[103] The irregularly laid brick walls weave a texture into the surface of the walls. The contrasting colors in the skylights above create a sensuousness that enhances the simple, spiritual quality of the space. The fortress-like, spiraling walls heightens one's sense of enclosure and void. The emptiness detaches one's mind, energy, and struggle: "One feels secure and serene in the expanding enclosure of the Tuskegee Chapel."[104]

FIGURE 3.9 Sanctuary interior, looking toward the pulpit, chancel, and choir, 2010.

Image from the Library of Congress, Prints & Photographs Division. Photograph by Carol M. Highsmith.

FIGURE 3.10 View of angled skylights in masonry wall at the meditation chapel, 2014.

Photograph by the author.

The lower level and mezzanine level house the office of the dean of the chapel, the choir director, and a tiered practice room for the Golden Voices Choir. A large, double-height, multi-purpose room, named in honor of the Rev. Dr. Martin Luther King, Jr., hosts various classes, student activities, chapel functions, and community meetings. Today, the Tuskegee University Chapel continues to serve as the religious, cultural, and community center for the campus.

Conclusion: the legacy of Rudolph's Tuskegee Chapel

The Tuskegee University Chapel is an architectural treasure, that has aged well, and unlike several of Rudolph's other modernist buildings, is not in danger of demolition. The chapel is a building of singular significance, as Rudolph predicted nearly fifty years ago in his presentation to the trustee board in April 1960.[105] Several factors can be attributed to its success. First, Dr. Foster resisted his initial impulse to replicate the original chapel and instead embraced the new chapel as a symbol of his vision to transform Tuskegee into a modern university. Second, Foster assembled a stellar ensemble of advisors, including Moreland Smith and John A. Welch, who collaborated with Rudolph to help his design blossom. Indeed, Rudolph was initially challenged by the presence of a national Advisory Committee.[106] Blending influences of Wright and Le Corbusier, Rudolph created an expressive, sculptural design for a concrete chapel. A long gestation period followed, which, coupled with Tuskegee's decision to switch to brick, allowed the chapel design to mature through two sets of construction documents deftly managed by Fry & Welch, who preserved Rudolph's design intent.[107] Fry & Welch orchestrated the brick detailing which made Rudolph's expressive chapel feel palatable to a Tuskegee community accustomed to brick buildings. The third reason contributing to the success of the chapel is its alignment with Rudolph's key design themes of monumentality and decoration. For example,

(a) the sheer brick walls accentuate the verticality and uplift of the building;
(b) the unified materiality of both the exterior and interior finishes enrich the relationship between the outside symbol of the chapel and its spiritual interior. Indeed, the russet-orange brick is used throughout the chapel on all four levels, on all four elevations, and on the exterior cascading stairs and terraced walls;
(c) a dramatic use of indirect, natural light inside the sanctuary is an important feature found in other Rudolph's projects as well; and
(d) the bright, monochromatic color of the brick walls is like a Mark Rothko abstract painting from the 1950s. The decorative brick walls achieve a luminosity that grey, rough-finished concrete cannot match.

Tuskegee's new chapel emerged during a violent and tumultuous decade of Civil Rights demonstrations in Alabama. By 1964, Tuskegee capitalized on the successful collaboration between Fry & Welch and Rudolph by establishing the practice of pairing him with other African American architects as new projects moved from design development into preparation of construction documents.[108] John S. Chase & Associates in Houston, Texas was assigned the new administration building, later named the Kresge Center.

Robert Madison of Madison & Madison in Cleveland, Ohio was commissioned to finish the working drawings for the new engineering building, later named Foster Hall. The physical education building evolved over time into the General Chappie James Aerospace Center. Tarlee Brown, a Tuskegee graduate who was a principal in Millkey & Brown Architects in Atlanta, Georgia received the commission to collaborate with Rudolph. The most successful of these architectural pairings, however, was the one between Paul Rudolph and Fry & Welch on the new chapel. Rudolph, a Southern-born minister's son, willingly collaborated with Fry & Welch, and he hired two architectural students from Tuskegee as summer interns in 1967.[109] Thus, Tuskegee University set an important architectural precedent on its new chapel project that became prevalent during the 1970s when local, state, and federal governments began pairing white and black architects in joint ventures.[110]

Fry & Welch, whose roots went back to Robert R. Taylor and to Tuskegee's tradition of training African American architects and brick masons, permitted that tradition to be continued in the luminous brick walls that adorn the structure. The new chapel, therefore, is rooted in both Tuskegee's proud cultural landscape and in Modernist religious structures of the twentieth century. The Rev. Dr. James Earl Massey, former Dean of the Tuskegee University Chapel best described the structure's significance when he wrote:

> the Chapel interior reminds one of the roughness of life as its bricks, purposely irregular at points, sometimes call attention to themselves; but it also reminds one about the luminous quality of life as the light from above keeps one conscious of movement in the midst of what stands solid and fixed.[111]

Acknowledgments

The authors wish to thank the following individuals who assisted with our research: Dana Chandler, Tuskegee University Archives; Dean of the Tuskegee Chapel, Rev. Dr. Gregory Gray; former Dean, Rev. Dr. Edward Wheeler; Major L. Holland, FAIA; Booker Conley, former director of the Tuskegee University Physical Plant; and Dr. Mari Nakahara, Library of Congress, Curator, Architecture, Design & Engineering, Prints and Photography Division.

Notes

1 Sybil Moholy-Nagy, Introduction to, *The Architecture of Paul Rudolph,* by Paul Rudolph, *trans. Marie Kroll* (New York, NY: Praeger, 1970), 7–29.
2 The two comprehensive studies of Rudolph's œuvre by Timothy Rohan (*The Architecture of Paul Rudolph* (New Haven, CT: Yale University Press, 2014) and Tony Monk (*The Art and Architecture of Paul Rudolph* (Chichester, West Sussex: Wiley-Academy, 1999) do not focus on his religious buildings.
3 Rohan, *The Architecture of Paul Rudolph*, 15, 246. Rohan coined the term to describe how Rudolph compartmentalized different sides of his life, and used the crew cut haircut as his trademark for life.
4 "Early Morning Fire Destroys Institute Chapel," *Campus Digest* (Tuskegee Institute), January 30, 1957, 1.
5 Ellen Weiss, Robert R. Taylor and Tuskegee: An African American Designs for Booker T. Washington (Montgomery, AL: New South Books, 2012), 26, 146,

6 Ellen Daugherty, "Negotiating the Veil: Tuskegee's Booker T. Washington Monument," *American Art* 24, no. 3 (Fall 2010): 52–77.
7 Ibid.
8 Memorial and Interment Services for Luther Hilton Foster, Jr., Tuskegee University Chapel, December 8, 1994, Tuskegee University Archives.
9 Ibid.
10 David J. Garrow, Bearing the Cross: Martin Luther King, Jr., and the Southern Christian Leadership Conference (New York, NY: William Morrow, 1986), 11–82.
11 Annual Report of the President, 1956–1957, Tuskegee University Archives.
12 Roger G. Kennedy, *American Churches* (New York, NY: Stewart, Tabori & Chang, 1982), 47–59.
13 Rohan, *The Architecture*, 9; Paul Rudolph, "Excerpts from a Conversation," *Writings on Architecture* (New Haven, CT: Yale School of Architecture, 2008), 138. Originally published in *Perspecto* 22 (1996: 135–136).
14 Kennedy, *American Churches*, 47–59.
15 "Walter Netsch, Architect, Dies at 88," *New York Times*, June 17, 2008.
16 Association de l'Oeuvre Notre-Dame-du-Haut. Ronchamp: Notre-Dame du Haut: The Pilgrimage Church of Notre-Dame du Haut by Le Corbusier: History, Architecture, Spirituality. Translated by Katherine Taylor (Regensburg: Schnell & Steiner, 2008), 53–76.
17 Mildred F. Schmertz, "Sanctuary of Sculptured Concrete," *Architectural Forum*, September 1960, 117. According to Timothy Rohan, Rudolph first met Le Corbusier in 1948 in Paris while traveling in Europe on the Wheelwright Fellowship.: Rohan, *The Architecture of Paul Rudolph*, 18.
18 Minutes of the Annual Meeting of the Board of Trustees of Tuskegee Institute, April 13, 1957, Tuskegee University Archives.
19 Annette K. Carter, "Louis Edwin Fry, Sr." In Dreck Spurlock Wilson, ed. *African American Architects: A Biographical Dictionary 1865–1945* (New York, NY: Routledge, 2004), 159–161.
20 Ibid.
21 Ibid.
22 Thanksgiving Service for the Life of Colonel (ret.) John Austin Welch, Monday, November 18, 2002, Greenwood Missionary Baptist Church, Tuskegee, AL. Courtesy of the Tuskegee University Archives.
23 Ibid.
24 Joyce Phillips, "Farewell, Dean Welch," *Campus Digest*, March 25, 1972, vol. 40: 1. Courtesy of Tuskegee University Archives.
25 Ibid.
26 Ibid. Taylor served as Director of Tuskegee's Mechanical Industries from 1902 to 1932.
27 Minutes of the Annual Meeting, April 13, 1957. Tuskegee University Archives.
28 Ibid.
29 Minutes of the Annual Meeting of the Board of Trustees, Tuskegee Institute, March 29, 1958. Tuskegee University Archives.
30 Ibid.
31 James Earl Massey, A Bridge Between: A Centennial History of Campus Ministry at Tuskegee University, 1888–1988 (Tuskegee, AL: Tuskegee University Press, 1988), 32.
32 John A. Welch, Tuskegee, to Paul Rudolph, New Haven, September 16, 1959; in unprocessed papers, PR 13 CN 2001.126, PMR 3171-4. Library of Congress. In his letter, Welch enclosed the "Preliminary Program for Cultural Center and Chapel for Tuskegee Institute."
33 Minutes of the Annual Meeting of the Board of Trustees, Tuskegee Institute, October 31, 1958. Tuskegee University Archives.
34 Ibid.
35 Ibid.
36 Booker Conley (former director of the Tuskegee Physical Plant), in discussion with both authors, Jonesboro, GA, June 12, 2014.
37 Ibid.
38 Resume of Moreland G. Smith, FAIA, in American Institute of Architects, *Directory 1970*.
39 See credits given for the Tuskegee Chapel project in Mildred F. Schmertz, "Paul Rudolph's Chapel for Tuskegee Institute," *Architectural Record*, November 1969: 126.
40 Resume of Moreland G. Smith, FAIA, in American Institute of Architects, *Directory 1970*.

41 "Mr. Moreland G. Smith, 82, Retired Architect, Civil Rights Activist," *Atlanta Journal-Constitution*, June 27, 1989.

42 Minutes of the Spring Meeting of the Board of Trustees of Tuskegee Institute, March 21, 1959. Tuskegee University Archives. Rudolph served as Yale's Dean of the Architecture Dept. from 1958–1965.

43 Ibid.; Rudolph later presented the final campus plan report on December 24, 1959, "Master Plan for Tuskegee Institute," in unprocessed papers, PR 13 CN 2001:126, PMR 3090-6, Library of Congress.

44 Ibid.

45 Ibid.

46 John A. Welch to Paul Rudolph, September 16, 1959.

47 Ibid.

48 US Department of the Interior, National Park Service, *National Survey of Historic Sites and Buildings*, March 1, 1965.

49 Luther H. Foster, Jr., Tuskegee, to Moreland G. Smith, Atlanta, November 3, 1972, in unprocessed papers, PR 13 CN 2101:126, PMR 3107-2, Library of Congress.

50 Ibid.

51 Ibid.

52 Historic Sites and National Monument Establishment, Pub. L. No. 93-486, 88 Stat. 1461 (1974).

53 Ibid.

54 L. H. Foster, Tuskegee, to Paul Rudolph, New York, October 6, 1977, in unprocessed papers, PR 13 CN 2001:126, PMR 3092-3, Library of Congress.

55 Minutes of the Spring meeting of the Board of Trustees of Tuskegee Institute, April 9, 1960. Tuskegee University Archives.

56 Ibid.

57 Mildred F. Schmertz, "Sanctuary of Sculptured Concrete," *Architectural Forum* 113 (September 1960): 103.

58 Rohan, The Architecture, 8.

59 Ibid.

60 Ibid, 9.

61 Ibid,18.

62 Ibid.

63 Gelernter, Mark, *A History of American Architecture: Buildings in Their Cultural and Technological Context* (Hanover, NH: University Press of New England, 1999), 273–277; Robert A.M. Stern, *New Directions in American Architecture* (New York, NY: George Braziller, 1977), 30–41. As Dean of Yale's School of Architecture and former student of Rudolph, Stern lead the restoration of Rudolph's A&A Building in 2009.

64 Daniel L. Ledford, "The Religious Architecture of Paul Rudolph" (unpublished paper for Reading Course with Professor Karla Britton, Yale Divinity School, December 16, 2014), 2–7, 21–27.

65 Rohan, *The Architecture*, 93. He explains that Rudolph used the term corrugated concrete to describe his signature finish. See, for example the photograph of the interior of the meditation chapel in the Lindemann Mental Health Center; Rohan, *The Architecture*, 129.

66 Emory University, Cannon Chapel, http://arts.emory.edu/plan-your-visit/venues/cannon-chapel.html. Accessed October 29, 2012.

67 Ibid., 125.

68 Minutes of the annual meeting of the Board of Tuskegee of Tuskegee Institute, October 28, 1960. Tuskegee University Archives.

69 Trustee Minutes, April 13, 1957; March 29, 1958. Tuskegee University Archives.

70 Trustee Minutes, October 31, 1958. Tuskegee University Archives.

71 Weiss, *Robert Taylor*. Weiss devoted three chapters to describing Taylor's role as Director of Mechanical Industries at Tuskegee from 1901 to 1932.

72 Letters to John A. Welch passim, during the construction phase, in unprocessed papers, PR 13 CN 2001;126, PMR 3007-3 and 3007-4, Library of Congress. Multiple letters were written to and from Welch during the construction phase, 1967–69, demonstrating his role as the Owner's Representative.

73 Keith Coulbourn, "Chapel of Sculptured Brick," *Atlanta Constitution*, May 25, 1969, 25.

74 Actual drawing date for the Concrete Bid Documents was January 22, 1965, courtesy of Tuskegee University Physical Plant.

75 Major L. Holland, FAIA, in discussion with both authors, Tuskegee University Chapel, May 22, 2013.

76 Ibid.

77 Ibid. The bid documents called for a Stipulated Sum Agreement, AIA A101-1963 Edition, in unprocessed papers, PR 13 CN 2001:126, 3092-4. Library of Congress.

78 Meeting notes of meeting held February 5, 1966. Luther H. Foster, Jr., Tuskegee, to Paul Rudolph, New Haven, December 17, 1965; Rudolph to Foster, December 31, 1965, in unprocessed papers, PR 13 CN 2001:126, 3092-4. Library of Congress.

79 Minutes of the Spring meeting of the Board of Trustees of Tuskegee Institute, March 21, 1959. Tuskegee University Archives.

80 Holland, discussion with authors, May 22, 2013.

81 Ibid.

82 Ibid.

83 Rohan, *The Architecture*, 141–151.

84 Ibid.

85 Ibid., 2–4.

86 Holland, discussion with authors, May 22, 2013.

87 Ibid.

88 Ibid.; F. N. Thompson's original guaranteed contract was $1,659,400.00 per Change Order No. 5 executed on December 26, 1967, in unprocessed papers, PR 13 CN 2001:126, PMR 3007-4, Library of Congress.

89 Ibid.

90 Massey, A Bridge Between, 33.

91 Holland, discussion with authors, May 22, 2013.

92 Moreland Griffith Smith, FAIA, Atlanta, memorandum to Owner, Architects, Engineers, and General Contractor, December 20, 1967; in unprocessed papers, PR 13 CN 2001:126, PMR 3007-4, Library of Congress. The memo confirmed that the parties agreed to have a full-time, on-site representative from the office of the Donald J. Neubauer, PE, structural engineer, to resolve all outstanding structural steel matters by January 26, 1968

93 Schmertz, "A Chapel," 126.

94 Ibid.

95 Tribute by Major L. Holland at the memorial service for Cady Metcalf, July 11, 2015

96 Ibid.

97 Holland, discussion with authors, May 22, 2013.

98 The authors studied both sets of the Constructions Documents prepared by Fry & Welch, that are stored in the Physical Plan Archives at Tuskegee University.

99 Ibid.

100 Holland, discussion with authors, May 22, 2013.

101 *The Tuskegee University Chapel: A Heritage of Faith, 1975.* Tuskegee University Archives.

102 The Office of Paul Rudolph, Architect, Boston, created an undated sketch during construction showing the colored, glazed skylights in the Meditation Chapel and in two stairwells; in unprocessed papers, PR 13 CN 2001:126, PMR 3007-4, Library of Congress.

103 "The Space of Human Spirit: Interdenominational Chapel, Tuskegee," trans. Carl Black, Jr., *Global Architectural*, April 1973.

104 Ibid.

105 Trustee Minutes, April 9, 1960. Tuskegee University Archives.

106 Trustees Minutes, March 21, 1959. Tuskegee University Archives.

107 Holland, discussions with authors, May 22, 2013.

108 Moreland G. Smith, Montgomery, to L. H. Foster, Tuskegee, November 9, 1964; L. H. Foster to Moreland G. Smith, December 12, 1964, in unprocessed papers, PR 13 CN 2001.126, PMR 3092-4, Library of Congress. Both letters discuss the idea of selecting black architects to work with Rudolph on Tuskegee's new buildings.

109 John Wade, Tuskegee Architecture Department Chair, to Paul Rudolph, New York, October 18, 1967, in unprocessed papers, PR 13 CN 2001.126, PMR 3092-4, Library of Congress. Wade thanked Rudolph for hiring two Tuskegee students as summer interns.

110 As black mayors were elected in during the 1970s in cities such as Atlanta, GA, Richmond, VA, and Tuskegee, AL, the joint venture model between majority and minority architectural firms became prevalent for awarding public sector work.
111 Massey, *A Bridge Between*, 35.

References

Annual Report of the President, 1956–57, 1961–69. Tuskegee Institute. Tuskegee University Archives.

Association de l'Oeuvre Notre-Dame-du-Haut. *Ronchamp: Notre-Dame du Haut: The Pilgrimage Church of Notre-Dame du Haut by Le Corbusier: History, Architecture, Spirituality*. Translated by Katherine Taylor (Regensburg: Schnell & Steiner, 2008).

Carter, Annette K. "Louis Edwin Fry, Sr." In Dreck Spurlock Wilson, ed. *African American Architects: A Biographical Dictionary 1865–1945*, 159–161 (New York, NY: Routledge, 2004).

Coulbourn, Keith. "Chapel of Sculptured Brick." *Atlanta Constitution*, May 25, 1969.

Daugherty, Ellen. "Negotiating the Veil: Tuskegee's Booker T. Washington Monument," *American Art* 24, no. 3 (Fall 2010): 52–77.

"Early Morning Fire Destroys Institute Chapel." *Campus Digest* (Tuskegee Institute). January 30, 1957. Tuskegee University Archives.

Garrow, David J. *Bearing the Cross: Martin Luther King, Jr., and the Southern Christian Leadership Conference* (New York, NY: William Morrow, 1986).

Gelernter, Mark. *A History of American Architecture: Buildings in Their Cultural and Technological Context* (Hanover, NH: University Press of New England, 1999).

Historic Sites and National Monument Establishment, Pub. L. No. 93–486, 88 Stat. 1461 (1974).

Kennedy, Roger G. *American Churches* (New York, NY: Stewart, Tabori & Chang, 1982).

Ledford, Daniel L. *The Religious Architecture of Paul Rudolph*, Yale Divinity School, Reading Course, Fall 2014, Karla Britton, December 16, 2014.

Massey, James Earl. *A Bridge Between: A Centennial History of Campus Ministry at Tuskegee University, 1888–1988* (Tuskegee, AL: Tuskegee University Press, 1988).

Minutes of the Annual Meeting of the Board of Trustees, 1957–60. Tuskegee Institute. Tuskegee University Archives.

Moholy-Nagy, Sybil. Introduction to Paul Rudolph, *The Architecture of Paul Rudolph*, 7–29. Captions by Gerhard Schwab, translated into English by Maria Kroll (New York, NY: Praeger, 1970).

Monk, Tony. *The Art and Architecture of Paul Rudolph* (Chichester, West Sussex: Wiley-Academy, 1999).

"Mr. Moreland G. Smith, 82, Retired Architect, Civil Rights Activist." *Atlanta Journal-Constitution*, June 27, 1989.

Phillips, Joyce. "Farewell, Dean Welch," *Campus Digest*, March 25, 1972, vol. 40: 1.

Rogers, Stevens B. "The Frank Lloyd Wright Campus at Florida Southern College: A Child of the Sun," *Frank Lloyd Wright Quarterly* 12, no. 3 (Summer 2001): 4–23.

Rohan, Timothy M. *The Architecture of Paul Rudolph* (New Haven, CT: Yale University Press, 2014).

Rudolph, Paul. "Excerpts from a Conversation," *Writings on Architecture* (New Haven, CT: Yale School of Architecture, 2008; originally published in *Perspecto* 22 (1996): 135–136).

———. Unprocessed papers. PR 13 CN 2001:126. Paul Marvin Rudolph Archive. Library of Congress.

Schmertz, Mildred F. "Sanctuary of Sculptured Concrete," *Architectural Forum* 113 September 1960: 102–105.

———. "Paul Rudolph's Chapel for Tuskegee Institute," *Architectural Record* 11 November 1969: 117–126.

Stern, Robert A. M. *New Directions in American Architecture* (New York, NY: George Braziller, 1977).

"The Space of Human Spirit: Interdenominational Chapel, Tuskegee." Translated by Carl Black, Jr., with photographs by Yukio Futagawa. *Global Architecture*, Tokyo, April 1973.

Tuskegee Institute Bulletin, Catalogue Issue, 1962–63. Tuskegee University Archives.

The Tuskegee University Chapel: A Heritage of Faith. 1975. (Tuskegee, AL: Tuskegee University Archives).

US Department of the Interior, National Park Service, *National Survey of Historic Sites and Buildings,* March 1, 1965.

"Walter Netsch, Architect, Dies at 88," *New York Times,* June 17, 2008.

Weiss, Ellen. *Robert R. Taylor and Tuskegee: An African American Architect Designs for Booker T. Washington* (Montgomery, AL: New South Books, 2012).

PART II

The parabola, concrete, and modern sacred architecture

4

BOLD MODERN FORM

The parabola and St. Louis's sacred buildings

Mary Reid Brunstrom

> The strength of this great form is indicated by the hold it exerted on the community consciousness for so long before it had the slightest beginning as a physical fact.[1]

St. Louisans knew it when they saw the architect's drawings of the Gateway Arch—the consummate form that could activate a storied past and reconstitute the image of the region as a protagonist in the country's future. Yet in prospect, the form was as unfamiliar as it was exciting when the design was first announced in 1948. The Arch was dedicated in 1965 as the centerpiece of the winning re-development scheme for the Jefferson National Expansion Memorial (JNEM) on the riverfront in downtown St. Louis. Designed by Eero Saarinen and Associates, the JNEM (renamed The Gateway Arch National Park in February, 2018) featured a complementary landscape of biomorphic-shaped water features set in green space by the landscape architect Dan Kiley.[2] For the Arch, Saarinen (1910–61) had started out with the general form of a parabola in mind because of its pleasing simplicity and elegance. In light of mathematical, structural, and aesthetic considerations, the design was modified as a weighted catenary.[3] The fact that the Arch, as an abstract yet legible sculptural form, quickly became the "symbol of progress in St. Louis" was confirmed by the number of businesses that designed the motif into their corporate logos.[4] The beauty and refinement of its gleaming, modern material—stainless steel—unquestionably spoke to America's belief in a strong and positive future, one based on scientific and technological determinism. The Arch was also heralded as an engineering tour de force because of its pioneering use of stressed-skin construction.[5] Saarinen's sleek design seemed aerodynamic in the way it compelled the eye skywards, expanding the space of everyday consciousness and perhaps anticipating the central place that aviation would occupy in the daily lives of Americans. Indeed, the Arch stood ready as a pre-digested symbol as outer space transcended aviation space as the zone of imagination and aspiration. This chapter introduces the Gateway Arch as the essential expression of parabolic form in the region, one that foreshadowed its use in an array of buildings, both sacred and secular, that arose in the 1950s and 1960s.

The parabola, defined as an open, geometric figure with a central axis and arms extending symmetrically on both sides of the vertex, was one of many vital curvilinear forms to emerge in the decades following World War II across a range of building types.[6] Geometrically predictable and mathematically calculable, it could span significant spaces in the manner of historical arches and vaults, as well as enable modern roof designs of aesthetic and symbolic import. Its proponents implicitly carried forward the 1930s language of streamlining in which the leading curved edge evoked the speed and efficiency associated with technological progress.[7] The parabola's distinctive aesthetics elicited an emotional response to architecture, perhaps because the form could be connected to the infinite through its diverging and theoretically limitless arms. Saarinen himself seized upon the parabola in his quest for the quintessential form for the era. "Each age" he noted "must create its own architecture out of its own technology, and one which is expressive of its own Zeitgeist—the spirit of the time."[8]

At midcentury, with the Arch concept gaining recognition in the region, three significant parabola-based religious buildings breathed new life into St. Louis's built environment. B'nai Amoona Synagogue (1945–50) by the German émigré architect Eric Mendelsohn, featured a parabolic section; Resurrection of Our Lord Catholic Church (1949–54) by the St. Louis-based architectural partnership of Murphy and Mackey, used a parabolic plan, and the Abbey Church of St. Mary and St. Louis (1956–62)—known as Priory Church, and designed by the Japanese-American architect, Gyo Obata for the firm of Hellmuth, Obata & Kassabaum (HOK)—repeated the parabola in vertical tiers around a central axis. Within the typology of the sacred building, parabolic form accommodated a multiplicity of programmatic needs while simultaneously projecting an array of meanings.

This linear study encompasses three main concerns. First, it traces the architectural phenomenon of parabolic form in St. Louis's mid-twentieth-century building culture. Second, the study is an interrogation of form, analyzing the three sacred buildings already cited and tracing the diverse origins of the architects' interest in the parabola. Third, I examine how specific conjunctions of materials and technology, both new and traditional, enabled formal variations that carried meanings particular to the era.

The curve and the context of the case studies

In its spare elegance, the Arch consummated Saarinen's search for a simple form that would render it timeless as well as intelligible at midcentury. The symmetrical flourish of stainless steel would rise on the Mississippi riverfront to the east of the downtown grid of masonry warehouses and mercantile structures like an exotic harbinger of change (Fig. 4.1). While the ostensible purpose of the 91-acre urban national park was to memorialize President Thomas Jefferson and the pioneers of westward expansion, the local, more urgent imperative was to revive the historic riverfront using land clearance policies that were central to urban planning practice of the era.[9]

During the 17 years between the Arch design's public debut in 1948 and the monument's dedication in 1965, architects and the public alike were left to speculate on how the form would impact design in the overall region as well as the riverfront. At the same time, the architects of this chapter's three religious buildings looked to Europe and Latin America for applications of the form. I argue, therefore, that the blossoming of parabolic form in midcentury St. Louis resulted from a multiplicity of influences that converged in the creative climate generated by the advent of the Arch. I further show that the architects explored new

FIGURE 4.1 Jefferson National Expansion Memorial, 1948; Eero Saarinen and Associates; photomontage of post-competition model.

© HB-11125-D, Chicago History Museum, Hedrich-Blessing Collection.

formal expression with imaginative uses of steel, concrete, and glass technology, even as they maintained continuity with past practices. All three sacred buildings were designed more or less contemporaneously with the Arch and were completed ahead of it. Along with the Arch, they contributed to a modernist transformation of the built environment in St. Louis in both the public and private sectors. Moreover, the architects' choice of parabolic form attested to a spirit of originality and autonomy in the design of religious architecture in the region.

Saarinen's Arch exemplified an individualized modernism that introduced a discursive turn into an opinionated field. The parabola enabled the architects under discussion in this study to recover the prerogative to unify form and materials in strategies that privileged beauty while attending to function. Aesthetic concerns had been largely subordinated to function and austerity in the doctrinal modernism that had shaped progressive architecture since the 1920s and 1930s.[10] Saarinen was interested in the rhetorical power of the Arch as the archetypal civic monument and symbolic portal with roots in antiquity.[11] As a refinement of this historic type, the Gateway Arch was exceptional in monument building for its pared-down formal simplicity and its quintessentially modern material. Saarinen understood parabolic form from working with his architect father, Eliel, on the dual-parabola plan for Kleinhans Music Hall (1938–40), a state-of-the-art music complex in Buffalo, New York. Le Corbusier's unbuilt proposal for the 1931 competition for the Palace of

Soviets in Moscow also seems likely to have influenced Saarinen's design for the St. Louis riverfront.[12] The simplicity and visibility of Le Corbusier's momentous vertical parabola as the compositional anchor illustrated its potential for creating symbolism at urban scale.

Recent scholarship argues that in the mid-twentieth century, architects transitioned from Beaux-Arts orthodoxy which privileged harmony as the design objective, to an evolutionary biological paradigm which theorized a building in terms such as "vital," "organic" and "living."[13] Scientific concepts and terminology were applied to design concerns such as plan, space, and innovations in steel and concrete technologies. Notably, Mendelsohn echoed this thinking when he pointed to a shift in structural principles from the rigid traditional systems of load and support, thrust and counter-thrust, to a mode of tension and relaxation based on elasticity.[14] As if describing a living structure, he identified "an organic process similar to the interplay of the body's muscles" that would ring in new ways of thinking about design.[15] Architects further understood the potential of parabolic form to produce buildings that would respond to changing cultural, social, and liturgical conditions at mid-century. For their congregational houses of worship, religious denominations sought designs that would foster community identity and participation.[16] To this end, Mendelsohn strove for flexibility in his B'nai Amoona design after studying Frank Lloyd Wright's open plan concept for Unity Temple in Chicago (1904). In the context of the Catholic Church liturgical reform initiatives, the traditional Gothic cruciform layout based on the hierarchical, processional basilica plan with designated precincts, was superseded by single-room, column-free design. These new schemes aimed to encourage worshipper participation, thereby unifying the congregation in the experience of the Mass.[17] Modern Jewish and Christian sanctuaries each in their own ways attempted to facilitate direct communion between worshippers and God, underscoring the democratic values of equal access and participation.

B'nai Amoona Synagogue (1945–50)—steel and brick

In the same year the Saarinen Arch entered the public imaginary, B'nai Amoona Congregation announced Mendelsohn's design for a new synagogue complex for a suburban site on St. Louis's western border where Jewish families were settling. Eric Mendelsohn (1887–1953) was among the foremost Jewish architects of his generation, the designer of the Expressionist Einstein Tower (1920–24) in Potsdam, Germany and a pioneer of modern design in Germany in the 1920s and later in Britain and Palestine.[18] With this inaugural commission in the United States, St. Louis provided Mendelsohn with an American launching pad for his visionary modernism.[19] He acknowledged a climate of openness to modern ideas, writing, "your Congregation was the first in our country willing to accept a design for its synagogue which does not try to imitate the past."[20] That past included designs that followed one traditional style or another in response to circumstances and contemporary taste. Even though no synagogue design guidelines exist, faith protocols require the synagogue to face toward Jerusalem, to place the Ark housing the Torah scrolls at the focal point of the sanctuary, and to situate the Bimah in a specific relation with the Ark.[21]

Mendelsohn's design focused on function rather than style, integrating three core needs relating to the spiritual (a sanctuary), the social (an assembly hall) and the educational (a school) as part of the synagogue's program. This integration of functions in a community-focused complex serving modern Jewish life would become the norm in post-war synagogue design in the United States.[22] The design fulfilled the requirement for flexibility to expand the assembly spaces for the High Holy Days. To these ends, on the elevated corner site Mendelsohn orchestrated a play of rectilinear, flat-roofed, horizontally oriented volumes arranged around a green courtyard, with the roof heights varying according to interior function. In a bold tectonic gesture that established the building in St. Louis and elsewhere as a beacon of modernism, Mendelsohn enclosed the sanctuary with a signature architectural feature, namely a wing-like half-parabola reclining on its perpendicular axis (Fig. 4.2). The parabolic roof projected some 26 feet westward by means of a monumental cantilever supported at the sanctuary wall.[23] Not only was this startling configuration a departure from normative synagogue design, the roof was unlike any other in the area. The daring parabolic gesture harked back to Mendelsohn's exuberant, visionary drawings of three decades earlier, which featured futuristic forms that bristled with anticipation at the plastic potential of steel, concrete, and glass when integrated in modern design.[24] An adventurous patron, a visionary builder, and technological advances were three factors that converged to make Mendelsohn's concept for B'nai Amoona a reality.[25] Mendelsohn may have assimilated the parabolic motif from Dominikus Böhm's St. Engelbert's Church (1930–32) in Cologne-Riehl in Germany, which derived its vitality from vertical parabolas repeated around a central axis.[26] In St. Louis, the configuration of the parabolic roof in section so that it appeared to spring from the ground in an infinite skyward trajectory, constituted the inventive breakthrough that unlocked the dynamic potential of the form. As with Saarinen's Arch, Mendelsohn's fluid gestural iteration of parabolic form expanded the imaginative field in which architectural vision could germinate and grow.

Reinforced concrete was used for the roof throughout the complex. The parabolic curve over the sanctuary was formed with six colossal steel I-beams, each 140 feet in length, that taper from the base at the rear of the building towards the end of the cantilever.[27] This bold design exemplified the dynamic fusion of form and function in a building that, according

FIGURE 4.2 B'nai Amoona Synagogue, University City, Missouri, 1950; Eric Mendelsohn.

© Courtesy of W. Philip Cotton/FAIA/The American Institute of Architects, St. Louis Chapter.

FIGURE 4.3 B'nai Amoona Synagogue, University City, Missouri, c. 1949; Eric Mendelsohn; parabolic steel girders under construction.

Courtesy of B'nai Amoona Archives.

to Mendelsohn, was "proud . . . to show its structural method as its formative principle."[28] Constructability challenges undoubtedly added to the heroics of the modernist narrative (Fig. 4.3). While the great steel girders gave the building its distinctive roof, it was the material with less charismatic potential—brick—that served in multiple ways to unify the design. The walls are constructed of concrete block faced with buff-colored Norman brick. This use of brick related the entire complex to the masonry traditions in the neighborhood, even as the yellow hue and distinctive patterning flagged the building as a modern departure. For the brickwork, Mendelsohn specified a stacked bond pattern in which the line created by the continuous mortar joints between the vertical tiers enhanced the sense of lift.[29] The light color key further mediated the weight of the massing. For these reasons, the masonry application can be viewed as an exemplary integration of design and material.

Innovative use of glass further proclaimed the building's modernity. Glass was the medium that produced spatial expansiveness, including reciprocity between the exterior and interior, as well as a distinctive quality of lightness. Mendelsohn equated light with enlightenment, clarity and modernity, stating that "Temples should reject in their interior the mystifying darkness of an illiterate time and should place their faith in the light of day."[30] Light was therefore a key dynamic inside the sanctuary, where it streamed through the tall clerestory windows on the west wall to illuminate the Ark which was the sacred focus, centered on the Bimah. This incoming illumination, which was supplemented by the light monitor in the parabolic roof, bathed the sanctuary in warmth, in certain conditions creating an aura of ineffable space. Throughout the complex, Mendelsohn introduced modern lighting schemes that integrated natural light from lofty plate glass windows and clerestories with illumination from electric fixtures.[31]

The parabolic roof quickly became the building's signifying attribute for both members and outsiders alike. Its contour created an energetic field for the Star of David which was set in a ten-foot diameter armature and mounted high up on the north exterior wall of the sanctuary (Fig. 4.4). Visible to all, this sole ornament differentiated the precinct as a synagogue. Mendelsohn echoed the aspirations of many Jews when he wrote that the temple should "symbolize our spiritual renascence."[32] The dramatic roof therefore amounted to more than a dynamic compositional flourish or a rhetorical nod to modernity. It signified Jewish aspiration in the post-war context and served as a beacon for a congregation engaged in collectively summoning the integrity of their ancient faith.[33] How then did this daring design help engender a sense of community? As the first modern synagogue dedicated in North America, the building signaled leadership in advanced synagogue design, an accomplishment that made its largely progressive congregation proud.[34] Mendelsohn associated modern architecture with democratic values.[35] For a congregation engaged in revitalizing Judaism in the immediate aftermath of the Holocaust, B'nai Amoona's unfettered architectural expression testified to the centrality of freedom in American democratic ideals. One witness resorted to scripture to conceptualize the construction spectacle as follows: "As God said to the Prophet [Ezekiel]: 'Behold I will lay sinews upon you, and will bring flesh upon you, and I will cover you with skin, and put breath into you and ye shall live.'"[36] This association suggests that the congregation understood the new synagogue arising in their midst as a metaphor for regeneration.

FIGURE 4.4 B'nai Amoona Synagogue, University City, Missouri, 2000; Eric Mendelsohn; framing the Star of David.

Resurrection Church (1949–54)—brick meets glass

In 1949, a further iteration of parabolic form emerged in St. Louis in the plan for the Church of the Resurrection of Our Lord designed by the firm of Murphy and Mackey (Fig. 4.5). Resurrection Church was part of the Catholic Archdiocese of St. Louis, which was then under the progressive leadership of Archbishop (later Cardinal) Joseph E. Ritter.[37] A determined social reformer, Ritter integrated St. Louis's parochial schools in 1947, years ahead of public schools and comparable mid-western Archdioceses.[38] Later, he helped lead the reforms of the Second Vatican Council in Rome (1962–65). In St. Louis, Ritter engaged the contested issues that were transforming church art and architecture at mid-century, pointing to modern churches in the Archdiocese, including Resurrection, as "the result in each instance of the free collaboration of the pastor with his architect, the fruit of their own thinking and planning."[39] Ritter's words provided cover for stylistic innovation enacted at the parish level.

Resurrection Church was built to serve a young and predominantly German middle-class population on the city's south side.[40] Its Renaissance-derived, tri-partite scheme comprised a sanctuary, a separate baptistery in front, and a bell tower located at the apex of the parabola, in addition to a rectory and convent. At the time, the architects Joseph D. Murphy (1907–95) and Eugene J. Mackey, Jr. (1911–68) were on the faculty of Washington University School of Architecture where Murphy was dean from 1948–52. Both attended MIT. Murphy won the 1929 Paris Prize which gained him two years at the École des Beaux Arts in Paris. Mackey graduated with an M.Arch. in 1937.[41] Both men were keen to pursue modernist ideas in their work.[42] Mendelsohn's parabolic section at B'nai Amoona almost certainly played into Murphy and Mackey's plan for the sanctuary at Resurrection Church, as did the widely

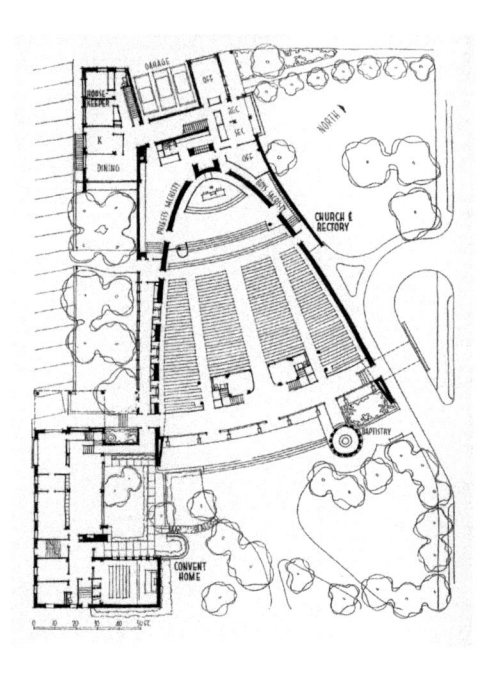

FIGURE 4.5 Resurrection Church, St. Louis, 1949; Murphy and Mackey; plan.
© Courtesy of the Murphy family.

disseminated design for Kleinhans Music Hall in Buffalo, New York which was based on dual parabolas connected through the base by a sweeping lobby.[43] A more certain and direct influence, however, came from Resurrection Church's pastor, Monsignor George Dreher who advocated for the parabolic plan published in a volume entitled *Vom Baue der Kirche* (later translated as *The Church Incarnate)*, by the German liturgical reform architect Rudolf Schwarz.[44] A German speaker, Dreher translated the text from the German for Murphy.[45] For Schwarz, the diverging wings of the parabolic plan symbolized the outstretched arms of Christ extending to the faithful a gesture of unconditional and infinite welcome in which liturgy and architecture coalesced.[46]

Whereas at B'nai Amoona, latent energy in the roof trajectory engages the viewer from both interior and exterior vantage points, the dynamics of parabolic form in Resurrection Church are felt more acutely on the interior. The converging walls draw the eye to the apex of the parabola where the altar is located (Fig. 4.6). The architects further emphasized the centrality of this most sacred precinct and the liturgical focal point of the Mass by concentrating copious natural and artificial light on this area from a lantern in the ceiling. Among Resurrection Church's architectural innovations was its open single-room sanctuary, a feature designed to enhance worshippers' engagement with the communal enactment of the Mass. Structural columns were held to the side, yielding unimpeded views of the celebrant at the altar. Column-free design also minimized spatial segmentation, even as the architects retained certain elements of the basilica plan, namely the central aisle on axis with the altar, and side aisles. The liturgical message was reinforced in an innovative approach to church furnishings. Led by the architects, a team of liturgical artists produced sculptures including Stations of the Cross, an altar mural, stained glass windows, furniture, and accouterments for the altar, all aesthetically and thematically integrated with the architecture (Fig. 4.6).[47] The building's principal material—brick—resonates with the surrounding residential architecture. In this masterly application that continued on the interior walls, the expansive, uninterrupted surfaces act as a perfect showcase for the infinite textural beauty of the dappled, rose-toned Roman brick that was set in running bond and faced with limestone.[48] The large expanses of brick on the exterior walls, both vertical and horizontal, could have seemed oppressive had Murphy and Mackey not deployed the parabolic footprint in a dynamic orientation that activates the composition on the block, integrating the building lightly and seamlessly with its site. The weight of the brick is additionally mediated by two strategic uses of glass, one in the wall-to-wall, ground-to-roof glazing of the façade, and the other on the clerestory level with a band of continuous grisaille-toned, biblically themed stained glass windows. The latter introduced visual interest and elevated the roof above the walls such that light could penetrate the sanctuary from both sides.

Upon examination, the unconventional use of glass as a counterpoint to brick in the façade can be interpreted as an expression of the existential fact that the Church in the early 1950s was poised between a tradition-based past and an expansive future. The challenge to design orthodoxy arose not so much in the choice of the material as in its application on the entire façade, which critics viewed as more appropriate for secular buildings such as supermarkets.[49] Light poured in, dissolving the customary separation between street and sanctuary. The entry experience was thereby transformed from a ritual of penetration of a dim interior to a fluent passage through a transparent threshold into an open, light-bathed, colonnaded space. The glass façade also underscored a new building truth, namely, that engineering had literally moved to the forefront of design. The lofty terracotta-clad steel columns that carried

FIGURE 4.6 Resurrection Church, St. Louis, Missouri, 1954; Murphy and Mackey; interior facing the altar at the apex of the parabolic plan, and liturgical furnishings.

© HB-17546-E, Chicago History Museum, Hedrich-Blessing Collection.

the roof exposed and celebrated the building's structural rationale. The transparent façade served also as an agent of the liturgy. Implying that the Church's boundless embrace extended through the glass to infinity, the parabola embodied an abstract but nonetheless engaging concept of "illimitable" space (Fig. 4.7).[50] This interpretation of the Church as an open rather than delimiting vessel may also have alluded to a policy of inclusiveness in the context of the racial integration of parochial schools noted earlier. When Archbishop Ritter pointed to the Church's historic reliance on the authority of its built forms, he implied that he would look to modern architecture to symbolize institutional leadership in the post-war era.[51]

Priory Church (1956–62)—the reinforced concrete shell

Priory Church was the first religious commission for the newly formed firm of Hellmuth, Obata & Kassabaum (HOK). Gyo Obata (1923–), a 1945 graduate of Washington University School of Architecture in St. Louis, was HOK's design partner and the designer of the Priory project.[52] The fact that the school had admitted Obata in 1941 enabled him to avoid World War II internment on the West Coast.[53] Obata went on to study at Detroit's Cranbrook Academy of Art, which was then under Eliel Saarinen's leadership.[54]

FIGURE 4.7 Resurrection Church, St. Louis, Missouri, 1954; Murphy and Mackey; façade elevation showing sanctuary, baptistery, and bell tower.

© Missouri History Museum, St. Louis/Mac Mizuki Photography Studio Collection.

The Priory site was an undeveloped tract in west St. Louis County some twenty miles from downtown St. Louis. The project was a new venture for the Catholic Monastic Order of Benedictines in England whom Archbishop Ritter had invited to establish a new school with exemplary spiritual and academic standards for Catholic boys. Convinced that progressive architecture could be instrumental in shaping modern faith, the Benedictines imagined a building that, as the spiritual and geographic focus of the monastic complex, would convey with strength and clarity the centrality of faith in contemporary Christian life.[55] The immigrant monks also wanted the architecture to read as American, meaning modern and advanced, and therefore using new materials and technology.

Obata had experienced first-hand the potential of thin-shell concrete as a means of optimizing light, spanning space and foregrounding aesthetics when he worked on the design of St. Louis's Lambert International Terminal (1951–56) for HOK's predecessor firm, Hellmuth, Yamasaki and Leinweber.[56] He was also aware of the vaulted thin-shell concrete structures of the Spanish-Mexican engineer, Félix Candela, and the lightweight spanning structures of the Italian engineer, Pier Luigi Nervi.[57] Lambert Terminal exemplified an innovative use of concrete shells in a series of three intersecting parabolic barrel vaults that soared over the passenger check-in and waiting areas.[58] The breathtaking expansiveness and gracefulness inherent in the terminal's spatial configuration would be re-imagined in the Priory Church sanctuary. When he visited the Lambert Terminal, the Benedictine Prior, Dom Columba Cary-Elwes apprehended in this secular building design a potential for aspiration that might enhance the religious experience in a church setting.[59]

Decades before thin-shell concrete was introduced, the parabola had been identified as the "true" modern form for concrete, largely because it required the smallest amount of material to support a given load.[60] Thin-shell technology breathed new life into the age-old and ubiquitous medium, enabling it to transcend its signature property, weight, with refinement and seemingly effortless grace in formal expression and across significant spans. The inherent challenges and contingencies of working with concrete arise from the manual or mechanical process of fusing sand, aggregate and cement.[61] Its fickleness is nowhere more evident than in the production of thin-shell concrete. The parabolic arches at Priory Church were formed

FIGURE 4.8 Priory Church, St. Louis County, Missouri, c. 1961; Gyo Obata/HOK; construction of parabolic shells.

© Missouri History Museum, St. Louis/Mac Mizuki Photography Studio Collection.

over plywood overlaid with reinforcing steel and steel mesh (Fig. 4.8). The ribs were poured first, after which wet-mix gunite—concrete which is pneumatically projected at high velocity through a hose—was blown onto the form to a uniform three-inch thickness. A dynamic routine of spraying and drying while controlling water content stabilized the concrete during the initial curing process.[62]

At Resurrection Church, verticality was achieved through the high walls that extend the parabolic footprint skyward. By contrast, at Priory Church, a remarkable sense of lift is accomplished without traditional walls, enhanced by the building's elevation on a platform. In a rising composition, three tiers of concrete parabolic shells are stacked in concentric circles, connected at the top by reinforced concrete ring beams (Fig. 4.9). Each register defines a precinct on the interior: the entry level houses twelve secondary altars, the organ and the ambulatory; the middle layer articulates the nave, and the uppermost layer features a skylight lantern. Positioned over the oculus on the central vertical axis, the lantern illuminates the interior and underscores the liturgical centrality of the altar. The column-free design spanning 140 feet in diameter responded to the new liturgical requirements for optimized sight lines to the altar and for the faithful to be seated close to, in this case literally encircling, the celebrant.[63] This dynamic fusion of structure and form epitomized the openness possible in a space conceived of as communal.

Bristling with formal vitality and permeated with diffused light, the building radiates spiritual ambiance. Obata's exploration of lightness resulted in a feat of illusionism whereby on the exterior the structure appears to levitate on its raised site. With light as a central design concern, Obata effectively reformulated the medieval arch as parabolic form, thereby embedding layers of historic reference for the Benedictines whose normative building style was Gothic Revival (Fig. 4.9). Moreover, the tripartite vertical layering engages the arcade, triforium, and clerestory hierarchy of the Gothic structure. For the "windows," Obata used Kalwall, an insulated, reinforced fiberglass product developed during World War II, that reads as black on the exterior but admits a suffused light evocative of Japanese Shoji screens.[64] These properties eliminated distraction from the outside, allowing the architect to harness the mesmerizing dynamics of light in its purity and abstraction. To the extent that the building embodied the Benedictines' intellectual and emotional engagement with tradition,

FIGURE 4.9 Priory Church, St. Louis County, Missouri, 1962; Gyo Obata/HOK; aerial view.
© HOK.

it acted as a metaphor for the indissoluble continuity of form, from medieval to modern. Obata's imaginative design reinforced the Benedictines' alignment of their groundbreaking mission in St. Louis with modern architecture.[65] The building's critical and functional success confirmed the Benedictines as leaders in modern church design in North America—Catholic and otherwise—a reputation they had inaugurated with their engagement of Marcel Breuer as the architect for St. John's Abbey in Collegeville, Minnesota (1953–61), that had been dedicated a year ahead of Priory Church.[66] Obata continued his exploration of thin-shell concrete with his design for McDonnell Planetarium which was named for James S. McDonnell, the aviation pioneer and cofounder of the St. Louis-based corporate aerospace leader McDonnell-Douglas. The building's spool-like hyperboloidal shell evoked the trajectories of space travel when it opened in 1963 at the height of the space race.[67] Obata would go on to consolidate his position as an architect who had insightfully interpreted the space age with his design of the Smithsonian Institution's National Air and Space Museum (1966–76) on the National Mall in Washington, DC.[68]

Conclusion

While the three sacred buildings discussed in this chapter originated in their architects' exploration of parabolic form, they each developed within the penumbra of Saarinen's archetypal scheme.[69] In the larger context of the Gateway Arch, they exemplify the versatility of the parabola. These applications of the curve expanded formal possibilities and along with successive secular uses of the form, they helped unify the design of the Arch with other St. Louis buildings of the period.[70] Of all the structures in this "parabola city," the one bearing the most distinct imprint of Saarinen's Arch was Busch Memorial Stadium (1964–66) which was designed as the new home for the St. Louis Cardinals baseball team. The ovoid design by Edward Durell Stone (1902–78) with Sverdrup & Parcel and Schwarz & Van Hoefen, featured a graceful coronet of thin-shell concrete parabolas at the roof line which explicitly acknowledged the Arch (Fig. 4.10).[71]

In the cases of the three houses of God discussed in this chapter, the innovative form of the parabola shaped the worshipper's relationship with the religious locale. From the exterior, the three buildings projected a sense of modernity that spoke variously to the regeneration of faith and to a focal shift from past to future. On the interior, the open sanctuary invited fresh experiences of worship, especially through more active participation in the ritual. Still, they differ dramatically because in each case the architect utilized a distinctive iteration of the parabola. Eric Mendelsohn used a parabolic section at B'nai Amoona Synagogue; Murphy and Mackey's Resurrection Church featured a parabolic plan, and at Priory Church, Gyo Obata arranged multiple vertical parabolas around a central axis.

Material opportunities and challenges are a continuous theme in this modernist narrative. At the time, the massive, curved steel girders that support the cantilevered concrete roof at B'nai Amoona were viewed as a tectonic triumph.[72] Construction images disseminated in the media sparked excitement at the advent of futuristic design in St. Louis. At Priory Church, the contractors solved constructability challenges posed by thin-shell concrete as the shaping agent for parabolic form.[73] Indeed, in its whiteness and lightness, the structure seemed to aspire to weightlessness. A parallel theme is the reprise of brick in modern building. Mendelsohn's use of light-hued brick, stacked vertically, gave the synagogue complex a modern geometric touch, while Murphy and Mackey exploited the familiarity

FIGURE 4.10 Busch Memorial Stadium with the Gateway Arch in downtown St. Louis, Missouri, 1966; Edward Durell Stone, Sverdrup & Parcel, and Schwarz & Van Hoefen.

of local brick to integrate Resurrection Church with masonry structures in the neighborhood. Both applications are essays in the subtle visual richness inherent in the medium of brick. Both buildings signaled their modernity by juxtaposing brick with expansive runs of plate glass. This strategy telegraphed transparency while underscoring the centrality of light in the experience of modern interior space.

Returning in conclusion to the Gateway Arch, its parabola-based configuration remains St. Louis's defining architectural form and its signifying civic attribute. Eero Saarinen expressed the aspirations of generations past and future in an exquisite form, one that transformed a civic eyesore into an icon. The Arch endures as a built expression of surpassing beauty, a source of pride, and one of the most visited monuments in the country and the entire world. An extensive renovation of the Arch grounds and ancillary facilities was opened to the public on July 3, 2018. With this expansive scheme, the design team led by Michael Van Valkenburgh Associates (MVVA) accomplished one of Saarinen's unrealized goals, namely the unification of the national park and downtown St. Louis. Moreover, it underscores the indispensable role of the Arch as a symbol of urban renewal. Historically, though, this dominant narrative of communal identity has overlooked a troublesome cultural dynamic, namely the widespread use of racial segregation in shaping urban infrastructure.[74] As this chapter demonstrates, the incidence of parabolic form in St. Louis in the mid-twentieth century is striking, its imaginative applications impressive. It is noteworthy that until their advent, St. Louis's architectural signature derived not necessarily from any particular form, but rather from the material, brick.

Without exception, modernist buildings stand as testaments to the individual vision and creativity that coalesced at mid-century in St. Louis when technological advances and postwar prosperity made their construction feasible. The result was a trove of unique, eye-catching structures that attest to a spirit of inventiveness in St. Louis. Collectively, they establish the region as a mid-century modern leader, a fact that was confirmed in consistent exposure in both the architectural and mainstream media of the time. Unlike many structures of the period, the future of the three sacred buildings in these case studies appears to be secure. In 1986, B'nai Amoona was repurposed as a community-based visual and performing arts center currently known as the Center of Creative Arts (COCA). An impressive expansion and renovation, including a state-of-the-art theatre in the original Mendelsohn sanctuary, is currently in process. A decade ago, Resurrection Church was saved from an uncertain future by a Vietnamese Catholic congregation who have infused it with life and invested in upgrades to the building while maintaining the integrity of Murphy and Mackey's design. Finally, more than a half century after its consecration in 1962, Priory Church continues uninterrupted in its original function as the vital focus of spiritual life on the Benedictine campus, known now as St. Louis Abbey.[75]

Notes

1 George McCue, "The Emerging St. Louis Symbol," *St. Louis Post-Dispatch*, June 10, 1962, 13G.
2 "Jefferson National Expansion Memorial Renamed Gateway Arch National Park," *St. Louis Construction News and Review*, February 27, 2018, http://stlouiscnr.com/departments/news/jefferson-national-expansion-memorial-renamed-gateway-arch-national-park/. Although the Arch itself was dedicated in 1965 with public access in 1967, the entire JNEM project would take until 1980 to complete. Robert J. Moore, Jr., *The Gateway Arch: An Architectural Dream* (St. Louis, MO: Jefferson National Parks Association), 2005, 126, 130–131.

3 The Arch measures 630 feet high by 630 feet across the base. Throughout the chapter, I use the term *parabola* in the generalized sense to make an argument about form rather than the mathematical specifics of the Arch as an inverted catenary. Robert Osserman, "How the Gateway Arch Got Its Shape," *Nexus Network Journal* 12, no. 2 (2010): 183.

4 James Neal Primm, *Lion of the Valley: St. Louis, Missouri, 1764–1980*, 3rd edn. (St. Louis: Missouri Historical Society Press, 1998), 456–457, and McCue, "Emerging," 13G.

5 Carl W. Condit, *American Building: Materials and Techniques from the First Colonial Settlements to the Present*, 2nd edn. (Chicago, IL: University of Chicago Press, 1982), 206–207. The Arch was designed in collaboration with the engineers Severud, Elstad, Krueger Associates.

6 Its order and symmetry differentiated it from biomorphic forms that constituted a parallel exploration of the curve. Eero Saarinen's design for the TWA Terminal at John F. Kennedy International Airport in New York City (1956–62) is a foremost example of the latter.

7 Meikle, Jeffrey L., *Twentieth Century Limited: Industrial Design in America, 1925–1939* (Philadelphia, PA: Temple University Press, 1979), 4.

8 Zeitgeist translates from German as the spirit of the time. The concept was engaged by leading modernists such as Le Corbusier and Mies van der Rohe to argue for architecture's unique role in expressing and animating the prevailing disposition of the era.

9 Joseph Heathcott and Máire Agnes Murphy, "Corridors of Flight, Zones of Renewal: Industry, Planning and Policy in the Making of Metropolitan St. Louis, 1940–1980," *Journal of Urban History* 31, no. 2 (January 2005), 174.

10 One strain of the discourse equated modern design with style, while the other tied modernism to social and political considerations. The former is associated with the Museum of Modern Art (MOMA) in New York, the latter with Bauhaus founder Walter Gropius, who after 1938 taught at Harvard's Graduate School of Design in Boston. Margaret Kentgens-Craig, "The Search for Modernity: America, the International Style, and the Bauhaus." In Keith L. Eggener, ed. *American Architectural History: A Contemporary Reader* (New York, NY: Routledge, 2004), 306–307.

11 Aline B. Saarinen, ed., *Eero Saarinen on His Work* (New Haven, CT: Yale University Press, 1962), 22.

12 Jean-Louis Cohen, *Le Corbusier and the Mystique of the USSR/Theories and Projects for Moscow 1928–1936* (Princeton, NJ: Princeton University Press, 1992), 164–203.

13 Catherine Rhiannon Osborne, "American Catholics and the Art of the Future, 1930–1975" (Ph.D. diss., Fordham University, 2013), 20–25.

14 Eric Mendelsohn, "The Great Adventure," *Marg* 4, no. 3 (1950–51): 33.

15 Ibid.

16 Kathleen James-Chakraborty, "Moderate Modernism: Sacred Architecture in St. Louis & Its Suburbs." In Eric Mumford, ed. *Modern Architecture in St. Louis: Washington University & Post-war American Architecture, 1948–1973* (St. Louis, MO: School of Architecture: Washington University in St. Louis, 2004), 27–28.

17 R. Kieckhefer, *Theology in Stone: Church Architecture from Byzantium to Berkeley* (New York, NY: Oxford University Press, 2004), 278–282.

18 In Germany, Mendelsohn's influential projects included the Schocken Department Store, Stuttgart (1928) and the Universuum Cinema, Berlin (1928); in England, the De La Warr Pavilion, Bexhill-on-Sea, Sussex (1935) with Serge Chermayeff; and in Palestine, the Hadassah University Medical Center, Jerusalem (1934–39), and the Chaim Weizmann House, Rehovot (1935–36).

19 Kathleen James-Chakraborty, *In the Spirit of Our Age: Eric Mendelsohn's B'nai Amoona Synagogue* (St. Louis, MO: Missouri Historical Society Press, 2000), 5.

20 Eric Mendelsohn to Barney Spitzer, September 1, 1950. B'nai Amoona Archives.

21 The Bimah is the raised platform housing the ark, the lectern and other sacred accouterments. It serves as a stage.

22 James-Chakraborty, *In the Spirit of Our Age*, 49.

23 L. Noelle Soren. "Congregation B'nai Amoona." National Register of Historic Places Registration Form (1984), Section 7, accessed February 18, 2018, https://dnr.mo.gov/shpo/nps-nr/84002698.pdf.

24 Bruno Zevi, *Erich Mendelsohn* (New York: Rizzoli, 1985), 26–28. St. Louisans may have seen these images in a 1944 MOMA-organized exhibition of Mendelsohn's drawings and photographs at the Saint Louis Art Museum.

25 The builder was I.E. Millstone, a member of the congregation and a legendary builder of St. Louis's civic infrastructure.

26 James-Chakraborty, *In the Spirit of Our Age,* 30.

27 Ibid., 36.

28 Mendelsohn, quoted in Rosalind Mael Bronsen, *B'nai Amoona for all Generations* (St. Louis, MO: Congregation B'nai Amoona, 1982), 151.

29 Mendelsohn, Dinwiddie and Hill, "Specifications and Contract Documents for Temple B'nai Amoona, St. Louis, Missouri," set 8, 1946, 49. B'nai Amoona Archives, St. Louis, MO.

30 Eric Mendelsohn, "In the Spirit of Our Age," *Commentary,* January 1, 1947: 541.

31 For example, the classrooms featured bilateral lighting with natural light entering through tall glass windows on the north wall opposite clerestory windows on the south, complemented by up lighting fixtures on the ceiling.

32 Mendelsohn, "In the Spirit of Our Age," 542.

33 James-Chakraborty, *In the Spirit of Our Age,* 48.

34 In addition to B'nai Amoona Synagogue (1945–50), Mendelsohn built three other synagogues in North America, all in the Midwest: Park Synagogue, Cleveland, Ohio (1946–50); Emanu-El Community Center, Grand Rapids, Michigan (1948–52); and Mount Zion Synagogue and Community Center, St. Paul, Minnesota (1950–54).

35 Mendelsohn, "In the Spirit of Our Age," 542. These precepts were personal to Mendelsohn who was part of a generation of modern architects and artists who left Germany under threat of Nazi persecution.

36 "Our Dream Comes True," brochure, B'nai Amoona Archives, quoted in James-Chakraborty, *In the Spirit of Our Age,* 36.

37 Nicholas A. Schneider, *Joseph Elmer Cardinal Ritter: His Life and Times* (Liguori, MO: Liguori, 2008).

38 Ibid., 14–22.

39 Editorial, and Joseph E. Ritter, "Toward a Living Climate of Religious Art," *Liturgical Arts* 23 (November 1954): 1, 4.

40 John F. Knoll, "Resurrection Church: Msgr. George Dreher's gift," *Newsletter,* (Society of Architectural Historians, Missouri Valley Chapter) XIV, no. 2 (Summer 2010): 2–3.

41 Mary Reid Brunstrom, "Faith's Midwest Modern Forms: Midcentury Catholic Churches by Murphy and Mackey, Architects" (Ph.D. diss., Washington University in St. Louis). In progress.

42 Murphy and Mackey's two other contemporaneous modernist churches are St. Ann Catholic Church, Normandy (1948–52) and St. Peter Catholic Church, Kirkwood (1949–53).

43 As already noted, parabolic form in the Kleinhans project was a likely influence on the Gateway Arch design.

44 Knoll, "Resurrection Church," 3. Monsignor George Dreher (1888–1962) was instrumental in liturgical reform at Resurrection Church. He followed the work of German liturgical reform theologians along with Rudolf Schwarz, their leading architect. Rudolf Schwarz, *The Church Incarnate,* trans. Cynthia Harris (Chicago, IL: Henry Regnery Company, 1958), 154–179.

45 Knoll, ibid.

46 Schwarz, *The Church Incarnate,* 154–179.

47 *Church of the Resurrection of Our Lord Silver Jubilee: 1930–1955.* Reprinted by Class of 1955 in 2005. Archives of the Catholic Archdiocese of St. Louis, MO. Resurrection Church Parish File.

48 "Resurrection Church Will Be Dedicated Tomorrow," *St. Louis Post-Democrat,* June 18, 1954.

49 Monsignor Richard Lubeley, interview by author, tape recording, January 6, 2010.

50 Murphy and Mackey quoted in press release, June 16, 1954, 4. "Murphy Family Papers."

51 Ritter, "Toward a Living Climate of Religious Art," 4.

52 Abbot Luke Rigby, O.S.B., interview by author, tape recording, April 12, 2007.

53 Marlene Ann Birkman, *Gyo Obata: Architect/Clients/Reflections* (Mulgrave, Australia: The Images Publishing Group, 2010), vii–viii.

54 Ibid, viii.

55 Timothy Horner, O.S.B., *In Good Soil: The Founding of Saint Louis Priory School, 1954–1973* (St. Louis, MO: Saint Louis Abbey Press, 2001), 144.

56 Gyo Obata, interview by author, tape recording, March 12, 2007.

57 Ibid. These projects highlight the indispensable role of the engineer in the production of architectural vision. As a consultant to the Benedictines, Nervi endorsed Obata's parabolic design.

58 "The New Lambert-St. Louis Air Terminal: The Theory and Criteria of its Design," *St. Louis Construction Record,* April 3, 1956, 11.

59 Dom Colomba Cary-Elwes, O.S.B., "Planning a Monastery and Monastic School," *Liturgical Arts* 26, no. 2 (February 1958): 49.

60 Adrian Forty, "A Material Without a History." In Jean-Louis Cohen and Martin Moeller, Jr., eds. *Liquid Stone: New Architecture in Concrete*, 34–37 (New York, NY: Princeton Architectural Press, 2006).
61 Ibid., 35, 37.
62 "Thin Shell Scallops Roof a Unique House of Worship," *Building Construction*, December 1962: 16.
63 Cary-Elwes, "Planning a Monastery and Monastic School," 49.
64 Birkman, *Gyo Obata*, 5.
65 Cary-Elwes, "Planning a Monastery and Monastic School," 48–49.
66 Victoria M. Young, *Saint John's Abbey Church: Marcel Breuer and the Creation of a Modern Sacred Space* (Minneapolis, MN: University of Minnesota Press, 2014).
67 Condit, 278. Also, "Creative Design in Contemporary Construction," *St. Louis Construction Record*, March 13, 1962, 6. Hyperbolic paraboloids are closely related to the parabola through their shared origins in conical form. Architects could and did move freely between them in their exploration of curvilinear form.
68 Birkman, *Gyo Obata*, 54–61.
69 I borrow the term "penumbra" from W. Arthur Mehrhoff's illuminating text, *The Gateway Arch: Fact & Symbol* (Bowling Green, OH: Bowling Green State University Popular Press, 1992), 4.
70 Mary Reid Brunstrom, "Four Decades of Modern Architecture in St. Louis, 1928–1968." In David Conradsen and Genevieve Cortinovis with Mary Reid Brunstrom. *St. Louis Modern*, exh. cat. (St. Louis, MO: Saint Louis Art Museum, 2015), 25–31.
71 Although Busch Stadium was part of the logic of the modernized riverfront and was formally attuned to the Gateway Arch, it was demolished in 2005 to make way for an updated facility.
72 "Our Dream Comes True."
73 Obata, interview.
74 Heathcott and Murphy, "Corridors of Flight," 179–182.
75 The original design was modified in 2000 by the addition of an enclosed walkway (not envisaged in the Obata plan) that connects the church to the monastery.

References

Birkman, Marlene Ann. *Gyo Obata: Architect/Clients/Reflections* (Mulgrave, Australia: The Images Publishing Group, Pty. Ltd., 2010).
Bronsen, Rosalind Mael. *B'nai Amoona for all Generations* (St. Louis, MO: Congregation B'nai Amoona, 1982).
Brunstrom, Mary Reid. "Faith's Midwest Modern Forms: Midcentury Catholic Churches by Murphy and Mackey, Architects" (Ph.D. diss., Washington University in St. Louis). In progress.
———. "Four Decades of Modern Architecture in St. Louis, 1928–1968." In David Conradsen and Genevieve Cortinovis with Mary Reid Brunstrom. *St. Louis Modern*, exh. cat., 10–53. (St. Louis, MO: Saint Louis Art Museum, 2015).
Cary-Elwes, Dom Colomba, O.S.B. "Planning a Monastery and Monastic School," *Liturgical Arts* 26, no. 2 (February 1958)
Cohen, Jean-Louis. *Le Corbusier and the Mystique of the USSR/Theories and Projects for Moscow 1928–1936* (Princeton, NJ: Princeton University Press, 1992), 164–203.
Condit, Carl W. *American Building: Materials and Techniques from the First Colonial Settlements to the Present*. 2nd edn. (Chicago, IL: University of Chicago Press, 1982).
"Creative Design in Contemporary Construction," *St. Louis Construction Record*, March 13, 1962, 6.
Forty, Adrian. "A Material Without a History." In Jean-Louis Cohen and Martin Moeller, Jr., eds. *Liquid Stone: New Architecture in Concrete*, 34–45 (New York, NY: Princeton Architectural Press, 2006).
Heathcott, Joseph and Máire Agnes Murphy. "Corridors of Flight, Zones of Renewal: Industry, Planning and Policy in the Making of Metropolitan St. Louis, 1940–1980." *Journal of Urban History* 31, no. 2 (January 2005): 151–189.
Horner, Timothy, O.S.B. *In Good Soil: The Founding of Saint Louis Priory School, 1954–1973* (St. Louis, MO: Saint Louis Abbey Press, 2001).
James-Chakraborty, Kathleen. *In the Spirit of Our Age: Eric Mendelsohn's B'nai Amoona Synagogue* (St. Louis, MO: Missouri Historical Society Press, 2000).

————. "Moderate Modernism: Sacred Architecture in St. Louis & Its Suburbs." In Eric Mumford, ed. *Modern Architecture in St. Louis: Washington University & Post-war American Architecture, 1948–1973*, 27–40 (St. Louis, MO: School of Architecture, Washington University in St. Louis, 2004).

"Jefferson National Expansion Memorial Renamed Gateway Arch National Park," *St. Louis Construction News and Review*, February 27, 2018. http://stlouiscnr.com/departments/news/jefferson-national-expansion-memorial-renamed-gateway-arch-national-park/.

Kentgens-Craig, Margaret. "The Search for Modernity: America, the International Style, and the Bauhaus." In Keith L. Eggener, ed. *American Architectural History: A Contemporary Reader* (New York, NY: Routledge, 2004).

Kieckhefer, R. *Theology in Stone: Church Architecture from Byzantium to Berkeley* (New York, NY: Oxford University Press, 2004), 294–312.

Knoll, John F. "Resurrection Church: Msgr. George Dreher's Gift," *Newsletter* (Society of Architectural Historians, Missouri Valley Chapter) XIV, no. 2 (Summer 2010): 2–3.

McCue, George. "The Emerging St. Louis Symbol," *St. Louis Post-Dispatch*, June 10, 1962, 13G.

Mehrhoff, W. Arthur. *The Gateway Arch: Fact & Symbol* (Bowling Green, OH: Bowling Green State University Popular Press, 1992).

Meikle, Jeffrey L. *Twentieth Century Limited: Industrial Design in America, 1925–1939* (Philadelphia, PA: Temple University Press, 1979).

Mendelsohn, Eric. "In the Spirit of Our Age," *Commentary*, January 1, 1947.

————. "The Great Adventure," *Marg* 4, no. 3 (1950–51).

Moore, Robert J., Jr. *The Gateway Arch: An Architectural Dream* (St. Louis, MO: Jefferson National Parks Association, 2005).

"The New Lambert-St. Louis Air Terminal: The Theory and Criteria of its Design," *St. Louis Construction Record*, April 3, 1956, 11.

Osborne, Catherine Rhiannon. "American Catholics and the Art of the Future, 1930–1975." Ph.D. diss., Fordham University, 2013.

Osserman, Robert. "How the Gateway Arch Got Its Shape," *Nexus Network Journal* 12, no. 2 (2010): 183.

Primm, James Neal. *Lion of the Valley: St. Louis, Missouri, 1764–1980*. 3rd edn. (St. Louis, MO: Missouri Historical Society Press, 1998).

"Resurrection Church Will Be Dedicated Tomorrow," *St. Louis Post-Democrat*, June 18, 1954.

Ritter, Joseph E. "Toward a Living Climate of Religious Art," *Liturgical Arts* 23 (November 1954).

Saarinen, Aline B., ed. *Eero Saarinen on His Work* (New Haven, CT: Yale University Press, 1962).

Schneider, Nicholas A. *Joseph Elmer Cardinal Ritter: His Life and Times* (Liguori, MO: Liguori, 2008).

Schwarz, Rudolf. *The Church Incarnate: The Sacred Function of Christian Architecture*. Translated by Cynthia Harris (Chicago, IL: Henry Regnery Company, 1958).

Soren, L. Noelle. "Congregation B'nai Amoona." National Register of Historic Places Registration Form (1984). Accessed February 18, 2018. https://dnr.mo.gov/shpo/nps-nr/84002698.pdf.

"Thin Shell Scallops Roof a Unique House of Worship," *Building Construction*, December 1962: 16.

Young, Victoria M. *Saint John's Abbey Church: Marcel Breuer and the Creation of a Modern Sacred Space* (Minneapolis, MN: University of Minnesota Press, 2014).

Zevi, Bruno. *Erich Mendelsohn* (New York: Rizzoli, 1985).

5

THE STRUCTURAL MODELING AND DESIGN OF ST. MARY'S CATHEDRAL, SAN FRANCISCO, 1963–71

Gabriele Neri

> What would Michelangelo have thought of this cathedral? He could not have thought of it. This design comes from geometric theories not then proved. It could only have been conceived today.[1]

The Cathedral of St. Mary of the Assumption in San Francisco, consecrated in 1971, is the principal church of the local Roman Catholic Archdiocese (Fig. 5.1). It is a highly significant example of sacred architecture of mid-twentieth century, specifically the 1960s, a decade notable for major changes in the Catholic Church in America and worldwide. The project to replace the old cathedral destroyed by fire in September 1962 took off in the years of Vatican Council II (1962–65). As such, the goal was to create one of the first major religious buildings to showcase the new liturgical prescriptions. The challenge was entrusted to two noted designers, architect Pietro Belluschi (1899–1994) and engineer Pier Luigi Nervi (1891–1979), who worked with the local architectural firm McSweeney, Ryan & Lee (MSRL) and the engineer Leonard F. Robinson (1915–2013). The aim was to shape a particularly ambitious architectural and engineering complex.[2]

The structural design is one of the building's outstanding features, a characteristic factor in the history of cathedrals. It embodied a fusion of various constructional strands in the architecture of the period, notably the use of reinforced concrete hyperbolic paraboloid. Its intricate political and social context during the time of tension at a turning point in American Catholic history has been carefully analyzed by other scholars.[3] The purpose of this chapter is rather to examine the genesis and evolution of the cathedral project. Specifically, it explores the cathedral's structural factors, from the first design ideas to the start of construction (1963–67). This investigation draws not only from the bibliography devoted to the building but also examines documents in Italian and American archives.[4] They reveal Nervi's point of view of the project, one of the most interesting perspectives given the structure's importance, and his interaction with architect Belluschi. The archives of various Italian and American research laboratories also preserve the technical reports on the sophisticated experimental tests conducted to define and assess the cathedral's structural form.

FIGURE 5.1 St. Mary's Cathedral, San Francisco, California, 2011.
Photograph by the author.

Analysis of these documents in addition to the context of the project and the succession of events made it possible to reconstruct the complex design process from different viewpoints as it unfolded in various parts of Italy and the United States. While highlighting the experimental value of the design process, this chapter is a testament to the cathedral's importance in a crucial transitional phase in the field of large structures design, and more generally in the management of such projects. On the one hand, computing and new methods of analysis used in California in the final phase of the project would soon supersede the earlier techniques of structural analysis, making them obsolete and opening up new frontiers for architecture and engineering. On the other hand, the management of the project reveals the potential but also the difficulties and resistances inherent in the international design processes.

Description of the work

St. Mary's Cathedral is located in the Western Addition neighborhood. Its exterior is characterized by the profile of an imposing dome, shaped by the intersection of eight concrete hyperbolic paraboloids that creates a Greek cross. They are faced with slabs of travertine marble and soar above the horizontal band of the base (Figs. 5.2, 5.3). Each of the eight hyperbolic paraboloid shells is approximately 130 feet high and 50 feet wide on average.[5] They were built using shotcrete deposited on precast concrete ribbed forms, a structural system typical of Pier Luigi Nervi's work. This technique defines the internal appearance of the dome, patterned with 1,680 precast concrete triangular coffers. These shells rest on four massive reinforced concrete piers with variable sections. This was achieved by means of a structure of hollow perimetric arches, likewise determined by the geometry of the hyperbolic paraboloid. Supported by this lower structure, the dome rises to a height of 191 feet.

This impressive structural system is comprised of a base with a square plan measuring 205 feet per side. It is left almost completely unobstructed, creating a large nave that can seat 2,500 worshippers. The nave, taking the form of a Latin cross in spite of the central plan is bathed in light penetrating from the transparent glass corners of the perimeter and by slender vertical 6 feet wide by 130 feet long stained glass strips that separate the pairs of

FIGURE 5.2 St. Mary's Cathedral, 2011.

Photograph by the author.

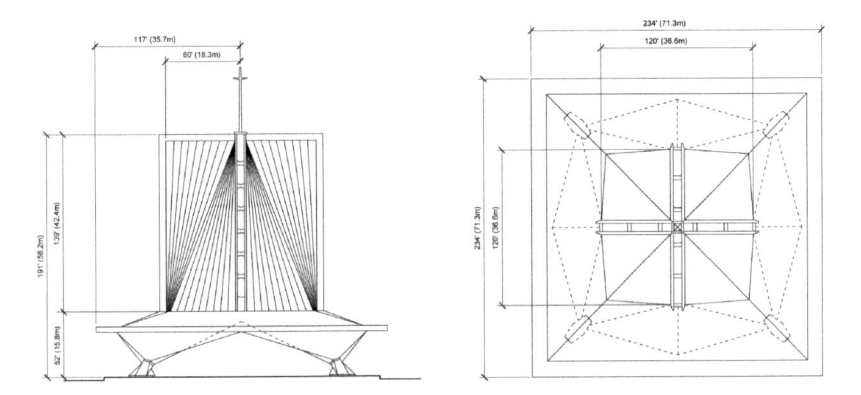

FIGURE 5.3 Schematic section and plan of the cathedral, 2018.

Drawing by the author.

paraboloids in the dome. The stained glass was designed by the Hungarian artist György Kepes (1906–2001), Professor of Visual design at MIT. The shimmering baldacchino sculpted from aluminum rods by Richard Lippold (1915–2002) stands in the great nave.[6] Suspended from the dome, it is a symbol of unity between the Church and the worshippers, in keeping with Vatican Council II's instructions to promote *actuosa participatio* (active involvement or participation) in the liturgy.

Genesis of the project

Development of the design began in 1963, a few months after the destruction of the old Victorian Gothic redbrick cathedral. In April that year, the Archdiocese of San Francisco, which in previous months had held a successful fundraising campaign, announced that the new building would be commissioned from MSRL architectural firm. The city, and notably the most influential donors, rejected MSRL's proposal, which essentially reprised traditional images of neo-Romanesque and missionary churches in California. The debate was further stoked by some pungent articles in the newspapers.[7]

Pressured by the polemics, Archbishop Joseph T. McGucken (1902–83), representing the commissioning body,[8] soon realized that unless a well-known name was paired with MSRL, public opinion and the city council's opposition would not subside. McGucken's choice was Pietro Belluschi, "Italian by birth, engineer by training, architect by choice and long experience, Catholic by upbringing, and designer of some of this country's most distinguished churches."[9] Belluschi served as the Dean of the School of Architecture and Planning at the Massachusetts Institute of Technology since 1951. He was a well-known architect in the field of American religious buildings, largely because of the many churches he had built in Oregon starting with the Equitable Building in Portland (1948).[10] He had been recommended to McGucken by Fr. Godfrey Diekmann (1908–2002), a distinguished theologian and editor of the monthly *Worship*, who was invited to review MSRL's preliminary drawings.[11]

Belluschi was appointed as the design consultant of the project in 1963.[12] Realizing the importance of the structural design on such an ambitious work, he immediately sought to involve Luigi Nervi, whom he had known since the previous decade, as a structural design consultant.[13] He asked to commission Nervi as a condition for taking part in the project.[14]

As hoped by the Archbishop, the partnership between the two renowned designers finally won over the press. Moreover, Nervi was already well known in the city: in 1961, he had a solo exhibition devoted to his work at the San Francisco Museum of Art, entitled "Pier Luigi Nervi. Space and Structural Integrity."[15] From the client's point of view, his close ties with the Vatican also favored the Italian engineer. In the same year, Nervi, based in Rome, was commissioned by Pope Paul VI to design the Audience Hall at the Vatican (1963–71), which later became celebrated.[16] The first letters exchanged between Italy and the United States immediately reveal the complexity of a design process being conducted on several fronts and in different parts of the world.[17] Already in the autumn of 1963, with work on the Cathedral in the preliminary phase, the geographical separation created an awkward situation. The client and the MSRL office were in California, Belluschi in Cambridge Massachusetts, and Studio Nervi in Rome. The number of professionals involved in the project would increase, creating a ramified network of spheres of competence in Italy and the United States, which made the project's management cumbersome.

Belluschi was officially appointed to the project in September 1963, but a few weeks earlier he had already begun to develop his first ideas for the design. Most of his church designs had mediated between a modern and regional architectural vocabulary. As his sketches show, his first conception was still quite rigid and traditional.[18] A scheme consisting of a large nave placed behind a tripartite façade, with two tall and almost completely blind side towers separated by a transparent central band, slightly recessed, giving access to the interior of the church. This design met the initial requests of the commissioning body, eager to symbolically rebuild an updated version of the old cathedral rather than adopting more disquieting and innovative forms. In a letter dated November 12, 1963, Belluschi described his design philosophy to the Archbishop in relation to his first proposal, focusing on the towers in the façade: "the two front towers are not strange forms; they are found in most old Gothic structures, but they have the cleanliness of our time."[19] Although this first version was not immediately shelved, in September of the same year a more advanced scheme was presented, leading to the final form of the cathedral.[20] This clearly brings out the predominance of the structural conception within the project: "here was a need for a strong structural concept—an engineering form as an expression of the modern age, comparable in scale and size to the cathedrals of the past, a form that could only be done now."[21]

The sketches drafted by Belluschi depict a composition based on a square plan defining a single nave.[22] It was topped by a roof approximating the form that was eventually built. His studies for the cathedral elevation clearly express recourse to the hyperbolic paraboloid as the generating form of the central dome. Also already evident are the vertical bands of glass separating the individual paraboloids to shed light inside. Belluschi's scheme appears daring, especially considering that the client favored close ties with the old cathedral. However, it turned out to be surprisingly in accordance with the liturgical guidelines laid down in the same months by Vatican Council II (1962–65), which endorsed a centrally planned church: "The new design concept had, fortuitously, prefigured the architectural implications of the Council's directive that the priest and people should be united with the altar as their focus."[23] The proposal appealed to the Archbishop due to the fact that this would be the first cathedral in the United States designed in accordance with the new liturgical guidelines, coupled with the guarantees offered by the reputations of Belluschi and Nervi. He approved the scheme in the fall of 1963.[24]

References of the design of the structural form

Belluschi made no secret of the origin of the hyperbolic paraboloid design, dictated by the "effort to have a short nave capable of grouping the faithful around the altar, and then devising a form that would express this concept seamlessly."[25] As he openly declared more than once, it was suggested by St. Mary's Cathedral in Tokyo (1961–64) designed by Kenzo Tange (1913–2005), which was surmounted by a hyperbolic paraboloid.[26] Also influential were the studies by the Argentinean architect Eduardo Catalano (1917–2010), whom Belluschi appointed to teach at Cambridge in 1956. Catalano's influence was of fundamental importance for the formal and structural design of the San Francisco cathedral.[27] After studying with Walter Gropius (1883–1969) at Harvard in the mid-1940s, in 1952 Catalano became professor at the School of Design at North Carolina State College in Raleigh, and explored the field of application of quadrics to architecture, in particular the use of hyperbolic paraboloids.[28] He is known to have been engaged in the early phases of work on the cathedral project, and would certainly have participated willingly, given his admiration for Nervi, whom he had already met on various occasions.[29] Catalano contributed, for example, to the construction of the first architectural model of the cathedral, consisting of wires simulating the imagined ruled surfaces. [30] In the fall of 1963, Belluschi and the Archbishop went to Rome for their first meetings with Nervi. The Archbishop's visit coincided with the second session of Vatican Council II, in which he took part.[31]

Structural models of the cathedral

Belluschi's September 1963 design was adopted enthusiastically, and preliminary studies of the structure began in the following months.[32] Understanding its complexity, Nervi immediately stressed the need to supplement traditional methods of study with structural modeling.[33] This was a special experimental technique that he had used since the mid-1930s in collaboration with Arturo Danusso (1880–1968), an eminent professor of structural engineering at the Milan Polytechnic.[34] This technique was also used by other celebrated structural engineers such as Eduardo Torroja (1899–1961) in Spain.[35] It rested on the use of special reduced-scale structural models that reproduced not only the geometry of a particular project, but also the behavior of the materials used in the actual building, while respecting the complex laws of similitude.[36] This made it possible to test the models as if they were miniature construction projects, overcoming (at least this was the intention) the limitations inherent in a purely theoretical approach to structural design.

Behind this method there also lay a clear philosophy, in which Danusso's scientific curiosity and Nervi's experimental design met.[37] Models, as Danusso thought, were the best answer to a basic condition. He wrote:

> Building means working in reality, and if reality – as we discover every day from physical experience – is highly complex and interrelated . . . science, by the poverty of its instruments, is forced to work by means of limitations and simplifications, leaving an abyss between it and reality.[38]

Hence it was necessary to look attentively and patiently at nature, to achieve what could not be enclosed within a theoretical framework. Nervi expressed a similar concept:

> No theoretical demonstration can clarify the elastic functioning of a structure as well as following the results of experimental research, and no procedure can be as effective in verifying the accuracy of our theoretical deductions.[39]

Then, in 1963, Nervi was appointed President of the Institute for Experimental Models and Structures (ISMES) in Bergamo, Italy. This was an internationally renowned research laboratory in the field of structural modeling, founded in 1951 by Arturo Danusso.[40] For the cathedral project, Belluschi planned to take advantage of the equipment at MIT in Cambridge, but the reputation of ISMES and Nervi's convictions persuaded everyone to have the models tested in Bergamo, Italy.[41] In early 1964, he began the preliminary study of the structure in Rome, at his office, increasingly stressing the difficulties and the need for experimental research:[42]

> With all sorts of feelings, we began studies of the hyperbolic paraboloid for San Francisco. But the theoretical problem was more fearsomely complex than I thought and I will not deny that the first results actually gave rise to some doubts about the intrinsic efficiency of the structure. We immediately had a model made of a first approximation at the lab in Bergamo, in order to get a preliminary qualitative and roughly quantitative idea of the whole.[43]

Nervi's caution and concerns were conveyed to the Archbishop, partly to justify and push through all the necessary stages of experimentation with models.[44] At the same time, in February 1964, Belluschi and the MSRL firm were required to officially present the project to the public.[45] For this occasion, a little architectural model was made with the building placed in its urban setting. It was still a general model, which did not provide precise information about the structural solution for the roof or an accurate representation of it. However, as Belluschi declared, "It is an idea; and a strong idea."[46]

The years 1964 and 1965 were critical to the exact definition of the geometry of the cathedral. Once the formal approach was defined, it became dependent to a large extent on issues of statics. In this period, careful tests were conducted on four different structural models, accompanied by various kinds of analysis, which would help to define the final form.[47]

Having received approval from the client, on March 16, 1964, the expert craftsmen at ISMES began making a first elastic model on a scale of 1:40.[48] Made of a sand and synthetic resin mix, the model reproduced only the upper part of the cathedral (the dome). The tests on it were conducted to roughly assess the states of stress induced in the cupola by its dead load and the lateral loads (wind load).[49] The work was done under the guidance of Enzo Lauletta (1927–71) and the supervision of Guido Oberti (1907–2004), two of the most experienced engineers in this field in Italy.[50] The first results showed the intrinsic stability of the overall structure, but also revealed the need for further study with other models, primarily because "As far as we can see," Nervi wrote to the Archbishop, "it is the first time in the world that a structure of this type and of such dimensions has been studied."[51]

The second structural model of the cathedral, in an epoxy resin mix (scale 1:100), was made in Bergamo but tested in 1964 in the wind tunnel at the Turin Polytechnic, with preliminary aerodynamic tests determining horizontal wind pressure (Fig. 5.4).[52] While the aerodynamic model was being tested in Turin, at ISMES in Bergamo the workers were crafting the third model, a true masterpiece of modeling aimed at studying the effects of dead loads (Fig. 5.5). Since this was made of a concrete mix, on a scale of 1:15, it was possible to reproduce the performance of the full-scale structure in the elastic range and beyond it to failure.[53]

The splendid photos now kept in ISMES's historical archives record its patient construction using wood and gypsum formwork. Begun in August, the model was fully completed by about late October 1964, when Pietro Belluschi and the Archbishop came to visit ISMES from the United States (Fig. 5.6).[54]

FIGURE 5.4 The aerodynamic model of the cathedral (1:100), 1964, restored in 2011.
Photograph by CEMED, Turin.

FIGURE 5.5 Construction of the third model of the cathedral scale 1:15, 1964.
ISMES Historical Archive, Italy.

FIGURE 5.6 Third large model of the cathedral (scale 1:15), in reinforced microconcrete, 1964.

ISMES Historical Archive, Italy.

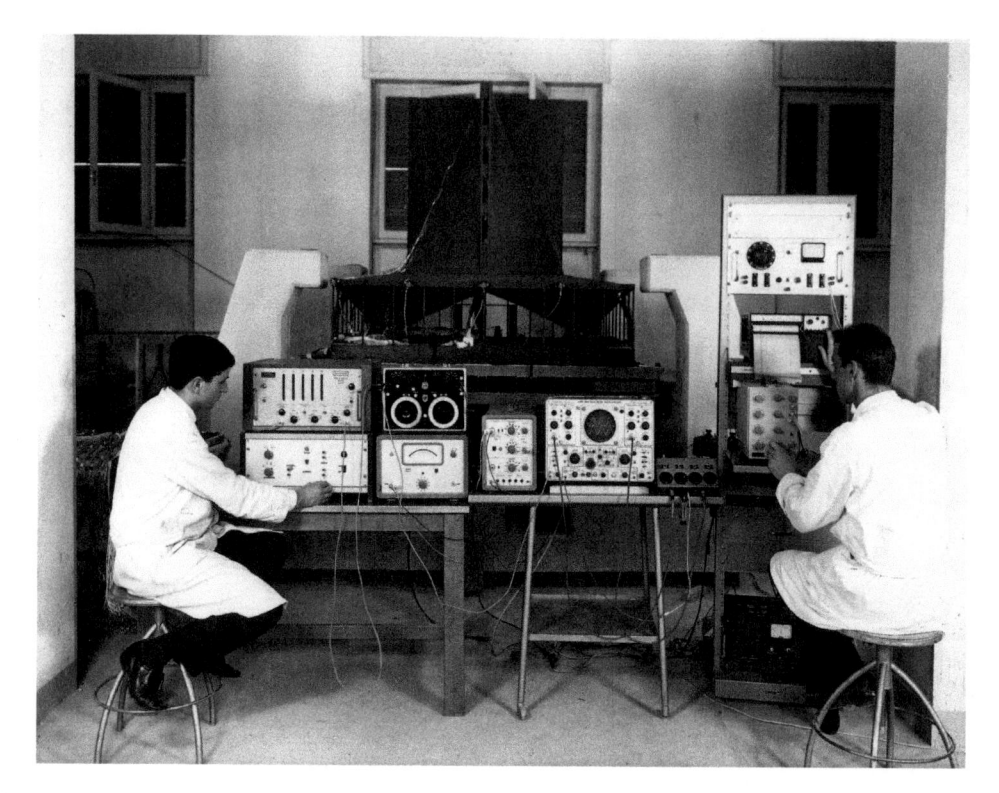

FIGURE 5.7 Fourth model of the cathedral (scale 1:36.89) during dynamic testing on a shake table at ISMES in 1965.

ISMES Historical Archive, Italy.

Three series of tests were made on this model.[55] In the first series, conducted at working load, the study concerned the pattern of strains and displacements, the cracking of the resisting sections, as well as plasticization and cracking due to stress concentration. In the second series (again at working load), the study concerned the relation between the deformation pattern variation in the cupola and the deformability of the cupola base. Finally, the third series was conducted at higher loads, to test the presence of an appreciable safety margin for the dome when the rigidity of the lower part was considerable, and to study the failure procedure if the rigidity was gradually decreased. On June 4 and 5, 1965, the model was brought up to failure, getting good results, with arrows of deformation that were very small and fully proportional to the loads.[56]

Between the second and third series of tests on the model on a scale of 1:15, experiments were also conducted on a fourth elastic synthetic resin model of the cathedral, on a scale of 1:36.89.[57] This reproduced the changes made in the meantime and was based on drawings of the project that the Studio Nervi had supplied to ISMES in February 1965 (Fig. 5.7).[58] In this way, various models and versions of the project were combined: the complexity and logistics of the project involved a continuous updating of ideas and results (Fig. 5.8).

The fourth model was the result of the adaptation of the first model on a scale of 1:40.[59] This was done to cut the time needed to make the model and record the slight reduction of the dimensions in the plan of the upper part of the church. Static and dynamic tests were carried out on this model.[60] In particular, it supplied significant data about the building's response to

FIGURE 5.8   Pier Luigi Nervi giving indications to ISMES engineers in front of the fourth model
of the cathedral, 1965.

ISMES Historical Archive, Italy.

seismic activity (a crucial issue in San Francisco). The experiments on structural models of the
cathedral at ISMES finally came to an end in October 1965, the date of the last lab report.[61]

Comparisons between the third and fourth model clearly bring out the development of
the structural design. Compared to the cement-mix model, the new elastic model presented
a highly different section and proportions, much closer to the appearance of the built work.
It is worth noting the reduction in the overall height of the dome and the altered inclination
of the structural system that forms the impost structure of the vaults.

Tensions between Rome and San Francisco

Experiments with the third and fourth models were far from easy, partly because of the
continuous changes to the project described above. The correspondence between Nervi and
Belluschi brings out the former's concern at the initial results produced at ISMES:

> I will not, however, conceal the fact that I had failed to fairly assess, at the beginning,
> the difficult path we had set out on for the Cathedral. The novelty of the design, the
> difficulties encountered at every step in terms of the design or the calculations and the
> incurable slowness of research on models when the structure is so complex, will still
> hinder the definitive drafting of the project. Hence it might be advisable (if you are
> agreed) to mention this to the Bishop so that he will not misinterpret the slowness with
> which we are proceeding.[62]

By mid-February 1965, Nervi was feeling alarmed by this situation.[63] In recent weeks, he
had been busy finalizing the details of the Audience Hall at the Vatican.[64] Now he began
to devote himself full time to the design of the cathedral, seeking a way out of the impasse.
In the following months, there was a particularly intense study of the project by the various figures involved in the work. The fundamental issue on which all others turned was the
proportion between the base of the cathedral and the dome, which risked appearing to lack
upward thrust.[65]

In spring 1965, while the tests on the third and fourth model were going ahead, Nervi betrayed his vexation with MSRL, which was pressing for progress in the project, revealing a certain impatience and some doubts over the time being taken over the studies of the building's statics in Italy.[66] His irritation increased following publication in the journal *Engineering News-Record* (January 28, 1965) of a photograph of an architectural model of the cathedral:

> True, we agreed right from the start to be presented as consultants, but to read that the work was designed by Messrs. McSweeney, Ryan & Lee, while we're here racking our brains to find a solution amid so many difficulties, and they . . . sit smoking their pipes, hardly testifies to their professionalism.[67]

Apart from the actual difficulty of the static and architectural problem, geographical distances complicated relations between the various parties. Issues were caused by the differences in time zones, the cost of intercontinental calls, the time taken by flights between Italy and the United States, the different languages, and different units of measurement. All this made communications between Rome, Bergamo, Cambridge, and San Francisco slow and fragmented. During the years of work on the project, several meetings took place on both sides of the Atlantic. But the exchange of information, and especially drawings, was done mainly by mail. This dragged out the drafting and revision work. At the same time, it was awkward to keep up contacts with the client and the various offices involved in the project. This situation was a feature of the period and naturally very different from the present, when a medium such as the Internet can transmit information, drawings, and data in real time.

Leonard Robinson's model

Despite the difficulties, the tests on the structural models at the ISMES came to an end in the fall of 1965 and their results were made available.[68] At the same time, in San Francisco, Leonard F. Robinson, the engineer in charge of developing the final design, was conducting a mathematical analysis of the structure on the four large piers of the cathedral, using a method of calculation based on the finite element method with the help of a computer; these were innovative processes not yet in use at ISMES (Fig. 5.9).[69]

The finite element method (FEM), which emerged in those years as a fundamental method of numerical analysis, made it possible to solve the problem of determining the state of stress (and related deformation) of specific elements in load conditions.[70] This would have been difficult to solve analytically. In this specific case, FEM could be used to decompose the surface of the vault of a hyperbolic paraboloid, like the one designed for the San Francisco cathedral, into a set of triangular elements yielding a finite static problem that was far more easily resolved.

In this way, for the cathedral, "a mathematical model – an equivalent three-dimensional space truss with approximately fourteen hundred members – was analyzed for vertical and horizontal loads, for spreading of supports and for unequal settlements of supports."[71] As Robinson observed, the computations for the analysis of this space truss were not difficult, but very lengthy: for this reason it was done on a large electronic computer, using the well-known "STRESS" program. The data processed by the computer furnished the values of the reactions and forces in all members of the structure and the relative displacements at each of the nodes.[72] To calculate seismic actions, Robinson instead took as his scale of reference the

FIGURE 5.9   Three-dimensional space truss simulated by L. F. Robinson in San Francisco, 1965.

MAXXI Museo nazionale delle arti del XXI secolo, Roma. Collezione MAXXI Architettura. Archivio Pier Luigi Nervi.

results obtained from the dynamic tests at ISMES, considered "the most advanced method of seismological design in use today."[73] He emphasized: "Such a thorough analysis would not have been possible a few short years ago."[74] Based on these calculations, the structure proved to be three times stronger than required by law in San Francisco, and the novelty of the procedure profoundly impressed Nervi, as he himself wrote to Robinson:

> We examined the final project of the St. Mary's Cathedral you sent me . . . and the very interesting calculation method you developed with the computer. I sincerely congratulate you. Your study is a real contribution to the constructions science and the correspondence of the results you obtained analytically and those that ISMES' experimental research has given, demonstrate the goodness and efficacy of both the methods.[75]

A further test of the cathedral's design

Since the project envisaged a maximum height that would be 31 feet higher than the limit set by San Francisco's Building Code for reinforced concrete structures, the design was not yet definitive.[76] Belluschi and his colleagues had hoped to wing this problem without much difficulty, but it proved more troublesome than expected. In early 1966, the Archbishop and the designers became seriously concerned, a mood clearly expressed by the letter Belluschi sent Nervi in February:

> Dear Nervi, We are still having problems with the San Francisco cathedral! As you already know, City Hall's regulations prohibit the construction of any concrete building more than 160 feet high. We had always hoped to get permission to reach a height of about 190 feet by demonstrating that the structure was completely resistant. Since City Hall's engineer is having trouble grasping the concept we have developed, he has asked the San Francisco Society of Engineers to appoint a panel of three engineers to advise City Hall . . . It seemed to me that both the City and the supervisors lack the

confidence to take responsibility to defend what they regard as a strange structure. Robinson tried to explain clearly the meaning of the calculations and tests that have been done, showing the structure is three times stronger than the requirements of the building code. But since the supervisors are not paid for their "advice" and the structure is not easy to understand, and because the steel industry has closed ranks against reinforced concrete, I'm afraid we will fail to get the permit we need. As things stand, perhaps they would allow us to build it in steel (which would be absurd and contrary to all logic), or else they will simply deny us a permit.[77]

To get a building authorization in California, it was necessary to submit the results to the scrutiny of the San Francisco Department of Public Works, and in particular of Robert C. Levy (1921–85), Secretary of the relevant Board of Examiners, to obtain the essential variant to section 2303.10 of the City's Building Code.[78]

The issue, concerning such an important building for the city of San Francisco, soon became public knowledge and was reported in the local press.[79] Though with the necessary caution, the final decision was favorable. The authorities suggested approving the variant, subject to additional guarantees, which Levy conveyed to Robinson on April 18, 1966.[80] The most important requirement was to conduct a further verification of the structure, independent of the designers involved, which the commission would entrust to a Review Board selected by the Bureau of Building Inspection.[81] This would have to consist of a structural engineer, active in San Francisco for at least ten years, an expert on reinforced concrete shells, and an expert on the vibrations caused by earthquakes.[82] This inspection was carried out by Frank Baron (1914–94) and Ray W. Clough (1920–2016), both professors of civil engineering of the University of California, and the engineer George Arthur Sedgwick of San Francisco.[83] It took several months and was presented to Robinson a year later, on May 8, 1967.[84]

The analysis in the inspection report produced by the three engineers is particularly interesting. First, it assesses the work of Nervi and ISMES from an external viewpoint and second, it enables us to compare Nervi's modus operandi with the methods used in scientifically advanced circles of California, and the English-speaking world in general.

After examining the preceding analyses, the Review Board made further studies to better determine the stress patterns in the structure.[85] While an interpretive study was made (based on a close examination of the results obtained by tests of the model at ISMES and an independent analysis), a more detailed computer analysis of the cupola was carried out: "This approach was feasible because a computer program for the analysis of rib-stiffened shell structures had been developed previously at the University of California and was readily available to the Board."[86] Its use was made possible by the assistance of Alexander C. Scordelis (1923–2007), professor of structural engineering at the University of Berkeley.[87] He contributed greatly to the development of the finite element method for structural analysis with the computer, developing several programs for the calculation of increasingly complex structures.[88]

Based on these studies, the Review Board also revised the working drawings and structural details of the cathedral. The Review Board concluded its report by advising the San Francisco Board of Examiners to accept the structural designs for the building, but recommended that the construction should be planned under Robinson's control.[89] Above all, it required the introduction of a pair of steel beams in the vertical bands of the dome, an element not strictly necessary—and conceptually unrelated to the design philosophy of Nervi, a master of reinforced concrete—but required for additional safety.

Finally, after nearly four years of analysis in offices, laboratories, and universities in Rome, Bergamo, Cambridge, Turin, San Francisco, and Berkeley, the structural design of St. Mary's Cathedral could be described as complete. The detailed drawings developed in laboratories and universities could be closed and construction of the building could begin. The foundation stone was blessed on December 13, 1967, and the building was eventually inaugurated in 1971.

Conclusion

In conclusion, the analysis of the design of St Mary's Cathedral, begun in 1963, raises several points. First, the difficulty of defining the form, entailing a broad and varied range of scientific analyses, demonstrates the boldness of its structural design. This lay not so much in its formal novelty (the hyperbolic paraboloid was common at the time, as we have seen) but its dimensions. Second, the complex verification of the project reveals the excellence achieved in the field of structural modeling by Nervi and the engineers at ISMES, that is, Arturo Danusso's students who were capable of dealing with such a difficult structural problem in a seismic region like California. Nevertheless, the case of San Francisco highlights the fact that in those years, especially in English-speaking academic and professional circles, methods and instruments of analysis were spreading. This knowledge would soon revolutionize structural design. The innovative instruments of analysis used by Robinson and the Review Board of San Francisco would soon eclipse the methods in which ISMES excelled. In many sectors, the physical model, much more expensive and less versatile than the virtual one, started to fade. The new horizons of engineering also meant the decline of the golden age of structural modeling.

The times were changing not only in terms of experimental techniques. The episodes recounted reveal the difficulty of managing a project whose actors were scattered in different localities in the United States and Italy. The problem, however, lay not in the internationalization of the design process, which was not a new phenomenon and one that would intensify in the coming decades. Rather, it was due to the inability of some individuals to adapt to new models of project management.

The Studio Nervi was emblematic in this respect. The engineer, by that time more than seventy years old and at the height of his fame, ran his office on a patriarchal model. His sons Antonio and Mario worked under him, and he was reluctant to delegate. Almost every decision was kept in his own hands, preventing any real change or innovation in response to the new demands arising globally.

This would change at least to some extent in the 1970s, when Pier Luigi's health gradually kept him away from the office, which he turned over to his sons. In particular, Antonio Nervi (1925–79) sought to upgrade the business to manage all the projects now spread across several continents.[90] Despite this, he was unable to match the services offered by more highly organized firms. Studio Nervi closed shortly after its founder's death, followed tragically by Antonio's own death just six months later. We might compare this with the example of Ove Arup (1895–1988), another major structural engineer almost coeval with

Pier Luigi Nervi. In the 1960s, Arup took a step back, preferring not to be directly involved with the projects.[91] Rather, he wanted to raise a new generation of engineers who would follow his design philosophy, such as Peter Rice (1935–92) and Ted Happold (1930–96). Today Studio Nervi no longer exists, while Ove Arup has 92 offices in 40 countries with 13,000 employees.[92]

In addition, Nervi's construction systems, designed as brilliant answers to the particular Italian building context, raised different problems when translated into the American context.[93]

Because of these above-mentioned factors, Nervi's role during the phase of construction was marginal. He was very skillfully kept at a safe distance by Belluschi, who probably feared slowdowns, knowing his colleague's intransigence.

Robinson was therefore in charge of the construction site. In 1971, at the work's end, he summed up the experience in a brief but significant article. In the conclusion he stated:

> 1. Because of some very sophisticated computer programs recently developed for the solution of three dimensional problems it is possible to design shell structures to a high degree of refinement in a relatively short time. 2. The construction of double-curvature shells is simpler than most people would assume.[94]

Almost two years had been spent conducting experimental tests on four models of the cathedral and Nervi had struggled to develop an adequate construction system. He had even proposed to have the whole dome structure shipped from Italy, which would have meant transporting 1,600 triangular reinforced concrete elements.[95] Bearing this in mind, Leonard Robinson's words may sound rather disrespectful, but they were well founded. Between 1963, the start date of the project, and 1971, the date of the building's completion, many things had changed. And as testament to this change, as well as in the tangible form of its reinforced concrete, lies a subtler fact about St Mary's Cathedral. It was a transitional work and fell between two periods. It was designed by means of (relatively) old techniques of investigation and the new: the brainchild of different generations of architects and engineers working in different contexts. At the same time, the cathedral itself was anchored in the tradition of sacred architecture yet guided by new ways of understanding the liturgy.

Notes

1 Pier Luigi Nervi, in "Saint Mary's Cathedral, San Francisco," *Architectural Record* 9 (1971): 114.
2 Gabriele Neri, *Capolavori in miniatura. Pier Luigi Nervi e la modellazione strutturale* (Mendrisio: Mendrisio Academy Press, 2014), 219–273.
3 James P. Gaffey, "The Anatomy of Transition: Cathedral-Building and Social Justice in San Francisco, 1962–1971," *The Catholic Historian Review* 1 (1984): 45–73.
4 The Pier Luigi Nervi Archive in Rome contains several folders of his Italian-American correspondence.
5 Neri, *Capolavori*, 219.
6 "Saint Mary's Cathedral, San Francisco," 118.
7 Cf. Alan Temko, "S. F.'s New Cathedral: A Critical Essay," *San Francisco Chronicle*, June 15, 1963.
8 "The Anatomy of Transition."
9 "Saint Mary's Cathedral, San Francisco," 114.
10 Meredith L. Clausen, *Spiritual Space: the Religious Architecture of Pietro Belluschi* (Seattle, WA and London: University of Washington Press, 1992).

11 Neri, *Capolavori,* 265.
12 PLN Archive, Rome (PLN-A), Letter from Belluschi to Nervi, July 26, 1963.
13 Ibid.
14 Ibid.
15 Henry J. Lagorio, *Pier Luigi Nervi. Space and Structural Integrity* (San Francisco, CA: Associated Arts Foundation, 1961).
16 Sergio Pace, "Papal Audience Hall" In Carlo Olmo and Cristiana Chiorino, eds. *Pier Luigi Nervi: Architecture as Challenge* (Cinisello Balsamo: Silvana Editoriale 2010), 182–185.
17 Neri, *Capolavori,* 222.
18 "Saint Mary's Cathedral, San Francisco," 114.
19 PLN Archive, Rome (PLN-A), Letter from Belluschi to McGucken, November 12, 1963.
20 Neri, *Capolavori,* 223.
21 "Saint Mary's Cathedral, San Francisco," 116.
22 Ibid, 114.
23 Ibid, 116–118.
24 In January 1964, Nervi and Belluschi were already trying to manage the structural problem of the new solution. See PLN-A, Letter from Belluschi to Nervi, January 8, 1964.
25 PLN-A, Letter from Belluschi to Nervi, December 9, 1963.
26 Ibid.; Yoshikatsu Tsuboi and Ryohei Nasukawa, "Hyperbolic Paraboloidal Shell Structure for Tokyo Roman Catholic Cathedral," *Bulletin of IASS* 28 (1966): 37–52.
27 Neri, *Capolavori,* 223–225.
28 Eduardo Catalano, "Two Warped Surfaces," *The Student Publication of the School of Design* 1 (1955); Ibid., "Structures of Warped Surfaces," *The Student Publication of the School of Design* 1 (1960).
29 PLN-A, Letter from Ciampi to Nervi, February 6, 1957.
30 Neri, *Capolavori,* 223–225.
31 PLN-A, Letter from McGucken to Nervi, December 10, 1963.
32 PLN-A, Letter from Belluschi to Nervi, January 8, 1964.
33 Ibid.
34 Neri, *Capolavori,* 15–67.
35 Ibid., 26–31.
36 Harry G. Harris and Gajanan M. Sabnis, *Structural Modeling and Experimental Techniques* (Boca Raton, FL: CRC Press, 1999).
37 Gabriele Neri, "Per il corretto costruire. Introduzione." In Gabriele Neri, ed. *Pier Luigi Nervi, Ingegneria, architettura, costruzione. Scritti scelti 1922–1971* (CittàStudi Edizioni, Torino 2014), 103–117.
38 Arturo Danusso, "Scienza delle costruzioni. Premesse e concetti fondamentali." In Piero Locatelli, ed. *La scienza e lo spirito negli scritti di Arturo Danusso* (Brescia: Morcelliana, 1978), 7.
39 Pier Luigi Nervi, *Costruire correttamente* (Milano: Hoepli, 1955): 39.
40 Neri, *Capolavori,* 69–129.
41 PLN-A, Letter from Belluschi to Nervi, December 9, 1963.
42 Gabriele Neri, "Pier Luigi Nervi's Reduced Scale Models for HP Shells," *Journal of the IASS* 176–177 (2013): 149–158.
43 PLN-A, Letter from Nervi to Belluschi, March 6, 1964.
44 PLN-A, Letter from Nervi to McGucken, March 31, 1964.
45 "Monumental Cathedral for the Modern Age: Project for San Francisco's New Roman Catholic Cathedral," *Architectural Forum* 3 (March 1964): 11.
46 Ibid.
47 Neri, *Capolavori,* 219–273.
48 ISMES Archive, Seriate (ISMES), "San Francisco Cathedral. Report on the Static Tests Carried Out on the Preliminary Model," Job No. 436, August 1964.
49 Ibid.
50 Neri, *Capolavori.*
51 PLN-A, Letter from Nervi to McGucken, May 12, 1964.
52 ISMES, "Wind Tunnel Tests on the Model of the San Francisco Cathedral," Job No. 449, October 1964.
53 ISMES, "San Francisco Cathedral. Dead Loading Tests on the Cement Mix Model," Job No. 486, July 1965.

54 PLN-A, Letter from Nervi to McGucken, October 22, 1964.
55 ISMES, Job No. 486.
56 Ibid.
57 ISMES, "San Francisco Cathedral. Dynamic Tests on Elastic Model," Job No. 502, October 1965; ISMES, "San Francisco Cathedral. Static Tests on Elastic Model," Job No. 503, October 1965.
58 Ibid.
59 Neri, *Capolavori*, 246–248.
60 ISMES, Job No. 502 and Job No. 503.
61 Ibid.
62 PLN-A, Letter from Nervi to Belluschi, February 24, 1965.
63 PLN-A, Letter from Nervi to Oberti, January 27, 1965.
64 PLN-A, Letter from Nervi to Belluschi, February 24, 1965.
65 PLN-A, Letter from Nervi to McGucken, March 15, 1965.
66 PLN-A, Letter from Nervi to Belluschi, April 14, 1965.
67 PLN-A, Letter from Nervi to Belluschi, April 7, 1965.
68 ISMES, Job No. 502, and Job No. 503, October 1965.
69 PLN-A, Letter from Nervi to McGucken, March 15, 1965.
70 Ray W. Clough and Edward L. Wilson, "Early Finite Element Research at Berkeley," paper presented at the Fifth US National Conference on Computational Mechanics (University of Colorado at Boulder, CO, August 4–6, 1999).
71 Leonard F. Robinson, "Saint Mary's Cathedral in San Francisco." in *Concrete Thin Shells*, eds. S. J. Medwadowski, W. C. Schnobrich and A. C. Scordelis (Farmington Hills, MI: American Concrete Institute, 1971), 186.
72 PLN-A, Leonard F. Robinson, "St. Mary's Cathedral Structural Computations," s.d., received August 18, 1967.
73 Letter from Robinson to Review Board, February 7, 1966, in Frank Baron, Ray W. Clough, George A. Sedgwick, "Report of the Board Appointed to Review the Structural Design of the proposed Saint Mary's Cathedral," technical report (San Francisco, CA: 1967), 32–34.
74 Leonard F. Robinson, "Saint Mary's Cathedral in San Francisco," 186.
75 PLN-A, Letter from Nervi to Robinson, April 21, 1967.
76 PLN-A, Letter from Belluschi to Nervi, February 19, 1966.
77 Ibid.
78 Letter from Graham, Pregnoff, and Rinne to Levy, March 4, 1966, in "Report of the Board," 28–29.
79 "Experts Approve St. Mary's Design," *San Francisco Chronicle*, March 8, 1966.
80 Letter from Levy to Robinson, April 18, 1966, in "Report of the Board," 26–27.
81 "Report of the Board."
82 Ibid.
83 Ibid.
84 Ibid., 2.
85 Ibid., 13–14.
86 Ibid., 14.
87 Ibid.
88 Alexander C. Scordelis, "General Analysis Using Discretizing Methods," *Bulletin of IASS* 71/72, December 1979–April 1980: 67–72.
89 Letter from Levy to Robinson, April 18, 1966, 26.
90 Carlo Olmo and Cristiana Chiorino, eds., *Pier Luigi Nervi: Architecture as Challenge* (Cinisello Balsamo: Silvana Editoriale, 2010).
91 Peter Jones, *Ove Arup: Masterbuilder of the Twentieth Century* (New Haven, CT and London: Yale University Press, 2006), 266–281.
92 www.arup.com/our-firm consulted on February 27, 2018.
93 Alberto Bologna and Gabriele Neri, "Pier Luigi Nervi in the United States. The Height and Decline of a Master Builder." In Paulo J. S. Cruz, ed. *Structures and Architecture – Concepts, Applications and Challenges* (London: CRC Press, Taylor and Francis Group, 2013), 1900–1906.
94 Robinson, "Saint Mary's Cathedral in San Francisco," 187.
95 PLN-A, Letters from Nervi to Delfino Brothers, between July 19 and October 8, 1965.

References

Baron, Frank, Ray W. Clough, and George A. Sedgwick. "Report of the Board Appointed to Review the Structural Design of the proposed Saint Mary's Cathedral," technical report (San Francisco, CA: 1967).

Bologna, Alberto and Gabriele Neri. "Pier Luigi Nervi in the United States. The Height and Decline of a Master Builder." In Paulo J. S. Cruz, ed. *Structures and Architecture – Concepts, Applications and Challenges*, 1900–1906 (London: CRC Press, Taylor and Francis Group, 2013).

Catalano, Eduardo. "Two Warped Surfaces," *The Student Publication of the School of Design* 1, 1955.

———. "Structures of Warped Surfaces," *The Student Publication of the School of Design* 1, 1960.

Clausen, Meredith L. *Spiritual Space. The Religious Architecture of Pietro Belluschi* (Seattle, WA, and London: University of Washington Press, 1992).

Clough, Ray W., and Edward L. Wilson. *Early Finite Element Research at Berkeley*. Paper presented at the Fifth US National Conference on Computational Mechanics, University of Colorado at Boulder, CO, August 4–6, 1999.

Danusso, Arturo. "Scienza delle costruzioni. Premesse e concetti fondamentali." In Piero Locatelli, ed. *La scienza e lo spirito negli scritti di Arturo Danusso* (Brescia: Morcelliana, 1978).

"Experts Approve St. Mary's Design," *San Francisco Chronicle*, March 8, 1966.

"Focus: St. Mary's Cathedral," *Architectural Forum* 133, no. 5 (December 1970): 5.

Gaffey, James P. "The Anatomy of Transition: Cathedral-Building and Social Justice in San Francisco 1962–1971," *The Catholic Historian Review* 1 (January 1984): 45–73.

Harris, Harris G., and Sabnis, Gajanan M. *Structural Modeling and Experimental Techniques*, 2nd edn. (Boca Raton, FL: CRC Press, 1999).

ISMES Archive, Seriate (ISMES). "San Francisco Cathedral. Report on the Static Tests Carried Out on the Preliminary Model," Job No. 436, August 1964.

———. "Wind Tunnel Tests on the Model of the San Francisco Cathedral," Job No. 449, October 1964.

———. "San Francisco Cathedral. Dead Loading Tests on the Cement Mix Model," Job No. 486, July 1965.

———. "San Francisco Cathedral. Dynamic Tests on Elastic Model," Job No. 502, October 1965.

———. "San Francisco Cathedral. Static Tests on Elastic Model," Job No. 503, October 1965.

Jones, Peter. *Ove Arup. Masterbuilder of the Twentieth Century* (New Haven, CT, and London: Yale University Press, 2006).

Lagorio, Henry J. *Pier Luigi Nervi. Space and Structural Integrity* (San Francisco, CA: Associated Arts Foundation, 1961).

"Monumental Cathedral for the Modern Age: Project for San Francisco's New Roman Catholic Cathedral," *Architectural Forum* 120, no. 3 (March 1964): 11.

Neri, Gabriele. "Pier Luigi Nervi's Reduced Scale Models for HP Shells," *Journal of the IASS* 176–177 (2013): 149–158.

———. *Capolavori in miniatura. Pier Luigi Nervi e la modellazione strutturale* (Mendrisio: Mendrisio Academy Press, 2014).

———. "Per il corretto costruire. Introduzione." In Gabriele Neri, ed. *Pier Luigi Nervi, Ingegneria, architettura, costruzione. Scritti scelti 1922–1971*, 103–117 (CittàStudi Edizioni, Torino 2014).

Nervi, Pier Luigi. *Costruire correttamente* (Milano: Hoepli, 1955).

Olmo, Carlo and Cristiana Chiorino, eds. *Pier Luigi Nervi: Architecture as Challenge* (Cinisello Balsamo: Silvana Editoriale, 2010).

Pace, Sergio. "Papal Audience Hall." In Carlo Olmo and Cristiana Chiorino, eds. *Pier Luigi Nervi: Architecture as Challenge*, 182–185 (Cinisello Balsamo: Silvana Editoriale, 2010).

"Powerful Cathedral for San Francisco," *Progressive Architecture* 45, no. 3 (March 1964): 69.

Robinson, Leonard F. "Saint Mary's Cathedral in San Francisco". In S. J. Medwadowski, W. C. Schnobrich, and A. C. Scordelis, eds. *Concrete Thin Shells*, 185–192 (Farmington Hills, MI: American Concrete Institute, 1971).

Scordelis, Alexander C., "General Analysis Using Discretizing Methods," *Bulletin of IASS* 71/72 (December 1979–April 1980): 67–72.

"St. Mary's Cathedral, San Francisco," *Architectural Record* 150, no. 9 (September 1971): 113–119.

Temko, Alan. "S. F.'s New Cathedral: A Critical Essay," *San Francisco Chronicle*, June 15, 1963.

Tsuboi, Yoshikatsu, and Nasukawa, Ryohei. "Hyperbolic Paraboloidal Shell Structure for Tokyo Roman Catholic Cathedral," *Bulletin of IASS* 28 (1966): 37–52.

6

CHARLES HAERTLING'S ST. STEPHEN'S LUTHERAN CHURCH, NORTHGLENN, COLORADO, 1963–64

Heather Seneff

American architect Charles Haertling (1928–84) started his practice in Boulder, Colorado, in 1957 and designed over forty structures in Colorado in an organic and dynamic mid-century modern style.[1] By the time he was commissioned to design St. Stephen's in 1962, Haertling was already establishing a name for himself. He was included in an article in *Zodiac*, an international magazine of contemporary architecture, in 1961 as one of their noted "Young Architects in the United States."[2] The article mentions his 1958 Noble House—explored again in the Italian architecture magazine *Casabella* in 1965—as well as three churches in Colorado: a Quaker Meeting House in Boulder, Zion Lutheran Church in Brighton, and an expansion of Our Savior's Lutheran Church in Denver. Most of the (scant) recent scholarship on Haertling considers his residential architecture, mostly in Boulder, such as the Brenton House (1969), Volsky House (1964), and Kahn House (1970).[3] However, Haertling did complete a handful of religious buildings that have not been studied as much as his houses. The focus of this chapter is his most unusual design of St. Stephen's Lutheran Church (1963–64) in Northglenn, a suburb of Denver, Colorado. St. Stephen's has a striking roof profile—four enormous concrete beams are draped from a tall central pier, and catenaries swoop dramatically down and then back upward to form a roof with a diagonal span of 155 feet (Fig. 6.1).

While the structure is still in use as a church today, the original congregation now worships in a more traditional brick building on the same lot. This chapter will investigate the context of the exuberant organic modernist architecture of St. Stephen's; the original congregation's feelings about its design and functionality; and why a more sedate, traditional building was constructed for the congregation in the 1990s. Did Charles Haertling "push the envelope" of mid-century modern architecture too far in the innovative, expressive structure of St. Stephen's? The temptation to exploit mid-century building technologies and create unusual forms not traditionally associated with religious architecture may have proved too much for a suburban Denver congregation. Was his experimental design for a traditional suburban congregation too controversial, or was the design of this local architect celebrated? Examining primary resources from local archives and libraries concerning

FIGURE 6.1 St. Stephen's Lutheran Church, Northglenn, Colorado, 2016.

Photograph by the author.

St. Stephen's Lutheran Church,[4] and conducting interviews with members of the church congregation and the Haertling family,[5] provided some answers to these questions.

Context: new suburbs

Denver experienced a boom in industries related to World War II (in ordnance production and atomic energy, for example), which changed the city's economy in ways that lasted into the post-war decades. During this time, Denver attracted attention from the aerospace industry, petroleum companies, and entities from other burgeoning industries. As a result, the population of the Denver metropolitan region increased at a rapid rate, and living in the suburbs became an attractive option, as it did nationwide.

The movement of Americans to the suburbs in the prosperous post-war period was stimulated by many factors. Homeownership was one of the main components of the "American Dream," a phrase coined by historian James Truslow Adams in 1931.[6] Post-war mortgage insurance programs like the Federal Housing Administration enabled more Americans to purchase single-family houses and encouraged developers to invest in homebuilding[7] for the growing population.[8] Unfair lending practices that favored white middle-class homebuyers, plus two large waves of migration by African Americans from the poor rural South to industrialized northern cities, increased racial tensions in urban housing. Land outside the city limits was less costly, and the rapid expansion of roads and highways nationwide encouraged access to that land, especially after the Interstate Highway Act of 1956.[9] Federal and local governments were less interested in urban renewal projects and more supportive of development outside urban centers.[10] Kathleen Tobin suggests in her article "The Reduction of

Urban Vulnerability: Revisiting 1950's American Suburbanization as Civil Defence" that the federal government was actively engaging in decentralizing the American population in response to the Cold War threat of nuclear warfare.[11] The association of suburban homes with economic stability, a healthy environment, and security contributed to a rising middle-class desire to own a home in the suburbs.

As American suburbs were constructed and populated in the post-war years, the need for new churches rose substantially. A marked increase in church attendance occurred after the war, stimulated by the "baby boom" population growth spurt, a general strengthening of faith after World War II, and the general insecurity of the atomic era.[12] Jay Price comments in his book *Temples for a Modern God: Religious Architecture in Postwar America*, "The Lutherans were among the most active and organized Protestant groups when it came to denominational support for construction."[13]

Northglenn suburb and its St. Stephen's Lutheran Church

In the spring of 1959, Denver-based developers Perl-Mack Enterprises responded to these post-war stimuli by beginning construction of their most ambitiously planned suburban community.[14] It was located about 15 miles north of downtown Denver in unincorporated Adams County, which saw a population growth of over 11 percent between 1950 and 1960 (the largest growth spurt since 1900). The development was to be called Northglenn and would eventually include a shopping mall. Houses in Northglenn were priced from $13,500 to $20,350 and were unremarkable in their design. The first Perl-Mack houses were single story, from 600 to 800 square feet, with generous lots.[15] Five model homes opened in June 1959 on the corner of Grant Street and 104th Avenue. By October 1962, 3,000 homes formed the new community.[16]

In the same month, Robert D. Beard, the pastor of a Lutheran congregation in Northglenn, and Charles Haertling, an architect from Boulder, Colorado, signed a contract for a new church.[17] The contract proposed to introduce something remarkable to Northglenn: St. Stephen's Lutheran Church. The plans for St. Stephen's promised to be so unusual that, according to a letter written on August 9, 1962 by Robert Beard,[18] the developers initially refused to approve the church project. Representatives from Perl-Mack Enterprises worried that the church would "stick out like a sore thumb" and disrupt the "external harmony" of the community.[19]

In his letter, Beard describes how the tone of the debate had changed during a second meeting on August 8, when the developers expressed specific concerns about the "color of the roof."[20] Haertling informed them he was considering a non-glare finish in a soft white. This apparently softened the opinions of the builders, one of whom admitted he "liked the plans" (Fig. 6.2). Pastor Beard's August 9th letter includes a paragraph expressing his indignation with the developer for "imposing his conceptions of architectural beauty . . . upon this community, in which he only has a commercial interest." He added that the "*people* in the community" have the "right to have within the community buildings which are just a bit out of the ordinary, which attempt to bring beauty and meaning in addition to being a shelter from the elements."[21]

Pastor Beard's congregation had first organized in April 1961; they were temporarily meeting in a Northglenn elementary school and wanted a new church building on a corner plot of land. A Preliminary Study Proposal[22] that was created in conjunction with financing the construction of a new Northglenn church building reported that the average value of the 63 members' homes was $15,500, and the estimated average annual income was $6,000. The parishioners were predominantly "white collar, clerical, sales, some mechanics, management." Sunday school attendance included 43 elementary school children, 10 toddlers, and 19 high school students. St. Stephen's was a young congregation with a population typical of the growing Denver suburb of Northglenn.

This ordinary congregation and housing development served as the context for Charles Haertling's out-of-the-ordinary church design (Fig. 6.3). He was an architect with a persistent and growing local reputation for atypical, boundary-pushing, and often controversial architecture. In fact, his Volsky House (which was being built in Boulder concurrently with St. Stephen's in 1964) was vilified by its neighbors while it was still under construction. Later, the house was featured in *Life* magazine in 1966, and led to Haertling "being pegged as one of America's most promising architects."[23]

FIGURE 6.2 St. Stephen's Lutheran Church, view looking southwest, 2016.
Photograph by the author.

FIGURE 6.3 St. Stephen's Lutheran Church, detail of the exterior showing the southwest
support and overhanging roof beam, 2016.
Photograph by the author.

Charles Haertling: a local architect

Charles Haertling was born in 1928 in Missouri and attained his architecture degree from Washington University in St. Louis in 1952 after a two-year stint in the US Navy. Haertling was a devout Lutheran[24] and a participant in the Lutheran Society for Worship, Music and the Arts. Pastor Robert Beard of Northglenn probably knew Charles ("Chuck") Haertling through Lutheran events in the Denver area. For instance, the Lutheran Society for Worship, Music and the Arts sponsored a seminar called "The Creative Parish" for all Denver-area Lutherans at Our Savior's Lutheran Church in Denver in November 1963.[25] The schedule included sessions on "Art in the Church—Abstract or Realistic" and "Banners and Symbolism in the Church," and concluded in the evening with "two award-winning contemporary films."

In 1953, Haertling moved to Boulder to teach architecture, and he opened his own practice there in 1957. Over the span of his short career (Haertling died at the age of 55), he contributed 40 unusual structures to the Boulder area. While Haertling did not have direct contact with architect Frank Lloyd Wright, he was influenced by Wright's organic and imaginative design, and by architect Bruce Goff, whose eccentric modernism produced several controversial buildings. Haertling's children recalled visiting with Goff in Oklahoma for an afternoon while on a family trip to Missouri.[26] Haertling includes a Bruce Goff quote on the first page of a self-published, undated pamphlet about his architectural practice:

> the usual definition of organic architecture is "that which grows from within outward through the natural use of materials so the form is one with function." However [Haertling adds], we must go further, and continue with "as directed and ordered by a creative spirit."[27]

Haertling himself had strong views about his own architectural style. After St. Stephen's was constructed, Haertling was interviewed for the *Rocky Mountain News* on March 14, 1965. In an article entitled "Exciting Church Design Urged," he is quoted as saying, "These are exciting times in architecture and we should be able to do almost anything we want to, especially in church architecture." Haertling described the congregation of St. Stephen's as a "tremendous group, interested, alive and excited about their church building."[28]

St. Stephen's Lutheran Church

St. Stephen's striking roof has been variously described as an upside-down Easter lily, praying hands,[29] elephant tusks,[30] "Flying Nun-like,"[31] a replica of the Rocky Mountain skyline, and a collapsing tent.[32] Haertling himself described it as an "inside-out dome"[33] (Figs. 6.1, 6.2, 6.3). Thomas Noel in his *Buildings of Colorado* (1997) includes St. Stephen's as only one of two buildings of note in Northglenn, describing the church as follows:

> Four concrete catenary roofs with 120-foot spans rise into a central spire, creating a concave dome centered over the altar of this church in the round. The Boulder architect, an admirer of Frank Lloyd Wright and Bruce Goff, created organic architecture according to Goff's definition: "that which grows from within outward through the natural use of materials . . ." This eye-catching church in an open field has been likened to everything from a sagging tent to soaring sculpture that suggests the snowcapped Rockies.[34]

Indeed, at the time of its construction, St. Stephen's might well have been quite eye-catching from its position above Denver, before the Valley Highway[35] corridor suburbs filled in (the roof is visible still from across the interstate from certain vantage points). Haertling's own notes about the church describe it as

> a small mission church on a gently rolling, exposed site set slightly above a rap-idly growing housing development . . . It seats 150 people in a communal seating arrangement (symmetry expressed by form), with encircling classrooms, offices, and social area.
>
> The altar is located directly below the 25-foot high intersection of the post-tensioned girders which meet at right angles which are only supported at four outside points. Glass above 7-feet-6-inch high nave walls allows views from all surrounding rooms into the upper part of the nave [signifying the centeredness upon the worship function of the church].
>
> The design is a sculpturing of structural elements to fulfill interior purpose. Limitation on building cubage also served to minimize space. Roof is a self-formed concrete slab (2½ inches) supported by catenaries and mesh slung between post-tensioned girders.[36]

The symmetrical nature of the church is revealed in a preliminary plan.[37] Under the diamond shape of the roof, the central altar in the chancel is placed on a hexagonal dais, surrounded by seating for the parishioners (Fig. 6.4). Around this central nave are passageways and an open space for assembly, and then finally, an outer ring of classrooms, with a nursery, office, kitchen, and bathrooms (Fig. 6.5). The irregularly shaped working rooms echo the hexago-nal dais under the altar. The central placement of the altar reflects Lutheran liturgical trends of the period, and the nurturing cocoon of the social spaces around the sacred reflects the celebration of community.

The plans and architectural drawings for St. Stephen's illustrate the level of detail that Haertling put into the church.[38] An unnumbered sheet describes carefully designed built-in office and kitchen furniture, with shelving and the baptismal font delineated as well. "Sheet 1: Plan of the Structure" includes a side note presumably by Charles Haertling himself: "Catenary (cable) sag should equal 1/10 of span for greatest economy. Max sag improves design & thus will be used."

Examination of these drawings also reveals that St. Stephen's was originally designed as the first building in a complex of structures for the parish. This is corroborated in an article from the *Denver Post* of January 22, 1964, "Tusk Beams Support Roof," which states that the church is the first unit of a complex.[39] The "future expansion" was intended to have been to the west, in the form of two diamond-shaped structures linked to the church by corridors around a small courtyard.

Perhaps the most elegiac description of St. Stephen's is found in the 8mm home movies shot by Charles Haertling during the construction of the church. In 1990, the architect's son Joel Haertling, director of the Cinema Program at the Boulder Public Library, created a 66-minute silent 8mm film, *Design Process of Charles A. Haertling, Architect*. He used the footage of the construction film, supplemented by sketches, drawings, and plans.[40] The film features five of the architect's projects, with St. Stephen's appearing first. While the footage

FIGURE 6.4 St. Stephen's Lutheran Church, interior showing the central altar, after 1964.

Unattributed contemporary photograph in the Boulder Public Library Carnegie Branch for Local History, Haertling Papers, 706-4-9, https://boulder library.org/cwjpgs/706-4-9photo_2.jpg.

FIGURE 6.5 Preliminary plan by the architect of St. Stephen's Lutheran Church, c. 1963.

Boulder Public Library Archives, courtesy of Joel Haertling.

is grainy and rough, it clearly illustrates the architect's joy in the swooping energetic roof beams, which rest on concrete pyramids at each end and are topped by a tall spire (Figs. 6.1, 6.2, 6.6). The camera also concentrates on details like the central altar and the chicken-foot decorations on the exterior walls (Fig. 6.7). Joel Haertling explained in a phone interview that these birdlike details are a deliberate reference to the New Testament's Matthew 23:37: "How often would I have gathered your children together as a hen gathers her brood under her wings . . . ."

Text written by Charles Haertling appears at the beginning of the film celebrating the power of organic architecture and the creative process:

> The design process is one of painful exhilaration where one gives ultimate importance to the problem being solved, letting the problem itself be an integrated solution which uses materials and structure void of distortion of uses untrue to the nature of the material or process, testing the boundaries of the application so as to give excitement, variety, adventure, human interest, and human relation to the project.[41]

The daring design seems to have been a success. Russ Skillings, a longtime member of the St. Stephen's congregation, stated in an e-mail on May 14, 2016, that "most everyone

FIGURE 6.6 St. Stephen's Lutheran Church, detail of the exterior showing the northeast "pyramid" support for the parabolic support "tusk," 2016.
Photograph by the author.

FIGURE 6.7 St. Stephen's Lutheran Church, exterior showing the "chicken feet" detail, 2016.
Photograph by the author.

liked [the building] and felt as though we were part of the wave of the future—the cutting edge . . . Frank Lloyd Wright was quite popular then and architecture was quite high in the consciousness of many." Barbara Sieckman, whose husband succeeded Robert Beard as pastor of St. Stephen's, corroborated this recollection on May 5, 2016: "When the church was first built, it was an attraction to the area because of how different it was. Generally everyone liked it, but it was an expensive structure to build and maintain."[42]

August 9, 1967: surviving a disaster

During World War II, the US Army created the Rocky Mountain Arsenal on the northeastern edge of Denver,[43] about 12 miles southeast of St. Stephen's Lutheran Church. After the war, the arsenal became a chemical weapon manufacturing site until 1967.[44] Disposal of the waste from this production was a problem. In 1961, a 12,000-foot well was drilled and injection of the waste and water into the earth began in March of the following year, halting in October 1963, and resuming in 1965[45] before ceasing permanently in 1966.[46] Two seismograph stations were located in the Denver area at the time; the one at the Colorado School of Mines in Golden, Colorado (about 15 miles west of downtown Denver), recorded over 1,300 earthquakes between 1963 and August 1967.[47] It was widely accepted that the injection of wastewater at the Arsenal caused these unusual earthquakes. The authors of a 1968 study published in *Science* magazine conclude, "Prior to 1967, the frequency of occurrence of earthquakes of different magnitudes in the Denver area was such that the likelihood of a really destructive earthquake could reasonably be considered remote."[48]

On August 9, 1967, a tremor measuring at 5.3 on the Richter scale was recorded at 6:25 in the morning. An article in Denver's *Westword* magazine on the fiftieth anniversary of the earthquakes reported that the quake "caused the most serious damage at Northglenn, where concrete pillar supports to a church roof were weakened."[49] Barbara Sieckman confirmed that this unnamed church was St. Stephen's. She recalled in an e-mail on May 5, 2016 that she and her husband "arrived at St. Stephen's about five hours after the earthquake struck. We did not enter the building for several days until it had been determined to be structurally safe."

In a phone call on May 27, 2016, the architect's widow, Mrs. Viola Haertling remembered the day of the earthquake as well. Her husband was out of town, but in a phone conversation with Viola he was not overly concerned about the structure of St. Stephen's, reassuring her and the church's congregation that the consulting engineer for the church, Ib Falk Jorgensen, was the best structural engineer in the state of Colorado. Viola recalled that Governor John Love later appointed Jorgensen to the committee formed to investigate the unusual earthquakes.

Barbara Sieckman described in her May 5, 2016 e-mail that

> There was no damage inside the building, but the four pillars that supported the roof were cracked.[50] The repair consisted of lifting the roof beams off the pillars, inserting a "Y" inside each pillar and placing the beams on top of the "Y" so the roof would "rock" on top of the pillars if the earth moved under it.

Charles Haertling's bold organic modernism[51] had survived a most unusual Colorado event. The integrity of the structure under duress suggests that the organic modernist design was truly farsighted, thoughtful, and far from "self-indulgent and undisciplined."[52]

The influence of changes in liturgy and modernism

The mid-century decades were indeed "exciting times in architecture,"[53] as Haertling recognized. Devotional architecture was especially ready for change, since an evolution in liturgy began in Europe before World War I.[54] Architects in Europe began to unite liturgical change and emerging technological developments in church design during the interwar period. The application of new materials and techniques to redesign traditional features of the medieval cathedral resulted in a Modern Gothic style,[55] which is characterized by Gothic arches,[56] spires,[57] high nave walls,[58] and a traditional altar at the nave wall with congregational seating facing it.[59] In his 1960 book *Modern Church Architecture*, historian and critic Joseph Pichard exhorted his mid-century audience to explore "contemporary forms" instead of looking only to the past for architectural inspiration.[60] Pichard's illustrations of modern church architecture and art include interwar churches by the German architects Dominikos Böhm and Otto Bartning, French architect August Perret (who, Pichard claims, "glorie[d] in the reinforced concrete [of the vaulting in his iconic 1923 Catholic Church at Le Raincy] and shows no false shame"[61]), and Swiss architect Le Corbusier. These examples exploited concrete and other emerging materials in new and expressive ways.

Religious leaders and organizations of many faiths encouraged this interest in modern design. Changes in liturgy inspired more centralized, intimate places of worship. This liturgical evolution witnessed unprecedented cooperation across denominations—a cooperation strengthened by the common emphasis on a more active participation of the faithful within their respective communities.[62] In "The Architectural Setting of the Liturgy," Peter G. Cobb points out that the "corporate nature of the [modern] worshipping community demands that the altar and lectern be much more in the midst of the people."[63] While the Catholic Church's Second Vatican Council (1962–65) is perhaps the most structured response to these liturgical changes, most Protestant denominations were also impacted by this evolution.[64]

Historian Gretchen Buggeln, in her article on a chapel constructed in 1956–59 at Valparaiso University (a Lutheran university founded in 1859), describes a 1958 16mm film created by the Church Architecture Group of the American Institute of Architects (AIA) called *A Place to Worship*, which was distributed to church building committees around the country.[65] The 13-minute film began with images of Classical Greek religious architecture and then "abruptly threw the viewer into the confusing speed and congestion of the modern world."[66] The AIA's Church Architecture Group strongly encouraged congregations to reflect the modernity of the post-war period in their churches. Other religious organizations and conferences were doing the same. In 1954, the Department of Church Architecture of the United Lutheran Church in America developed *Organizing and Operating the Building Program,* a manual (revised in 1958) including references "intended to enhance the congregation's understanding of worship and architecture."[67] As a result, more mid-century architects were inspired to reject traditional basilican churches and to embrace "organic, playful forms that went beyond the rectilinear and entered the realm of expressionism."[68]

Alan Hess writes in *Organic Architecture: the Other Modernism* (2006) that "[t]he birth of modernism had provoked experiment and debate; now its [post-war] reassessment stimulated even more ferment."[69] Hess includes Charles Haertling in his book—describing the Willard-Schapiro House (1961) and the Brenton House (1969)—as an example of one of these architects participating in this "matrix of rationalism and revolution."[70] He argues that the "spirit of individualism in the American myth was closely tied to the popularity of Organic architecture"[71] in the mid-century decades. Haertling's comment in the 1965 interview with the *Rocky Mountain News* seems to be an expression of his own individualistic credo: "we should be able to do almost anything we want to."[72] Suburban devotional architecture, which required "ease of access and high visibility,"[73] provided a blank slate, since no specific architectural vocabulary accompanied the new requirements of the liturgy. It seems in character that Haertling would aspire to create a highly visible, inspirational, and exciting Organic Modern building for the congregation of St. Stephen's.

The influence of modern concrete roofs

It is equally understandable that Haertling would have chosen to embellish his design with a commanding roof. Many of the icons of mid-century organic modernism used unusual and audacious rooflines. Frank Lloyd Wright, for example, designed a steeply sloping pitched roof in the First Unitarian Church in Madison, Wisconsin (1949–51), and whose Annunciation Greek Orthodox Church in Wauwatosa, Wisconsin (1956–61) has a vast, shallow dome. Le Corbusier's Notre-Dame-du-Haut at Ronchamp (1952–55) displays a magnificent undulating sculptural concrete roof. Oscar Niemeyer's Cathedral of Brasilia (1958–60) in Brazil is formed by 16 upright hyperbolic concrete beams which give the roof a crown-like appearance; and Eero Saarinen's North Christian Church (1964) in Columbus, Indiana is dominated by a towering spire.[74] Jay M. Price remarks that "Theologian James White suggested that [mid-century] religious architecture became 'a study in comparative roofs,' finding that the high and dramatic roof of the church of the 1960s is almost a trademark of the era."[75]

The exploration of new materials and technologies—especially concrete—in the late 1950s and 1960s contributed to this celebration of "high and dramatic" roof profiles. Joseph Pichard points out that the "revitalized liturgical programs . . . lead [the architect] to think in plastic terms. [The architect] is given the opportunity to experiment with the hitherto unknown possibilities of new materials and to create moving forms."[76] Architects and engineers experimented with hyperbolic paraboloids, catenary and parabolic arches, and thin-shell concrete to reach their most arresting heights in roofs of commercial, religious, and educational buildings. The new materials and technologies of the modern age were catalysts for an organic architecture that embraced conspicuous cantilevers, beehive geometries, circular pods,[77] parabolas, and catenaries—features that identified each building as an individual celebration of material and humanity.

The experimentation with modern materials and plastic shapes was not always well received. Organic modern architects were also criticized for being intentionally unconventional, self-indulgent, and undisciplined.[78] The exuberance and flamboyance of organic modern architecture could be interpreted as arrogance or hubris, or as Meredith Clausen describes it in her book *Spiritual Space*, "structural exhibitionism."[79] In *Organic Architecture: the Other Modernism*, Alan Hess mentions the contemporary criticism of the "eccentricities" of organic modernism by architectural journalists, and the censure of Oscar Niemeyer's mid-century modern work in Brazil.[80] The influence of Mies van der Rohe's rational international modern style was a powerful pedagogy for organic modernism to combat.[81] Post-war suburban church construction in Northglenn (and other places) was dominated by familiar basilican buildings,[82] which addressed the new liturgical requirements without combining those changes with the new forms of organic modernism. Cost would have been a factor in many communities, and only a wealthy congregation could afford a church designed by a "name" architect like Frank Lloyd Wright. In fact, Haertling noted in a description of St. Stephen's that the "cost was $70,000 for construction only."[83]

Sculptural roof forms were appearing in the new architecture of Denver as well, as the city's 1950s urban renewal projects demolished older more conventional city buildings. The huge hyperbolic paraboloid entrance canopy to the May D&F Department Store in Denver[84] was used as an illustration for an August 1958 *Architectural Forum* article, "The Rise of Thin Shells."[85] A number of church buildings with unusual rooflines appeared in Denver in the 1950s,[86] including the Most Precious Blood Catholic Church in Denver designed by architect James Paull, in 1951, which has a tall, spiked, crown-like roof, and Calvary Temple Church (Ralph Peterson, 1958), which has a sweeping parabolic roof that appears to spring from the ground.

Haertling employed both the parabola and the catenary structural systems in St. Stephen's. The two forms can be very similar; Galileo demonstrated the former with the trajectory of a thrown object and the latter with a hanging chain.[87] Both arching forms exploit the qualities of concrete that made the material so prevalent in mid-century architecture. While the structural properties of and mathematical equations for parabolas and catenaries had been known for centuries,[88] they were not exploited as a visible vocabulary until Spanish architect Antonio Gaudi employed them in several of his buildings, perhaps most famously in Sagrada Familia (1898–1915) in Barcelona. Catenaries and parabolas are related visually to arches, but, unlike the arch, which is historically imbued with symbolic meaning, they are visually neutral and suitable for all types of architecture. In the mid-twentieth century, these evocative arc shapes created with concrete appear ubiquitous and seem to be synonymous with modernity and progress.[89]

Haertling's "painful exhilaration" in the design of St. Stephen's is expressed in the parabolic beams, which soar energetically into the sky like spiritual hope, and the gentle, calm swoops of the catenary roof surfaces. In Joel Haertling's film showing the construction of the church, the excitement at the Tri-L Construction Company site is apparent. First, the ground is prepared by compaction and the foundation poured. The four permanent support pyramids for the roof are poured and the central temporary support is created. The complex wooden forms for the four enormous concrete beams are created by the crew and then are precast on-site. "When the compressive strength of the beam cement reaches a strength of 4,000 psi, the two tendons along the center line of the beam are pre-tensioned"[90] and the beams are lifted by two cranes (one 60-ton, the other 41-ton) into position on the concrete support pyramids (Fig. 6.8). The internal central support structure—upon which the interior (highest) ends of the roof "tusks" rested before post tensioning—is dismantled, and the massive tusks defy gravity over the central space (Fig. 6.9). The roof catenary cables are then

FIGURE 6.8 St. Stephen's Lutheran Church during construction, placing the cast-on-site roof beams; 35mm slide probably taken by Charles Haertling, 1963.

Boulder Public Library Carnegie Branch for Local History, Haertling Papers, 706-9-18, https://boulderlibrary.org/cwjpgs/706-9-18photo_1.jpg.

FIGURE 6.9   St. Stephen's Lutheran Church during construction, catenary cables draped in a diamond pattern; photograph probably taken by Charles Haertling (digital image cropped to remove damage to print), 1963.

Boulder Public Library Carnegie Branch for Local History, Haertling Papers, 706-4-9, https://boulderlibrary.org/cwjpgs/706-4-9photo_3.jpg.

draped from the beams in a diamond pattern, and concrete is troweled on the roof deck, creating a smooth, silky surface. At last the spire is added to the roof by crane with much care under a blue Colorado sky. In a May 27, 2016 phone conversation with the architect's widow, Mrs. Haertling remembered a local news station being on site to film that final step, in which everything had to meet just right. The completed building stands prominently on its open site, with the vast skyline of Colorado beyond, a symbol of St. Stephen's youthful congregation and Haertling's excitement in the materials and forms of modern architecture.

St. Stephen's in the twenty-first century

Did Charles Haertling "push the envelope" too far in designing his adventurous Northglenn church? The "painful exhilaration" of the design process allowed for a successful exploration of the forms and techniques of mid-century architecture. What resulted was a joyful, extraordinary building that not only catered to the changes in liturgy of the era but also elicits a gasp of surprise in the mundane suburb that surrounds it. The *structural* envelope of the design was not pushed too far either, as St. Stephen's survived a highly unusual seismic event. The audacity of the architect to defy gravity with the massive, parabolic beams of the roof was not overreaching hubris but calculated engineering.

St. Stephen's congregation at the time of its construction seems to have appreciated the design and even enjoyed it. The local news media covered the construction of the church with an enthusiasm that suggests the larger Denver community took an interest in the eye-catching roofline and unusual form. Strong bonds are often forged between a community and the architecture that defines or enhances it—buildings that are "just a bit out of the ordinary."[91]

Pastor Robert Beard's choice of a dynamic young local architect for his new church reveals the optimism of the time. The congregation embraced Haertling's "pushing of the envelope"— and perhaps perceived the building as a symbol of their own prosperity and the growth of their spiritual community. The church is an example of the excitement, individualism, and adventure of mid-century modernism. The emphatic roofline, the reliance on concrete and the use of the parabola and catenary place St. Stephen's firmly in the spirit of its time.

There should always be a place for architecture that extends beyond the mundane—"directed and ordered by a creative spirit"—and the mid-twentieth century provided a perfect environment for such innovative thinking, even in the suburbs of Denver.

St. Stephen's Lutheran Church stands today in a more crowded suburban environment than its original setting. The church is immediately surrounded by a parking lot, with a school across the street. Haertling's exuberant building no longer serves as the St. Stephen's parish church, but is rented to another congregation. Thus, it continues to serve as a house of worship. A more traditional nave-and-crossing church—its conservative façade almost invisible—stands on the same plot of land as Haertling's "praying hands" and now serves the congregation (Fig. 6.10). As Barbara Sieckman explained in a September 6, 2015 e-mail, "The construction of the [original] building was not energy-efficient and maintenance is costly. About 1999, a new, more conventional building was built on the property and the Haertling building has been rented to a Spanish-speaking congregation." When asked if the original congregation grew tired of the novelty of Haertling's unconventional building, Mrs. Sieckman commented in a May 14, 2016 e-mail, "No, I don't think the congregation grew tired of it. There was a fierce loyalty to the building. Especially in the face of a few snide comments by non-members."

The "new, more conventional building" more closely resembles the style of parish church that appeared in Northglenn in the 1960s. In a history of Northglenn written for the series *Images of America* (2013), Elizabeth Moreland Candelario makes no reference to St. Stephen's at all. The three churches featured in the "Religious and School Life" chapter are all traditional post-and-lintel, rectangular nave buildings: Northglenn Lutheran Church (now Gethsemane Lutheran Church), completed in 1961, with a 1965 addition; Calvary Community Baptist Church, built in 1967, and Northglenn Christian Church, which held its first service in 1960.[92] The nostalgic images of historic suburbia sought by *Images of America* seem to have no room for the daring of mid-century Modern Organic extravaganzas like Haertling's St. Stephen's.

In spite of the loyalty inspired by their cutting-edge, modern church, the congregation chose to build a more conventional structure three decades later. In this, St. Stephen's also reflects the growing cynicism of the latter part of the twentieth century as the prosperity

FIGURE 6.10 St. Stephen's Lutheran Church, view to the 1990s structure on the left beneath the beam of the earlier church by Haertling, 2017.

Photograph by the author.

and optimism of the post-war decades faded. The mundane practical realities of Organic Modernism that make the aging structures impractical or at worst undesirable—leaky roofs and energy inefficiencies—seems as metaphors for the faded promises of the post-war era. As Jay Price describes:

> many of the features that were supposed to make "up to date" churches and synagogues so attractive became liabilities . . . The vast vaulted interiors of modern houses of worship Modern Gothic were exorbitantly expensive to heat and cool. Lofty ceilings, especially those with complicated angles, also had a nasty tendency to leak.[93]

Price also notes that mid-century construction materials often did not age as well as traditional materials. He comments that "[m]any a mainline Protestant [church] of the 1950s has come to share a building with a congregation of Korean Evangelicals or Latino Pentecostals."[94] Practicality, it seems, sometimes overrules creativity.

Many of the American mid-century modern churches that pushed the envelope of construction and design have not survived.[95] The upside-down Easter lily, St. Stephen's, has been lucky, perhaps due in part to the strength of Charles Haertling's local reputation. Not all mid-century organic architecture has fared as well.[96] For example, much of Bruce Goff's Oklahoma architecture, an inspiration to Haertling, has suffered over time. His Hopewell Baptist Church—known as the "Wigwam" Church (1951)—has been abandoned, and Bavinger House (1955)—an iconic spiral structure—has been destroyed.

Eero Saarinen's North Christian Church in Columbus, Indiana, on the other hand, was built at the same time as St. Stephen's and is now on the National Register of Historical Places. Pietro Belluschi's Zion Lutheran Church (1951) in Portland, Oregon is also on the National Register. Likewise, Boulder has rallied around preserving Charles Haertling's domestic architecture several times. The Haertlings' own house (originally built for Richard and Helen Wilson) became a Boulder landmark in 2010, and his Roitz House (1978) was landmarked in 2007. The preservation of Boulder's historic buildings is frequently (if sporadically) a hot topic and, in 2006, a M.S. student at the Chicago Art Institute, Jessica Lee Fasick, even wrote an (unpublished) thesis on Haertling entitled "A Preservation Plan for the Work of Charles A. Haertling in Boulder, Colorado." While St. Stephen's does not seem endangered except perhaps from neglect, admirers of St. Stephen's Lutheran Church and Charles Haertling may be able to rally support for its preservation if the church is ever endangered.

Notes

1 L. Marshall, "Outside the Box: Architect Charles Haertling Left a Controversial Organic Footprint on House Design in Boulder," *Rocky Mountain News*, January 19, 2008. Retrieved from http://infoweb.newsbank.com/resources/doc/nb/news/11E52A8545D9C5B0?p=AWNB.
2 Esther McCoy, "Young Architects in the United States," *Zodiac* 8 (January 1961): 168.
3 These buildings were recognized and admired in the decades following their construction and still generate controversy today. The Brenton House, also known as the Mushroom House, featured briefly in Woody Allen's 1973 movie *Sleeper*.
4 Boulder Public Library Archives; Boulder Public Library Carnegie Branch for Local History; and Western History Collection, Denver Public Library.
5 Conversations with Joel Haertling (several live and by telephone); telephone conversation with Viola Haertling, May 27, 2016; e-mail exchanges with Barbara Sieckman, June 19, 2015, and with Russ Skillings, June 4, 2015 and May 14, 2016.

6 Bernadette Hanlon, *Once the American Dream: Inner-Ring Suburbs of the Metropolitan United States* (Philadelphia, PA: Temple University Press, 2009), 1.

7 Ibid., 3.

8 Forty percent of homes sold between 1947 and 1957 were financed by FHA and Veterans Administration loans: G. Scott Thomas, *The United States of Suburbia: How the Suburbs Took Control of America and What They Plan to Do with It* (Amherst, NY: Prometheus, 1998), 37.

9 Ibid., 37–38.

10 Kathleen A. Tobin, "The Reduction of Urban Vulnerability: Revisiting 1950's American Suburbanization as Civil Defence," *Cold War History* 2, no. 2 (January 2002): 2, http://dx.doi.org/10.1080/71399949.

11 Ibid., 4.

12 Jay M. Price, *Temples for a Modern God: Religious Architecture in Post-war America* (Oxford: Oxford University Press, 2013), 51, https://doi.org/10.1093/acprof:oso/9780199925957.001.0001.

13 Ibid., 87.

14 "History," City of Northglenn, accessed June 5, 2017, www.northglenn.org/history.

15 Jared Jacand Maher, "Change of Plans," *Westword*, November 30, 2006, accessed June 14, 2016, www.westword.com/news/change-of-plans-5091132.

16 "History," *City of Northglenn*, accessed December 12, 2016, www.northglenn.org/history.

17 "Standard Form of Agreement Between Owner and Architect," Papers of Charles Haertling, Boulder Public Library Archives.

18 Letter from Robert Beard to Robert Krass, Board of American Missions, Division of Church Extensions, New York, New York, August 9, 1962; Papers of Charles Haertling, Boulder Public Library Archives.

19 Letter from Robert Beard, August 9, 1962.

20 Ibid.

21 Ibid.; original emphasis.

22 "Preliminary Study Proposal," Papers of Charles Haertling, Boulder Public Library Archives.

23 Marshall, "Outside the Box."

24 In 1952, he met his future wife Viola Brase in the basement of Grace Lutheran Church in Boulder.

25 "Registration Form," *The Creative Parish*, Papers of Charles Haertling, Boulder Public Library Archives.

26 Mimi Zeiger, "We Love [Charles] Haertling," *Dwell* 8, no. 8 (July 2008): 112.

27 "Charles Haertling, Architecture," Western History Collection, Denver Public Library.

28 Wes French, "Exciting Church Design Urged," *Rocky Mountain News*, March 14, 1965, 48.

29 Ibid.

30 "'Tusk' Beams Support Roof," *Denver Post*, January 22, 1964.

31 Zeiger, "We Love Haertling," 116.

32 Thomas J. Noel, *Buildings of Colorado* (Oxford: Oxford University Press, 1997), 122.

33 French, "Exciting Church Design Urged," 48.

34 Noel, *Buildings of Colorado*, 122.

35 As Interstate 25 was then called.

36 Boulder Public Library Carnegie Branch for Local History, Boulder, Colorado, #706-4-9.

37 Preliminary plan (sketch), Papers of Charles Haertling, Boulder Public Library Archives.

38 "St. Stephens Lutheran Church, Northglenn Architectural Drawings, 1963," Boulder Public Library Carnegie Branch for Local History, Boulder, Colorado.

39 "'Tusk' Beams Support Roof."

40 Joel Haertling, *Design Process of Charles A. Haertling, Architect*, 8mm silent film, 66:00, 1990, accessed June 16, 2015, www.youtube.com/watch?v=lHo5uuWxqz0.

41 Ibid., 0:35–0:50.

42 Barbara Sieckman, email to the author, May 5, 2016.

43 Patricia Calhoun, "Denver Earthquakes 40 Years Ago Were Caused by Uncle Sam, Not Mother Nature," *Westword*, para. 7, accessed June 11, 2015, www.westword.com/news/denver-earthquakes-40-years-ago-were-caused-by-uncle-sam-not-mother-nature-5833488

44 J. H. Healy, W. W. Rubey, D. T. Griggs, and C. B. Raleigh, "The Denver Earthquakes," *Science* 161, no. 3848 (September 27, 1968): 1301, doi:10.1126/science.161.3848.

45 Ibid.

46 Ibid.

47 Calhoun, "Denver Earthquakes," para. 7.

48 Healy et al., "Denver Earthquakes," 1309.

49 Calhoun, "Denver Earthquakes," para. 11.

50 As shown in an undocumented, misidentified photograph of the time, accessed December 10, 2015, www.dailykos.com/story/2011/08/24/1010130/-I-Experienced-a-Man-Made-Quake-in-1967-Caused-by-Fluid-Injection-in-a-Chemical-Weapons-Facility-Well.

51 Architect and historian Alan Hess writes, "[t]he freedom to explore new forms, varied images, free-flowing spaces, and new materials marked the course of Organic design. This resulted in an astonishing range of forms and plans, of aesthetics and attitudes": Alan Hess and Alan Weintraub, *Organic Architecture: The Other Modernism* (Layton, UT: Gibbs Smith, 2006), 81. The very vagueness of the "definition" of organic modernism reflects the stylistic energy, imagination, and plasticity of its structures.

52 Hess and Weintraub, *Organic Architecture*, 77.

53 French, "Exciting Church Design Urged," 48.

54 Meredith L. Clausen, *Spiritual space: the religious architecture of Pietro Belluschi* (Seattle, WA: University of Washington Press, 1992), 21.

55 Price, *Temples for a Modern God*, 121.

56 Ibid., 127.

57 Ibid., 130.

58 Ibid., 133.

59 Ibid., 134.

60 Joseph Pichard, *Modern Church Architecture* (New York, NY: Orion Press, 1960), 9.

61 Ibid., 34.

62 Michael Joseph Gibson, "Creating Sacred Spaces in the Suburbs: Roman Catholic Church Architecture in Post-war Southern California" (M.A. thesis, University of Southern California, 2009), 58.

63 Peter G. Cobb, "The Architectural Setting of the Liturgy." In Cheslyn Jones et al., eds. *The Study of Liturgy* (New York, NY: Oxford University Press, 1978), 528–542.

64 Gibson, "Creating Sacred Spaces in the Suburbs," 63.

65 Gretchen Buggeln, "The Shape of a New Era: Valparaiso's Chapel of the Resurrection in Historical Context," *The Cresset* LXXIII, No. 3, para. 3 (2010), accessed May 26, 2016, http://thecresset.org/2010/Lent/Buggeln_L10.html#_.

66 Ibid.

67 Mark A. Torgerson, *An Architecture of Immanence: Architecture for Worship and Ministry Today* (Grand Rapids, MI: William. B. Eerdmans Pub. Co., 2007), 92.

68 Victoria M. Young, *Saint John's Abbey Church: Marcel Breuer and the Creation of a Modern Sacred Space* (Minneapolis, MN: University of Minnesota Press, 2014), 33.

69 Hess and Weintraub, *Organic Architecture*, 76.

70 Torgerson, *An Architecture of Immanence*, 48.

71 Hess and Weintraub, *Organic Architecture*, 76.

72 French, "Exciting Church Design Urged," 48.

73 Price, *Temples for a Modern God*, 59.

74 A number of Saarinen's secular structures display sculptural roofs as well: the TWA terminal in New York City (1962) being perhaps the most well-known; and his Gateway Arch in St. Louis, Missouri, could be considered all roof.

75 Price, *Temples for a Modern God*, 136.

76 Pichard, *Modern Church Architecture*, 74.

77 Hess and Weintraub, *Organic Architecture*, 76.

78 Ibid., 77.

79 Clausen, *Spiritual Space: The Religious Architecture of Pietro Belluschi*, 21.

80 Hess and Weintraub, *Organic Architecture*, 77.

81 Ibid., 77.

82 Clausen, *Spiritual Space*, 22.

83 Boulder Public Library Carnegie Branch for Local History, #706-4-9.

84 At the time, the largest such structure in the United States: Tyler S. Sprague, "'Beauty, Versatility, Practicality': The Rise of Hyperbolic Paraboloids in Post-war America," *Construction History 28*, no. 1 (2013): 178, http://du.idm.oclc.org/login?url=http://search.proquest.com/docview/16642 43087?accountid=14608.

85 Ibid.
86 Although the Church of the Risen Christ (James Sudler), nicknamed "Ski Jesus," or "the Ski Jump," which looks like a ski jump, wasn't built until 1969.
87 Robert Osserman, "How the Gateway Arch Got its Shape," *Nexus Network Journal* 12, no. 2 (2010): 167.
88 Expressed in the sixteenth century by Galileo and defined in the seventeenth century by a number of mathematicians.
89 The 1962 Seattle World's Fair (the Century 21 Exposition) was replete with paraboloid roof structures (including Paul Thiry's Washington State Coliseum and Minoru Yamasaki's Science Pavilion), suggesting the forms were exploited as symbols of the future.
90 Haertling, *Design Process of Charles A. Haertling* (film), 9:25.
91 Letter from Robert Beard to Robert Krass, Board of American Missions, Division of Church Extension, New York, NY; Papers of Charles Haertling, Boulder Public Library Archives.
92 Elizabeth Candelario, *Northglenn* (Charleston, SC: Arcadia Publishing, 2013), 63–70.
93 Price, *Temples for a Modern God*, 182.
94 Ibid., 175.
95 Sheba Wheeler, "Seeking Salvation: Too Modern to be Historic, Boulder's First Christian Church Faces Demolition. Preservationists Want to Save It and Others," *Denver Post*, July 2, 2006, accessed June 23, 2015, http://search.proquest.com/docview/410834504?accountid=14608.
96 Ibid., 184.

References

Buggeln, Gretchen. "The Shape of a New Era: Valparaiso's Chapel of the Resurrection in Historical Context," *The Cresset* LXXIII, no. 3 (2010): 6–14. Accessed May 26, 2016, http://thecresset.org/2010/Lent/Buggeln_L10.html#_.

Calhoun, Patricia. "Denver Earthquakes 40 Years Ago Were Caused by Uncle Sam, Not Mother Nature," *Westword*, August 24, 2011. Accessed June 11, 2015, www.westword.com/news/denver-earthquakes-40-years-ago-were-caused-by-uncle-sam-not-mother-nature-5833488.

Candelario, Elizabeth. *Northglenn* (Charleston, SC: Arcadia Publishing, 2013).

City of Northglenn. "History." Accessed June 5, 2017, www.northglenn.org/history.

Clausen, Meredith L. *Spiritual Space: The Religious Architecture of Pietro Belluschi* (Seattle, WA: University of Washington Press, 1992).

Cobb, Peter G. "The Architectural Setting of the Liturgy." In Cheslyn Jones, Geoffrey Wainwright, and Edward Yarnold, eds. *The Study of Liturgy*, 528–542 (New York, NY: Oxford University Press, 1978).

French, Wes. "Exciting Church Design Urged," *Rocky Mountain News*, March 14, 1965.

Gibson, Michael Joseph. "Creating Sacred Spaces in the Suburbs: Roman Catholic Church Architecture in Post-war Southern California." M.A. thesis, University of Southern California, 2009.

Haertling, Joel. *Design Process of Charles A Haertling, Architect*, 8mm silent film, 66:00, 1990. Accessed on June 16, 2015, www.youtube.com/watch?v=lHo5uuWxqz0.

Hanlon, Bernadette. *Once the American Dream: Inner-Ring Suburbs of the Metropolitan United States* (Philadelphia, PA: Temple University Press, 2009).

Healy, J. H., W. W. Rubey, D. T. Griggs, and C. B. Raleigh. "The Denver Earthquakes," *Science* 161, no. 3848 (September 27, 1968): 1301–10. doi:10.1126/science.161.3848.1301.

Hess, Alan, and Alan Weintraub. *Organic Architecture: the Other Modernism* (Layton, UT: Gibbs Smith, 2006).

Maher, Jared Jacand. "Change of Plans," *Westword*, November 30, 2006. Accessed on June 14, 2016, www.westword.com/news/change-of-plans-5091132.

Marshall, L. "Outside the Box: Architect Charles Haertling Left a Controversial Organic Footprint on House Design in Boulder," *Rocky Mountain News*, January 19, 2008. Retrieved from http://infoweb.newsbank.com/resources/doc/nb/news/11E52A8545D9C5B0?p=AWNB.

McCoy, Esther. "Young Architects in the United States," *Zodiac* 8 (January 1961): 168–185.

Noel, Thomas J. *Buildings of Colorado* (Oxford: Oxford University Press, 1997).

Osserman, Robert. "How the Gateway Arch Got its Shape," *Nexus Network Journal* 12, no. 2 (2010): 167–189.

Pichard, Joseph. *Modern Church Architecture* (New York, NY: Orion Press, 1960).

Price, Jay M. *Temples for a Modern God: Religious Architecture in Post-war America* (Oxford: Oxford University Press, 2013).

Sprague, Tyler. S. "'Beauty, Versatility, Practicality': The Rise of Hyperbolic Paraboloids in Post-war America," *Construction History* 28, no. 1 (2013): 165–184, http://du.idm.oclc.org/login?url=http://search.proquest.com/docview/1664243087?accountid=14608.

Thomas, G. Scott. *The United States of Suburbia: How the Suburbs Took Control of America and What They Plan to Do with It* (Amherst, NY: Prometheus, 1998).

Tobin, Kathleen A. "The Reduction of Urban Vulnerability: Revisiting 1950's American Suburbanization as Civil Defence," *Cold War History* 2, no. 2 (January 2002): 1–32, http://dx.doi.org/10.1080/713999049.

Torgerson, Mark A. *An Architecture of Immanence: Architecture for Worship and Ministry Today* (Grand Rapids, MI: William. B. Eerdmans Pub. Co., 2007).

"'Tusk' Beams Support Roof," *Denver Post*, January 22, 1964.

Wheeler, Sheba. "Seeking Salvation to Modern to be Historic, Boulder's First Christian Church Faces Demolition. Preservationists Want to Save It and Others," *Denver Post*. July 2, 2006. Accessed June 23, 2015, http://search.proquest.com/docview/410834504?accountid=14608.

Young, Victoria M. *Saint John's Abbey Church: Marcel Breuer and the Creation of a Modern Sacred Space* (Minneapolis, MN: University of Minnesota Press, 2014).

Zeiger, Mimi. "We Love [Charles] Haertling," *Dwell* 8, no. 8 (July 2008): 112–118.

7

A MONUMENTAL ABSENCE

Paul Rudolph's Christian Science Building, 1965 (demolished 1986)

Scott Murray

In 1962, the Christian Science Organization at the University of Illinois commissioned one of America's best-known architects to design a new building in Champaign, Illinois, with spaces for religious study, meetings, and ceremonies. When he began the design, Paul Rudolph was still a relatively young architect at 44 years of age, but he had already achieved professional prominence.[1] He had completed more than forty built projects and was in the fourth year of his seven-year tenure as chair of the Department of Architecture at Yale University.[2] As Timothy Rohan writes in his monograph, *The Architecture of Paul Rudolph*: "In the firmament of post-World War II American architecture, few stars shone brighter than Paul Rudolph's."[3] Robert A. M. Stern claims Rudolph "possessed the greatest talent of his generation of American architects."[4] By the time construction of the Christian Science Building[5] was completed in 1965, Rudolph had resigned his position at Yale and moved his office permanently to New York City to focus on his rapidly expanding practice.[6]

Despite its architect's renown, the Christian Science Building existed for only twenty years until it was demolished. At the time of its destruction in 1986, a postmodernist critique of Rudolph's brand of modernism was ascendant within the discipline, and Rudolph's practice and reputation had significantly declined. He had, in fact, virtually disappeared from the architectural scene.[7] Thus, the demolition of the Christian Science Building after just two decades echoed Rudolph's professional fall from grace and the diminishing influence of his work. Today, however, a resurgent interest in mid-twentieth-century modernism in general, and in Rudolph's work in particular, calls for a re-examination of his now obscure but still striking design of the Christian Science Building (Fig. 7.1).[8]

The Christian Science Building (1965) was designed at a pivotal time in Rudolph's career. The project represents a critical link between the architect's engagement with the monumental scale of his institutional buildings of the 1960s and the more intimate scale of his residential work of the 1940s and '50s. The project deployed a pinwheel plan anchoring a corner site, signature walls of vertically corrugated concrete exposed inside and out, and sectional variety in interior spaces. As such, the Christian Science Building shared several defining characteristics with Rudolph's perhaps best-known work, the much larger Art & Architecture Building at Yale (completed in 1963).

FIGURE 7.1 Christian Science Building, Champaign, Illinois, exterior.

HB-29509-Q, Chicago History Museum, Hedrich-Blessing Collection.

One of only a few religious buildings that Rudolph completed during his extensive career, the Christian Science Building was an important example of mid-century modern sacred architecture. Today, thirty years after its untimely demise, the building remains one of Rudolph's lesser-known works, often excluded from discussions of his œuvre, likely due to its small scale and short lifespan.[9] This chapter attempts to address this oversight by examining

Rudolph's design and the circumstances surrounding its commission, construction, and eventual demolition. In addition, it illustrates the design's relationship to both Christian Science architecture and the modernist ethos that shaped Rudolph's work during that era.

The background of the Christian Science Building project

Rudolph's concept for the design was concisely articulated in a letter he wrote in December 1968, three years after the building's completion, in response to two architecture students at the University of Illinois. They had asked him about his design process for the Christian Science Building and his assessment of the completed project. In his reply, Rudolph provides a direct statement of his primary objectives and a frank appraisal of its relative success:

> The building is scaleless, attempts to turn the corner, reads as a series of planes rather than a linear composition . . . [it] is purposely many charactered on the inside, although it can be opened up to form almost one continuous space, subjugates clarity of structure for spatial variety, and depends on the introduction of lighting and color for its effect. In many ways the intentions are not carried out successfully, and in other ways they seem to me more successful than I had dreamed, but this is for you to decide.[10]

From this description emerges a set of principles that were at the forefront of Rudolph's thinking at the time and became evident in several of his 1960s projects. Chief among these were the manipulation of perceived scale, the creation of internal spatial variety, and the symbolic importance of natural light. In addition, Rudolph explained his design as an attempt to engage what he called the psychological and emotional aspects of architectural space.

Although the building was comparatively small-scaled among the much larger and higher-profile institutional commissions in Rudolph's growing portfolio, it garnered positive critical reaction upon its completion. It was featured, for example, on the cover of *Architectural Record* in February 1967. In an interview conducted in 1986—one month before the demolition of the Christian Science Building and shortly after he had revisited the University of Illinois[11]—Rudolph said of this project: "I feel it's one of the more successful of my buildings."[12] Recalling its design and construction in the 1960s, he elaborated: "At that time I liked the building, and I still like it, which I can't say about all my buildings. I will be unhappy if it's demolished but I'm not in control of that."[13] After only two decades in use, the fate of the building had indeed taken a dramatic turn. The original owners moved out and sold the property to a developer who demolished the building to construct an unremarkable apartment complex in its place.

The commission and the client

An article published on October 12, 1965, in the University of Illinois student newspaper, *The Daily Illini*, announced the imminent opening of the campus's new Christian Science Building. The article also reveals an interesting fact not subsequently recounted in publications about the building: the first architect commissioned to design the building was not Paul Rudolph, but Frank Lloyd Wright.[14] The 91-year-old Wright was first contacted about designing the building during what turned out to be the final months of his life. The archives of Wright's correspondence include several letters exchanged in 1958 and 1959 between Nancy Houston, who served as advisor to the Christian Science Organization at the University of Illinois and Director of its Building Trustees, and the office of Frank Lloyd Wright.[15] Houston first wrote to the architect about the Christian Science Building project in September 1958, following up a month later with an offer to drive to Wright's office at Taliesin in Spring Green, Wisconsin, to discuss it in person. It is not clear to what extent Wright began designing the project before he died on April 9, 1959.[16] However, a letter from Houston to Wright on January 19, 1959, indicates that they had discussed the site and that Houston was preparing to send site surveys and photos to Wright for his use in the design process.

Nancy Houston may have sought out Wright based on his recent involvement with other Christian Science congregations. Wright designed unbuilt projects for a Christian Science Reading Room in Riverside, Illinois (1954), and a Christian Science Church in Bolinas, California (1956).[17] Although Wright's death in 1959 ended the Champaign project in its earliest phase, it is evident that Houston's intention from the beginning was to engage a prominent architect at the forefront of American modernism.[18] It is further reported in *The Daily Illini* article that after Wright's death, the suggestion to commission Paul Rudolph came from David Hanser, a church member who was also an architecture student at the University of Illinois. Hanser, who later became a professor of architectural history at Oklahoma State University, recently confirmed that he did in fact suggest to Houston that Rudolph be selected as the architect for the project.[19] Hanser recalls that approximately ten architects were under consideration for the job, including Philip Johnson and A. Richard Williams (then a professor at the University of Illinois). Apparently Houston, who was responsible for overseeing the building project, compiled research on each architect's recent work and sought input from students before finally offering the commission to Rudolph. It was also noted in *Inland Architect* that Rudolph won the commission "because he was felt to be sensitive to the needs and interests of young people."[20] One may speculate that the prior involvement, however brief, of Frank Lloyd Wright Wright—whom Rudolph considered the greatest American architect[21]—may have attracted Rudolph to the project and influenced his decision to accept this relatively small commission.

The working relationship between Paul Rudolph and Nancy Houston, as architect and client, appears to have been mutually satisfactory and enriching. In a later interview, Rudolph referred to Houston as "really quite a remarkable woman" whom he greatly respected.[22] He continued: "As a client she was marvelous because she understood why I thought something should be done," and "it's not everyone who takes that attitude." Although the architect-client relationship can sometimes be confrontational due to tensions over budget and schedule, especially when out-of-the-ordinary design or construction concepts are proposed, Rudolph clearly saw Houston as an ally in the process. Houston must have likewise enjoyed the collaboration with Rudolph, as in 1975 she hired him again, this time to design a house for her in Westerly, Rhode Island.[23] Following completion of the Christian Science Building, Houston remained an advisor there until 1972, when she became a member of the Christian Science Board of Lectureship, traveling widely to lecture on the Church's teachings in the United States, Europe, and Africa.[24] As the person in charge of overseeing the procurement of the new Christian Science Building in Champaign, Nancy Houston appears emblematic of the prominent position of women in the governance of the Christian Science Church throughout its history, dating back to its founder Mary Baker Eddy, whom Houston greatly admired.[25] Writing about the early development of the Christian Science denomination, founded in 1879, the historian Paul Eli Ivey specifically notes that leadership roles in the construction of new branch church buildings were often fulfilled by women.[26] He notes that an "attraction of Christian Science to women was the opportunity to have a real say in the designs and features of church buildings."[27] The successful completion of a nationally recognized Christian Science facility in Champaign can be attributed to Houston's leadership and tenacity, as was acknowledged and appreciated by the architect.[28]

The building

Construction of the Christian Science Building on the campus of the University of Illinois at Urbana-Champaign began in October 1964, and the building opened for use in October 1965 (Fig. 7.2). The reported budget of $150,000 was funded by private donations.[29] Rudolph's office worked with Champaign-based Delbert R. Smith as the local Architect of Record, and the Felmley-Dickerson Company served as contractor.[30] The new building occupied the northwest corner at the intersection of Fourth Street and Gregory Drive in Champaign, Illinois. It replaced two existing wood-framed houses that were demolished (one of which had previously been used as the meeting location for the Christian Science Organization). The two residential lots were consolidated to create one site measuring 109

FIGURE 7.2   Christian Science Building, exterior.
HB-29509-A, Chicago History Museum, Hedrich-Blessing Collection.

by 115 feet.[31] The floor area of the new building totaled 5,630 square feet, distributed on two main levels.[32] The primary structure consisted of load-bearing walls and foundations of cast-in-place reinforced concrete, with floors and roofs of plywood over exposed wood beams and joists.

The building was designed as a composition of interlocking rectangular spaces of various sizes, united by a common material palette of exposed concrete, painted wood, and glass. The program included spaces for religious study, services, and meetings, for an organization comprising 150 Christian Science students at the university and other local residents.[33] The ground level included a lobby, reception area, large meeting room, study room, small kitchen, and lounge (Fig. 7.3). The upper level included committee rooms, restrooms, and a private studio apartment for a staff member (Fig. 7.4). A pair of staircases, one internal and one external, linked the two levels. The minimal grounds surrounding the building accommodated plantings of trees and lawn. Two outdoor paved courtyards were formed by low garden walls on the north and south sides, with a compact arrangement of nine parking spaces on the west side.

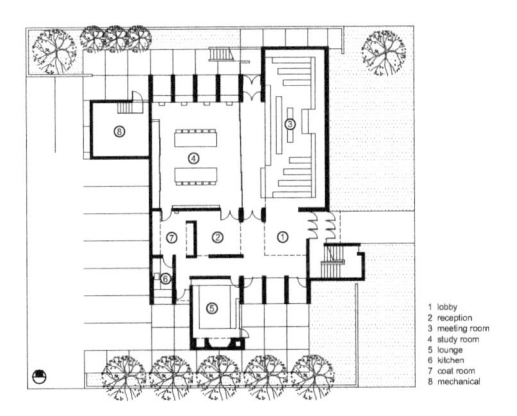

1 lobby
2 reception
3 meeting room
4 study room
5 lounge
6 kitchen
7 coat room
8 mechanical

FIGURE 7.3 Christian Science Building, ground floor plan.

Drawing by author based on construction documents in the Paul Marvin Rudolph Archive, Library of Congress.

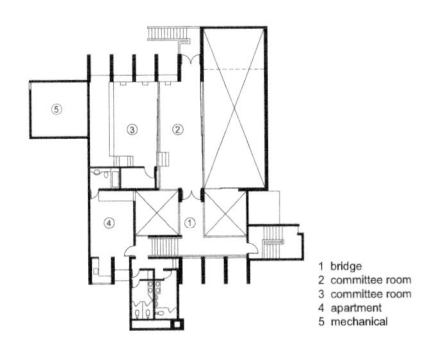

1 bridge
2 committee room
3 committee room
4 apartment
5 mechanical

FIGURE 7.4 Christian Science Building, upper floor plan.

Drawing by author based on construction documents in the Paul Marvin Rudolph Archive, Library of Congress.

FIGURE 7.5 Christian Science Building, section-perspective drawing.

Paul Rudolph Archive, Library of Congress, Prints & Photographs Division, PMR–2120.

The key to understanding Rudolph's design lies in grasping the intricate spatial variations of the interior (Fig. 7.5). Although it may generally be described as a two-story building, the actual volumetric arrangement of the building was far more complex than that. In fact, there were seven distinct floor levels within the building, and ceilings heights varied from just over 7 feet to 42 feet.[34] On the ground level, the meeting room and lounge were recessed 12 inches below the entry elevation, while on the upper level, the committee work room comprised three platforms, stepping up 2 feet and then 4 feet. The rest rooms and apartment were raised 6 feet from the main second level.[35] Skylights and clerestory windows, oriented in different directions, were positioned within three periscope-like "towers," as Rudolph's drawings refer to them, with various roof heights. These towers transmitted natural light—ranging from subtle to dramatic in quality—down through the multi-height spaces to create a variety of experiential conditions throughout the day. They also included planters near the ceiling, from which vines dangled downward into the spaces. Dynamic daylighting effects heightened the sense of movement induced by interior spatial volumes connected one to the next, both horizontally and vertically, a manifestation of Rudolph's belief that "space flows much in the manner of water from one volume to another."[36]

As shown in Figures 7.3 and 7.4, upon entering the building through the vestibule on the east façade, beneath a cantilevered canopy 7 feet, 4 inches above the floor, a visitor would arrive in the lobby, with a ceiling height of 15 feet. To the left was the main interior stair, leading to the upper levels. Above this stair was the first clerestory tower, rising to a height of 35 feet. Straight ahead was the reception area, naturally lit from above by a clerestory tower 42 feet high, and a coatroom. To the left was a lounge, with its floor recessed two steps down, surrounded by built-in seating and a fireplace. Beyond that was a small kitchen. Turning to the right, one would enter the largest space of the building, the meeting room, fitted with bench-style pews, where services and lectures were held.[37] Here the ceiling was 22 feet high, extending to 35 feet at the north end, where the third tower was positioned. The concrete walls of this space contained no windows, giving it an inward focus, yet the room was bathed in natural light from above. A linear skylight was positioned along the east wall in addition to the clerestory windows at the north tower. To the west of this space were two committee rooms, each separated from the meeting room by movable partitions, which could slide aside to connect all three spaces. Thus the meeting room could be transformed into a much larger auditorium-like space. On the upper level, a circulation bridge connected the stair to the committee workrooms. Low railings along the bridge and additional sliding partitions at the work rooms made it possible for the upper level to serve as a balcony for the double-height meeting room below (Fig. 7.6).

The monochromatic aesthetic of the building's concrete exterior was contrasted by a colorful interior. Exposed wood joists and ceiling panels were painted in vivid hues of orange and magenta, and bright carpets covered the floors.[38] Most of the furniture and light fixtures, designed by Rudolph, were similarly colorful. When asked why the interior colors were so vivid, Rudolph replied: "My father, who was a Southern Methodist minister, had his effect on me with regard to religious matters. I thought, as reaction, that religion should have some joyfulness in it."[39] Artwork was also integrated in the building in two discrete locations. The three main entrance doors, made of brass and weighing over 200 pounds each, featured an abstract relief created by sculptor Roger Majorowicz, who taught in the art school at the University of Illinois. And prominently placed on a wall in the reception area, beneath a clerestory window, was a bronze-relief portrait of Mary Baker Eddy, founder of the Christian Science Church.

FIGURE 7.6 Christian Science Building, upper-level interior.

HB-29509-J, Chicago History Museum, Hedrich-Blessing Collection.

In designing the public assembly spaces of the building, Rudolph considered the need for flexibility resulting from the changing day-to-day occupancy conditions inherent to a religious facility. He said that "many religious groups need to have the intimacy of not very many people being there, making that seem okay, and then on special days having a lot of people."[40] The main spaces of the building—the meeting room, the study room, and the committee rooms—could each function independently, but could also be combined into one communal space through the operation of more than 80 linear feet of sliding partitions. The pews of the meeting room would normally seat 75 people, but by opening the adjacent spaces on both levels and arranging movable chairs, in less than an hour's set-up time, up to 350 could be accommodated for larger events.[41] Despite this attention to the flexibility of spaces, an argument of inflexibility to other uses would later be used as a justification for demolishing the building.

Concrete and form

From the exterior, the building had a monumental presence, suggesting solidity and permanence, which Rudolph deemed appropriate for a religious program. The form embodied an assemblage of interlocking cubic volumes and planar elements united by a singular material:

cast-in-place concrete. The varied and dynamic profiles of the building form exploited the plasticity of poured concrete. But the presiding aesthetic of the building's exterior derives not just from the prominent use of concrete but also from the extensive treatment of its surface with vertically striated ridges. Rudolph often referred to this as "corrugated concrete," and published descriptions also called it corduroy, textured, or grooved concrete.[42] A purely ornamental feature, the finely corrugated surface would simultaneously catch and reflect sunlight while casting shadows upon itself. The effect was achieved by pouring concrete in corrugated forms, and then, after the concrete cured and formwork was removed, the resulting ridges of concrete were bush-hammered by hand. This chiseling action exposed the aggregate and created irregularly angled facets that would reflect sunlight in different directions. It is worth quoting Rudolph at length as he describes this technique, which he first employed at Yale's Art & Architecture Building, then at the Christian Science Building and several other projects:

> The nature of concrete and its lack of weathering capability . . . led me to corrugated forming systems, which allowed the forwardmost edges of the concrete to be broken away, thereby exposing the aggregate with its multitudinous beautiful colors. The stain of the concrete was contained within the grooves, whereas the leading edges were constantly washed by the rain. It broke down the scale of the walls and caught the light in many different ways . . . Light was fractured in a thousand ways and the sense of depth was increased. As the light changed the walls seemingly quivered, dematerialized, took on additional solidity.[43]

Rudolph said that he was fascinated by architectural scale and how it is perceived, and he described the Christian Science Building's exterior as "purposely scaleless"[44] (Fig. 7.7). He designed it to be read as many different sizes in response to the wide range of scales embodied by existing buildings within the site's immediate context. Across Fourth Street from the building site was the University's Armory (a massive fieldhouse), while to the west was a residential neighborhood of detached houses. To enable an ambiguity of scale, components which typically convey a sense of scale, such as doors and stairs, were recessed

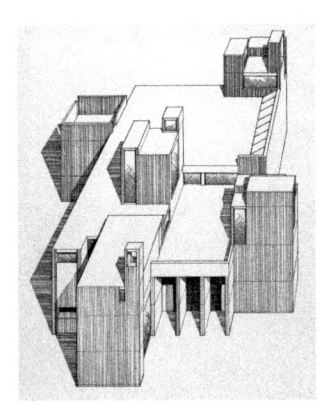

FIGURE 7.7 Christian Science Building, axonometric drawing.

Paul Rudolph Archive, Library of Congress, Prints & Photographs Division, PMR-2120.

and de-emphasized. The simple material palette of finely corrugated concrete surfaces was also intentionally devoid of recognizable scale as compared to unit materials like brick or concrete block, for instance.[45] Although the horizontal joint lines in the concrete walls implied floor levels, the two-story building appeared from different viewpoints as having three or even four levels, thanks to the multiple clerestory towers that extend a full story above the main roof level. Rudolph acknowledged that the space inside the upper portion of these towers, which contained no usable floors, could be considered by some as "wasted space."[46] However, he argued that such space was important "because it nourishes the subconscious,"[47] particularly so in the Christian Science Building because the towers were a primary source of natural light.

In several ways, Rudolph's design for the Christian Science Building can be seen as reflective of a critique of modernism that he began articulating in the 1950s. Rudolph wrote in 1958 that "the essential element in architecture is the manipulation of space," but that "modern architecture is tragically lacking in eloquent space concepts."[48] He challenged architects to create "different kinds of space—quiet, enclosed space; hustling, bustling space pungent with vitality . . . vast, sumptuous, even awe-inspiring space; mysterious space; and transitional space which defines and separates yet joins juxtaposed spaces of contrasting character."[49] He believed that architecture should celebrate the richness and complexity of life.[50] Within the

FIGURE 7.8 Christian Science Building, central tower interior.

HB-29509-H, Chicago History Museum, Hedrich-Blessing Collection.

relatively compact footprint of the Christian Science Center, Rudolph designed a complex set of interlocking spaces of varying dimensions in plan and section. The design conveys his interest in dynamic volumes, or "space which has a thrust horizontally and vertically," resulting in the pinwheel plan in which "each wing has strong horizontal thrust around a vertical thrust."[51] Rudolph identified another of "modern architecture's greatest failings" as "its lack of interest in the relationship of the building to the sky."[52] This concern is addressed in the design by the verticality of the building's tower elements, which extend upward from the main mass of the building. The towers' dual purpose is to open the interior spaces to daylight from above and to create a symbolic gesture upwards toward the heavens, also a common feature in the tradition of earlier Christian Science architecture (Fig. 7.8).

The Christian Science architectural tradition

Rudolph's Christian Science Building design was clearly related in its form and materiality to other Rudolph projects of the era (most notably the Art & Architecture Building at Yale), and he never articulated a direct relationship between his design and the principles of Christian Science.[53] Still, the building can be read as a modern re-interpretation or abstraction of certain distinguishing characteristics of the architecture of earlier Christian Science churches.

The construction of new churches was an important part of the rapid growth and expansion of the Church of Christ, Scientist, as it was officially named, in the decades following its founding in Massachusetts in 1879. The founders of this new Protestant denomination promoted an understanding of the Christian faith rooted in the healing power of spirituality.[54] They believed that comprehension of spiritual laws could heal the sick and redeem the sinner, and that the teachings of Jesus could reveal a method of healing that was at once spiritual and scientific. They also came to view the construction of churches as an important means of attracting members and providing a public face for the new denomination. Within 15 years of its founding, their first large-scale purpose-built edifice was completed: the First Church of Christ, Scientist (also referred to by members as the Mother Church) in Boston in 1894. It was designed by Franklin Welch, with a major addition in 1906 by Solon Beman. The Christian Science denomination grew rapidly: there were about 250 branch organizations in 1895, and by 1910 this number had grown to approximately 1,100.[55] To accommodate its popularity (membership was estimated at 300,000 by 1912), new branch churches were built across the United States, eventually expanding overseas as well. The Christian Science building boom of the early twentieth century attracted the attention of architects and builders; it was not uncommon to have up to 15 architects competing for the commission to design a branch church.[56]

The early churches were often designed in Romanesque, Gothic-revival, or Classical styles, lacking a coherent aesthetic. Church-founder Mary Baker Eddy expressed a preference for buildings that clearly conveyed their purpose for religious worship, that presented a traditional outward appearance, and that included tower elements "pointing heavenward."[57] Stone façades predominated, which contributed to a perception of "substantiality and permanency" that became an important and desired attribute of Christian Science church buildings, perhaps in reaction to the relative newness of the denomination.[58] And the symbolic importance of light—nearly universal across many religions—was likewise a common interior feature in Christian Science buildings. But the central leadership of the Church in Boston did not dictate how branch churches should be designed or built; those decisions were left to the local congregations. This allowed for regional differences and the occasional emergence of a forward-looking and even modernist approach in some locations, particularly in California. A prime example is Bernard Maybeck's First Church of Christ, Scientist, in Berkeley, completed in 1911 and now a National Historic Landmark. Far from the textbook classicism of other early Christian Science churches, Maybeck's design is an eclectic composition incorporating reinforced concrete, industrial steel-sash windows, and exposed heavy-timber beams. The critic Allan Temko wrote that Maybeck's church showed how "the new architecture of the technological age . . . could use functionalist aesthetics and industrial materials . . . to express deep spiritual meanings for modern society."[59] Another key modernist example is Maynard Lyndon's 1955 design for the Twenty-eighth Church of Christ, Scientist, in Los Angeles, which features a distinctive curved concrete wall perforated by a grid of small, circular apertures. The history of Christian Science architecture also includes notable unbuilt church projects in the modernist vein, such as Eliel Saarinen's 1925 proposal for Minneapolis, and Frank Lloyd Wright's 1956 proposal for Bolinas, California.

Paul Eli Ivey describes the typical characteristics of the denomination's branch churches of the late nineteenth and early twentieth century as presenting a heavy, authoritative exterior contrasted by a comfortable, light-filled interior.[60] Without reference to the historically derivative styling of the early churches, this depiction of architectural character also aligns with Rudolph's design—as does Temko's description of Bernard Maybeck's materiality noted before. The dominant exterior element of Rudolph's building was of course its massive cast-in-place concrete walls (once likened to "a medieval fortress"[61]), with clerestory towers reaching skyward to transmit natural light to the interior spaces. This light would wash the concrete walls and reflect off brightly painted wood surfaces, infusing the interior spaces with constantly shifting light throughout the day. Rudolph believed in a concept he termed "the humanism of reflected light,"[62] which he described as a connection created between a building's interior surfaces and its occupants through reflected light. This became a central feature of the Christian Science Building.

It may be assumed that for Rudolph, then, the design was focused not on an interpretation of the specific tenets of the Christian Science denomination, but rather more generally on the spiritual dimensions of a space for religious contemplation. Rudolph's architecture is not characterized by explicit historic references (as the earliest Christian Science branches were), but nevertheless he did claim to be influenced by traditional architecture, much more so than by modern architecture.[63] He attributed this to his interest in "feeling and understanding," which he found abundant in traditional architecture but lacking in most modern architecture, aside from the work of two architects he admired: Frank Lloyd Wright and Le Corbusier.[64] The architectural historians Lydia Soo and Robert Ousterhout describe Rudolph's design of the Christian Science Building as both a challenge to and an expansion of the twentieth-century modernist dictum of objective functionalism, moving it beyond the quotidian and "widening the definition of function to include the fulfillment of man's spiritual and psychological needs."[65] Rudolph had previously said that architects are obligated to address both the everyday needs *and* the spiritual needs of a building's users and that therefore "mere functionalism is never enough."[66] He argued that architects must be concerned with symbolism and content, and he sought to create what he described as "living, breathing, dynamic spaces of infinite variety, capable of helping man forget something of his troubles"[67] (Fig. 7.9).

FIGURE 7.9 Christian Science Building, meeting room interior.
HB-29509-M, Chicago History Museum, Hedrich-Blessing Collection.

Criticism and demolition

Upon completion, the Christian Science Building received national attention through publication in professional journals, where the work was generally reviewed positively if not glowingly. *Architectural Record* called it a demonstration of Rudolph's virtuosity in the manipulation of space and scale.[68] In the same article, however, a contradiction was observed between the "delicacy and precision" of Rudolph's pen-and-ink drawings of the project and the "rough, irregular, and raw" qualities of the completed concrete structure.[69] *Inland Architect* found the work daring, positively inspired, and "a strong, bright, flexible building that has served the students well since its completion."[70] Rudolph had delivered spaces that were "fluid and energetic," designed "with imagination and sensitivity."[71] And, at least by some measures, the building was well-received locally. In 1969, the Champaign County Development Council's Community Improvement Program gave Rudolph's building an award for excellence in church design, citing its exemplary coordination of "color, form, texture, flow of space, relationship of interior to exterior, [and] light to dark."[72]

Given such positive assessments of its architecture, why was the building demolished after only twenty years of use? Two main factors appear to have led to the eventual destruction of the Christian Science Building, as purported by those who were in a position to save the building but chose not to. They argued that the building was, first, too costly to operate and maintain and, second, too inflexible to adapt for re-use with a different function or program. In effect, the building's cultural value was overshadowed by its lack of profitability.[73]

By the 1980s, student membership in the Christian Science Organization had declined significantly, and the costs of operating the building became untenable for the group.[74] The most commonly noted problem was the expense of heating the building, which eventually led to its partial closure during winter months.[75] Heat loss through the walls and roofs of the building was inevitable. As designed, the building envelope consisted of 12-inch-thick monolithic cast-in-place concrete walls which provided thermal mass but contained no thermal insulation, with single-pane glazing and a tar-and-gravel roof over plywood with minimal insulation.[76] Additional insulation could have been easily added to the roof, and the glass could have been upgraded to double-pane insulating units (albeit at significant cost), but the corrugated concrete walls were a different story. Because the walls were monolithic and exposed to view on the inside as well as the outside, covering them with a thick layer of insulation and additional cladding would have drastically changed the aesthetic and the architectural integrity of the building. The formal and material qualities for which it was known would be seriously compromised. The irony of this situation, however, is that Rudolph had initially proposed building these walls with two wythes of fluted concrete masonry units (CMU), with an interstitial air cavity and layer of rigid-foam insulation.[77] This would have provided significantly higher thermal resistance, but was deemed too expensive by the builders. Through a process that would today fall under the euphemistic term "value engineering," the double-layer block wall was revised in the plans to be a single, solid layer of site-cast concrete.[78]

These operational issues finally led the Christian Science Organization to offer the building for sale, and a private local developer named Gloria Dauten purchased it.[79] Dauten intended to construct a new apartment building and clearly found the land to be of more value than the building, which she judged unusable for her purposes. Dauten was not completely unsympathetic to the architectural significance of Rudolph's design, however. When opposition to her plans by preservationists became apparent, she offered to sell the building to the University of Illinois or to trade it for another site of equal economic value. University administrators declined, saying the building "could not accommodate any of [the university's] urgent needs for space without considerable modification to the building as it exists."[80] In retrospect, these claims of the building's inflexibility seem dubious, as the university includes many smaller academic units that surely could have utilized the building for lectures and receptions, as a branch library, or as meeting or study spaces for other student organizations. The charge of inflexibility was also ironic considering Rudolph's expressed desire to design architecture that could accommodate future changes through modification. He wrote that "the complexities of our time suggest that buildings should not be thought of as complete within themselves—they should have an open end, and should change."[81]

Public support for the preservation of Rudolph's building was voiced by faculty and students at the university's School of Architecture and by the local chapter of the American Institute of Architects.[82] Nevertheless, Dauten proceeded with her plan to completely demolish the building in March 1986 and then constructed an undistinguished six-story apartment complex on the site.

The robust concrete structure of the Christian Science Building apparently did not go away easily, however. It was reported that the first swing of the wrecking ball simply bounced off

FIGURE 7.10 Demolition of the Christian Science Building, 1986.

Photograph by Myra Kaha.

the solid concrete walls, and the demolition process, which had been initially scheduled for two days in duration, ultimately took two weeks to complete.[83] Back in 1965, a local newspaper's review of the newly completed building had remarked on its "solid, long-lasting appearance";[84] indeed, its solidity was confirmed, but the building proved to be long-lasting in appearance only (Fig. 7.10). Unlike many currently celebrated examples of mid-century modern religious architecture still extant, Rudolph's Christian Science Building exists now only in archival photographs, publications, and drawings, and in the memories of those who encountered the building during its brief twenty-year existence.

When Rudolph died in 1997, his obituary in the *New York Times* stated that he "leaves behind a perplexing legacy that will take many years to untangle."[85] An important part of that legacy includes Rudolph's buildings that have been demolished, such as the Christian Science Building, the Riverview High School in Sarasota, Florida (1958, demolished 2009), and multiple houses. Additionally, several existing works face an uncertain future due to physical deterioration, lack of maintenance, perceived inflexibility, or economic forces. Even amid the extensive catalog of a prolific architect like Rudolph, the absence of these buildings is significant and a poignant reminder of the role that historic preservation could play in maintaining the cultural heritage of twentieth-century modern architecture.

The design of the Christian Science Building can be read as an essay on architectural principles centered around monumental form, use of concrete, spatial character, decoration, and light, that preoccupied Paul Rudolph at the apex of his career in the early 1960s. Despite the purported shortcomings that led to its destruction, the building remains a historically important and instructive example of the mid-century movement toward brutalism[86] and away from the dominant glass-box aesthetic of high modernism. Beyond that, Rudolph's design embodies a personal approach that stood against the universal, abstract space of high modernism[87] in favor of an eclectic, expressive modernism focused on direct human experience of variations in space, light, and material. As Rudolph conceived the project, it was an attempt to expand the impact of modern architecture beyond objective functionalism and rationalism toward an architecture that "fires the imagination" and "provides a world of perceptions and sensation."[88] Within a relatively compact footprint, the Christian Science Building offered a unique, complex, and carefully orchestrated architectural experience marked by not only visual but also haptic sensory engagement. The fact of its severely shortened lifespan has obscured an important work of architecture that deserves recognition as a paradigm of Rudolph's quest for "eloquent space concepts"[89] and its implicit critique of post-war modernism.

Notes

1 For example, Rudolph was featured in a *Time* magazine article calling him "the most exciting new arrival" on the architectural scene: "Bright New Arrival," *Time* (February 1, 1960): 60.
2 For biography and project list, see Timothy Rohan, *The Architecture of Paul Rudolph* (New Haven, CT: Yale University Press, 2014). A project list is also provided by the Carney Library at the University of Massachusetts: http://prudolph.lib.umassd.edu/chronological_list.
3 Ibid., 1.
4 Robert A.M. Stern, Foreword, in Paul Rudolph, *Writings on Architecture* (New Haven, CT: Yale University Press, 2008), 6.
5 In publications, the building has been called by various names: the Christian Science Building, Christian Science Student Center, and Christian Science Center. Rudolph's construction drawings use the project title "Christian Science Building at the University of Illinois," and so it is herein referred to as the Christian Science Building.
6 Between 1965 and 1970, Rudolph completed an additional forty projects.
7 Rohan writes that "at a time when modernism was being questioned, Rudolph became more symbolic of its failures than any other architect of his generation," and he spent the last three decades of his career on the periphery of the profession: *The Architecture of Paul Rudolph*, 1. For a discussion of Robert Venturi's critical attack on Rudolph's work, see Lydia M. Soo and Robert Ousterhout, "Has Functionalism Triumphed? The Destruction of Paul Rudolph's Christian Science Building," *Reflections* 4, no. 1 (Fall 1986): 43.
8 The publication of Rohan's monograph in 2014 followed a major exhibition and symposium on Rudolph at Yale University in 2008 to mark the renovation of Rudolph's Art & Architecture Building at Yale University, which was renamed Rudolph Hall in his honor.
9 For example, the Christian Science Building is not included in Rohan's *The Architecture of Paul Rudolph*, which is described in its introduction as the first comprehensive monograph on Rudolph.
10 Paul Rudolph to Joseph Martinez and Thomas Heinz, December 17, 1968. Letter provided to the author by the Anthemios Chapter of Alpha Rho Chi at the University of Illinois at Urbana-Champaign.
11 Rudolph served as Plym Distinguished Professor of Architecture at the University of Illinois during the fall semester of 1983.
12 Robert Bruegmann, "Interview with Paul Rudolph," February 28, 1986. Chicago Architects Aural History Project. The Art Institute of Chicago, 48–50. http://digital-libraries.saic.edu/cdm/ref/collection/caohp/id/9861.
13 Ibid., 48.
14 Ed McCahill, "Finish New Reading Room," *The Daily Illini* (Urbana-Champaign, Illinois), October 12, 1965, 3.

15 Letters in the Frank Lloyd Wright Archives include: Nancy Houston to Eugene Masselink (Secretary to Frank Lloyd Wright), October 15, 1958; Houston to Wright, January 19, 1959; Wright to Houston, January 27, 1959; and Masselink to Houston, April 13, 1959.

16 The Christian Science project in Champaign does not appear among Wright's published projects lists.

17 Wright produced two different schemes for each of these projects. See Yukio Futagawa, ed., *Frank Lloyd Wright Monograph 1951–1959* (Tokyo: ADA EDITA, 1988), 262–263, and Anat Geva, *Frank Lloyd Wright's Sacred Architecture: Faith, Form, and Building Technology* (London: Routledge, 2012), 185, 262–264.

18 David Hanser, e-mail message to author, April 5, 2017.

19 Ibid.

20 Nory Miller, "Rudolph's Rich Molding of Space at the U of I," *Inland Architect* 17, no. 9 (September 1973): 18.

21 Paul Rudolph, "Excerpts from a Conversation," *Perspecta* 22 (1986): 103. Republished in Rudolph, *Writings on Architecture*, 135.

22 Bruegmann, "Interview with Paul Rudolph," 48.

23 See Project List in Rohan, *The Architecture of Paul Rudolph*, 254.

24 Obituary of Nancy Houston, *Troy Record* (Troy, New York), April 19, 2003.

25 Houston wrote a piece for the *Christian Science Journal* calling on church members to emulate Mary Baker Eddy's qualities of humility, sincerity, and courage. Nancy Evans Houston, "What a Calling!" *Christian Science Journal* 106, no. 4 (April 1988).

26 Paul Eli Ivey, *Prayers in Stone: Christian Science Architecture in the United States, 1894–1930* (Chicago, IL: University of Illinois Press, 1999), 31.

27 Ibid., 31.

28 Bruegmann, "Interview with Paul Rudolph," 46–48.

29 This was the reported budget before construction began; it is likely that the number increased, but a final construction cost was not published. See "Christian Science Foundation Plans New Building," *Daily Illini* (Urbana-Champaign, Illinois), May 21, 1963, 10; and McCahill, "Finish New Reading Room," 3.

30 Other consultants included Herman D. J. Spiegel as Structural Engineer and Van Elm Heywood & Shadford, as Mechanical Engineers, as noted on construction documents in the Paul Marvin Rudolph Archive, Library of Congress, Washington, DC.

31 Ibid.

32 Ground-floor area was 3,500 square feet, while the upper floor, with several open-to-below areas, was 2,130 square feet.

33 See Miller, "Rudolph's Rich Molding of Space," 18.

34 The provision of seven different floor levels was commonly noted in published reviews of the building. See, for example, Miller, "Rudolph's Rich Molding of Space," 18–19.

35 Built 25 years before the Americans with Disabilities Act and lacking an elevator or ramps, clearly the building would not meet current accessibility standards. Because the entry doors were at grade, the main entrance, lobby and study room on the ground floor would have been accessible to a visitor using a wheelchair, but the remainder of spaces required using stairs to access them.

36 Paul Rudolph, "Enigmas of Architecture," in Toshio Nakamura, ed., *100 by Paul Rudolph: 1946–74* (Tokyo: A+U Publishing, 1977), 320.

37 David Hanser, a member of the organization in the 1960s, recalls that Wednesday night services were regularly held in the meeting room, while on Sundays, members attended local churches in the area: David Hanser, e-mail message to author, April 5, 2017.

38 See "An Architecture Strongly Manipulated in Space and Scale," *Architectural Record* 141, no. 2 (February 1967): 137–142, and Miller, "Rudolph's Rich Molding of Space," 18–19.

39 Bruegmann, "Interview with Paul Rudolph," 48.

40 Ibid., 49.

41 Noted in Miller, "Rudolph's Rich Molding of Space," 19.

42 See "Rudolph's Rich Molding of Space," and "An Architecture Strongly Manipulated."

43 Rudolph, "Enigmas of Architecture," 318.

44 Paul Rudolph, *The Architecture of Paul Rudolph*, introduction by Sibyl Moholy-Nagy, captions by Gerhard Schwab (New York: Praeger, 1970), 138. Also see Johann Albrecht, "A Conversation with Paul Rudolph: December 9, 1983," *Reflections* 2, no. 1 (Fall 1984): 77, and John W. Cook and Heinrich Klotz, *Conversations with Architects* (New York: Praeger, 1973), 104.

45 Noted in "Paul Rudolph's Elaborated Spaces: Six New Projects," *Architectural Record* 139 (June 1966): 146, and Miller, "Rudolph's Rich Molding of Space," 18.

46 Rudolph, "Enigmas of Architecture," 320.

47 Ibid. Furthermore, he wrote of unused space: "Perhaps it is, paradoxically, the most important of all." Also noted in Soo and Ousterhout, "Has Functionalism Triumphed?" 43.

48 Paul Rudolph, "To Enrich Our Architecture," *Journal of Architectural Education* 13, no. 1 (Spring 1958): 10.

49 Ibid.

50 Paul Heyer, *Architects on Architecture: New Directions in America* (New York, NY: Walker and Company, 1966), 303.

51 Rudolph speaking about the Yale A&A Building, as quoted in John W. Cook and Heinrich Klotz, *Conversations with Architects* (New York, NY: Praeger, 1973), 98.

52 Quoted in Heyer, *Architects on Architecture*, 297.

53 In fact, Rudolph remarked in 1986, "Does it have anything to do with Christian Science? Not that I can think of": Bruegmann, "Interview with Paul Rudolph," 48. He also notes, however, that his memory has somewhat faded. David Hanser, who was a student member of the organization, wrote: "I don't think there is any aspect of the building particularly related to Christian Science. Symbolism was never of special importance in the religion, just acoustics, sight lines, and a sense of community": David Hanser, e-mail message to author, April 5, 2017.

54 Ivey, *Prayers in Stone*, 14–17.

55 Ibid., 16.

56 Ibid., 119.

57 Ibid., 55.

58 Ibid., 35.

59 Allan Temko, *No Way to Build a Ballpark and Other Irreverent Essays on Architecture* (San Francisco, CA: Chronicle Books, 1993), 264. Temko also quotes Maybeck as saying: "Christian Scientists are wonderful clients. They have the fervor of early Christians, and they always pay their bills": ibid., 265.

60 Ivey, *Prayers in Stone*, 3.

61 McCahill, "Finish New Reading Room."

62 Rudolph, "Enigmas of Architecture," 320.

63 Bruegmann, "Interview with Paul Rudolph," 53.

64 Ibid.

65 Soo and Ousterhout, "Has Functionalism Triumphed?" 42.

66 Cook and Klotz, *Conversations with Architects*, 96–97.

67 Paul Rudolph, "Changing Philosophy of Architecture," *Architectural Forum* 101 (July 1954): 120.

68 "An Architecture Strongly Manipulated in Space and Scale," 137–142.

69 "Rudolph's drawings, sharp as steel engravings, suggest that he didn't want his *beton* to be quite so *brut* as this": ibid., 137.

70 Miller, "Rudolph's Rich Molding of Space," 18.

71 Ibid., 18.

72 Carl Schwartz, "UI Improves Amenities," *Daily Illini* (Urbana-Champaign, Illinois), January 11, 1969, 9.

73 Soo and Ousterhout, "Has Functionalism Triumphed?" 43.

74 Confirmed by David Hanser, e-mail message to author, April 5, 2017.

75 Soo and Ousterhout, "Has Functionalism Triumphed?" 40.

76 As shown in archival construction documents in the Paul Rudolph Archive at the Library of Congress.

77 Archival construction documents at the Paul Rudolph Archive at the Library of Congress; Bruegmann, "Interview with Paul Rudolph," 49.

78 Ibid.

79 J. P. Bloomer, "With Demolition Approaching, Landmark Doesn't Have a Prayer," *News Gazette* (Champaign, Illinois), February 2, 1986, 1–2.

80 University of Illinois Chancellor T. E. Everhart, letter to architecture students, March 1986, as quoted in Soo and Ousterhout, "Has Functionalism Triumphed?" 44.

81 Heyer, *Architects on Architecture*, 304.

82 Soo and Ousterhout, "Has Functionalism Triumphed?" 40.

83 Ibid., 40.

84 McCahill, "Finish New Reading Room."
85 Herbert Muschamp, "Paul Rudolph is Dead at 78; Modernist Architect of the 60s," *New York Times*, August 9, 1997. www.nytimes.com/1997/08/09/arts/paul-rudolph-is-dead-at-78-modernist-architect-of-the-60-s.html.
86 The term "brutalism" (from the French *béton-brut* for raw concrete) generally describes a modernist architectural movement of the 1950s–70s "characterized by bold geometries, the exposure of structural materials, and functional spatial design," as described by the World Monument Fund, www.wmf.org/project/british-brutalism.
87 Compare, for example, the contemporary work of Skidmore, Owings & Merrill and Mies van der Rohe.
88 Rudolph, "To Enrich Our Architecture," 12. These words were written before Rudolph designed the Christian Science Center but are a retrospectively apt description of its affects.
89 Rudolph, "To Enrich Our Architecture," 10.

References

Albrecht, Johann. "A Conversation with Paul Rudolph: December 9, 1983," *Reflections* 2, no. 1 (Fall 1984): 70–77.
"An Architecture Strongly Manipulated in Space and Scale," *Architectural Record* 141, no. 2 (February 1967): 137–142.
Bloomer, J.P. "With Demolition Approaching, Landmark Doesn't Have a Prayer," *The News Gazette* (Champaign, Illinois), February 2, 1986, 1–2.
"Bright New Arrival," *Time*, February 1, 1960, 60.
Bruegmann, Robert. "Interview with Paul Rudolph," February 28, 1986. Chicago Architects Aural History Project. The Art Institute of Chicago, 48–50. http://digital-libraries.saic.edu/cdm/ref/collection/caohp/id/9861.
"Christian Science Foundation Plans New Building," *Daily Illini* (Urbana-Champaign, Illinois), May 21, 1963, 10
Cook, John W. and Heinrich Klotz. *Conversations with Architects* (New York: Praeger, 1973).
Futagawa, Yukio, ed. *Frank Lloyd Wright Monograph 1951–1959* (Tokyo: ADA EDITA, 1988).
———, ed. *Paul Rudolph: Architectural Drawings* (New York, NY: Architectural Book Publishing, 1972).
Geva, Anat. *Frank Lloyd Wright's Sacred Architecture: Faith, Form, and Building Technology* (London: Routledge, 2012).
Heyer, Paul. *Architects on Architecture: New Directions in America* (New York, NY: Walker, 1966).
Houston, Nancy Evans. "What a Calling!" *Christian Science Journal* 106, no. 4 (April 1988).
Ivey, Paul Eli. *Prayers in Stone: Christian Science Architecture in the United States 1894–1930* (Chicago, IL: University of Illinois Press, 1999).
McCahill, Ed. "Finish New Reading Room," *Daily Illini* (Urbana-Champaign, Illinois), October 12, 1965, 3.
Miller, Nory. "Rudolph's Rich Molding of Space at the U of I," *Inland Architect* 17, no. 9 (September 1973): 18–19.
Muschamp, Herbert. "Paul Rudolph is Dead at 78; Modernist Architect of the 60s," *New York Times*, August 9, 1997. www.nytimes.com/1997/08/09/arts/paul-rudolph-is-dead-at-78-modernist-architect-of-the-60-s.html.
Nakamura, Toshio, ed. *100 by Paul Rudolph: 1946–74* (Tokyo: A+U Publishing, 1977).
"Paul Rudolph's Elaborated Spaces: Six New Projects," *Architectural Record* 139 (June 1966): 135–150.
Rohan, Timothy M. *The Architecture of Paul Rudolph* (New Haven, CT: Yale University Press, 2014).
Rudolph, Paul. *The Architecture of Paul Rudolph*. Introduction by Sibyl Moholy-Nagy, captions by Gerhard Schwab (New York: Praeger, 1970).
———. "Changing Philosophy of Architecture," *Architectural Forum* 101 (July 1954): 120–121.
———. "Enigmas of Architecture." In Toshio Nakamura, ed. *100 by Paul Rudolph: 1946–74* (Tokyo: A+U, 1977).

———. "Excerpts from a Conversation," *Perspecta* 22 (1986): 102–107.

———. *Paul Rudolph: Architectural Drawings* (London: Lund Humphries, 1974).

———. "To Enrich Our Architecture," *Journal of Architectural Education* 13, no. 1 (Spring 1958): 9–12.

———. *Writings on Architecture*. Nina Rappaport, ed. (New Haven, CT: Yale School of Architecture, 2008).

Schwartz, Carl. "UI Improves Amenities," *Daily Illini* (Urbana-Champaign, IL), January 11, 1969, 9.

Soo, Lydia M., and Robert Ousterhout. "Has Functionalism Triumphed? The Destruction of Paul Rudolph's Christian Science Building," *Reflections* 4, no. 1 (Fall 1986): 40–45.

Stern, Robert A.M. Foreword, in Paul Rudolph, *Writings on Architecture* (New Haven, CT: Yale University Press, 2008).

Temko, Allan. *No Way to Build a Ballpark and Other Irreverent Essays on Architecture* (San Francisco, CA: Chronicle Books, 1993).

PART III

Denominations, identity, and modern sacred architecture

8

CREATING SACRED SPACES IN THE SUBURBS

Roman Catholic architecture in post-war Los Angeles, 1948–76

Michael J. Gibson

In his 1959 study, *The Church and the Suburbs*, Catholic sociologist Andrew M. Greeley declared the Archdiocese of Los Angeles to be the "most suburban of all dioceses" in the country.[1] During the three decades following World War II, the general population of the four-county region covered by the Archdiocese boomed, increasing by 138%. Concurrently, the region's Catholic population increased by an astounding 253%, from 625,000 to 2.2 million.[2] By some estimates, new Catholic residents were arriving at a rate of more than a thousand a week throughout the 1950s. Most of these new arrivals chose to settle in newly developed suburban neighborhoods where Catholic churches were either non-existent or too small to accommodate the influx. Accordingly, between 1948 (when Cardinal James Francis McIntyre became archbishop) and 1976 (when Orange County became a separate diocese) the Archdiocese established 98 new parishes and constructed more than 250 new churches.

Today, these churches with their associated parish campuses are familiar landmarks in the region's post-war suburban landscape. Despite their ubiquity, they have attracted scant scholarly attention individually, and none as a group. This is surprising given the questions they pose for architectural historians: Why are the characteristic design elements and architectural vocabularies of these churches so different from those of pre-war churches? Why are earlier post-war churches so different from later ones? Are these numerous differences related to changes in the purpose of these buildings, or in how they function? Do these differences stem from changes in belief, or in how Catholics understood themselves? This chapter addresses these questions and demonstrates that these churches, as a group, reflect and exemplify a much larger story. They represent the transformation of American church building during the 1950s, 1960s, and 1970s. They also illustrate, through the prism of architecture, how one highly visible and influential denomination addressed the challenges posed by post-war religious, social, and cultural changes in one of the country's most dynamic regions. As recent scholarly studies indicate, the experiences of particular denominations, especially in a regional context, offer a promising field of inquiry for expanding our understanding of this architecture, especially with regard to evolving post-war religious identities and local adaptation.[3]

The research for this chapter began with field visits to more than a hundred churches. Each was analyzed in terms of the "four ways of looking at a church" and the three church-building traditions identified in Richard Kieckhefer's wide-ranging study of Christian architecture, *Theology in Stone*.[4] Post-war commentaries on church design, historical and sociological studies of American Catholicism, and biographies of McIntyre and his successor Cardinal Timothy Manning[5] were then consulted to develop a general framework for interpretation. These preliminary steps were followed by my original research in the Archdiocesan archives focused on 45 individual churches, selected because they were typical of many similar churches or because they were distinctive for one reason or another. Building committee records, contemporary newspaper accounts (especially architect interviews), commemorative church dedication booklets, and parish fundraising materials proved to be the most useful sources of information.

The Catholic architectural program

The key to understanding the Los Angeles Archdiocese's portfolio of post-war churches lies in an appreciation of three historic phenomena that drove their underlying architectural program: (1) the swift growth of the local Catholic population in the rapidly developing suburbs, which created a need for churches that could be built quickly and economically; (2) the desire of Church leaders to develop parishes that would attract the next generation of American Catholics—young, educated, middle-class, and suburban—just as ethnic urban parishes had once drawn their working-class, immigrant grandparents and parents; and (3) a new theological and pastoral emphasis on congregational participation in worship, both before and after the Second Vatican Council.

Accommodating population growth and suburban development

On the most basic level, the Archdiocese's church-building program was a practical response to population growth and suburban sprawl. These conditions were not unique to Los Angeles. During the post-war years, the entire nation was engaged in, as one observer put it, "the most frantic, extensive church building boom since the London fire of the 17th century."[6] But unlike most other metropolitan regions, Southern California was forced to cope with hundreds of thousands of immigrants from other parts of the country. Many had visited the area while serving in the military during or immediately after the war, returning later to pursue educations, establish careers, and start families. Others came looking for work in the region's booming post-war economy, as its wartime aircraft and shipbuilding infrastructure were converted to such peacetime uses as aerospace, electronics, consumer products manufacturing, and commercial shipping. Still others succumbed to the popular image of "Southern California living" burnished by decades of promotion by real estate developers and the film industry.[7] These new arrivals—at least one-fourth of whom were Catholic—found homes in the new suburban developments sprawling across the Los Angeles Basin and its neighboring valleys. Thus, there was an unprecedented demand for new churches to serve small town and rural parishes whose territories were being transformed into suburbs, as well as newly formed parishes created to accommodate newly built residential subdivisions.

Even so, for the recently arrived Archbishop McIntyre, church building was not the top priority. He believed that, in a region experiencing growth without parallel "in any country at any time," the greatest need was for new Catholic schools that would prepare children to "crusade against [the] Communistic tendencies of our times and against all forms of ideology that beggar the individual of his freedom under God."[8] Consequently, no parish was allowed to build a permanent church until all other parish facilities had been completed and, to an appreciable extent, paid off. These typically included a temporary church suitable for eventual conversion into a multipurpose social hall or gymnasium, a full school, a convent to house the sisters teaching in the school, and a rectory to house the priests serving in the parish.

Thanks to McIntyre's penchant for careful management, by the late 1950s "the ecclesial building program in the Los Angeles archdiocese had become a model for other areas of the Church in the United States."[9] Because decision-making authority was concentrated in a few individuals, the design and construction process was an efficient one. Following a set of written directives, a parish's pastor proposed the project and the architect. The Archbishop and his Board of Consultors reviewed the proposal and if approved, confirmed the choice of architect and a preliminary budget. Initial plans were submitted to the Archdiocesan Building Committee for review, revision, and ultimate approval. Minutes suggest that one of the committee's key functions was to keep ambitious pastors and architects in check by prescribing reductions in size, seating capacity, artistic program, and cost. A professional director of construction operations supervised the bidding process and the actual construction. The Archbishop could intervene at any point and ultimately all decisions belonged to him.[10]

The Archdiocese maintained a list of approved architects from which pastors were encouraged to choose.[11] As a result, a small but versatile pool of architects designed the vast majority of churches. Occasionally, a pastor selected a member of his parish or another local architect, and these selections were usually approved after an informal investigation of the proposed architect's credentials.[12] Within these parameters, a pastor's choice of architect reflected his personal preferences, sophistication, and taste; his familiarity with each architect's previous work; and his willingness to seek out advice from other pastors.

Remarkably, this process did not include any formal mechanism for receiving input from parishioners, including seeking their review or approval once plans had been drawn. Thus, it stood in marked contrast to the process prevailing in most Protestant denominations and in Jewish synagogues, where decisions were made at the local level, typically by a committee of members. However, any proposed project that lacked broad appeal was bound to fail for one simple reason: unenthusiastic parishioners would not volunteer time for, nor give generously to, the massive fundraising drives that became a regular feature of post-war suburban parish life.[13]

Attracting and serving a new generation of Catholics

American Catholics underwent a tremendous transformation during the three decades that followed World War II. The waves of European immigrants who brought Catholicism to America on a large scale in the late nineteenth and early twentieth centuries settled in ethnic enclaves in the big cities, where their churches became religious, social, cultural, and educational centers. To support and preserve Catholic identity and practice, Church leaders created a comprehensive network of Catholic organizations, including schools, youth groups, unions, professional associations, social clubs, athletic leagues, charities, hospitals, and retirement homes. They enabled Catholics, in the words of historian Charles Morris, to "live almost their entire lives within a thick cocoon of Catholic institutions."[14] After the war, this separatist culture began to dissipate as a new generation of native-born Catholics chose the "melting pot" suburbs over homogenous immigrant neighborhoods. These Catholics were better educated—thanks to the G.I. Bill—and more affluent than their parents and grandparents.

This assimilation into the mainstream coincided with a broader acceptance of Catholics in American politics and popular culture. During the two decades following the war, the country's Catholic bishops were in the forefront of the crusade against atheistic communism.[15] John F. Kennedy's election to the presidency in 1960 marked the demise of any lingering nativist suspicions that Catholics could not be loyal Americans.[16] The civil rights, anti-war, and labor movements of the late 1960s and '70s featured many prominent Catholic leaders, including Robert Kennedy, Eugene McCarthy, Cesar Chavez, and the Berrigan brothers.[17] Catholic writers ranging from Thomas Merton to Dorothy Day attracted the attention of intellectuals.[18] Popular films portrayed priests and nuns as kind, wise, and heroic.[19] Catholic inspirational messages, from Father Patrick Peyton's assurance that "the family that prays together, stays together,"[20] to Bishop Fulton Sheen's insistence that "life is worth living!"[21] permeated the airwaves.

At the same time, assimilation was a cause for alarm. In the suburban "melting pot," there was a danger that Catholics might embrace the notion that one religion is practically as good as another. Catholic leaders desired to ensure that Church members would retain their religious identities even as they cast their ethnic and working-class identities aside.[22]

The solution was a new model for Catholic congregations: the post-war suburban parish.[23] The measure of this model's success would be its ability to attract the young Catholic families who were now putting down roots in the suburbs in astonishing numbers. Thus, it was designed to promote, support, and celebrate marriage, parenting, and especially, children. Although parish life centered around the school, a full range of activities was designed to attract parishioner participation, from the very young to the very old.[24] These activities cultivated a sense of parish loyalty and, more importantly, a sense of personal and group identification as Catholic.

Throughout the 1950s and into the mid-1960s, America's post-war suburban parishes flourished. Initially, Catholics appeared to have survived changing demographics, relocation to the suburbs, and assimilation into the mainstream with their distinctive identities intact. But in the late 1960s and early 1970s, a new set of challenges emerged. The theological and institutional reforms introduced after 1965 following the Second Vatican Council proved to be wide-ranging and sometimes controversial. They embraced matters such as internal organization and decision making, relations with other religious groups and civil governments, worship, ministerial roles, teaching methods, individual moral behavior, and intellectual dissent.[25] These internal reforms unfolded against a backdrop of broader political and social controversies, including unrest over the Vietnam War, racial tensions, student rebellion, changing sexual mores, and the women's and gay liberation movements.[26]

The convergence of these circumstances ushered in a period of disorientation and fragmentation for American Catholics. The percentage of Catholics attending Mass every Sunday declined from 75% in 1958 to just over 50% by 1978.[27] Large numbers of men and women left their vocations as priests and sisters. Some former priests became outspoken critics of the Church's leadership, while high-profile conflicts emerged between conservative bishops and groups of sisters attempting to reform their religious orders. One such conflict, heavily publicized, roiled the Archdiocese in 1967. The Immaculate Heart Sisters, desiring to update their ministry and lifestyle in the spirit of Vatican II, adopted several reforms, including a more democratic form of governance and allowing members to choose careers other than teaching.[28] Cardinal McIntyre opposed several of these changes; his attempts to exert his authority over the order, and disagreements within the order itself, eventually resulted in an exodus of sisters from Archdiocesan schools and a division of the order into two independent groups.[29] These and other events contributed to a crisis of authority. By 1977, Greeley heralded the emergence of the "communal Catholic," loyal to the community and sensitive to his or her spiritual heritage but refusing "to take seriously the teaching authority of the leadership of the institutional church."[30]

Embracing the liturgical reform movement

A third phenomenon that played a role in the post-war building boom was not a function of changing local conditions or shifting national demographics, but rather an international movement within the Catholic Church that placed a new theological and pastoral emphasis on congregational participation in worship. Although the "liturgical movement," as it came to be known, originated in Europe in the mid-nineteenth century, it came into full flower in the mid-1940s.[31] Many of its principles were officially adopted at Vatican II in the early 1960s, resulting in a series of reforms that stretched into the mid-1970s.[32] These reforms touched every aspect of Catholic worship, including texts, ritual actions, choice of language and music, and the roles played by the clergy and members of the congregation.[33] Although the great majority of Catholics embraced these reforms, for others they were profoundly unsettling. For them, the liturgy had symbolized and demonstrated the universal and unchanging nature of Catholicism. These changes appeared to signal that other aspects of the Church's belief and practice, also once thought to be permanent, were mutable as well.[34]

Each bishop was granted some degree of latitude in implementing liturgical changes in his diocese. Indeed, some judged the relative liberalism or conservatism of individual bishops by the speed at which these changes were carried out.[35] Cardinal McIntyre had a general reputation as a conservative, and was criticized by some as "recalcitrant in liturgical reform."[36] But according to his biographer, Msgr. Francis Weber, although McIntyre retained an "affection for the old" and "never apologized for his penchant towards retaining Latin in the Mass," he was nonetheless "a good sport and a loyal churchman and, when his preferences were not followed, he supported the majority view."[37] According to Weber, because of the careful, steady pace at which reforms were implemented, "the archdiocese probably fared better liturgically in those years than did the majority of its sister jurisdictions in the United States."[38]

Analytic framework

Richard Kieckhefer proposes that a church be analyzed in terms of four basic elements: (1) *spatial dynamics* refers to the overall configuration of the space within a church, chiefly determined by the liturgical action that takes place within that space; (2) *centering focus* concerns the object that serves as the central focus of the church, and how the church's architecture signals the centrality of that object; (3) *aesthetic impact* refers to the overall impression the architecture creates, and the emotional response it evokes in the visitor, and (4) *symbolic resonance* denotes the symbolic associations of the church's structure, furnishings, and decoration.[39]

Using this analytic approach, Kieckhefer identifies three basic models or "traditions" in church building, each of which combines these four elements in a distinctive way: the *classic sacramental* tradition, the *classic evangelical* tradition, and the *modern communal* tradition.[40] These models or traditions provide a useful tool for understanding the evolution of church building in the Archdiocese during the post-war era in two key respects. First, prior to the early 1960s, all Catholic churches in the Archdiocese conformed to the *classic sacramental* model. This model underwent a transformation after World War II when local architects—and the Archdiocese's leadership—finally began to embrace modernist design principles and vocabularies as an appropriate choice for church building. Second, by the mid-1960s, churches conforming to the *modern communal* model began to appear. Within a decade, this model had replaced the *classic sacramental* one, principally due to the impact of liturgical reform.

This chapter now addresses, first, the *classic sacramental* tradition, and the post-war adaptation of this tradition to accommodate both the need for modernist simplicity and the desire for a contemporary architectural image. Next, it examines the characteristic elements of this tradition by analyzing representative local churches in terms of spatial dynamics, centering focus, aesthetic impact, and symbolic resonance. Then, it considers the emergence of the *modern communal* tradition as a response to the call for increased congregational participation in the liturgy. Finally, it analyzes representative examples of this tradition in terms of spatial dynamics, centering focus, aesthetic impact, and symbolic resonance.

The classic sacramental tradition

According to Kieckhefer, *classic sacramental* churches are characterized by complex spatial dynamics,[41] a singular centering focus,[42] rich and dramatic aesthetic impact,[43] and high symbolic resonance.[44] These characteristics are particularly well illustrated by three post-war Los Angeles area churches designed by local architect J. Earle Trudeau:[45] St. Charles Borromeo in North Hollywood (1959) (Fig. 8.1), St. Therese in Alhambra (1951) (Fig. 8.2), and St. Mel in Woodland Hills (1958) (Fig. 8.3).

Perhaps the most remarkable thing about these three churches is their diversity, which reflects and illustrates the transformation of the *classic sacramental* tradition in the post-war

FIGURE 8.1   St. Charles Borromeo, North Hollywood, California, façade.
Photograph by the author, 2007.

FIGURE 8.2 St. Therese, Alhambra, California, façade.
Photograph by the author, 2007.

FIGURE 8.3 St. Mel, Woodland Hills, California, façade.
Photograph by the author, 2008.

years as it shifted from historic revivalism to modernism. This transformation is directly linked to two aspects of the Archdiocese's architectural program: a need for churches that could be built quickly and economically, and a need for churches that would attract young, educated, middle-class, suburban Catholics.

Modernist simplicity

The desire of the Archdiocese to build new parish churches as rapidly and inexpensively as possible was readily accommodated by three of modernism's key tenets: simplicity of design, integrity and honesty in materials, and technological innovation.[46]

Local Catholic architects eagerly embraced modernism's emphasis on simplicity and its rejection of superfluous ornamentation. Trudeau's position was clear: "Should Catholic churches of today be constructed to reflect the sober permanence of tradition built up around

Christianity? Tradition, yes, but not borrowed form and ornament promiscuously applied to any building material, fake or showy."[47]

These sentiments were later echoed by local architect J. George Szeptycki,[48] who criticized the "fakery" of architects who were continuing "to build a box and then hang embellishments on it" so that it would appear to be "Gothic" or "Spanish American."[49]

Modernism's preference for new materials and technology similarly facilitated the dual goals of speed and low cost. Trudeau, affirming that the "the first requisite in respect to tradition is sound, honest construction," stated that "we in Southern California turn to reinforced concrete," since "cement is inexpensive and aggregate plentiful."[50] Taking an even broader view, Szeptycki declared:

> I believe we face a truly great era in architecture. For the first time in more than 500 years, revolutionary and imaginative structural methods and materials are simultaneously available . . . Everyone . . . should be fascinated by the vast array of new materials and new methods of construction which ought to be allowed to speak for themselves.[51]

Contemporary image

Building a modernist church projected a vital, contemporary image for the post-war suburban parish. Local Catholic architects were quick to point out that the great church architecture of the past was "contemporary" or "modern" in its day, and that its greatness was directly related to its ability to express the spirit and meet the needs of the people of its time. As Szeptycki succinctly expressed it, "It [is] not in the best tradition to repeat architectural forms that had a meaning in the past but none in the present."[52] When defending modernism, local architect Ross G. Montgomery[53] likewise made an appeal to tradition:

> The Church spoke to the Roman slave; to the knight and serf of the Middle Age[s]; and she spoke to them in their own tongue. If today we know more than our fathers did of machinery, metallurgy and medicine, the Church has a language for us too; for She is the Church of the modern man as She was of men now gone, and as She will be of every man to come.[54]

Judging by the overwhelming success of the fundraising drives that financed their construction, Southern California's new generation of Catholics—educated, affluent, and fully sensitized to the virtues of modernist design in every other aspect of their lives—enthusiastically welcomed the modernist designs proposed for their new parish churches. If there were any outspoken critics of these designs, it seems their protests have been left unrecorded.

Classic sacramental spatial dynamics and centering focus

The spatial dynamics of a *classic sacramental* church are complex, having developed over the centuries to accommodate the intricate ritual action of the medieval liturgy and to reinforce the strict hierarchical arrangement of the clergy, choir, assisting ministers, and congregants.[55] Although the liturgy was simplified over the years, two key aspects of this spatial organization persisted.[56] The first is a dominant longitudinal axis designed to accommodate liturgical processions that connects the narthex with the sanctuary at the opposite end of the building. Repetitive architectural features – arches, columns, rows of side chapels – reinforce a sense of forward movement. The second is articulation into distinct segments, allocated according to use and user: sanctuary, main nave, transept, choir loft, side chapels, baptistery, shrines, and narthex. Observation and comparison reveal that during the 1950s and early 1960s this longitudinal emphasis and complex articulation of space gradually softened and eventually disappeared. By opening up sightlines and adjusting conventional floor plans, architects sought to bring the ritual action in the sanctuary closer to the congregants, both visually and physically, thereby facilitating the participation advocated by early, pre-Vatican II liturgical reformers.[57]

The centering focus of a *classic sacramental* church is its main altar, where the chief ritual actions of the Mass take place. The centrality of the main altar is signaled by several architectural and artistic features: location at the end of the church's processional axis, demarcation from the rest of the church by a communion rail, elevation on a platform, sheltering by a baldacchino, and placement in front of a reredos or other eye-catching backdrop.

The characteristic spatial dynamics and centering focus of the *classic sacramental* tradition are on full display at Trudeau's three churches. Both St. Charles and St. Therese follow a cruciform plan. At St. Charles, a central dome resting on four massive arches divides the interior into five distinct spaces: nave, semitransepts, crossing, and sanctuary. Arches lining the nave reinforce the processional axis, while drawing attention to the altar at its terminus. A carved oak reredos with an outsized crucifix, framed by a baldacchino whose curve echoes the massive curve of the decorated arch which delineates the sanctuary from the crossing, provides a backdrop for the altar. At St. Therese, a relatively shallow dome integrated into the ceiling structure covers the crossing where the nave, sanctuary, and transept intersect, unifying these otherwise distinct spaces. The sanctuary extends into the nave, increasing both the visibility and proximity of the ritual action at the altar. A floor-to-ceiling reredos composed of matched marble slabs, and highlighted with gold fleur-de-lis and ribbon designs, incorporates the tabernacle, a crucifix, and a monumental sculpture of St. Therese. In contrast to these two churches, St. Mel is essentially an A-frame design. The steeply pitched, 60-foot-high ceiling creates a strong processional axis that places an unrelenting focus on the altar. A series of eight shrines, most arranged as miniature side chapels, line the nave, reinforcing the axis and focusing attention on the sanctuary.

Classic sacramental aesthetic impact

Classic sacramental churches are intended to be places where, in Kieckhefer's words, "the ascending curve of human transcendence and the descending curve of divine immanence intersect."[58] Architects have long employed time-honored conventions to orchestrate a rich and dramatic aesthetic impact that shifts the visitor's attention from ordinary, everyday experience to considerations of existence beyond space and time. The use of height and spatial volume to convey a sense of aspiration, and the employment of filtered light to create a feeling of ambiguity or mystery, are two such conventions.

New building technologies allowed post-war architects to draw attention to ceiling height by accentuating massive concrete beams and folded-plate roofs, and to create new and dramatic lighting effects. At St. Therese, for example, clerestory windows placed high in the dome admit natural light, illuminating both the dome's cross-beamed superstructure and the space below. The striking reredos is similarly bathed in natural light streaming through concealed tinted windows lining the sanctuary walls. St. Mel's verticality, combined with varicolored light filtering through the floor-to-ceiling stained glass panels that enclose the side-chapels, similarly produces a highly dramatic effect.

Classic sacramental symbolic resonance

Kieckhefer views the symbols that are incorporated into a church as being closely tied to the congregation's cultural identity.[59] These symbols, especially in the form of representational images, provide instruction in religious history and doctrine; they focus attention, and inspire thoughtful and emotional responses; and they reinforce the connection between the liturgy and "the network of symbols and narratives in which that liturgy is grounded."[60]

Because of their characteristically profuse use of such symbols, *classic sacramental* churches "look like churches." On the outside, their status as sacred buildings is conveyed by their massing and scale, and by their incorporation of towers and prominent porticos. Inside, they typically display a rich collection of images rendered in sculpture, painting, mosaic, and stained glass, often having identifiable connections to the congregation. Observation and comparison reveal that, as period-revival styles gave way to modernism, artistic images became increasingly abstract, and reliance on decorative architectural elements was replaced by an emphasis on the building's basic structural elements and the inherent qualities of its materials.

In Southern California, the building material of choice was concrete. The exteriors of the three Trudeau churches demonstrate its virtues and versatility. St. Charles Borromeo is the most traditional in appearance, incorporating oversized cast-stone ornamentation reminiscent of the great Baroque cathedrals of Mexico (Fig. 8.1). St. Therese, by contrast, is minimalist in design, with carefully selected symbols embedded in the expanses of concrete. The streamlined 120-foot-tall tower enshrines a sculpture of St. Therese at its apex, and incorporates decorative screens displaying the fleur-de-lis, a symbol associated with the saint (Fig. 8.2). At St. Mel, the use of gunite, poured concrete, and concrete masonry techniques, combined with an underlying steel frame, have created distinctive front, side, and rear elevations that reflect the configuration of the interior spaces (Fig. 8.3).

Throughout the Archdiocese, concrete, especially tilt-up construction, was combined with a wide range of materials, including faceted glass, mosaic, tile, metallic sculpture, and even simple brick veneer, to create a contemporary, yet recognizable look for post-war churches. Concrete itself was molded, shaped, or finished to achieve a range of architectural effects, as exemplified by Our Lady of the Holy Rosary in Sun Valley, designed by Victor J. Spotts and Thomas V. Merchant (1964) (Fig. 8.4). A concrete and faceted glass sculpture of the Crucifixion by Los Angeles artist Roger Darricarrere is seamlessly integrated into the center of the rectangular façade, flanked by panels subtly etched with tall, narrow Gothic arches. The building's corners have been cut away and replaced with concrete screens composed of rows of tall, narrow elliptical shapes, enclosing planted areas visible within the building through clear glass windows.

Perhaps the Archdiocese's most distinctive post-war monument to the possibilities of concrete and new technology is St. Basil in Wilshire Center, a modernist masterwork in the *classic sacramental* tradition designed by Albert C. Martin & Associates[61] and completed in 1969 (Fig. 8.5). St. Basil was conceived as a set of twelve adjoining, 80-foot-tall "towers," each incorporating 10,000 cubic yards of poured concrete.[62] The exterior concrete surfaces have been bush-hammered, and the interior concrete surfaces sand-blasted. The towers are separated from one another by 13 sculptural constructs of Cor-Ten steel framing, created by artist Claire Falkenstein, that incorporate panes of colored glass arranged in seemingly random overlapping and multi-angled patterns to create a kaleidoscopic effect. These constructs are visible from within the church through floor-to-ceiling windows of clear glass. The repetitive, although irregular, pattern provided by the alternating concrete and glass panels of the side walls reinforces the church's strong processional axis. The high, open beam ceiling is partially concealed by a network of trusses, to which 2,400 aluminum tubes have been fastened in dynamic, twisting patterns to create what is essentially a hanging sculpture.[63] These patterns are echoed in an assemblage of aluminum tubes projecting from the sanctuary wall which functions as both a reredos and a baldacchino, framing a fourteenth-century Italian crucifix.

FIGURE 8.4   Our Lady of the Holy Rosary, Sun Valley, California, façade.
Photograph by the author, 2008.

FIGURE 8.5   St. Basil, Wilshire Center (Los Angeles), California, façade.
Photograph by the author, 2007.

The modern communal tradition

By the mid-1960s, liturgists and architects were concluding that if a reformed liturgy based on congregational participation was going to succeed, a new approach to church building was needed—one that would not only facilitate participation but would also confirm the status of the assembly, in and of itself, as a key signifier of God's presence.[64] Architectural historian Mark Torgerson calls this new approach an "architecture of immanence," based on "a fusion of ideas emerging from the ecumenical movement, the liturgical movement, and the modern architecture movement," and emphasizing "the presence of God in people communally engaged in worship and ministry."[65]

Kieckhefer views this new approach as the foundation of a new church-building tradition, which he identifies as the *modern communal* model. Unlike the *classic sacramental* church, which "works on multiple levels," the *modern communal* church is "ultimately grounded in a single and readily appreciated principle," making it "easily understandable and widely understood."[66] Its distinctive characteristics are a spatial dynamic of "gathering in and sending forth,"[67] more than one centering focus,[68] an aesthetic impact focused on hospitality and celebration,[69] and moderate symbolic resonance.[70]

Modern communal spatial dynamics and centering focus

The spatial configuration of a *modern communal* church is intended to address the practical problem of gathering a diverse group of individuals together, helping them worship as a united community, and then sending them out into the world again.[71] Although the sanctuary and its furnishings continue to be the primary focus, the assembled congregants are given almost equal attention. Thus, the entire space is treated as an integrated whole. Congregants are seated as closely as possible to the ritual action, which is clearly visible from any perspective. At the same time, congregants are visible to one another, facilitating awareness of their status as members of a single worshipping community. In a *modern communal* church, then, the congregational seating arrangement is critical. For post-war architects, the biggest challenge was providing enough seats. Suburban parishes had large memberships—the average seating capacity in the fifty churches built between 1960 and 1965 was a thousand.[72] In the early 1960s, architects experimented with T-shaped, arrow-shaped, and diamond-shaped floor plans. Each featured a high-ceilinged nave and two low-ceilinged semitransepts. But in a 1965 interview, Thomas Kelly, the Archdiocese's construction coordinator, expressed dissatisfaction with plans like these because they tended to divide the congregation into groups instead of a "single community of worship."[73]

Three churches completed in the mid-1960s illustrate how creative architects addressed this challenge. Corpus Christi in Pacific Palisades designed by Albert C. Martin & Associates (1964) takes the shape of a paraboloid formed by a continuous, free-standing brick sidewall (Fig. 8.6). The open ends of the paraboloid intersect with a curving aluminum-framed glass wall that encloses the interior space without visually closing the geometric figure. The sanctuary is situated in the curve of the paraboloid, opposite the glass wall. Banks of pews radiate from the sanctuary, spanning the width of the paraboloid as it expands. A free-standing structure located adjacent to the glass wall serves as an organ and choir loft. St. Jerome in Westchester designed by Prescott, Whalley & Weit[74] (1966) takes its form from a substructure consisting of sixteen steel columns arranged in a circle (Fig. 8.7). Each column supports a steel roof beam which projects to the center of the circle, where the beams meet to form an oculus topped with a lantern and spire. The building has 16 sides, grouped into pairs to form eight gabled bays. One of these bays forms the backdrop for the sanctuary, which projects into the essentially circular nave. Several banks of pews, set at varying angles, converge on the sanctuary. The ceiling, with its central skylight and tent-like folds, envelops the entire interior space. The plan of Sacred Heart in Ventura designed by John Bartlett[75] (1968) has been compared to "a tunic with spread sleeves" (Fig. 8.8).[76] The curved sanctuary is located at the neck of the tunic; the square nave corresponds to the tunic's body; and a pair of semitransepts pivoted at an angle to the sanctuary correspond to the tunic's sleeves. The nave's ceiling is highest at the church's façade, slanting downward towards the sanctuary; in contrast, the semitransepts' ceilings slope upward toward the sanctuary. The sanctuary itself is set within a vast open space, lit from above by an unusually tall, triangular skylight paneled with stained glass.

FIGURE 8.6   Corpus Christi, Pacific Palisades, California, interior.

Photograph by the author, 2007.

FIGURE 8.7   St. Jerome, Westchester, California, roofline.

Photograph by the author, 2007.

FIGURE 8.8   Sacred Heart, Ventura, California, exterior.
Photograph by the author, 2008.

Observation and comparison reveal that, by the late 1960s, the *modern communal* tradition had replaced the *classical sacramental* tradition as the model for new churches constructed throughout the Archdiocese. Most of these churches are not as distinctive as the three just discussed. The most common floor plans place the sanctuary at either the middle of one of the long sides of a rectangle or the top of a bell-shaped footprint. Rows of pews then radiate from the sanctuary in a roughly fan-shaped configuration. Subtle architectural touches create an impression of expanding space overhead and a sense of contracting space at floor level. This enhances the feeling that the congregation is being gathered in and around the sanctuary. A ceiling's height may rise as it moves from the narthex to the sanctuary. At the same time, a floor's slope may be raked from back to front, a feature that has the added benefit of improving sight lines. Banks of pews may become progressively narrower as they approach the sanctuary, creating a sense of contraction. Whatever the details, the objectives are excellent visibility, a feeling of closeness to the ritual action, and a sense that the members of the congregation—gathered together in a single, simply defined, unbroken space, and fully visible to one another—comprise one united community.

Modern communal aesthetic impact and symbolic resonance

In order to create a sense of hospitality and celebration, the interiors of *modern communal* churches are designed to a human scale. Light is abundant. Even when stained glass is used, the overall effect is one of brightness rather than mystery. The inherent properties of construction materials are showcased for maximum visual impact. Corpus Christi's interior design exemplifies this, relying heavily on the textures and colors of brick, glass, metal, and wood, and the qualities of natural light (Fig. 8.6). Its flat, steel-framed roof is supported by seven 30-foot-tall, star-shaped, textured concrete columns, leaving a 2-foot-tall gap between the top of the 28-foot-high parabola-shaped brick wall and the wooden ceiling. This gap is glazed with clear glass, creating the impression that the ceiling is floating above the interior space. Additional natural light enters through the glass wall that forms the church's façade, and a crown-shaped skylight above the sanctuary.

Because the *modern communal* tradition emphasizes the symbolism of the gathered assembly, artistic and architectural symbols are often used sparingly. At the same time, symbolism is sometimes attributed to the form of the building itself. Corpus Christi's project architect, Joseph L. Amestoy, explained that the transparent curved façade that intersects with the church's parabola-shaped brick sidewall allows the parabola "to reach out to infinity, without closing in on itself, thus symbolizing the reaching out of Christ to all men."[77] Symbolic value might also be ascribed to the distinctive folded plate, tent-like roof that shelters and enfolds the congregation at St. Jerome (Fig. 8.7). Given this approach, it is not surprising that a *modern communal* church doesn't always "look like a church." Typically, exterior elevations simply express the interior arrangement. Sacred Heart's symmetrical façade, with its cantilevered eave, segues into a gently sloping roof that intersects with a tall, triangular skylight. This skylight serves the visual function of a steeple while blending into the curved rear elevation (Fig. 8.8). In many cases, the church building itself does not display any traditional indicator of ecclesiastical purpose, relying exclusively on a steeple or free-standing tower for identification.

By 1970, the *modern communal* tradition had evolved to the point that it was producing masterworks like St. Rita in Sierra Madre designed by John Gougeon.[78] St. Rita is a text-book illustration of concrete fabrication techniques: cast-in-place, precast, tilt-up, gunite, and slip-forming. Its architect describes it as "a piece of spiritual sculpture" where "almost nothing is vertical."[79] Its asymmetrical exterior elevations, which defy any systematic ver-bal description, display a series of remarkable juxtapositions of straight and curved lines (Fig. 8.9). The interior's relatively intimate scale, extensive use of wood, and harmonious combination of earth tones are illuminated by abundant natural light, which enters through stained glass panels lining the nave, a hidden skylight above the sanctuary, and clerestories of transparent glass. Although these clerestories appear to open onto a second-floor gal-lery, they, in fact, offer a view of the undersides of the sheltering eaves outside. Shaded from direct sunlight, they admit light, promote cross-ventilation, and permit the release of heated air (Fig. 8.10).

FIGURE 8.9 St. Rita, Sierra Madre, California, façade.
Photograph by the author, 2008.

FIGURE 8.10 St. Rita, interior.

Photograph by the author, 2008.

Conclusion

The Catholic churches of suburban Los Angeles comprise an unsurpassed resource for gaining insight into how the architectural program of a fast-growing denomination, grappling with an evolving identity and a new approach to worship, inspired mid-century architects to develop a fresh approach to American church building in the post-war era. They evidence the transformation of the *classic sacramental* tradition as it shed period-revival conventions in favor of modernist design principles and architectural vocabularies. At the same time, they illustrate the emergence of the *modern communal* tradition, from the earliest experiments to the fully developed template that guides Catholic church building up through the present day.

One of the most striking aspects of these churches is how well suited the principles of modern design proved to be in helping the Archdiocese achieve its architectural program. Simplicity, honest materials, innovative technology, a contemporary aesthetic, and an emphasis on functionality satisfied the demand for rapid and inexpensive construction, an up-to-date image for the post-war suburban parish, and an architecture tailored to the reformed liturgy.

In these churches, the ideals of the "post-war suburban parish" found concrete expression. They were, in their heyday, the architectural crown jewels of parish campuses that bustled with a range of spiritual, educational, charitable, social, and recreational activities. They showcased the family, especially children, as the main focus of suburban Catholic life. For Catholics who were rapidly assimilating into the American political and cultural mainstream, they reinforced religious identity. To non-Catholics, they communicated the message that their Catholic neighbors were community-minded, fashionable, and economically thriving.

At the same time, the values of the twentieth-century liturgical movement are embodied in these churches. They bear witness to the desire for full and active congregational participation both before and after Vatican II. Churches designed prior to the mid-1960s in the *classic sacramental* tradition feature open sightlines and modified floor plans intended to bring ritual action closer, although a degree of spatial differentiation and segmentation persists. Later churches based on the *modern communal* model eliminate these distinctions, focusing on the assembled congregation as a central symbol of God's presence.

Despite the updates and remodels they have endured over the years, these churches remain the definitive architectural expression of the suburban, middle-class, family-oriented Catholic subculture that flourished in Southern California during the post-war era. They are tangible links to a time within living memory when Sunday Masses were crowded, Catholic schools were bursting at the seams, sisters were teaching in nearly every classroom, one or two boys from every graduating eighth-grade class went off to the junior seminary, and new churches (it seemed) were under construction everywhere.

Notes

1 Andrew M. Greeley, *The Church and the Suburbs* (New York, NY: Sheed & Ward, 1959), 65 n. 3.
2 *The Official Catholic Directory 1948* (New York, NY: Kennedy, 1948), statistical insert following 1360; *The Official Catholic Directory 1976* (New York, NY: Kennedy, 1976), statistical insert following 5C.
3 Gretchen Buggeln, *The Suburban Church: Modernism and Community in Postwar America* (Minneapolis, MN: University of Minnesota Press, 2015); Jay M. Price, *Temples for a Modern God: Religious Architecture in Postwar America* (New York, NY: Oxford University Press, 2013); Robert Proctor, *Building the Modern Church: Roman Catholic Church Architecture in Britain, 1955 to 1975* (Farnham, UK: Ashgate Publishing Limited, 2014).
4 Richard Kieckhefer, *Theology in Stone: Church Architecture from Byzantium to Berkeley* (New York, NY: Oxford University Press, 2004), 10–11.
5 Francis J. Weber, *His Eminence of Los Angeles: James Francis Cardinal McIntyre* (Mission Hills, CA: St. Francis Historical Society, 1997); Francis J. Weber, *Magnificat: The Life and Times of Timothy Cardinal Manning* (Mission Hills, CA: St. Francis Historical Society, 1999).
6 John E. Morse, *To Build A Church* (New York, NY: Holt, 1969), xvii.
7 Merry Ovnick, *Los Angeles: The End of the Rainbow* (Los Angeles, CA: Balcony Press, 1994), 274–288.
8 Weber, *His Eminence*, 250.
9 Ibid., 243.
10 Building Regulations circa 1937 in file marked "Materials Pertaining to the Building Committee 1928–1944," Archdiocesan Archives; Building Regulations promulgated September 14, 1959, in file marked "Materials Pertaining to the Building Committee 1945–1961," Archdiocesan Archives; Weber, *His Eminence*, 242–243.
11 Ibid.; Binder titled "Church Buildings 1960–1965," Archdiocesan Archives.
12 Ibid.
13 Greeley, *Church and the Suburbs*, 63–66.
14 Charles R. Morris, *American Catholic: The Saints and Sinners Who Built America's Most Powerful Church* (New York, NY: Times Books, 1997), VII.
15 Morris, *American Catholic*, 230; James T. Fisher, *Communion of Immigrants: A History of Catholics in America* (New York, NY: Oxford University Press, 2008), 119–123; Patrick W. Carey, *Catholics in America: A History* (Westport, CT: Praeger, 2004), 103.
16 Morris, *American Catholic*, 281; Carey, *Catholics in America*, 111.
17 Fisher, *Communion of Immigrants*, 143–150.
18 Ibid., 124–125, 128–130.
19 Ibid., 125.
20 Carey, *Catholics in America*, 100–101.
21 Ibid.; Fisher, *Communion of Immigrants*, 125–127.
22 Greeley, *Church and the Suburbs,* 56–62; Morris, *American Catholic*, 257, 281; Fisher, *Communion of Immigrants*, 124.
23 Greeley, *Church and the Suburbs*, 58–69; "Modern Suburban Parish Faces Unique Problems," *Tidings*, May 9, 1958, 5; Morris, *American Catholic*, 276; Carey, *Catholics in America*, 95.
24 Greeley, *Church and the Suburbs*, 66–67.
25 John W. O'Malley, *What Happened at Vatican II* (Cambridge, MA: Belknap Press, 2008).
26 Carey, *Catholics in America*, 115.
27 Morris, *American Catholic*, 307–308.
28 Weber, *His Eminence,* 416–437; Weber, *Magnificat*, 361–383; Anita Caspary, *Witness to Integrity: The Crisis of the Immaculate Heart Community of California* (Collegeville, MN: Liturgical Press, 2003).

29 Ibid.

30 Andrew M. Greeley, *The American Catholic: A Social Portrait* (New York, NY: Basic Books, 1977), 272.

31 Keith F. Pecklers, S.J., *The Unread Vision: The Liturgical Movement in the United States of America: 1926–1955* (Collegeville, MN: Liturgical Press, 1998).

32 Ibid.

33 Joseph P. Chinnici, O.F.M., "The Catholic Community at Prayer, 1926–1976," in *Habits of Devotion: Catholic Religious Practice in Twentieth Century America*, ed. James M. O'Toole (Ithaca, NY: Cornell University Press, 2004), 9–88.

34 Carey, *Catholics in America*, 116.

35 Thomas T. McAvoy, C.S.C., *A History of the Catholic Church in the United States*, (Notre Dame, IN: University of Notre Dame Press, 1969), 465.

36 Weber, *His Eminence*, 200; see also Morris, *American Catholic*, 260.

37 Weber, *His Eminence*, 200.

38 Ibid., 197.

39 Kieckhefer, *Theology in Stone*, 10.

40 Ibid., 11.

41 Ibid., 22–43.

42 Ibid., 64–84.

43 Ibid., 108–119.

44 Ibid., 135–143.

45 Educated at the Beaux-Arts Institute of Design and Princeton, Trudeau (a St. Therese parishioner) designed churches, schools, rectories, and convents for the Archdiocese, as well as a wide range of commercial and residential projects for other clients.

46 Mark A. Torgerson, *An Architecture of Immanence: Architecture for Worship and Ministry Today* (Grand Rapids, MI: William B. Eerdmans Publishing Co., 2007), 49.

47 "Newton & Trudeau" [Display Advertisement], *Tidings*, December 16, 1938, 25.

48 Prior to immigrating to the United States in 1948, Szeptycki restored historic churches, was active in the Polish underground, and served time in a Nazi concentration camp. After earning a graduate degree in architecture at USC in 1952, he built a successful practice in Southern California specializing in church and school design.

49 "New Renaissance Seen in Design of Churches: Southland Architect Who Has Created 20 Urges 'Education' of Building Commission" [Interview with J. George Szeptycki], *Los Angeles Times*, July 26, 1964, K5.

50 "Newton & Trudeau," 25.

51 "New Renaissance Seen," K5.

52 Ibid.

53 Montgomery was a versatile and prolific architect whose work for the Archdiocese in the 1920s and 1930s included churches and chapels in the Byzantine, Romanesque, Spanish Colonial, Pueblo, and Art Deco styles.

54 "Bishop Will Dedicate New St. John's Church," *Tidings*, December 26, 1947, 2.

55 Kieckhefer, *Theology in Stone*, 25.

56 Ibid.

57 Torgerson, *An Architecture of Immanence*, 115.

58 Ibid., 102.

59 Ibid., 143.

60 Ibid.

61 This firm, led by three generations of the Martin family, has been designing churches since it was formed in 1906. Among its numerous Los Angeles area landmarks is the region's tallest building, Wilshire Grand Center, completed in 2017.

62 Francis J. Weber, *Christ on Wilshire Boulevard: A Guide to St. Basil's Catholic Church* (Los Angeles, CA: Westernlore, 1969).

63 Ibid.

64 Michael E. DeSanctis, *Building from Belief: Advance, Retreat, and Compromise in the Remaking of Catholic Church Architecture* (Collegeville, MN: Liturgical Press, 2002), 39.

65 Torgerson, *An Architecture of Immanence*, 49.

66 Kieckhefer, *Theology in Stone*, 16.

67 Ibid., 52–60.

68 Ibid., 93–96.
69 Ibid., 124–126.
70 Ibid., 143.
71 Ibid., 56.
72 "Churches Designed for New Liturgy," *Tidings*, October 1, 1965, 1.
73 Ibid.
74 Raymond Whalley, a St. Jerome parishioner, maintained a diverse practice that included church design.
75 Bartlett, an Arcadia-based architect, also designed buildings for the Archdiocesan seminary.
76 "Cardinal to Bless New Church," *Tidings*, June 4, 1976, 11.
77 "Groundbreaking Planned for Palisades Church," *Tidings*, February 15, 1963, 5.
78 Pasadena-based Gougeon, noted for his mid-century residential designs, also designed Pasadena Presbyterian Church (1976).
79 Chris Bertrand, "When Architecture Becomes Sculpture and Landmark: Architect Gougeon Speaks on St. Rita Church Design," *Mountain Views-Observer*, August 29, 2008, 13.

References

Bertrand, Chris. "When Architecture Becomes Sculpture and Landmark: Architect Gougeon Speaks on St. Rita Church Design," *Mountain Views-Observer*, August 29, 2008, 13.
"Bishop Will Dedicate New St. John's Church," *Tidings*, December 26, 1947, 2.
Buggeln, Gretchen. *The Suburban Church: Modernism and Community in Postwar America* (Minneapolis, MN: University of Minnesota Press, 2015).
"Cardinal to Bless New Church," *Tidings*, June 4, 1976, 11.
Carey, Patrick W. *Catholics in America: A History* (Westport, CT: Praeger, 2004).
Caspary, Anita. *Witness to Integrity: The Crisis of the Immaculate Heart Community of California* (Collegeville, MN: Liturgical Press, 2003).
Chinnici, Joseph P., O.F.M. "The Catholic Community at Prayer, 1926–1976." In James M. O'Toole, ed. *Habits of Devotion: Catholic Religious Practice in Twentieth Century America*, 9–88 (Ithaca, NY: Cornell University Press, 2004).
"Churches Designed for New Liturgy," *Tidings*, October 1, 1965, 1.
DeSanctis, Michael E. *Building from Belief: Advance, Retreat, and Compromise in the Remaking of Catholic Church Architecture* (Collegeville, MN: Liturgical Press, 2002).
Fisher, James T. *Communion of Immigrants: A History of Catholics in America* (New York, NY: Oxford University Press, 2008).
Greeley, Andrew M. *The American Catholic: A Social Portrait* (New York, NY: Basic Books, 1977).
———. *The Church and the Suburbs* (New York, NY: Sheed & Ward, 1959).
"Groundbreaking Planned for Palisades Church," *Tidings*, February 15, 1963, 5.
Kieckhefer, Richard. *Theology in Stone: Church Architecture from Byzantium to Berkeley* (New York, NY: Oxford University Press, 2004).
McAvoy, Thomas T., C.S.C. *A History of the Catholic Church in the United States* (Notre Dame, IN: University of Notre Dame Press, 1969).
"Modern Suburban Parish Faces Unique Problems," *Tidings*, May 9, 1958, 5.
Morris, Charles R. *American Catholic: The Saints and Sinners Who Built America's Most Powerful Church* (New York, NY: Times Books, 1997).
Morse, John E. *To Build A Church* (New York, NY: Holt, 1969).
"New Renaissance Seen in Design of Churches: Southland Architect Who Has Created 20 Urges 'Education' of Building Commission" [Interview with J. George Szeptycki], *Los Angeles Times*, July 26, 1964, K5.
"Newton & Trudeau" [Display Advertisement], *Tidings*, December 16, 1938, 25.
The Official Catholic Directory 1948 (New York, NY: Kennedy, 1948).
The Official Catholic Directory 1976 (New York, NY: Kennedy, 1976).
O'Malley, John W. *What Happened at Vatican II* (Cambridge, MA: Belknap Press, 2008).

Ovnick, Merry. *Los Angeles: The End of the Rainbow* (Los Angeles, CA: Balcony Press, 1994).

Pecklers, Keith F., S.J. *The Unread Vision: The Liturgical Movement in the United States of America: 1926–1955* (Collegeville, MN: Liturgical Press, 1998).

Price, Jay M. *Temples for a Modern God: Religious Architecture in Postwar America* (Oxford: Oxford University Press, 2013).

Proctor, Robert. *Building the Modern Church: Roman Catholic Church Architecture in Britain, 1955 to 1975* (Farnham, UK: Ashgate Publishing Limited, 2014).

Torgerson, Mark A. *An Architecture of Immanence: Architecture for Worship and Ministry Today.* (Grand Rapids, MI: William B. Eerdmans Publishing Co, 2007).

Weber, Francis J. *Christ on Wilshire Boulevard: A Guide to St. Basil's Catholic Church* (Los Angeles, CA: Westernlore, 1969).

———. *His Eminence of Los Angeles: James Francis Cardinal McIntyre* (Mission Hills, CA: St. Francis Historical Society, 1997).

———. *Magnificat: The Life and Times of Timothy Cardinal Manning* (Mission Hills, CA: St. Francis Historical Society, 1999).

9

CRITIQUING MODERNISM

The unorthodox Orthodox, 1950s–60s

Dean G. Lampros

During the mid-1950s, Eastern Orthodox congregations throughout the United States, like other religious groups with immigrant roots, began their exodus to the suburbs. This meant leaving behind the previous generation's downtown churches, in which they'd worshiped for many decades. To complete the move, building committees, clergy, and architects collaborated to construct new buildings for the next generation. The resulting creations combined modern materials and construction methods, an emphasis on simplicity and abstraction, and a sleek, space-age aesthetic with a bold historicism so that a connection to the past was readily apparent. From Boston to the Bay Area, mid-century Orthodox churches blended modernist and traditional idioms, resulting in a hybridity that was immediately recognized and largely celebrated. This hybridity reflected the congregations' assimilationist aspirations as well as their attachment to their roots,[1] and it featured prominently in newspaper descriptions and promotional materials whenever a new church broke ground or was completed; in fact, it was often the first quality that was mentioned. This chapter's exploration of the hybridity of mid-century Orthodox churches as an expression of group identity thus follows a specific thread: hybrid churches for hyphenated Americans.

The designs drew inspiration from two seemingly disparate but surprisingly compatible streams: the complex architectural legacy of Byzantium and mid-century modernism. More importantly, the completed churches took liberties with both. A survey of mid-century Orthodox church buildings in the United States reveals that for the architects and building committees whose joint visions they embodied, a reliance upon a varied, flexible, and vernacular interpretation of Byzantine architecture was the norm. It is also apparent that, in many communities, ethnic and regional ties played a significant role in selecting which traditional elements and forms were borrowed and, ultimately, modified, re-imagined, and abstracted. Often the Byzantine influence was subtle, playful, and artful. At times the modernist forms and motifs employed were controversial and, in some cases, reconfigured or reversed by later generations. In each instance, however, the unorthodox products were created for, and in collaboration with, congregations that were simultaneously forward-looking and proud of their Old World roots.

Writing about mid-twentieth-century Greek churches, architect and historian Steven Papadatos acknowledges that while these buildings "included the traditional elements which express the theology of the church," they also used "contemporary materials, state-of-the art church construction methods and contribute[d] new dimensions which are pleasing to the eye and the tastes of contemporary man."[2] Theodore Saloutos also acknowledges a new direction in church architecture during the mid-twentieth century and emphasizes how Greek Americans relied upon architectural modernism to communicate progress, respectability, and belonging. "A church in the old immigrant neighborhood," Saloutos concludes,

> would no longer do. The parishioners were Americans, in many instances they had carved out successful niches for themselves in the business and professional worlds. They wanted their churches to reflect their new status in American society. Perhaps the most striking example of the new departure in architecture was that of the Annunciation Church of Milwaukee, designed by Frank Lloyd Wright.[3]

A similar argument was made by Charles Moskos: "The Americanization of the Greek Church is also apparent in its aesthetic side . . . an American idiom [being] found in the architecture of new Greek churches."[4] None, however, address hybridity; nor do they attempt to identify patterns within the broader landscape of Orthodox America beyond the Greek community.

Frank Lloyd Wright's Annunciation Greek Orthodox Church of Wauwatosa, Wisconsin

The Annunciation Greek Orthodox Church of Wauwatosa (1961), just outside of Milwaukee, symbolizes the paradoxical way in which modernism and tradition could be joined together in a single feature or motif (Fig. 9.1). In other words, the same design elements could be used to express both modernism and tradition. The elements themselves, like the congregations whose stories they told, were bilingual. They emphasized geometric forms (especially circles and lunettes), simplicity, and minimalism. It was, however, the Annunciation's shallow concrete dome that most effectively spoke the language of modernism. Its flatness was consistent with the horizontality long associated with Wright. By the late 1950s, moreover, domed structures were being created for domestic, civic, and entertainment applications.[5] The dome spoke the language of functionalism, offering a practical and graceful solution for covering a space in which large groups of people congregated. It also spoke the language of history and of Byzantium, which appealed to Greek Americans and other groups from the Eastern Mediterranean.

If the stories are to be believed, it was Frank Lloyd Wright's carefully overturned saucer that quelled the tempest brewing when the men who hired him had grown uneasy about the famed architect's creative process. The saucer, placed over a teacup during the architect's meeting with the church's building committee in 1956, represented the shallow dome Wright had in mind; the teacup, its concave base.[6] It was the finished drawings, however, that eventually won them over.[7] The design spoke to the community's collective sense of history as well as their identity as second-generation, upwardly mobile Greek Americans. According to the teacup story, Wright convinced these particular clients that the use of a

FIGURE 9.1 Annunciation Greek Orthodox Church, Milwaukee, Wisconsin.
Photograph by Stephen Matthew Milligan.

flattened dome, as illustrated by the overturned saucer, was a stroke of artistic genius, a singular and unique spark of inspiration. In reality, his design utilized a developing architectural idiom, examples of which were appearing in other Orthodox communities throughout the United States.[8]

Time magazine echoed the teacup theme in a 1961 article entitled "Teacup Dome."[9] Wright was already dead by then, and the design of the church, one of his final commissions, was getting attention for its striking blend of architectural modernism and the distinct architectural tradition of Byzantium. The article noted the Annunciation's connection to the sixth-century Church of the Holy Wisdom in Istanbul (Hagia Sophia), the archetype of the domed Byzantine church, to which Wright looked for inspiration. It explained that in designing the "concrete and steel teacup church," Wright had also taken advice from his wife, Olgivanna, who was raised Eastern Orthodox in Montenegro.[10] Still, Church authorities outside of Milwaukee were concerned initially that their ecclesiastical tradition demanded "greater fidelity to existing Byzantine structures."[11] Wright countered with a declaration that it was "never necessary to cling slavishly to tradition."[12]

Wright appears to have understood the Byzantine tradition, though he denied that the building was a copy of the Hagia Sophia, asserting that it was "better than a copy."[13] Instead, he treated it as an homage to an architectural icon. A "little St. Sophia," he called it.[14] The finished church took the form of a rotunda consisting of a wide, shallow dome atop a concrete bowl resting on the four equal arms of a Greek cross. The Annunciation's connection to the Hagia Sophia was not vague, as some have claimed.[15] Rather, the connection, embodied primarily in the structure's dome, was both figuratively and literally concrete.

Its bold historicism challenged a tenet of orthodox modernism, which sought a clean break with historical styles. The *Time* article captured the tension between modernism and tradition that the building committee wrestled with and the collaboration between these two opposite poles, which Wright so successfully wrought.

Some deem Wright's Annunciation an anomaly within the landscape of Greek Orthodox America.[16] Others place the structure within the wider context of Greek Orthodox church building at mid-century but overstate the structure's reliance on a modernist idiom.[17] Accordingly, they credit Wright's design with ushering in a new emphasis on architectural modernism within America's Greek Orthodox Church. For example, Robert Nelson has argued that "[the Annunciation] began a new phase of Greek Orthodox architecture in America. Within a few years, its design was being imitated for new Greek churches locally and nationally."[18] Virtually no one, however, connects the design of the Annunciation with the ongoing tension between modernism and tradition that shaped a new Eastern Orthodox landscape—not just Greek—spanning the nation for the next two decades.[19]

Architectural historians have not paid close enough attention to the creative, experimental hybridity displayed in the Annunciation and countless other Orthodox (and Byzantine-rite) churches across the United States, a hybridity that was immediately recognizable to contemporary observers. Consequently, they have missed an opportunity to explore the way in which mid-twentieth-century sacred architecture was used to resolve and communicate complicated questions of identity and the tension between the New World and the Old. The familiar, formal language of Byzantium by itself no longer accurately expressed who assimilating communities were becoming. At the same time, they also found the language of strict, ahistorical modernism insufficient. Together, however, the two languages were able to communicate the complex and nuanced identities of Orthodox congregations throughout the United States at mid-century.

Even before pencil ever touched paper, the process of selecting an architect revealed the ambivalence with which the Milwaukee parish grappled. One of the candidates under consideration was a Greek from Chicago; another firm promised them "a perfect Byzantine," recommending that they remain true to their traditions. In the end, the parish chose an architect known for his innovative designs. They wanted Wright in part because they believed his notoriety and prominence would lend respectability to a community that was still seen—and saw itself—as a struggling immigrant church.[20] Of the congregation, John Gurda writes, "its adjustment to America was not yet complete; Greek was often spoken at church council and parish assembly meetings . . . Despite the success of a few families, Annunciation was not a well-heeled community."[21] Equally important, they believed that Wright would deliver "something unusual," in the words of one of the committee members.[22] He guaranteed them a departure from tradition, a continuation of the journey they had already begun by leaving behind their immigrant roots and moving to the suburbs. A church designed by the famous Frank Lloyd Wright would express the progress they had made as a community. They had, writes one observer, "a progressive spirit that was ready to be expressed in concrete."[23]

Nonetheless, they also were mindful of their roots and the architectural heritage of Byzantium. The committee provided Wright with a list of 28 specifications outlining, among other things, the spatial requirements of Orthodox liturgy. "Being of the Eastern Orthodox persuasion," began the last of the specifications, our traditions are exemplified in the Church of St. Sophia in Constantinople and St. Mark's in Venice, which have a cruciform plan, barreled vaults and domes characterizing the Byzantine style of architecture. The architect for our church is at liberty to design an edifice carrying forth the basic traditions in a modern or organic setting, bearing in mind that the majority of our parishioners are of Greek extraction who have come to America to become a permanent part of the American scene.[24]

What the committee was asking for was, strictly speaking, a departure from modernism—they wanted tradition and modernity together, because that combination defined who they were.[25] How to blend the two was up to Wright.

Not everyone thought he succeeded. Some parishioners were shocked by his design and referred to it as a "flying saucer," a designation that is often repeated today.[26] Others saw only progress, no history. Archbishop Michael, the head of the Greek Orthodox Church in North and South America, penned a strongly worded objection when he became aware of Wright's design. He eventually withdrew his opposition, but his successor, Archbishop Iakovos, reportedly told the Milwaukee community that had he been in charge at the time, he would not have approved the plan.[27] At the celebratory banquet following the church's formal opening, he claimed to have accepted the church "without reservations" but spoke about how the church was "a complete departure from traditional Greek Orthodox architecture."[28] Two decades later, he continued to emphasize the church's modern design. "Yet like St. Sophia, the Milwaukee structure is for our times akin to the fabled great church in Constantinople," he said, speaking with Steven Papadatos, "which for the time of Justinian was innovative and daring."[29]

Many others, however, saw a "modern Byzantine" hybrid when they beheld the Annunciation and liked what they saw.[30] "The overall plan is just what we want," Father Emmanuel Vergis, Annunciation's pastor, later told the *Milwaukee Journal*. "It follows traditional forms, and yet it can be said that this is something of today."[31] The newspaper's editors likewise considered the finished church "an architectural marvel" and wrote that "Wright's basic conception was as thoroughly Byzantine as the great Saint Sophia built at Constantinople . . . But Wright was informed by tradition, not enslaved."[32] Architectural historians too were quick to point out the modern structure's reliance upon tradition. "In the design of this church," wrote Richard W. E. Perrin in his 1967 book *The Architecture of Wisconsin*

> Wright probably came closer to an established tradition than in any other situation. This was necessarily so, because of the positive requirements of the Orthodox liturgy, but in addition there was the love he professed for the Byzantine of Hagia Sophia.[33]

Likewise, when the church was nominated to the National Register of Historic Places in 1974, Mary Ellen Wietczykowski, the chairman of the Milwaukee Landmarks Commission, described the structure in similar terms: "For his design Frank Lloyd Wright drew upon time-honored Eastern Orthodox traditions, and yet Annunciation Church is wholly of this century."[34]

The paeans to Wright's genius notwithstanding, there is an aspect of the Annunciation that was entirely predictable. A hybrid church was, after all, exactly what was requested by

Milwaukee's Greek Americans, proud of their roots but rapidly Americanizing and bound for suburban Wauwatosa. Thus, while it cannot be said that Wright's aesthetic, his unique design, or the precise way in which he executed his commission were at all predictable, there was predictability in the blending of architectural modernism and historical tradition in a mid-twentieth-century Orthodox church. In the end, the Greek Americans of Milwaukee were not so unique. Their regional access to Wright notwithstanding, the building committee would not have been governed by a radically different set of criteria or standards. Thus, the Annunciation represents not a departure, but a product of the same hybrid identity shared by other Orthodox communities nationwide. "In the post-war years," Jay Price rightly points out, "Orthodoxy was still primarily an immigrant community, its members wrestling with how to be both American and part of centuries-old religious traditions."[35]

Moreover, by the time the Annunciation was completed in 1961, hybrids had already been built by Orthodox congregations in other parts of the United States, and many more had been designed and were awaiting construction. Robert Nelson explains:

> After World War II, the character of new Greek churches changed as the American-born children of immigrants began to play a larger role and as English was heard more frequently in services. During the prosperous post-war period, the Greek Orthodox were increasingly accepted in American society, and Greek Orthodox architecture parted from tradition and became more innovative. Now, instead of continuity with Greece, congregations permitted architects and painters to mingle originality and personal experience with traditional forms. The results were predictably diverse.[36]

Although the Annunciation is undeniably an iconic masterpiece, when placed within the context of the entire corpus of mid-twentieth-century Orthodox church buildings, it quickly becomes apparent that it is not exceptional.[37] Many other architects were busy working within Orthodox communities nationwide to achieve the same artful blend of modernism and Byzantine architecture.

The best of two worlds

For America's Orthodox Christians at mid-century, the pull of Byzantium was strong. Depending on the community's roots, however, Byzantium could mean the Hagia Sophia or the monasteries of Mount Athos; Athens or Asia Minor; the cathedrals of Russia or Ukraine; the churches of Serbia, Romania, or the Levant.[38] Architects had their own, more academic understanding of the Byzantine tradition, too. When blending the era's modernist idiom with historical and vernacular elements from a variety of sources, they had to join their own modernist vision with the wishes of particular congregations and operate within the parameters set by the building committees that had hired them.

But whether it was presented in a set of sketches and plans or embodied in a finished church, hybridity worked because it was familiar territory. The Chalcedonian Christology central to Orthodox theology is based upon the notion of hybridity: the paradox of divinity and humanity joined in the person of Christ, the two natures existing without separation or confusion. In the case of individual mid-century Orthodox churches, each time an architect and a building committee came together to articulate a common vision, modernism and tradition were joined harmoniously in a single structure, a marriage of opposites. Across the nation, architects and building committees found creative ways to make a familiar Byzantine form speak the language of architectural modernism.

Two West Coast churches, the Ascension Greek Orthodox Cathedral (1960) in Oakland and Holy Trinity Greek Orthodox Church (1963) in San Francisco—both designed by the San Francisco firm of Reid Rockwell Banwell & Tarics—utilize a bilingual dome as their principle form. However, if the Hagia Sophia served as the inspiration, the architects interpreted it differently than did Wright. In the former example, the steel-ribbed, copper-covered dome, with its four rounded dormers, sits not on a concave base like Wright's Annunciation, but on a low drum, and is surrounded by a minimalist, four-sided portico. The architect, Robert Olwell (1917–88), described the church as "a contemporary expression of a Byzantine church,"[39] language that is echoed today on the Ascension's website.[40] Covering the dome's interior is a modernist depiction of the Christ *Pantokrator*, designed by Brian Tivel and executed by Cedric Bourboulis (Fig. 9.2). The mosaics were completed by Lucienne Bloch Dimitroff, who spoke at length about the affinity between modernism and Byzantine art when it came to abstraction, a language shared by both: "It is a very marvelous thing for us in the modern and abstract art world. [Byzantine art] is much closer to the modern and the abstract."[41]

When it was dedicated in January 1964, Holy Trinity was described as "a contemporary design with a Byzantine look."[42] It utilizes a shallow dome but employs distortion to exaggerate the tholobate, or drum. The heavy buttresses around the drum's perimeter evoke those found in many early Byzantine churches, including the Hagia Sophia, the "Little Hagia Sophia" (the Church of SS. Sergius and Bacchus), and the Hagia Irene in Istanbul. Looking back in 2001, almost four decades after the church was constructed, Holy Trinity's priest described the hybrid identity of the parish during the post-war years: "They were now Greek Americans, Greek at heart but American in outlook."[43] Holy Trinity symbolized the advances that the San Francisco Greek Americans had made. In 1956, the city had elected its first Greek American mayor, George Christopher (1907–2000), who was still in office when Holy Trinity was dedicated.

FIGURE 9.2 Christ *Pantokrator*, interior of dome, Ascension Greek Orthodox Cathedral, Oakland, California.

Photograph by Michael Dickens.

FIGURE 9.3 St. George Greek Orthodox Cathedral, Manchester, New Hampshire.
Photograph by the author.

The domes used in the design of St. George Greek Orthodox Cathedral (1966) in Manchester, New Hampshire (Fig. 9.3), appear less a copy of the Hagia Sophia than an abstraction of a ciborium (the four-pillared domed structure depicted in icons of the infant Jesus' presentation in the temple). The form, used over the main sanctuary as well as repeatedly in the exonarthex and community center, is fluent in both modernism and Byzantine.[44] Familiar as it was to Orthodox worshippers, it was executed using modernism's space-age aesthetic and is similar to the original canopy over the Golden Rondelle Theater (1964) in Racine, Wisconsin.

Paul Thiry's design for St. Demetrios Greek Orthodox Church (1962) in Seattle (Fig. 9.4) employed a gracefully undulating octapartite roof similar to Felix Candela's Los Manantiales (1958).[45] A modernist celebration of fluidity and volume, it paid homage to the barrel-vaulted interiors and cupola domes of Greece's Middle Byzantine period.[46] The design expressed the community's Old World roots, which were still strong in the 1960s; three years into their new structure, they hosted their annual bazaar with a "Greece in Seattle" theme.[47] Newspaper coverage from the event included an image that shows two smiling women, neither with Greek last names, holding up a tray of Greek pastries.[48] The article makes extensive reference to Greek culinary traditions. In spite of assimilation and intermarriage, this was a community that knew and loved its roots, and this love was reflected in the church building, just as it reflected the community's success, assimilation, and prosperity.

The hybridity of St. Sarkis Armenian Apostolic Church (1962) in Dearborn, Michigan, was instantly recognized by its building committee. While the octapartite roof and lantern cupola used angles instead of curves to evoke the geometry and conical domes of medieval

FIGURE 9.4 St. Demetrios Greek Orthodox Church, Seattle, Washington.
Photograph by Joe Mabel.

Armenia, the design was nonetheless seen as a reflection of the community's assimilationist aspirations. "We live in a new place, and not in the old country. It is necessary to blend the traditional symbols with the contemporary society,"[49] explained the secretary of the building committee, Percy Sarkisian.

The Church of SS. Peter and Paul (1964) in Glenview, Illinois (a suburb of Chicago), utilizes a form that can be found in a handful of other midwestern Greek churches, whose aesthetic connection to the Hagia Sophia was tenuous at best.[50] Rather, they seem to have taken their inspiration from the eighth-century church of the same name in the northern Greek city of Thessaloniki. Designed by James Economou (1928–2014), SS. Peter and Paul consists of a brick building whose footprint is a largely unadorned Greek cross topped by a central dome. One observer described how it "was at the same time modern and faithful to the tenets of Byzantine architecture" and compared it not to either of the Hagia Sophias, but to the eleventh-century church of St. Theodore in Athens:

> Both employ the high center dome and arched doorways and narrow arched windows. Both are also made of brick, and contain a main room in the shape of a Greek cross . . . But here the similarity ends. SS. Peter and Paul is simpler and more functional, with clean, uncluttered lines that are strictly 20th century.[51]

For Greek and non-Greek observers, Byzantium meant more than simply the Hagia Sophia.

Furthermore, SS. Peter and Paul is a good example of how modernist minimalism influenced not just exterior form, but interior spaces as well. To minimize divisions between the different worship spaces and emphasize the sense of airy openness, a glass wall topped by metallic arches was used between the narthex and the nave. The iconostasis—the icon screen separating the nave from the altar—was remarkably simple in its execution, employing light, metallic arches, broad gaps between the icons, and a short, framed gate affording a clear and unobstructed view of the altar table. SS. Peter and Paul was not alone, moreover, in its rejection of the traditional heavy and ornately carved wooden iconostasis in favor of a sleeker, more minimalist, streamlined version. While voids framed by round arches were used in SS.

Peter and Paul, a similar effect was achieved by the doors of the iconostasis in the Dormition of the Virgin Mary Church in Minneapolis, Minnesota (1957), which were executed in metalwork lattice using a cross-in-circle pattern. However, even solid screens were sometimes pared down to their most basic elements, namely the icons themselves, with no decorative embellishments of any kind.[52]

Suburban churches like SS. Peter and Paul were symbols of how progress and modernity commingled with history and tradition in the community's collective identity. They were a product of "the assimilative suburbs," concluded one historian in 1974.[53] Referring specifically to the Glenview community, he wrote about how the exodus to the suburbs, "as second and third generations climbed the socioeconomic scale," was prompting exiles to shape a nuanced vision of themselves. "Some second and third generation Greek-Americans relocating in the suburbs were apathetic about the perpetuation of the Greek ethos . . . wanting to have the best of two worlds—Greek and American."[54]

Still other churches, like the brick and concrete Holy Apostles Greek Orthodox Church (1965) in suburban Westchester, Illinois, designed by Edward Dart (1922–75), used a dome in abstract. Over the low, octagonal baptistery, Dart placed a shallow dome. What a 1966 analysis in *Progressive Architecture* termed a "half-dome" over the sanctuary is actually a curved cylinder coming up from the roof, bending at a 90-degree angle before opening as a half circle. It simulates the two-dimensional silhouette of a dome.[55] Father Chiganos, the priest during the construction of the new church, saw the building's hybridity as theologically and liturgically correct:

> The Byzantine era was a Golden Period in our church history . . . I can honestly say, however, that Holy Apostles is truly a "neo-Byzantine" church in design. That is to say, its architecture reflects something of the old by the use of modern materials. In this respect, Dart has successfully interpreted Orthodox tradition. The materials used are earthy and simple, representing the strength indicative of the church of Christ, while at the same time they are rich in elegance, symbolizing the ritual and tradition of the Greek Orthodox Church.[56]

For Father Chiganos, the structure's hybridity was less about his flock's hyphenated identity than it was about the paradoxical nature of their faith. Two other excellent examples of abstracted domes are Jovan Tomich's (1929–2001) brutalist evocation of the Serbian Byzantine tradition in Pittsburgh's Holy Trinity Cathedral (1971) and Tasso Katselas's Assumption Greek Orthodox Church (1968) in Poughkeepsie, New York. Both accomplished with abstracted domes what Michail Georgiou and Theresa Kwok achieved half a century later in the Peter the Apostle and Helen the Martyr Chapel in Paphos, Cyprus (2015).

Finally, the dome referenced by some churches within the Orthodox fold was not the great dome of the Hagia Sophia or the domes of medieval Greece, but the onion domes of Mother Russia and Kievan Rus'. Many communities and architects looked to the Orthodox landscape of Eastern Europe; many to their own places of origin, some to large urban churches, others to small rural churches. One illustrative example of this can be found in Manhattan. At the edge of Stuyvesant Square stands the glass and concrete church built to house the congregation of St. Mary's Byzantine Catholic Church (1963). It is capped at one corner by a modernist interpretation of a traditional onion dome (Fig. 9.5). Housing the church bell and rendered sculpturally in strips of steel, which appear almost as if caught up in a whirlwind, the dome creates an overall effect of being dematerialized, more spirit than matter. St. Mary's also demonstrates that hybridity was not limited to the suburbs.

Constantin Pertzoff's (1899–1970) Holy Trinity Russian Orthodox Cathedral (1960) in Boston (Fig. 9.6) took the opposite approach, emphasizing materiality in its modernist make-over of an onion dome, making it speak the streamlined language of the atomic age.[57] By 1994, church members no longer spoke that language, and the main dome was removed and replaced with a historically accurate onion dome (Fig. 9.7). Perhaps the most playful example is the conical dome of Philadelphia's St. Vladimir Ukrainian Orthodox Cathedral (1966), which offers a sleek, modernist take on the familiar tented roofs and *kokoshniki* of Russian and Ukrainian cathedrals.

FIGURE 9.5 St. Mary's Byzantine Catholic Church, New York City.

Photograph by the author.

FIGURE 9.6 Holy Trinity Russian Orthodox Church, Boston, showing original domes.

Photograph from the author's private collection.

FIGURE 9.7 Holy Trinity Russian Orthodox Church, Boston, showing 1994 exterior renovations.

Photograph by Daderot.

Beyond the dome

Some communities eschewed the dome entirely, like the Greek Americans of Lynn, Massachusetts. They opted instead for a flattened basilica in beige brick with a tall bell tower (Fig. 9.8).[58] Arched at its top, the tower was pierced by a double Byzantine window and crowned with a budded cross. The wide horizontality of the façade and the relative minimalism of the interior were broken up by three stained glass windows. Separated and framed in aggregate concrete, the windows depicted Christ flanked by the Virgin Mary and St. George—to whom the church was dedicated—in a sublime, abstract, mid-century modern take on Byzantine iconography. Completed in 1954, the church housed a community that had reason to be proud and to demand a church that embodied the progress they felt. They had raised up the nation's "Golden Greek," Harry Agganis, the starting first-baseman for the Boston Red Sox that year.[59]

FIGURE 9.8 St. George Greek Orthodox Church, Lynn, Massachusetts, prior to renovations.

Photograph from the author's private collection.

For at least some of the city's Greek Americans, most notably the sizable contingent whose roots could be traced to the Greek island of Lesvos in the northern Aegean, St. George Greek Orthodox Church likely evoked the island's renowned pilgrimage church, the *Panagia Vrefokratoussa* in the hill town of Agiassos. The Lynn church would have been a familiar sight to anyone acquainted with the wide, eleventh-century basilica and its prominent bell tower.[60] Sadly, it did not suit twenty-first-century parishioners, for whom the structure evoked not a beloved pilgrimage church from the Old Country but rather a dated embarrassment, a product of the previous generation's misguided modernism.[61] In 2008, the structure was "modernized"[62] after a new generation and new leadership, driven by zeal for Byzantine purity, embarked on an ambitious campaign to correct what they considered past errors. The result is a mangled façade, Byzantinized through the removal of the stained glass window, the addition of an exonarthex, and the cropping of the stately bell tower, which was modified into a squatter domed tower matching one of slightly smaller proportions that was built on the other side to create a lopsided symmetry.

For Christ Kamages, the architect who designed and oversaw the renovation, the 1954 St. George with which he had to work fell into the category of "'half-baked,' 'Neo-Byzantine' concoctions that are neither fish nor fowl." Kamages is today one of the premier architects working with Greek Orthodox communities to build new churches or remodel older ones. He has criticized basilicas in particular, calling them "un-Orthodox,"[63] and he refuses to include them in his list of correct Byzantine Orthodox Church architecture. "I do not believe that the basilicas should be included in this grouping," he writes, "because it was a 'borrowed' church form . . . and does not relate or adequately support the Orthodox worship activity."[64] His position, while narrow, is consistent with what Kostis Kourelis and Vasileios Marinis describe as the third and most recent of the "three phases of distinct architectural change" in the landscape of Greek Orthodox America. Stretching from the 1980s to the present, it "consists of a centralized return to historicist correctness."[65]

The domes of some mid-twentieth-century churches often were subordinate to other features that consistently and reliably evoked the Byzantine tradition. Prophet Elias Greek Orthodox Church (1965) in San Bernardino, California; Holy Trinity Hellenic Orthodox Church (1966) in Chicago; and Holy Trinity Greek Orthodox Church (1966) in Bridgeport, Connecticut, all employed rippling arches, a common modernist motif.[66] Although all three possess domes, the arches dominate their façades, and while they give the churches an undeniably modernist look, the arches also echo the blind arcades found throughout the Balkans, Eastern Europe, and Asia Minor.[67] For the worshippers at St. Mary Romanian Orthodox Church in Chicago, built in 1963,[68] both the cupola dome and its rippling arches would have evoked the familiar Brâncovenesc style of the seventeenth-century Romanian Patriarchal Cathedral in Bucharest. Blind arcades also feature prominently in earlier structures, such as the fifteenth-century Dealu Monastery, the fifteenth-century St. Nicholas Princely Church in Iași, and the sixteenth-century Sucevița Monastery.

It was a very specific version of the Romanian vernacular that shaped Haralamb Georgescu's (1908–77) modern design for St. Mary's Romanian Orthodox Cathedral (1960) in Cleveland, Ohio (Fig. 9.9). He looked to the Maramureș region's rural, wooden churches with their steeply pitched roofs, deep eaves, prominent, rounded apses, and high steeples and rendered each one using clean lines, abstraction, minimalism, and familiar modernist forms, such as the A-frame.[69] "The church, while modern, is in the style of wooden churches of the Transylvanian Carpathians of Romania," declared the *Cleveland Plain Dealer* in its coverage of the dedication (Fig. 9.10). There is little doubt that Georgescu intended the church to be a hybrid, and it is not difficult to understand his reasoning. The ceremonies that accompanied the church's opening perfectly conveyed the congregation's mixed identity. On one hand, the festivities included a tour of the church's museum with its display of Romanian handicrafts and folk costumes. On the other, Ohio Senator Frank Lausche (in office: 1957–69) obtained an historic American flag, reportedly the first with fifty stars ever to fly atop the Capitol Building in Washington, for the flag raising. Later that same evening, the community hosted an informal banquet with the theme "A Night in Bucharest."[70] Among Cleveland's Romanian Americans, as was true elsewhere within Orthodox America, American patriotism and pride in one's roots coexisted.

FIGURE 9.9 St. Mary Romanian Orthodox Cathedral (ROEA), Cleveland, Ohio, the oldest Romanian Orthodox parish in the United States.

Photograph by the V. Rev. Dr. Remus Grama.

FIGURE 9.10 Village church, Şurdeşti, Maramureş, Romania.

Photograph by Albabos.

Conclusion: getting over the modernist impasse

Architectural hybridity presented a natural fit for second-generation Americans from Southern and Eastern Europe and the Eastern Mediterranean, many of whom were becoming increasingly ambivalent about their origins by the 1950s and 1960s. Forward-looking and assimilationist, they simultaneously celebrated their roots while keeping a certain distance from their past. This ambivalence, the desire to be both progressive and backward-looking, was communicated by building committees to architects, who subsequently employed hybridity in their designs to resolve the tension between past and present at the heart of each community's story. A hyphenated identity, combined with the fragmented nature of Orthodoxy and the emphasis on nationalism within its individual branches, populated America's Orthodox Christian landscape with hybrid churches that are often misunderstood and underappreciated today.

Frank Lloyd Wright's design of the Annunciation, and all of the completed structures discussed here, departed from strict modernism. For architects and their Orthodox clients, the vocabulary of modernism proved inadequate, as did the traditional Byzantine idiom. The solution to which they repeatedly turned was a combination of modernism and historicism. However, the approach was less about blending disparate elements into the same structure than it was about making the same design elements speak both languages.

There is no doubt that architects known for modernist structures were hired by building committees to create something modern. There were architects available who could have been called upon to produce traditional churches, if that had been what the committees wanted. Rejecting the safe choice, they took risks instead, knowing that the end result might be controversial. They were open to something new. At the same time, the historical orientation of Orthodoxy combined with its liturgical requirements compelled, but also allowed, architects to go beyond the existing vocabulary of modernism in their designs. A commission for an Orthodox church gave an architect permission to break free from the rules of mid-century modernism. It was an invitation to innovate.

As a result, the mid-century Orthodox churches they produced do not fit easily into any one category. They consistently featured abstraction, minimalism, a space-age aesthetic, and artfully incorporated historical elements that were often used in a playfully distorted fashion to suggest something fresh and modern. Likewise, it is ironic that well-established modernist motifs and forms were recruited to evoke centuries-old traditions. Distortion, irony, and hybridity were all hallmarks of what would later come to be called "postmodernism," at least as far as it was initially defined by Charles Jencks:

> [Postmodernism was] one-half Modern and one-half something else—usually a traditional or regional language of building. The major reason for this hybrid was clearly to do with the contrary pressures on the movement. Architects who wanted to get over the Modernist impasse, or failure to communicate with their users, had to use a partly comprehensible language, a local and traditional symbolism. But they also had to communicate with their peers and use a current technology.[71]

Whether or not we are comfortable categorizing mid-century Orthodox churches as postmodern or even proto-postmodern, they represented something new and bold and different. Consequently, both the architects who designed them and the communities that worshipped in them should rightly be deemed pioneers.

Notes

1 Because of the decentralized nature of Eastern Christianity and the lack of any centralized liturgical reform, identifiable ethnicities and linguistic differences persisted in the distinct Orthodox communities in the United States well past the mid-century mark. "While in principle Eastern Orthodoxy represented a single Church," writes Richard Kieckhefer, "the jurisdictions were distinct. What this meant for architecture was a somewhat greater degree of adherence to traditional ethnic forms": Richard Kieckhefer, *Theology in Stone: Church Architecture from Byzantium to Berkeley* (Oxford and New York, NY: Oxford University Press, 2008), 221.

2 Steven Peter Papadatos, "Development of Orthodox Architecture." In Miltiades B. Efthimiou and George A. Christopoulos, eds. *History of the Greek Orthodox Church in America* (New York, NY: Greek Orthodox Archdiocese of North and South America, 1984), 295.

3 Theodore Saloutos, *The Greeks in the United States* (Cambridge, MA: Harvard University Press, 1964), 373.

4 Charles C. Moskos, *Greek Americans: Struggle and Success* (New Brunswick, NJ: Transaction Publishers, 2009), 72.

5 Examples include London's Dome of Discovery (1951), the Gold Dome in Oklahoma City (1958), the Palomar College Dome in San Marcos, CA (1958), and Becker House (1959; later called the Shine Dome) in Canberra, Australia. Others followed during the 1960s.

6 John Gurda, *New World Odyssey: Annunciation Greek Orthodox Church and Frank Lloyd Wright* (Milwaukee, WI: The Milwaukee Hellenic Community, 1986), 76.

7 Ibid., 76–78.

8 Singularity cannot be applied to the Annunciation's form or dome. Wright and his associates recycled elements of the church in the design of the Marin County Civic Center (1962) in San Rafael, California. In 1967 when Taliesin architects reworked the Rondelle Theater (Lippincott & Margulies, 1964) in Racine, Wisconsin, they must have looked to the Annunciation for inspiration.

9 "Teacup Dome," *Time* 78 (August 18, 1961): 50.

10 Ibid.

11 Ibid.

12 Ibid.

13 Wright quoted in Gurda, *New World Odyssey*, 62.

14 Ibid.

15 Kostis Kourelis and Vasileios Marinis, "An Immigrant Liturgy: Greek Orthodox Worship and Architecture in America." In Teresa Berger, ed. *Liturgy in Migration: From the Upper Room to Cyberspace* (Collegeville, MN: Liturgical Press, 2012), 172.

16 This is the argument made by Jay M. Price, who does not see the Annunciation as part of a larger mid-century pattern. Still, he hints at hybridity with his brief discussion of what he calls "Mid-century Traditional" post-war Greek churches, which stood in contrast to what he sees as Wright's "ultramodern" Annunciation: Jay M. Price, *Temples for a Modern God: Religious Architecture in Post-war America* (Oxford: Oxford University Press, 2013), 179–180.

17 One exception is Anat Geva, who devotes significant attention to the Annunciation's Byzantine influences: Anat Geva, *Frank Lloyd Wright's Sacred Architecture: Faith, Form, and Building Technology* (London: Routledge, 2012), 94, 134, 145, 183.

18 Robert S. Nelson, *Hagia Sophia, 1850–1950: Holy Wisdom Modern Monument* (Chicago, IL: University of Chicago Press, 2004), 209.

19 A notable exception is Richard Kieckhefer (*Theology in Stone*, 200) who mentions this tension in several Serbian Orthodox Churches, but even here the emphasis is on the 1970s, by which time Orthodox communities had been building hybrid churches for more than a decade.

20 "In the twentieth century surely more than at any previous time, clients for church architecture were willing to engage the services of distinguished designers regardless of their beliefs, indeed regardless of whether they had any faith at all. Seeking to show their openness to the modern world, the Greek Orthodox might hire a Frank Lloyd Wright": Kieckhefer, *Theology in Stone*, 229.

21 Gurda, *New World Odyssey*, 40, 52.

22 Ibid., 52.

23 Ibid.

24 Ibid., 56.

25 Ibid., 40.

26 Gurda, *New World Odyssey*, 76; Anthony Cutler, "The Tyranny of Hagia Sophia: Notes on Greek Orthodox Church Design in the United States," *Journal of the Society of Architectural Historians* 31, no. 1 (March 1972): 44; and www.atlasobscura.com/places/annunciation-greek-orthodox-church. Referenced April 15, 2017.

27 Gurda, *New World Odyssey*, 80.

28 Ibid., 80, 103–104.

29 Papadatos, "Development of Orthodox Architecture," 296.

30 "Modern Byzantine," *The Living Church* 143 (July 23, 1961): 7.

31 Gurda, *New World Odyssey*, 76.

32 "Frank Lloyd Wright Church is an Architectural Marvel," *Milwaukee Journal*, July 16, 1961, 18.

33 Richard W. E. Perrin, *The Architecture of Wisconsin* (Madison, WI: State Historical Society of Wisconsin, 1967), 126–127.

34 Mary Ellen Wietczykowski, "Greek Orthodox Church of the Annunciation," National Register of Historic Places Inventory/Nomination Form, Milwaukee Landmarks Commission, October 1, 1974.

35 Price, *Temples*, 179–180.

36 Nelson, *Hagia Sofia*, 196.

37 Several others appear to have drawn inspiration directly from the Annunciation. For example, St. Nicholas Greek Orthodox Church (1967) in Jamestown, New York; the Annunciation Greek Orthodox Church (1970) in Atlanta, Georgia; and Holy Trinity Greek Orthodox Church (1973) in New Rochelle, New York; all possess shallow domes that may have been inspired by the Annunciation's flattened dome.

38 Cutler denies a diversity of inspiration existed and emphasizes the Hagia Sophia as the sole model, because building committees "knew too little of [historicism]": Cutler, "Tyranny," 41, 48–50.

39 Bruce Coleman, "Marinites Designers of Greek Church," *Daily Independent Journal* (San Rafael, CA), March 10, 1962, 4.

40 www.ascensioncathedral.com/our-history/. Accessed April 27, 2017.

41 Coleman, "Marinites," 4.

42 "Greek Orthodox Church to Dedicate Sanctuary," *The Times* (San Mateo, CA), January 22, 1964, 67.

43 www.sanfranciscogreeks.com/index.php/historical-society?id=248. Accessed April 27, 2017.

44 The form was also used in the bell tower of Lawrence Cuneo's Annunciation Melkite Catholic Cathedral (1966) in Boston.

45 Thiry (1904–93) was an American architect widely credited with having introduced modernism to the Pacific Northwest.

46 A similar example is St. George Byzantine Catholic Church (1968) in Youngstown, Ohio.

47 "Greek Church Slates Third Annual Bazaar," *Lynnwood Enterprise*, October 5, 1966, 8.

48 Ibid., 8.

49 "Church of 16 Pillars: St. Sarkis Armenian to Break Ground for $400,000 Dearborn Church," *Detroit Free Press*, July 15, 1961, 8.

50 Similar Greek examples are the Dormition of the Virgin Mary (1957) in Minneapolis, Minnesota; the Kimissis tis Theotokou (1966) in Racine, Wisconsin; St. George (1968) in St. Paul, Minnesota; SS. Constantine and Helen (1968) in Wauwatosa, Wisconsin, and Holy Cross (1969) in Pittsburgh, Pennsylvania.

51 "Greeks Sign Church Mortgage: Work Begins in Glenview," *Chicago Tribune*, June 4, 1964, 259.

52 See Edward Dart's Church of the Holy Apostles (1965) in Westchester, Illinois.

53 Andrew T. Kopan, "Education and Greek Immigrants in Chicago, 1892–1973: A Study in Ethnic Survival" (Ph.D. diss., University of Chicago, 1974).

54 Ibid.

55 Leonard J. Robilotti's Annunciation Greek Orthodox Church (1974) in Vestal, New York, uses this unusual feature and is a virtual copy of Dart's Holy Apostles.

56 "Reinterpreting an Ancient Liturgy," *Progressive Architecture* 47 (March 1966): 142, 145.

57 Pertzoff's design must have been the inspiration for Sergey Padukow's St. Nicholas Russian Orthodox Church (1968) in Whitestone, New York. Pertzoff also designed Three Saints Russian Orthodox Church (1966) in Ansonia, Connecticut, whose space-age spire evokes the tent roofs of Russian cathedrals.

58 St. George Antiochian Orthodox Church (1955) in Washington, D.C., was similar in form and feel, though it possesses a more steeply pitched gable.

59 Six months after the church was dedicated, Agganis's funeral was held there after his sudden death at the age of 26 from a pulmonary embolism.

60 This would have been true only for some. The Greek Diaspora in Lynn, as in other places, came from different parts of Greece and the Eastern Mediterranean. There were also some members of the community for whom the church's wide, flattened gable and prominent tower were evocative of the mill and smokestack/tower of the city's industrial landscape.

61 Christ J. Kamages, "Building an Architecture of True Orthodox Vision: Past, Present and Future," *The Christian Activist: A Journal of Orthodox Opinion* 10 (1997): 14.

62 See http://stgeorgelynn.org/renovation2008.htm. Accessed April 27, 2017.

63 Kamages, "True Orthodox," 9, 14.

64 Ibid., 8–9.

65 Kourelis and Marinis, "Immigrant Liturgy," 165.

66 Rippling arches feature prominently in New Formalism, examples of which include the Fontainebleau Miami Beach (1954), the Michigan State Medical Society headquarters (1961) in East Lansing, Butler University's Irwin Library (1963) in Indianapolis, Milwaukee Union Station (1965), the Metropolitan Opera House (1966) in New York, the Greater Refuge Temple (1966) in New York, and The Forum (1967) in Inglewood, California.

67 Holy Trinity (1960) in Indianapolis and Holy Trinity (1961) in Pittsburgh also employ rippling arches but dispense with the dome entirely. Even without domes, the Indianapolis and the Pittsburgh churches were recognized as hybrids that blended modern and Byzantine elements.

68 Chicago's Holy Resurrection Serbian Orthodox Cathedral (1975) is a virtual copy of St. Mary Romanian Orthodox.

69 The church may have served as the inspiration for the Presentation of Our Lord Romanian Church (1972) in Akron, Ohio.

70 Richard Wager, "Romanian Orthodox to Consecrate Church," *Cleveland Plain Dealer*, August 20, 1960, 16; "Saint Mary's Romanian Church is Dedicated," *Cleveland Plain Dealer*, August 22, 1960, 25.

71 Charles A. Jencks, *The Language of Post-Modern Architecture*, 5th edn. (New York, NY: Rizzoli, 1987), 6.

References

"Church of 16 Pillars: St. Sarkis Armenian to Break Ground for $400,000 Dearborn Church," *Detroit Free Press*, July 15, 1961, 8.

Coleman, Bruce. "Marinites Designers of Greek Church," *Daily Independent Journal* (San Rafael, CA), March 10, 1962, 4.

Cutler, Anthony. "The Tyranny of Hagia Sophia: Notes on Greek Orthodox Church Design in the United States." *Journal of the Society of Architectural Historians* 31, no. 1 (March 1972): 49–50.

"Frank Lloyd Wright Church is an Architectural Marvel," *Milwaukee Journal*, July 16, 1961, 18.

Geva, Anat. *Frank Lloyd Wright's Sacred Architecture: Faith, Form, and Building Technology* (London: Routledge, 2012).

"Greek Church Slates Third Annual Bazaar," *Lynnwood Enterprise*, October 5, 1966, 8.

"Greek Orthodox Church to Dedicate Sanctuary," *The Times* (San Mateo, CA), January 22, 1964, 67.

"Greeks Sign Church Mortgage: Work Begins in Glenview," *Chicago Tribune*, June 4, 1964, 259.

Gurda, John. *New World Odyssey: Annunciation Greek Orthodox Church and Frank Lloyd Wright* (Milwaukee, WI: The Milwaukee Hellenic Community, 1986).

Jencks, Charles A. *The Language of Post-Modern Architecture.* 5th edn. (New York, NY: Rizzoli, 1987).

Kamages, Christ J. "Building an Architecture of True Orthodox Vision: Past, Present and Future." *The Christian Activist: A Journal of Orthodox Opinion* 10 (1997).

Kieckhefer, Richard. *Theology in Stone: Church Architecture from Byzantium to Berkeley* (Oxford and New York, NY: Oxford University Press, 2008).

Kopan, Andrew T. "Education and Greek Immigrants in Chicago, 1892–1973: A Study in Ethnic Survival." Ph.D. diss., University of Chicago, 1974.

Kourelis, Kostis and Vasileios Marinis. "An Immigrant Liturgy: Greek Orthodox Worship and Architecture in America." In Teresa Berger, ed. *Liturgy in Migration: From the Upper Room to Cyberspace*, 155–175 (Collegeville, MN: Liturgical Press, 2012).

"Modern Byzantine," *The Living Church* 143 (July 23, 1961): 7.

Moskos, Charles C. *Greek Americans: Struggle and Success* (New Brunswick, NJ: Transaction Publishers, 2009).

Nelson, Robert S. *Hagia Sophia, 1850–1950: Holy Wisdom Modern Monument* (Chicago, IL: University of Chicago Press, 2004).

Papadatos, Steven Peter. "Development of Orthodox Architecture." In Miltiades B. Efthimiou and George A. Christopoulos, eds. *History of the Greek Orthodox Church in America*, 293–302 (New York, NY: Greek Orthodox Archdiocese of North and South America, 1984).

Perrin, W. E. *The Architecture of Wisconsin* (Madison, WI: State Historical Society of Wisconsin, 1967).

Price, Jay M. *Temples for a Modern God: Religious Architecture in Post-war America* (Oxford: Oxford University Press, 2013).

"Reinterpreting an Ancient Liturgy," *Progressive Architecture* 47 (March 1966): 141–145.

"Saint Mary's Romanian Church is Dedicated," *Cleveland Plain Dealer*, August 22, 1960, 25.

Saloutos, Theodore. *The Greeks in the United States* (Cambridge, MA: Harvard University Press, 1964).

."Teacup Dome," *Time* 78 (August 18, 1961): 50.

Wager, Richard. "Romanian Orthodox to Consecrate Church," *Cleveland Plain Dealer*, August 20, 1960, 16.

Wietczykowski, Mary Ellen. "Greek Orthodox Church of the Annunciation," National Register of Historic Places Inventory/Nomination Form, Milwaukee Landmarks Commission, October 1, 1974.

10

J. EUGENE WUKASCH AND MID-CENTURY LUTHERAN CHURCHES IN TEXAS, 1950–70

Jason John Paul Haskins

During the twentieth century, Lutheran ecclesial leadership shifted toward more centralized organizations as it worked toward the vision of its founder in America: "one church and one book."[1] The Commission on the Liturgy and Hymnal brought together eight major Lutheran bodies to create a shared English liturgy and hymnal.[2] In 1958, it authorized the *Service Book and Hymnal*, which quickly became the most widely used service book among the participating bodies.[3] The introduction to the 1958 *Service Book* clearly outlined the influence of the liturgical movements that were under way in other denominations:[4]

> At the same time that our Churches in America have come more fully to appreciate each other, they have also discovered through deepened scholarship a broader fellowship, the rich treasury of ecumenical liturgy . . . A vision clearer than was sometimes possible during the Reformation controversy has revealed the enduring value of some elements which were lost temporarily in the sixteenth century reconstruction of the liturgy.[5]

Collaborative efforts in liturgical matters facilitated the ecclesial consolidation. By 1963, the eight cooperating Lutheran bodies had merged into two: the American Lutheran Church and the Lutheran Church in America.[6] The patriotic nomenclature of these resulting denominations reflected the focus on American Lutheranism as the central identity.[7] The various denominational liturgical movements shared common themes including: an elevation of liturgical action over other forms of religious observance; the centrality of the Eucharist and frequent communion; the use of vernacular languages, where not already in use; the principal of *actuosa participatio* and emphasis of the participatory roles of all members of the church as the Mystical Body of Christ, and *ressourcement* or a renewal, by a return to the sources of previous practice and texts as a grounded source for newly composed or reformed liturgies. Methods of worship and architecture in particular, were a primary focus of cooperative efforts both within and between denominations. Lutheran ministers and architects participated as prominent members of the Church Architectural Guild of America and other national working groups that were considering the role of architecture in worship.[8]

Emphasis on liturgical principles guided architects to create a modernism infused with historical forms, objects, and actions. The consolidation of immigrant, regional Lutheran bodies in America followed cooperative efforts for liturgical renewal based on a *ressourcement*[9] of ancient and Reformation-era worship. A collaborative network of regional architects translated high-profile, avant-garde experiments into a common language of mainstream modernism that accompanied parallel shifts in ecclesial structures and liturgical practices. This chapter examines the work of J. Eugene Wukasch (1921–2001), a Lutheran architect at the forefront of modern church architecture in Texas, and illustrates fundamental principles that mid-century church-building shared with its contemporary liturgical movements. Like many Lutheran architects, Eugene Wukasch, a member of the Lutheran Church–Missouri Synod, worked with congregations across the spectrum of Lutheranism as well as with other denominations. Just as the renewed liturgies drew from traditional sources, Wukasch's new forms of art and architecture drew on the past in order to emphasize the centrality of sacrament in worship. Further, this study shows that Wukasch's work demonstrates how architectural change helped construct a new American Lutheran identity.

Architect J. Eugene Wukasch

The most prominent and prolific Lutheran architect in Texas during the church-building boom period (1950s–60s) was Joe Eugene Wukasch. He was a descendant of Wendish immigrants who settled at Low Pin Oak (now Serbin, Texas) in the mid-nineteenth century. They arrived motivated in part by the desire for linguistic and religious liberty.[10] These European Lutherans built the St. Paul Lutheran Church in Serbin, which became the first Lutheran Church—Missouri Synod (LCMS) congregation in Texas.[11] The church featured a two-story pulpit above the altar, a balcony surrounding the sanctuary, and an elaborate vernacular decorative painting.

Born July 12, 1921 in Austin, Texas, Wukasch attended grammar school at St. Paul's Lutheran Church, the principal LCMS church in Austin.[12] After he graduated in 1943 from the University of Texas at Austin with a Bachelor of Science in Architectural Engineering, he served in the US Navy during World War II and held "apprenticeships in nine divergent construction industry-related firms" before he officially started his own practice in 1954.[13] The new firm completed eight church projects in Texas, during its first year, including six for Lutheran congregations, one for a Reformed church, and one for a Methodist church.[14] Church projects represented the majority of Wukasch's work for the next two decades. During this time, he was an active member of the Church Architectural Guild of America and served as their Southwest Regional Director and board member.[15]

As the postwar church-building boom waned, Wukasch shifted his focus to capitalize on his engineering background and involvement in the nascent environmental and energy-efficient building field.[16] He renamed the firm Applied Environmental Research and championed passive solar housing and underground buildings.[17] Active in local politics, Wukasch was a charter member of the Heritage Society of Austin and the Citizen's Board of Natural Resources and Environmental Quality.[18]

The Church Architectural Guild of America

As an influential member of the Church Architectural Guild of America (CAGA) Wukasch interacted with other regional architects specializing in church buildings. CAGA formed in

1940 to promote excellence in church design.[19] The guild included theological and liturgical content in its work to disseminate its ideas through church congregations.[20] From its beginning, the guild championed modern architecture.[21]

CAGA was one of multiple cooperating organizations including the Department of Church Building and Architecture of the National Council of Churches of Christ, the AIA Committee on Religious Architecture, and the American Society of Church Architecture.[22] Together these organizations held an annual National Conference on Church Architecture in a different city each year.[23] The conference included business meetings between the various organizations, sessions on theoretical and practical considerations, and tours of recent local buildings.

CAGA's members included prominent modern-leaning architects including Pietro Belluschi and Paul Thiry in the Pacific Northwest, Charles Stade and Edward Dart in Chicago, Edward Anders Sövik in Minnesota, and Harold Waggoner in Philadelphia.[24] While a few of the members' practices were national, the majority of the members maintained regional practices specializing in religious buildings. The content of the National Conferences on Church Architecture reflected both developments in modern architecture and the Liturgical Movement as global phenomena, as well as the regionalism of the local practices.[25]

The liturgical movements in all major Christian denominations included a reconsideration of architecture as an integral component.[26] The spatial aspects of rituals and the relationship of the material artifacts of worship became the primary considerations.[27] Eugene Wukasch gained exposure to what he described as the "international grass-roots liturgical movement" through published texts and interactions with continental architects during the 1961 International Conference on Church Architecture.[28] On that trip, Wukasch met Peter Hammond, an Anglican priest and Secretary of the New Churches Research Group in London, who particularly influenced Wukasch's approach to liturgical architecture.[29]

As part of his involvement with CAGA and his service on the Board of Directors from 1962 to 1966, Eugene Wukasch gave multiple presentations at the guild's annual conferences. He maintained correspondence with other members of the guild and expanded on the travel opportunities the conferences afforded by visiting their practices and churches. The papers Wukasch presented at the conferences covered a wide range of topics that reflected the breadth of the guild's concerns. His paper on "The First Unit and the Master Plan"[30] covered a common strategy for new suburban churches. To save initial costs, these churches built a smaller multi-purpose hall that typically became the social space after the construction of a permanent sanctuary. Many of Wukasch's early projects were first units on this model. At the 1964 conference in Dallas, he chaired a session on fundraising, and in 1963 he discussed "Collaboration of Building Committee and Architect" with Rev. Edward Frey, the Executive Director of the Commission on Church Architecture for the Lutheran Church of America.[31] His papers culminated in a slide-focused presentation entitled "Art, Architecture, and the Liturgical Revival."[32] In it, Wukasch presented a synthesis of design theory, architectural history, and liturgical theology that applied lessons of the European Liturgical Movement to American church design.[33]

Integration of the arts

In 1961, Wukasch participated in CAGA's Study Tour of Contemporary European Churches, which culminated in his attendance at the International Conference on Church Architecture.[34]

At the national conference the following year, he co-presented a report on the trip entitled, "Echoes from the European Conference."[35] Wukasch gave the "Architect's Point of View" of this tour, while the Rev. A. R. Kretzmann presented the "Churchman's Point of View."[36] Wukasch's training as an engineer, his experience as a church designer, his frequent collaboration with artists, and his sensitivity to the civic role of the built environment led to observations under the following headings:

1.   Aesthetically Competent
2.   Quality of Construction
3.   Architect-contractor Relationship
4.   Dignity of the European Craftsmen
5.   Respect for the Past
6.   Integration of the Arts
7.   The Importance of the Pedestrian
8.   Civic Sensitivity and Civil Control in Construction
9.   Large Crosses[37]

His final observation pointed to a deficiency in American church architecture: "As an American, I was struck with the absence of large or free-standing crosses, a related, sometimes almost undisciplined expression or 'jargon' of American church design."[38] He contrasted this with the integrated arts observed in Europe where, "aside from the customary applied art, it was evident that the artist had an active part in the development of the total art expression of the building."[39]

Decades later, Wukasch similarly critiqued postmodern "embellishments" and the fact that the rejection of ornament had been taken to be the rejection of art.[40] In a lecture given to an American Concrete Institute Convention, he used the language of Genesis to celebrate the sculptural potential of concrete to merge art into the structure:

> Raw concrete "resembles the uncreated world at the beginning of time;" it is, to use the words of Genesis, "without form and void . . ." It takes us into the realm of art which transcends mortal bounds . . . Concrete is to the designer (architect/engineer) as marble and oils are to the sculptor and artist.[41]

Wukasch collaborated with artists early in the design process to ensure integration.[42] For Prince of Peace Lutheran Church in Austin, he worked with Mexican American artist Octavio Medellín,[43] who created the church's sand-blasted glass: "Truly an old-time religion is expressed in the idiom of modern art and contemporary architecture at the little church in South Austin."[44] Wukasch's approach embodied the idea that architecture was primarily a communal art, and the local Lutheran congregations who hired him presented ideal settings for participatory architecture.[45] These were congregations whose previous generations had executed the decorative interior paintings of churches they had built themselves.[46] Projects frequently involved labor from the members,[47] pastors' input on the liturgical arts, and discussion with building committees about how to develop a modern architecture that maintained continuity with the traditional elements valued by the church members. Wukasch's regionalism grew out of the strong local building traditions inherited from the Lutheran country churches of Central Texas, including St. Paul's, Serbin. The forms of these churches, abstracted by the exigencies of frontier settlement, readily transitioned to modern forms with integrated artworks.[48] The spontaneity and continuing activity of this approach answered Pietro Belluschi's criticisms of regionalism as merely "a naive and rather soft-headed variation of our architectural mainstream."[49]

Toward modern American sacred architecture

While Wukasch was "jealous" of the grand scale and ideal aesthetics of the buildings he saw in Europe, he recognized that the church in America had distinct challenges to address.[50] His church designs exemplified both a regionalism local to Texas and the pursuit of a national, modern, religious architectural identity. Wukasch participated in the emergence of a modern Central Texas regional architecture alongside architects such as O'Neil Ford and Fehr & Granger. Their works featured modern spatial arrangements abstractly rendered in similar materials with simple details: rough local masonry, expressed wood ceiling beams, and linear windows with minimal metal frames.[51]

Based on site observations, Wukasch also explored active and passive responses to local environmental conditions. He participated in early experimental residential applications of air-conditioning and incorporated an integrated sub-floor system in Windsor Park Presbyterian Church (1958) in Austin. Later in life, Wukasch was a strong proponent of subterranean architecture that used earth as a heat sink to provide passive cooling.[52]

Gethsemane Lutheran Church (1963) in Austin exemplifies both the influences of the European study tour and the efforts toward defining an American modern architecture (Figs. 10.1, 10.2). The architect collaborated with Gabriel Loire[53] to create a liturgical center in a luminous volume of Chartres blue *dalle de verre* perched atop a brick base. Between 1958 and 1961, the Texas State Capitol's expansion program displaced Gethsemane, as well as the German Evangelical St. Martin's Lutheran Church that built a new sanctuary in downtown Austin. Following a study of congregational membership movements and expectations for future growth,[54] Gethsemane chose to relocate to the fast-growing north Austin suburbs rather than rebuild in close proximity to St. Martin's Lutheran. Although members of different Lutheran denominations, both churches now held services in English, and the theological and cultural distinctions between them had diminished.[55] Their respective denominations participated in the preparation of a shared *Service Book and Hymnal* published in 1958.[56] Pastor Edward V. Long of St. Martin's, who was heavily involved in the design of that congregation's new structure, was the principal speaker at both the cornerstone ceremonies for Gethsemane[57] and the groundbreaking of its planted church Prince of Peace.[58]

Gethsemane's church historians described the new building as "Gothic in concept and contemporary in design," and noted them as being "modern buildings that retained their cathedral atmosphere when adorned with stained glass," a "contemporary" concept the architect "had observed . . . while studying church architecture in Europe."[59] Specific influences on the use of stained glass to comprise the entirety of the wall included Auguste Perret's Notre-Dame du Raincy and the work of Dominikus and Gottfried Böhm. Inspired by Böhm's St. Anna, Ehrenfeld, Wukasch achieved the full height, stained glass curtain walls of the cantilevered chancel through the first architectural application of post-tensioned concrete beams in Texas (Fig. 10.1).[60] The influence of the European Liturgical Movement had contributed to the prominence of the free-standing altar accentuated by the luminous stained glass surrounding it (Fig. 10.2).

FIGURE 10.1   Gethsemane Lutheran Church, Austin, Texas, 1963.

Photograph by the author.

FIGURE 10.2   Gethsemane Lutheran Church, 1963, interior.

Photograph by the author.

Gethsemane was not merely a copy of European models. As impressive as he found the European churches, Wukasch did not share the view held by other architects that American architecture lacked in comparison.[61] He championed American innovations in church architecture that responded to a different social situation and therefore focused more on functional solutions to outreach and education. He pointed to the Akron plan[62] as a functional innovation that stimulated a re-appraisal of American church design techniques and pre-dated the modern movement in Europe.[63]

Advocacy for a modern American architectural identity corresponded with the growing self-identification as "American Lutheranism" among those churches. Given the many changes that Gethsemane Lutheran Church had experienced between 1958 and 1962 (e.g., new location, new building, new *Service Book*, new denominational body), the congregation realized that "the premise of preserving Swedish traditions and language through the community of worship now was redirected to ecumenical opportunities. The concept of American Lutheranism became the new standard for the twentieth century."[64] At the same time, American Lutherans led the widespread adoption of modern church architecture to the surprise of contemporary observers.[65]

Whereas in Europe public institutions provided social centers, Wukasch saw this as the Church's domain in America. The master plan for Gethsemane included extensive educational facilities arranged on the hillside to engage the landscape.[66] His planning strategy represented an American adaptation of traditional "atrium architecture"[67] for a new suburban context and an application of his research into energy-efficient building through integration with the terrain. The design of Immanuel Lutheran Church in Giddings, Texas, built on the Akron plan in its contiguous sanctuary and hall with attached classrooms. An operable partition separated the hall where it intersected the front of the nave and provided flexible expansion, while maintaining the distinction between the ritual functions of the spaces. Increased attendance at English-language services in the 1940s led to rapid growth and the need for a new church building[68] that reflected the new worship and the church's status as a social center in the town.

In his support for distinctly American modern architecture, Wukasch greatly admired and emulated Frank Lloyd Wright. On promotional materials for his firm, and opposite a verse from Psalm 118,[69] he printed a quote attributed to Wright: "when we endeavor to make for ourselves an atmosphere in which to live and work according to our own faith and feeling for nature, we are performing a genuine service not only to our time but especially to the future."[70]

The master plan for Windsor Park Presbyterian in Austin (Fig. 10.3) incorporated site and climate considerations. As shown in archival material and analysis of his design, this plan is reminiscent of Wright's Taliesin West, where attention to orientation and ventilation strategies were adapted for the hot and humid climate of Central Texas. Wukasch organized the plan on the same grid of equilateral triangles used by Wright in some of his Usonian projects in the South.[71] The church's first unit, with its A-frame roof and projecting chancel, also drew on Wright's First Unitarian Society in Madison, Wisconsin. The A-frame or "Tent Form" popularized by Wright, as well as Eero Saarinen's Kramer Chapel at Concordia Theological Seminary in Fort Wayne, Indiana, became an icon of mid-century American church design and appeared in many Wukasch-designed churches.[72]

The 1965 design of the expansion and renovation of St. Paul's Lutheran, Brenham (1956–66) (Figs. 10.4, 10.5) implemented an integration of the arts and the civic role of the church building. Formally, the building was an idiosyncratic interpretation of European medieval, Western Christian architecture analogous to Frank Lloyd Wright's interpretation of Greek Orthodox architecture for Annunciation Greek Orthodox Church in Wauwatosa, Wisconsin (1956–61).[73] The new atrium's deep windows derived from Gothic geometry with pointed arches in the voids cut into the wall thickness. The figural motifs that tie the new windows

FIGURE 10.3 Windsor Park Presbyterian Church (First Unit), Austin, Texas, 1959.
Photograph by the author.

FIGURE 10.4 St. Paul's Lutheran Church, Brenham, Texas, 1966, addition and renovations.
Photograph by the author.

FIGURE 10.5 St. Paul's Lutheran Church, 1966, addition and renovations: interior.
Photograph by the author.

to the 1925 Gothic revival continue through the altar, ambo, candlesticks, and other custom liturgical fixtures.

Wukasch intended the layered sequence of the new forecourt (Fig. 10.4) and double-height atrium narthex (Fig. 10.5) to impart "a feeling of distance from the noise, the rush, the confusion of the workaday world."[74] He saw this as an antidote to the alienation of contemporary society and the automobile. It was to recover the social experience of both the churches of the Middle Ages, which "embodied the open space that fronted them in a manner consistent with man in his natural setting," and of the early days of the Church when the surrounding environment "served to introduce man to the wonders of the religious experience which lay outside the church proper."[75]

Wukasch's liturgical architecture: emphasis of sacraments over devotions

Some aspects of modern architectures broadly corresponded with the aims of the liturgical movements. For example, the minimalism and functionalism of the former could express the latter's emphasis on the liturgical over the devotional. However, there were limits to this correlation. Wukasch lamented that the rejection of additive ornament often entailed the wholesale rejection of art.[76] Whereas devotional art was extrinsic to architecture, integrated arts lent themselves to expression of and use in the celebration of the sacraments. Rudolf Schwarz, an architect who worked with Romano Guardini in the early stages of the German Benedictine Liturgical Movement, warned against the emptiness of mere functionalism of buildings as "machines for liturgy" instead of buildings as actual participants in the liturgy.[77]

Integrated modern arts, an emphasis on the altar, and architectural *ressourcement* were common features of mid-century religious architecture. Koenker echoed the sentiments of other advocates of modern religious art when he instructed that "the church should be interested in the best contributions of the most creative contemporary minds."[78] Wukasch incorporated contemporary art into his church designs as the congregation's budget and values permitted. His work with Octavio Medellín[79] at Prince of Peace in Austin (1955) provided a narrative, symbolic program around the theme of "Prince of Peace," with the images' locations coordinated to the liturgical use of space. Images of welcoming, creation, and initiation enveloped the entrance and acted as a luminous billboard (Fig. 10.6). The altar rail featured symbols elaborating the expanded scope of Lutheran Eucharistic theology. The inclusion of an innovative interpretation of stained glass with modernist figures elevated the humble suburban church. The collaboration with Loire at Gethsemane, Austin integrated modern developments in artistic, structural, spatial, and liturgical disciplines into a unified experience of worship focused on the altar (Fig. 10.2).

Lindemann has written, "The most consistent emphasis of the liturgical movement in all effected denominations has been on the Sacrament of the Altar."[80] It also had the most direct architectural implications. Simple, prominent, free-standing altars as the primary focus of the church were the dominant architectural manifestation of the new prioritization of the Eucharist. In his description of the building in the Dedication booklet for Immanuel Church in Giddings, Texas, Wukasch explained that "the altar, always the 'high point' both in function and interest, is dramatized as the place of atonement—specifically Christ's atonement for our sins."[81] The Lutheran sanctuary evolved from the prominence of the pulpit surmounting the altar, as seen in St. Paul's, Serbin where the pulpit occupies a second story above the altar.

FIGURE 10.6 Prince of Peace Lutheran Church, Austin, Texas, 1955.

Photograph by the author.

FIGURE 10.7 Our Redeemer Lutheran Church, Dallas, Texas, 1966–68, interior.

Photograph by the author.

In some cases, architects interpreted the emphasis on the altar by placing the altar in the geometric center of the church encircled by the assembly and then generating the volume of the church around this central focus. As an extreme example, fellow Lutheran architect Edward Anders Sövik came to advocate an adaptable "non-church" "centrum" model, wherein a movable altar was placed in a generic volume as needed.[82] By contrast, Wukasch's approach retained traditional basilica arrangements realized in new structural systems for the main body of the church and created luminous chancels as elevated places that were distinct but not separate from the nave (Figs. 10.2, 10.7, 10.8). A similar strategy guided the design of the Chapel of the Resurrection at Valparaiso University in Valparaiso, Indiana, which was a collaboration between architect Charles Stade and Rev. Kretzmann as liturgical consultant.[83]

At Gethsemane in Austin, Wukasch enveloped the chancel in the light from the full-height, stained glass windows (Fig. 10.2). The clerestory windows tied the nave and chancel together and directed worship toward the altar: "Emphasizing the Communion of Saints as being the Family of God, a free standing altar was placed in the chancel—an altar octangular in shape so as to have people kneeling all around it at the celebration of the Eucharist."[84] For the chancel at Our Redeemer Lutheran Church in Dallas, Texas, he used an opaque variation, with a circular extended predella and altar rail around an altar that sits as a threshold following ancient basilica models (Fig. 10.7). The integration of an architecturally distinct sanctuary creates a "trysting-place" of the temporal (nave) and eternal (apse) realms.

Similar to Eliel Saarinen's Christ Church Lutheran in Minneapolis, and Eero Saarinen's Chapel at Concordia Theological Seminary, Wukasch most frequently used a more shallow chancel with a concealed or otherwise dramatized light source. Combined with simple A-frame or bent-frame structures, this model provided a cost-effective means to achieve a sacred focus within a single-roof volume. Holy Trinity Lutheran Church in Irving, Texas (1956) and Prince of Peace in Austin (1955) (Fig. 10.6) illustrate Wukasch's application of this model.[85] In recognition of its high design on a tight budget, the building also appeared in the book *A Guide to Church-building and Fund Raising* from Augsburg Press, in trade magazines and advertisements, and in the 1957 exhibit Contemporary Religious Arts in Texas at the Witte Memorial Museum, in San Antonio.

Immanuel Lutheran Church in Giddings featured the most fully developed iteration of this model (Figs. 10.8, 10.9). According to the architect's own description, the design's emphasis was on the altar

FIGURE 10.8 Immanuel Lutheran Church, Giddings, Texas, 1958, interior.
Photograph by the author.

FIGURE 10.9   Immanuel Lutheran Church, 1958.

Photograph by the author.

by various means: from the skylight above, soft light filters down over the altar, adding a natural glow, like a benediction. From the dossal behind the altar, the large cross against the chalice in the background upholds the idea of revitalization through acceptance of the Christ as Lord of life and death.[86]

Variations in brick coursing further illuminate a liturgical hierarchy. A single brick color unified the building, while the more sacred spaces received the more elaborate and structurally expressive wall types. The office, social hall, and classroom volumes used modern stack bond surmounted by ribbon windows; the nave and bell tower were clad in running bond brick with narrow vertical windows, and the rear wall of the chancel was laid in Flemish bond and held off from the main body of the nave by a continuous window and skylight (Fig. 10.9). On the interior of the rear chancel wall, glass blocks replaced some of the headers on the subtly convex interior surface. These blocks and the chancel's stark white surfaces catch the light from the concealed strip window to give the church its terminus.

Wukasch's liturgical architecture: architectural *ressourcement*

Just as the liturgical movements looked to traditional worship practices to renew the liturgy in response to modern society, Eugene Wukasch was among those modern liturgical architects whose work explicitly engaged the past. Koenker praised these architects who "followed the Scriptural injunction to bring forth from their treasure 'things new and old.'"[87]

For some clergy, the appeal to tradition was insufficient, while for some architects, to speak of contemporary designs in historical concepts was a dilution of modernist principles.[88] However, Wukasch and other members of CAGA were entirely comfortable with the apparent contradiction of modernism that engages the past. He observed that there was "no need to mimic the past, but rather to build on it," and he admired St. Michael Cathedral in Coventry, England (Basil Spence, 1956–62) as "the grandest example of respecting and honoring the past while completely breaking architecturally from the past."[89] While resolutely modern, Wukasch's designs were not anti-historical; they achieved a continuity with the past through both overt forms and implicit programmatic structures. His approach to religious architecture echoed Frank Lloyd Wright, who described Annunciation Greek Orthodox Church in Wauwatosa, Wisconsin as "a complete work of modern art and science belonging to today but dedicated to ancient tradition—contributing to Tradition instead of living upon it."[90]

Coverage in the local press celebrated Wukasch's modern work, while highlighting its continuity with familiar church forms. The *American-Statesman* published an interior drawing of the nave of Immanuel in Giddings under the heading "Historical Church Styles Get Contemporary Look" and with the explanation that "Wukasch thoughtfully translated warm traditional forms of the past—such as a church tower and spire—into contemporary idiom."[91] An article on Prince of Peace in Austin noted that "Wukasch promised the building committee that the church he would design would have 'churchliness' but he did not promise 'colonialism.'"[92] Many such articles about Wukasch included quotes he provided from leading figures in the international liturgic and architectural discourses in place of direct quotes from the architect. A feature in the *American-Statesman* in 1961 proclaimed, "Church Design: a New Face" over an image of Windsor Park Presbyterian[93] and included a passage from Cardinal Lecaro:

> The artist who creates the church must deeply exemplify the idea of liturgic worship and must experience and assimilate its soul: then it will be easy and almost spontaneous for him to bring to the men of his time in their own language the echo of the Divine Word. It is necessary that the Catholic community realize the true sense of tradition which is not a crystalized form of a specific period of history. God is God of the Living and not of the dead.[94]

In the Immanuel Church's dedication booklet, Wukasch assured the congregation that

> indeed the presence and blessing of the Lord is the very essence and beauty of Immanuel Church. In its total concept, as envisioned by the architect and laid up, brick by brick, by the contractors and their artisans, "They (that is all who worship here) shall call his name 'Immanuel' . . . God with us." That this building, made up of so many bricks and bits of mortar and steel, be quickened by the eternal presence of the Living God and become a true spiritual sanctuary for the many souls of Immanuel Lutheran Parish— this is the prayer of its designers.[95]

To achieve this, Wukasch followed the approach common to architects of the liturgical movements: "To this end, certain pieces of furniture and specific symbols of various materials have been carefully incorporated into the basic design of integral parts of the whole plan."[96] In a letter to Rev. Max Studtmann, Pastor of Immanuel in Giddings, Wukasch explained his approach to integrating symbols into the architecture

> which represent basic ideas and concepts, [and] play a vital role, however subtle this may be. Always a symbol of this type must assist the worship toward better expression of the "fear, love, and trust" he feels for God, or it has no lasting value.[97]

Symbols with substantive traditional significance—not "undisciplined expression or 'jargon'" or devotional accretions—were to be directed toward worship and integrated into the architecture.

FIGURE 10.10 Our Redeemer Lutheran Church, Dallas, Texas, 1966–68.
Photograph by the author.

In other uses of historical references, Wukasch prefigured aspects of postmodernism, most notably in the design of Our Redeemer Lutheran Church (1966–68) in Dallas with its storefront apses, barrel vaults, and pop iconography (Figs. 10.7, 10.10). In explaining his use of the old with the new in church architecture, Wukasch points to Pietro Belluschi, who once wrote of church architecture:

> It has become increasingly apparent that even the conservative people are beginning to doubt the wisdom of blindly copying the historical styles. But freeing ourselves from the bonds of historical styles does not mean rejecting all past experience. The thoughtful architect will appraise the spirit which moves other ages, so that he may himself recapture such spirit, not by imitating it, but by truly understanding it, which means seeing the thousand ties which bond architecture to its own age.[98]

Wukasch's adherence to this concept informed all of his church work and became the basis of his paper "Art, Architecture, and the Liturgical Revival."[99] He made an argument for the clarity and functionalism of modern architecture applied to the rich symbolic traditions and revived liturgical practices of the Lutheran Church in America.

Conclusion

Reflecting in 1971 on the accomplishments of the preceding decades of liturgical renewal and denominational consolidation in the Lutheran Church, Herbert Lindemann noted the development of "completely new styles of church building."[100] He states:

> The results in some instances have been curious to behold, but taken as a whole the newer churches are the products of inquiring minds and adventurous spirits; there have been few stereotypes . . . It has become quite common, before even thinking of design, for architect and building committee to ask some basic questions concerning the purpose and use of a church building and only then to begin to sketch a structure which might efficiently meet these objectives. In other words, there has been a healthy replacement of traditionalism with honesty.[101]

The wide variety of new church forms Wukasch created for local Texas churches during this period reflected these larger trends.

In this work, Wukasch combined leading international liturgical scholarship and developments in building technology with local building traditions of rural Texas congregations. Whether rural or urban, Wukasch's churches share qualities of humble monumentality and a proclamatory stance in the landscape of rural vernacular churches of Central Texas. They contributed to the formal and material language of a nascent Central Texas modernism, particularly in the characteristic use of a loose ashlar masonry of local stone with minimal steel-framed glazing. Wukasch's churches incorporated innovative concrete and A-frame structures as well as modern art stained glass within new technologies in glazing systems. He also employed early examples of central air-conditioning combined with passive geothermal and ventilation strategies to address the local climate. Above all, Wukasch approached church-building as a communal art and thereby arrived at a true regionalism.

Wukasch actively participated in the Lutheran expression of the twentieth-century liturgical movements present in many Christian Churches intended to recover continuity with "the rich treasury of ecumenical liturgy."[102] In worship, art, and architecture, American Lutherans sought a "continuity with the whole church"—universal and denominational—that would "embody the tradition of worship during the early centuries of the Church . . . [that was] reaffirmed during the Reformation era."[103] Through his work and involvement with national organizations including the Church Architectural Guild of America, Wukasch contributed to a national dialogue among and between architects and church leaders that led to the dissemination of modern architecture across the full spectrum of theological confessions and congregational environments. Moreover, Wukasch worked for the revival of the liturgical arts as an integral component of architecture through respect for the past that rejected mimetic historicism.

Notes

1 "Introduction to the Common Hymnal," *Service Book and Hymnal* (Minneapolis, MN: Augsburg Publishing House, [1958] 1979), 287.

2 Edward T. Horn, "Preparation of the Service Book and Hymnal." In Edgar S Brown, Jr., ed. *Liturgical Reconnaissance* (Philadelphia, PA: Fortress Press, 1968), 91.

3 William R Seaman, "The Service Book and Hymnal Since 1958." In Edgar S Brown, Jr., ed. *Liturgical Reconnaissance* (Philadelphia, PA: Fortress Press, 1968), 105.

4 Timothy C. J. Quill, *The Impact of the Liturgical Movement on American Lutheranism* (Lanham, MD: The Scarecrow Press, 1997).

5 "Preface to the Liturgy," *Service Book and Hymnal*, vii.

6 E. Clifford Nelson, "The New Shape of Lutheranism, 1930–." In E. Clifford Nelson, ed. *The Lutherans in North America* (Philadelphia, PA: Fortress Press, 1975), 527.

7 "The Lutheran Churches in America are in the process of becoming the Lutheran Church in America. We share the rich endowments of a common faith, a common history, a common heritage of liturgy and hymnody, and the recognition of a common mission and destiny in the New World": "Introduction to the Common Hymnal," *Service Book and Hymnal*, 287.

8 Gretchen Buggeln, *The Suburban Church: Modernism and Community in Post-war America* (Minneapolis, MN: University of Minnesota Press, 2015), 11.

9 Many changes in the twentieth-century liturgical movements were intended to recover earlier practices rather than introduce novel inventions. For a discussion of *ressourcement* (return to sources) as a core principle of the liturgical movements and its impact on American Lutheranism specifically, see Quill, *The Impact of the Liturgical Movement*. "*Ressourcement*" was also specifically used as a name for a European Roman Catholic theological movement based on a return to ancient Patristic texts.

10 George R. Nielsen, *In Search of a Home: The Wends (Sorbs) on the Australian and Texas Frontier* (Birmingham, UK: University of Birmingham, 1977).

11 Buie Harwood, *Decorating Texas: Decorative Painting from the 1850s to the 1950s* (Fort Worth, TX: Texas Christian University Press, 1993), 17.; Anat Geva and Jacob Morris. 2010. "Empirical Analyses of Immigrants' Churches Across Locations: Historic Wendish Churches in Germany, Texas, and South Australia," *ARRIS – The Journal of South East Chapter of the Society of Architectural Historians* 21 (2010): 38–60.

12 Employment Application, Box 129, Folder 1, J. Eugene Wukasch records, Alexander Architectural Archives, University of Texas Libraries, The University of Texas at Austin.

13 "About the Author," Box 129, Folder 1, J. Eugene Wukasch records, Alexander Architectural Archives, University of Texas Libraries, The University of Texas at Austin.

14 A Listing of Building Construction for Client Owned Projects, Box 51, Folder 9, Wukasch & Associates Records and Drawings, Austin History Center, Austin, Texas.

15 "About the Author."

16 Ibid.

17 Ibid.

18 Ibid.

19 Twenty-fourth National Conference on Church Architecture Program, Box 130, Folder 2, J. Eugene Wukasch records, Alexander Architectural Archives, University of Texas Libraries, The University of Texas at Austin.

20 Ibid.

21 Buggeln, *The Suburban Church*, 2.

22 The Wukasch records in the Alexander Architectural Archives contain materials from his participation in the conferences in 1959, 1962, 1964, 1965, 1966, 1968, 1969, 1970.

23 Ibid.

24 Ibid.

25 Ibid.

26 Peter Hammond, *Liturgy and Architecture* (New York, NY: Columbia University Press, 1961) and Peter Hammond, ed., *Towards a Church Architecture* (London: The Architectural Press, 1962) document one expression of these trends that Wukasch was well acquainted with.

27 Ibid.

28 Eugene Wukasch and A. R. Kretzmann, "Echoes From the European Conference," paper presented at The National Conference on Church Architecture, Cleveland, Ohio, March 20–22, 1962.

29 Ibid.

30 Eugene Wukasch, "The First Unit and the Master Plan," paper presented at The National Conference on Church Architecture, Los Angeles, CA, February 17–19, 1959.

31 Edward Frey, Culver Heaton and Eugene Wukasch, "Collaboration of Building Committee and Architect," paper presented at The National Conference on Church Architecture, Seattle, WA, March 5–7, 1963.

32 Prints of the slides for the paper "Art, Architecture, and the Liturgical Revival" (or "Revival of Liturgical Traditions in Architecture") dated 1970 are included in Box 132, J. Eugene Wukasch records, Alexander Architectural Archives, University of Texas Libraries, The University of Texas at Austin.

33 Ibid.

34 Wukasch and Kretzmann, "Echoes."

35 Ibid.

36 Ibid.

37 Ibid.

38 Ibid.

39 Ibid.

40 Eugene Wukasch, "The Good, The Beautiful, and the Concrete," paper presented at the 1988 American Concrete Institute Fall Convention, November 3, 1988.

41 Ibid.

42 Anita Brewer, "Sand Blasted Glass Art Work Like a Billboard, Churchman Says," Box 51, Folder 13, Wukasch & Associates Records and Drawings, Austin History Center, Austin, Texas.

43 Octavio Medellín (1907 or 1908–1999) was a Mexican-born sculptor and mosaicist associated with the Texas Regionalists movement of the 1930s and 1940s. Active until the 1990s, Medellín

created many works for Texas churches: Stephanie Lewthwaite, "Modernism in the Borderlands: The Life and Art of Octavio Medellín," *Pacific Historical Review* 81, no. 3 (August 2012): 337–370.

44 Brewer, "Sand Blasted Glass Art Work."

45 "Church Builders," *Austin American-Statesman*, July 24, 1957; Marj Wrightman, "Cooperation Aids Art Job," *Austin American-Statesman*, January 13, 1961, 15.

46 Fifteen of these "Painted Churches of Texas" constitute the "Churches with Decorative Interior Painting Thematic Resource" listed on the National Register of Historic Places (NRHP 64000835). Further examples, including St. Paul's in Serbin, are documented at www.klru.org/paintedchurches/.

47 "Church Builders"; Wrightman, "Cooperation Aids Art Job."

48 Harwood, *Decorating Texas*.

49 Pietro Belluschi, "The Meaning of Regionalism in Architecture," *Architectural Record* 118, no. 6 (December 1955): 131.

50 Wukasch and Kretzmann, "Echoes."

51 Examples of Fehr and Granger's church work in this vein include Central Presbyterian and St Stephen's Episcopal School Chapel, both in Austin, Texas.

52 Eugene Wukasch, "Proposed: An Earth-Covered Dome Development," *Earth Shelter Living* no. 39, May/June 1985, 7–10.

53 Gabriel Loire (1904–96) was a stained glass artist from Chartres, France who specialized in impressionistic modern *dalle de verre* or slab glass installations for churches throughout the world. Loire's work and included the Kaiser Wilhelm Memorial Church in Berlin, First Presbyterian Church, Stamford, Connecticut, and Philip Johnson's Chapel of Thanksgiving in Dallas, Texas.

54 Dean Zellmer, *125 Years of Faith: A History, Gethsemane Lutheran Church*. Karl Gronberg, ed. (Austin, TX: Gethsemane Lutheran Church, 1993), 5.

55 Ibid., 3. See also Nelson, "The New Shape of Lutheranism, 1930–," 527.

56 *Service Book and Hymnal* (Minneapolis, MN: Augsburg Publishing House, [1958] 1979).

57 Gethsemane Cornerstone Ceremony Program, 21 October 1962, AF-3662 (G), Austin History Files, Austin History Center, Austin, Texas.

58 "Ceremony Today," *Austin American-Statesman*, September 11, 1955.

59 Zellmer, *125 Years of Faith*, 5.

60 Marj Wrightman. "New Construction Technique in Use," *Austin American-Statesman*, October 2, 1962.

61 Wukasch and Kretzmann, "Echoes," 7.

62 The Akron plan featured a centralized auditorium with integrated classrooms, often separated by operable partitions, and was first used for First Methodist Episcopal Church in Akron, Ohio in 1872: Lewis Miller, "The Akron Plan." In Jesse Lyman Hurlbut, ed. *Seven Graded Sunday Schools: A Series of Practical Papers* (New York, NY: Eaton & Mains, 1893), www.gutenberg.org/files/32278/32278-h/32278-h.htm.

63 Wukasch and Kretzmann, "Echoes," 7.

64 Zellmer, *125 Years of Faith*, 6.

65 Albert Christ-Janer and May Mix Foley, *Modern Church Architecture: A Guide to the Form and Spirit of 20th Century Religious Buildings* (New York, NY: McGraw-Hill 1962), 127.

66 Eugene Wukasch, "Outdoor Worship Areas," *Your Church* 15, no. 2 (March/April 1969): 14–19.

67 Eugene Wukasch, "Atrium Architecture," *Your Church* 15, no. 2 (March/April 1969): 16–19, 59.

68 Dedication: Immanuel Lutheran Church, 15 January 1961. Box 30, J. Eugene Wukasch records, Alexander Architectural Archives, University of Texas Libraries, The University of Texas at Austin.

69 Printed as: "the stone which the builders refused is becoming the head stone of the corner. this is the LORD'S doing; it is marvelous in our eyes."

70 This quote comes from a talk given to the Taliesin Fellowship, May 28, 1955, and was quoted in Frank Lloyd Wright, *An American Architecture*. Edgar Kaufmann, ed. (New York, NY: Horizon Press, 1955), 43.

71 Yukio Futagawa, ed., *Frank Lloyd Wright Monograph*, vols. 5–7 (Tokyo: A.D.A. EDITA, 1988).

72 "The Tent Form—A Village Gothic for Today," *Architectural Forum* 101, no. 6 (December 1954): 128–131.

73 Wukasch featured slides of St. Paul's, Brenham alongside Wright's Annunciation in his paper "Art, Architecture, and the Liturgical Revival."

74 Eugene Wukasch, "Atrium Architecture," 19, 17.

75 Ibid.
76 Wukasch, "The Good, The Beautiful, and the Concrete."
77 Rudolf Schwarz, *The Church Incarnate*, trans. Cynthia Harris (Chicago, IL: Henry Regnery Company, 1958), 200.
78 Ernest Koenker, *Worship in Word and Sacrament* (St. Louis, MO: Concordia Publishing House, 1959), 75.
79 Stephanie Lewthwaite, "Modernism in the Borderlands: The Life and Art of Octavio Medellín" *Pacific Historical Review* 81, no. 3 (August 2012).
80 Herbert Lindemann, *The New Mood in Lutheran Worship* (Minneapolis, MN: Augsburg Publishing House, 1971), 37.
81 Eugene Wukasch, "Immanuel Speaks in Symbols" in Dedication: Immanuel Lutheran Church, January 15, 1961, Box 30, J. Eugene Wukasch records, Alexander Architectural Archives, University of Texas Libraries, The University of Texas at Austin.
82 Edward Anders Sövik, *Architecture for Worship* (Minneapolis, MN: Augsburg Publishing House, 1973), 23, 73–88.
83 Buggeln, *The Suburban Church*, 47.
84 "New Gethsemane Lutheran Church Dedication Today," *Austin American-Statesman*, March 3, 1963.
85 Eugene Wukasch, "Representative Selection: Central Texas Chapter, AIA," *Texas Architect* 8, no. 1 (March 1958): 6.
86 Wukasch, "Immanuel Speaks in Symbols."
87 Koenker, *Worship*, 80.
88 Buggeln, *The Suburban Church*, 11.
89 Wukasch and Kretzmann, "Echoes," 6
90 Bruce Brooks Pfeiffer, *Frank Lloyd Wright Drawings: Masterworks from the Frank Lloyd Wright Archives* (New York, NY: Harry N. Abrams, Inc., 1990), 101.
91 "Historical Church Styles."
92 Anita Brewer, "Sand Blasted Glass Art Work."
93 Marilyn Prud'homme, "Church Design: A New Face," *Austin American-Statesman*, May 28, 1961, E-1.
94 Ibid.
95 Wukasch, "Immanuel Speaks in Symbols."
96 Ibid.
97 Eugene Wukasch to Rev. Max Studtmann, Immanuel Lutheran Church, November 18, 1960, Box 30, J. Eugene Wukasch records, Alexander Architectural Archives, University of Texas Libraries, The University of Texas at Austin.
98 "Historical Church Styles Get Contemporary Look," *Austin American-Statesman*, July 26, 1959.
99 Wukasch, "Art, Architecture, and the Liturgical Revival."
100 Lindemann, *New Mood*, 25.
101 Ibid.
102 "Preface to the Liturgy," *Service Book and Hymnal*, vii.
103 "Introduction," *Lutheran Book of Worship* (Minneapolis, MN: Augsburg Publishing House, 1978), 8.

References

Belluschi, Pietro. "The Meaning of Regionalism in Architecture," *Architectural Record* 118, no. 6. (December 1955),: 131–139.
Buggeln, Gretchen. *The Suburban Church: Modernism and Community in Post-war America* (Minneapolis, MN: University of Minnesota Press, 2015).
"Ceremony Today," *Austin American-Statesman*, September 11, 1955.
Christ-Janer, Albert, and Mary Mix Foley. *Modern Church Architecture: A Guide to the Form and Spirit of 20th Century Religious Buildings* (New York, NY: McGraw-Hill, 1962).
"Church Builders," *Austin American-Statesman*, July 24, 1957.
Frey, Edward, Culver Heaton and Eugene Wukasch, "Collaboration of Building Committee and Architect," paper presented at The National Conference on Church Architecture, Seattle, Washington, March 5–7, 1963.

Futagawa, Yukio, ed. *Frank Lloyd Wright Monograph* (Tokyo: A.D.A. EDITA, 1988).

Geva, Anat and Jacob Morris. "Empirical Analyses of Immigrants' Churches Across Locations: Historic Wendish Churches in Germany, Texas, and South Australia," *ARRIS – The Journal of South East Chapter of the Society of Architectural Historians* 21 (2010): 38–60.

Hammond, Peter. *Liturgy and Architecture* (New York, NY: Columbia University Press, 1961).

———, ed. *Towards a Church Architecture* (London: The Architectural Press, 1962).

Harwood, Buie. *Decorating Texas: Decorative Painting from the 1850s to the 1950s* (Fort Worth, TX: Texas Christian University Press, 1993).

"Historical Church Styles Get Contemporary Look," *Austin American-Statesman*, July 26, 1959.

Horn, Edward T. "Preparation of the Service Book and Hymnal." In Edgar S Brown, Jr., ed. *Liturgical Reconnaissance* (Philadelphia, PA: Fortress Press, 1968).

"Introduction." *Lutheran Book of Worship* (Minneapolis, MN: Augsburg Publishing House, 1978).

"Introduction to the Common Hymnal." *Service Book and Hymnal* (Minneapolis, MN: Augsburg Publishing House, [1958] 1979).

Koenker, Ernest. *Worship in Word and Sacrament* (St. Louis, MO: Concordia Publishing House, 1959).

Lewthwaite, Stephanie. "Modernism in the Borderlands: The Life and Art of Octavio Medellín," *Pacific Historical Review* 81, no. 3. (August 2012): 337–370.

Lindemann, Herbert. *The New Mood in Lutheran Worship* (Minneapolis, MN: Augsburg Publishing House, 1971).

Lutheran Book of Worship (Minneapolis, MN: Augsburg Publishing House, 1978).

Miller, Lewis. "The Akron Plan." In Jesse Lyman Hurlbut, ed. *Seven Graded Sunday Schools: A Series of Practical Papers* (New York, NY: Eaton & Mains, 1893). www.gutenberg.org/files/32278/32278-h/32278-h.htm.

Nelson, E. Clifford, "The New Shape of Lutheranism, 1930–." In *idem*, ed., *The Lutherans in North America*, 453–541 (Philadelphia, PA: Fortress Press, 1975).

"New Gethsemane Lutheran Church Dedication Today," *Austin American-Statesman*, March 3, 1963.

Nielsen, George R. *In Search of a Home: the Wends (Sorbs) on the Australian and Texas Frontier* (Birmingham, UK: University of Birmingham, 1977).

Pfeiffer, Bruce Brooks. *Frank Lloyd Wright Drawings: Masterworks from the Frank Lloyd Wright Archives* (New York, NY: Harry N. Abrams, Inc., 1990).

Prud'homme, Marilyn. "Church Design: A New Face," *Austin American-Statesman*, May 28, 1961.

Quill, Timothy, C. J. *The Impact of the Liturgical Movement on American Lutheranism* (Lanham, MD: The Scarecrow Press, 1997).

Schwarz, Rudolf. *The Church Incarnate*. Translated by Cynthia Harris (Chicago, IL: Henry Regnery Company, 1958).

Seaman, William R. "The Service Book and Hymnal Since 1958." In Edgar S Brown, Jr., ed. *Liturgical Reconnaissance* (Philadelphia, PA: Fortress Press, 1968).

Service Book and Hymnal (Minneapolis, MN: Augsburg Publishing House, [1958] 1979).

Sövik, Edward Anders. *Architecture for Worship* (Minneapolis, MN: Augsburg Publishing House, 1973).

"The Tent Form—A Village Gothic for Today." *Architectural Forum* 101, no. 6 (December 1954).

Wright, Frank Lloyd. *An American Architecture*. Edgar Kaufmann, ed. (New York, NY: Horizon Press, 1955).

Wrightman, Marj. "Cooperation Aids Art Job," *Austin American-Statesman*, January 13, 1961.

———. "New Construction Technique in Use," *Austin American-Statesman*, October 2, 1962.

Wukasch, Eugene. "Atrium Architecture," *Your Church* 15, no. 2 (March/April 1969): 14–19, 59.

———. "The First Unit and the Master Plan," paper presented at The National Conference on Church Architecture, Los Angeles, CA, February 17–19, 1959.

———. "The Good, The Beautiful, and the Concrete," paper presented at the 1988 American Concrete Institute Fall Convention, November 3, 1988.

———. "Immanuel Speaks in Symbols," dedication, Immanuel Lutheran Church, January 15, 1961.

———. "Outdoor Worship Areas," *Your Church* 15, no. 2 (March/April 1969): 14–19.

———. "Proposed: An Earth-Covered Dome Development," *Earth Shelter Living* 39 (May/June 1985): 7–10.

———. "Representative Selection: Central Texas Chapter, AIA," *Texas Architect* 8, no. 1 (March 1958): 6.

———, and Kretzmann, A. R. "Echoes From the European Conference," paper presented at The National Conference on Church Architecture, Cleveland, Ohio, March 20–22, 1962.

Zellmer, Dean. *125 Years of Faith: A History, Gethsemane Lutheran Church*. Karl Gronberg, ed. (Austin, TX: Gethsemane Lutheran Church, 1993).

11

THE NEXUS BETWEEN LITHUANIAN VERNACULAR AND AMERICAN MODERNISM

Milda B. Richardson

Mid-twentieth-century Lithuanian American church architecture stimulates a unique conversation by bringing tradition and modernism together without compromise on either of them. This chapter explores the contributions to the American ecclesiastical works and to the Lithuanian American cultural landscape by a core group of Lithuanian designers: Stasys Kudokas (1893–1988), Jonas Mulokas (1907–83), and Vytautas Jonynas (1907–97). They represent the generation of artists trained in Europe and forced by war to leave their homeland. They eventually immigrated to the United States where they set up architectural practices during the post-World War II period. Opportunities in America invigorated a desire to experiment with design choices and produced innovative work by immigrant architects.

Inherited tradition and non-violent resistance

The Lithuanian architects and designers born at the turn of the twentieth century spent their youth anticipating and, finally, welcoming Lithuanian independence from Russian Imperial control in 1918.[1] Although they were children, they understood the significance of the political events happening around them. The artists grew up in medieval towns rich in the history of the original polytheistic Baltic tribes with their reverence for the earth and ancient pagan nature worship.[2] They were exposed to medieval Gothic churches, to the popular Baroque style of the seventeenth century, as well as the Gothic Revival and Neoclassical churches of the nineteenth and early twentieth centuries. They also delved deeply into the history, folk art, and vernacular architecture of Lithuania as part of their university curriculum.[3] This context and their studies planted the seeds for design ideas in later years in America.

During the period of independence, 1918–40, three events deeply affected artists of this generation: the invigorated ethnographic research on the vernacular wayside shrines and folk art[4] and the occupation by Poland of the Vilnius district from 1919 to 1939.[5] Additionally, the artists participated in the development of modernist architecture and theory, as well as the founding of the avant-garde artists' organization in Kaunas, known as *Ars*.[6]

A vivid image in Lithuanian cultural memory was the wayside shrine. These were small-scale chapels ornately carved from oak and erected on a pole in the countryside, usually close to farms, and in churchyards and cemeteries. A triple-tiered artifact from 1885 illustrates the iconographic hybrid of Christian and pagan imagery (Fig. 11.1). Marija Gimbutas interpreted the origin of such chapels as an aspect of pagan worship displaying cult images.[7] For example, carved details of scrolls may represent ancient snake worship.[8]

Wayside shrines were the spiritual heartland of the domestic landscape, offering a venue for religious rituals and private and group worship. The shrine interior was fitted with miniature polychromatic religious figures, which were imbued with powers of protection. Because of their huge numbers and frequency of placement these shrines permeated the Lithuanian landscape with an omnipresent aura of sacredness.[9]

The documentation of wayside shrines began prior to World War I, while Lithuania was still under Russian rule. Many shrines had been destroyed under the czars, and there was concern for the deterioration of the remaining oak carvings.[10] The first monograph devoted to Lithuanian wayside shrines was published in 1912 and contained drawings by landscape artist L. Antanas Jarosevičius (1870–1956).[11] The painter Adomas Varnas (1879–1979) began photographing the shrines in 1905. He collaborated with students and ethnographers like Balys Buračas (1897–1972) and recorded over eight hundred images.[12] Eighty of his photographs were featured at the 1925 Second International Decorative Art Exhibit in Monza-Milan Royal Palace, Italy.

Preservation of these venerable layers of folk culture became a matter of honor and moral obligation for patriotic citizens. The intellectual elite devoted themselves to systematically researching and publishing on topics of traditional culture, raising aesthetic sensibilities of fellow citizens, reviving the crafts and adapting them to modern life.[13] Parliament established the official vehicle for this activity called the Hall of Agriculture, which operated from 1926 until the Soviet occupation in 1940.[14] Information was further disseminated in two widely read publications by Antanas Tamošaitis (1906–2005) on crafts and cottage industry.[15] In 1929, a special project for building technology was launched in Kaunas: an ensemble of six examples of rural architecture containing about six thousand artifacts of material culture. Although the exhibit was demolished by the Soviet Army in 1945,[16] these projects generated design ideas which would allow artists to integrate traditional arts into a modern architectural

FIGURE 11.1   Triple-tiered, roofed pole style of oak shrine in a farmyard of the Šešuoliai village, Ukmergė region, Lithuania, 1885.

Adomas Varnas, Lietuvos kryžiai (Crosses of Lithuania), Kaunas, 1926. Courtesy of the Varnas family.

expression of their homeland. In 1935, Tamošaitis wrote, "As we collect folk art which is disappearing from the village, we justify ourselves since in the future we will create a national style and return it once again to the village."[17]

World War I and the Bolshevik Revolution brought disruptive political changes to Lithuania. Although Poland initially recognized Lithuanian independence in 1918, fear of Bolshevik advances drove the Polish Army to illegally invade Vilnius on April 19, 1919, and occupy eastern Lithuania for the next twenty years.[18] The subsequent program of polonization inspired a renaissance of wayside shrines known as the "Crosses of Vilnius."[19] People were encouraged to erect authentic-style shrines in protest against foreign occupation and as signs of national unity. This movement demonstrated the value of folk art as instruments of non-violent political resistance.[20]

Opportunities for European education introduced modernism to Lithuania. Vytautas Landsbergis-Žemkalnis (1893–1993) and Stasys Kudokas (1893–1988) were among the leaders of a group of forty productive modernist architects working in the temporary capital of Kaunas.[21] Žemkalnis was educated in Rome, where he graduated from the Royal School of Architecture in 1926. He returned to Lithuania to complete major avant-garde commissions, including two churches which put younger designers on the modernist track.[22] The first was Christ the Redeemer, a Romanesque Revival parish church in Kybartai, 1928, with sculpture by Bronius Pundzius (1907–59). The second was the Sacred Heart of Jesus parish church in Mažeikiai, consecrated in 1935. The graphic artist Rimtas Kalpokas (1908–99) decorated its five-bay interior. The minimalist triple-nave brick building with a central tower and steep roof became a cynosure for future designers.

Stasys Kudokas also earned a Ph.D. in architecture from the Royal School of Architecture in Rome and was granted an international license to practice architecture in 1930. He was appointed city architect for Kaunas and completed more than a hundred efficiently planned, multi-functional, institutional as well as domestic commissions.[23] From 1941 to 1944 he served as Dean of Architecture at Vytautas Magnus University. His churches in Pažeriai (1936) and Pilviškiai (1939) are classically inspired. Their crisply articulated geometric shapes dominate the rural landscape.

World War II, refugee camps and new models

Lithuanian refugee artists who fled their country during the war benefited from the rich cultural life in the Displaced Persons camps in the French, British, and American zones. Frequent exhibitions featured modern art and sculpture, and libraries offered rich holdings. In addition, refugees were able to publish illustrated works as well as stage their own performances, and were further energized by the positive reception and medical treatment during this traumatic dislocation.[24] For example, the Displaced Persons camp in Augsburg, Germany, housed about two thousand Lithuanians and offered an extensive educational curriculum.[25] While in that camp, Jonas Mulokas taught drawing and art history in the camp's school from 1944 to 1948.[26] Mulokas carved miniature wooden shrines as presentation gifts for dignitaries (Fig. 11.2). The large-scale shrine he created in 1945 was recently restored and today stands on the site of the former refugee camp.

A major achievement was the founding in 1946 by Vytautas Kazimieras Jonynas of the Freiburg School of Arts and Crafts, at the Displaced Persons camp in Freiburg im Breisgau, in the French zone.[27] Jonynas was educated in Paris at the École Boulle and Conservatoire

FIGURE 11.2 Jonas Mulokas (center) with school children in the Augsburg Displaced Persons Camp, Germany, 1944–48. Handmade miniature shrines and folk art are displayed on the wall.

Photograph courtesy of Rimas Mulokas.

National des Arts et Métiers and had his first solo exhibit in the Galerie Zak in 1935;[28] his talent and originality were recognized once again in 1949 with a solo exhibit at the Ariel gallery in Paris.[29] The intensely productive Freiburg school ceased to operate in 1950.

While in Europe, the displaced artists absorbed modernist trends in ecclesiastical architecture based on the liturgical reform movement in the Roman Catholic Church, which had begun in Europe late in the nineteenth century.[30] The German priest-educator Hans Anscar Reinhold (1897–1968) studied the innovations of German architects and became a proponent of the "Dialogue Mass," which stressed active participation by the laity before the Vatican II era of 1962–65. Having been persecuted by the Nazis for his underground resistance activities, Reinhold arrived in the United States in 1936.[31] As a theologian, he advocated community liturgy centered on the altar. Liturgical participation was, according to Reinhold, the key to healing the world's rupture following the two World Wars.[32]

Displaced artists continued to follow theories of modern church design, such as those of Rev. Romano Guardini and Rudolf Schwarz (1881–1962), whose book *Vom Bau der Kirche* was published in 1947.[33] Schwarz produced a variety of plans and sleek geometric designs for church buildings in his treatise on sacred geometry. As a supporter of Schwarz and others, Reinhold introduced the work of German modernists to the United States.[34] In 1947, Pope Pius XII issued an encyclical "On the Sacred Liturgy" (*Mediator Dei*), acknowledging new possibilities for church art and architecture.[35]

Two churches by Maurice Novarina (1907–2002), a Savoyard architect of the same generation as the refugees, attracted their attention with his particularly innovative designs.[36] Our Lady of Léman, built 1933–35, inspired Lithuanian artists not only with its A-frame structure and glazed gable, but also with its Arts and Crafts ornamentation. The polychromatic interior includes Christian and French nationalistic and folk art motifs carried through in mosaics, stained glass, tiles, and wainscoting.

The chalet-style church of Our Lady Full of Grace of the Plateau d'Assy (1937–46), facing Mont Blanc, was designed by Novarina with Édouard Malot.[37] This historical site is famous for the interior decorative program contributed by avant-garde artists, such as Rouault, Léger, Braque, Chagall, and the Lithuanian-born Jacques Lipchitz (1891–1973).[38] At the time the DP camps were being dissolved, Matisse began working in Vence on the Chapel of the Rosary, completed in 1951.[39]

Lithuanian architects in post-war America

Designers who arrived from Europe participated in professional discussions on liturgy and the arts, and read professional American journals.[40] They were especially influenced by the 1951–54 issues of *Liturgical Arts*, in which Joseph Cardinal Ritter (1892–1967), Archbishop of St. Louis, urged church designers to adopt modern expression.[41]

Stasys Kudokas arrived in the United States in 1949, and was granted architectural licenses in Ohio and California where he designed a number of ecclesiastical, institutional, and residential projects.[42] He designed All Saints (closed 1989), in the Chicago suburb of Roseland in the early 1950s. Chicago was the largest urban center of Lithuanian American culture in the United States. By 1927, there were a dozen parishes for a colony of 125,000 Lithuanian immigrants.[43] The new arrivals to Chicago were attracted by well-paying jobs on the railroads, and in stockyards and coal mines. The simple massing of All Saints Church echoes Landsbergis's Sacred Heart from 1935 and rural wooden churches in the homeland. The addition of an abstracted lantern style of wayside shrine to the central entrance tower of All Saints is a conspicuous symbol of the homeland collective memory of the parish.[44]

This example of Lithuanian symbolism on the exterior of churches represents a new element. St. Casimir Church in Shenandoah, Pennsylvania, was the earliest Lithuanian parish for a congregation formed in 1872.[45] Its interior was completely covered with frescoes of Lithuanian folk designs copied from publications by Antanas Tamošaitis.[46]

The post-World War II immigrants considered themselves political refugees living abroad temporarily in a status commonly referred to as the Lithuanian Church in Exile.[47] Adding symbols of Lithuanian traditional culture and history to the exterior of churches became a way to publicly highlight their parishes as belonging to the Lithuanian Church in Exile. It is worth noting that Vytautas Jonynas was commissioned by the Vatican in 1967 to design the Lithuanian chapel in the grottoes of St. Peter in Rome dedicated to the Churches of Silence behind the Iron Curtain.[48]

Stasys Kudokas's most notable American project is the extensive complex for Our Lady of Perpetual Help in Cleveland (Fig. 11.3).[49] Construction for the church began in 1950 with designs by Kudokas, who worked under the auspices of Michael G. Boccia, a licensed architect, shortly before Kudokas earned his own license. The site includes a school, convent, rectory, and community center. The entire complex was completed in 1967 by the parishioners themselves in order to contain costs. Artist Kazys Varnelis (1917–2010) designed the interior liturgical furnishings and fabricated the stained glass windows, with a dominant theme of the Madonna (Fig. 11.4). The Romanesque Revival parish church acknowledges both the work of Landsbergis as well as the American version of this German-influenced movement.[50]

Jonas Mulokas arrived in the United States in 1949 and first lived in South Boston.[51] His major commissions in America were the Nativity of the Blessed Virgin Mary Church in Chicago and the Church of the Transfiguration in Queens, New York. In addition to residential and commercial projects, he designed numerous wayside shrines for private patrons.

FIGURE 11.3   Our Lady of Perpetual Help, Cleveland, Ohio, 1950–67, Stasys Kudokas, designer.
Photograph courtesy of Algis Lukas.

FIGURE 11.4   Our Lady of Perpetual Help, chancel after 1987 renovations.
Photograph courtesy of Algis Lukas.

Vytautas Jonynas immigrated to the United States in 1951, and settled in New York. There he opened the Jonynas and Shepherd Art Studio specializing in ecclesiastical arts.[52] He taught painting, graphic art and art history at Fordham University in New York City from 1956 until his retirement in 1973.[53] In 1956, Jonynas collaborated with Mulokas on the small Immaculate Conception Church for about a thousand Lithuanian families in St. Louis, Missouri.[54] The massing of the church, constructed by members of the parish, recalls Kudokas's All Saints in Chicago and restates in metal the Lithuanian wayside shrine motif on the central entrance tower. The interior boasts stained glass windows with images of the Madonna by Jonynas, sculpture by Vytautas Kašuba (1915–97) and folk-style wood carvings.[55]

While these artists were working in St. Louis, they became acquainted with the Resurrection of Our Lord, a German parish church designed by Joseph D. Murphy (1908–95), trained at MIT. Murphy's modern designs were reviewed enthusiastically in professional journals and reinforced the connection to German modernism.[56]

FIGURE 11.5 Nativity of the Blessed Virgin Mary Church, Chicago, Illinois, 1957–62, Jonas
Mulokas, designer.

Photograph courtesy of Algis Lukas.

A collaboration of immigrant engineers, architects, contractors and designers, with
Mulokas and Jonynas in the lead, designed Nativity of the Blessed Virgin Mary Church in
Chicago (1957–62). This is a Lithuanian church continuing the Marian theme with devotion to Mary as the Patroness of the United States (Fig. 11.5).[57] The folk Baroque curves of
the transept facades recall the seventeenth-century Baroque churches of Lithuania. Together
with the stylized wayside shrines which terminate the twin towers and the spire over the
crossing, they are the most recognizable Lithuanian elements (Fig. 11.5). The yellow-faced
brick and cut stone exterior is otherwise plain, except for the colorful mosaics by Jonynas,
depicting historical events such as "The Coronation of Mindaugas."

The vaults of the interior echo the volumes of urban Baroque sites in Lithuania. Jonynas
set up a hierarchy for the decoration by using bands of stucco with repetitive floral patterns
which articulate the vaults and arches as well as the curved choir loft (Fig. 11.6). The vaults
spring from squared capitals with stylized tulip designs, immensely popular in folk art. The
patterns based on nature are further articulated by a subtle two-tone cream-colored painting
scheme. Brilliant color enters the space through the Cubist-inspired stained glass windows in
which Jonynas depicted images of Mary and various saints.

The repeated elements of the stucco patterns merge into the overall form of the interior.
These borders delimit the "field of force," and together with the subtle weaving pattern of
all three aisles, lead to the polygonal chancel in which the decoration is greatly intensified.[58]
The 45-foot high, double-tiered white marble retable reaches the height of the chancel.
Below, an image of Crucified Christ is set in a chapel with chain-type colonnettes, while
above, an 8-foot gold-plated icon of Our Lady of Šiluva appears in an elaborate architectural
frame under a canopy with Rosso Levanto marble columns and a broken pediment. The
icon commemorates the 1608 apparition of Mary in Šiluva, Lithuania. Wrought-iron filigree
decorations appear throughout. Snodin and Howard noted that appropriating ornamentation
of another world for a new world and claiming to invent a new species is, essentially, an
extension of a triumphant past.[59] Gombrich echoes this when discussing the tenacity of conventions in the traditional crafts through ritualizing behavior: "The movements and actions

FIGURE 11.6   Nativity of the Blessed Virgin Mary Church, 1957–62, chancel; Vytautas
K. Jonynas, liturgical arts.

Photograph courtesy of Algis Lukas.

the craftsmen perform must not only be performed correctly, they must also be correctly
handed down to the next generation."[60]

Much of the criticism against twentieth-century modernist sacred spaces has to do with
stark interiors and abstract designs which, according to traditionalists, results in "imageless
thought."[61] The anthropological argument is that it is necessary to access images to convert to
new mental images in order for humans to know.[62] Deep symbolic language in liturgical art
produces a synergy of the observer's senses, intellect, memory, imagination and emotions.[63]

Further developments in materials and structural systems

Corning Glassworks of New York acquired Steuben, a small art glass studio, in 1918. This
acquisition became crucial to industrial production of high-quality architectural glass.[64]
Architects became acquainted with examples of large-scale glazing such as the commission by
the Tolleri Studio for Chester F. Wright's Novitiate in Ipswich, Massachusetts, in 1962.[65] In
1963–64, Belli & Belli designed the Immaculate Conception Lithuanian Church in Chicago,
with stained glass by Conrad Schmitt Studios.[66]

Inspired by the possibilities of large-scale glazing, Mulokas remodeled Holy Cross Parish
Church in 1964. Founded in 1914, in Dayton, Ohio, it is listed on the National Register
of Historic Places. This project gave Adolfas Valeška (1905–94) the opportunity to produce
a dramatic glazed chancel wall with faceted French stained glass featuring a full range of
wayside shrine typology (Fig. 11.7). Each of the nave windows set between Stations of

FIGURE 11.7 Holy Cross Parish Church, Dayton, Ohio, chancel, remodeled in 1964; stained glass by Adolfas Valeška.

Photograph courtesy of Algis Lukas.

the Cross shows a different style of shrine. The geometric weaving patterns popular on Lithuanian sashes decorate the façade and are repeated on the tiles of the central aisle. In the church garden, architect Alfredas Kulpa-Kulpavičius (1923–2007), designed wayside shrines representing each of three of the ethnic regions of Lithuania.[67] The commemorative plaque is dedicated to "all the martyrs for the faith in the countries occupied by the Soviet Communists."[68]

Lithuanian architects arriving in the United States encountered for the first time the American Colonial Revival and the Shingle Style with its emphasis on the prominent gables.[69] It is understandable they perceived this phase of American architecture as reminiscent of vernacular structures in their homeland. A flourishing phenomenon in the Midwest that caught their particular attention was the variety of structural solutions with the frequent use of the A-frame for Lutheran and Roman Catholic denominations.[70]

The Church of the Transfiguration (1957–62), is considered one of the notable buildings in Queens, New York (Fig. 11.8). Mulokas and Jonyas were the designers and collaborated with Stankus Construction Company.[71] The A-frame structure itself with its predominant glazed gable is based on typical Lithuanian vernacular dwellings and farm buildings. The gentle contours of thatched rooflines of the villages, almost literally touching the earth, are favorite motifs in Lithuanian art because of their organic relationship with the natural landscape.[72]

The modernity of this building was not derived from any compromise with the tradition: "Modernity, rather than always eliminating folk beliefs and practices, often reinforces them in people."[73] As instruments of cultural discourse, these often "modern"-looking designs subtly invoked tradition with a contemporary connection to the past. For a long time, small-scale shrines were confined within the enclosed spaces of the immigrant domestic interiors in America.[74]

The ridgepole of the Church of the Transfiguration is steel and glass, while the base of the building is laid with orange and ivory brick. The glazed ridgepole creates dramatic effects on the interior (Fig. 11.9). Natural light from the glazed ridgepole falls directly on the retable in the center of the chancel wall and illuminates a stylized sunburst type of wayside shrine.

FIGURE 11.8   Church of the Transfiguration, Maspeth, New York, 1957–62; Jonas Mulokas, designer.

Photograph courtesy of Algis Lukas.

A bas-relief of Christ's Transfiguration appears in the center of the sunburst, totally enveloped in light. Two asymmetrical groups of the prophets and saints are on secondary surfaces of the cross. The illumination enhances the warm tones of the African wood.

The cubist-inspired stained glass and liturgical arts are by Jonynas, who chose religious and historical figures for the forty nave windows. The glass on the front façade, recessed under the projecting eaves of the A-frame, highlights figures such as Our Lady of Šiluva.[75]

The majestic figure against the glazed façade is an aluminum sculpture by Aleksandras Marčiulionis (1911–98) (Fig. 11.10). Marčiulionis had been educated in Kaunas, and later taught sculpture at the Freiburg School founded by Jonynas.[76] He moved to the United States in 1956 and worked on numerous ecclesiastical projects from his studio in Chicago.[77] His aluminum sculpture of the Transfiguration of Jesus departs from the tradition of the Pensive Christ carved in wood by itinerant craftsmen and placed in the wayside shrines. (Fig. 11.10) Beginning in the Middle Ages, the seated figure of the Pensive Christ served

FIGURE 11.9   Church of the Transfiguration, 1957–62, chancel; Vytautas K. Jonynas, liturgical arts.

Photograph courtesy of Algis Lukas.

FIGURE 11.10 Church of the Transfiguration, *Transfiguration of Jesus*, aluminum; Aleksandras Marčiulionis, sculptor.

Photograph courtesy of Algis Lukas.

primarily religious purposes. From the mid-nineteenth century through the twentieth, sculptures of Christ became a symbol of Lithuanian national identity.[78] The figures created by professional artists became more sophisticated.[79] The Transfiguration, as narrated in three of the Gospels, describes Jesus enveloped in bright light as He spoke to His disciples preparing them for the events to come. Marčiulionis's choice of shining metal for the figure set above bold red doors with an undulating canopy brings a sign of hope to immigrant worshippers as they are reminded of terrible ordeals to be followed by a joyous return home.

Collective memory and theoretical background

Youthful impressions have a powerful effect on the formation of adult memories: "The terrain of late childhood is especially potent, nurturing the developing intellect and dwelling in adult memory as a guiding image of coherence."[80] This was particularly relevant for Lithuanian American designers, and their mature art was festooned with religious iconography—especially wayside shrines—as they portrayed the terrain and images of their homeland. The church buildings in this chapter provided a spatial framework for the retrieval of life stories. The philosopher Yi-Fu Tuan analyzes such stories as defensive strategies of communication or collective memory, a form of inner geography.[81]

Forced and destabilizing exile frequently produces increased memories of the past and the persistence of specific memories.[82]

The designers and the environments they built became instruments for organizing past experiences into monuments of a stable cultural memory providing meaning, sense, emotion, and values. According to Michael Owen Jones, creativity is a tool for coping with anxiety. He describes the process: "Grieving and creativity have much in common … Intense mourning and introspection discharge the emotions of loss, hostility, and guilt, and ultimately lead to reintegration of the self."[83] The churches provided a corpus of clarifying architectural forms of remembrance by showing that a past that has slipped out of reach can be reclaimed.

The modern Lithuanian designs were frequently based on familiar vernacular forms, but they also reflected an understanding of French architectural theory.[84] In his essay "Architecture, Essay on Art" (c. 1794), Etienne-Louis Boullée demanded regularity, proportion, and symmetry—qualities that resulted in what he labeled architectural "character."[85] Boullée suggested simple geometric shapes as the proper foundation for modernism.

Lithuanian American designers were inspired by their own collective memory and the vernacular similar to Le Corbusier's vision of modernism as related to the people's relationship to artifacts and material surroundings.[86] Ultimately, "he was able to see the relation of the structures of a specific period to the period's contemporary life, both seen and unseen, openly expressed and striving for expression."[87]

Conclusion

The Lithuanian American designers achieved their creative goal of a synthesis between vernacular forms and modernist vocabulary by translating elements of traditional wooden architecture into masonry, glass, and steel structures. The way in which a community relates to its built environment further defines its identity and connects it with the uniqueness of its culture. In this sense, the Lithuanian American experience is similar to that of other immigrant ethnic groups.[88] Lithuanian immigrants established a coherent identity for themselves in the United States through the deployment of metaphors of architecture in expressing their collective memory. The complexes they built provided a secure venue for the preservation of cultural values and a free productive life in their new land.

Acknowledgments

The author dedicates this chapter to the memory of the following friends and colleagues: Vacys Milius, Feliksas Marcinkas, Marija and Jurgis Gimbutas, and Kazys and Gabriela Varnelis.

Notes

1 Saulius Suziedelis, *The Sword and the Cross. A History of the Church in Lithuania* (Huntington, IN: Our Sunday Visitor, Inc., 1988), 146–157; Albertas Gerutis, ed., *Lithuania 700 Years* (New York, NY: Manyland Books, 1984), 145–165.

2 Ibid., 13–18; Jonas Puzinas, "The Origins of the Lithuanian Nation." In Albertas Gerutis, *Lithuania 700 Years* (New York, NY: Manyland Books, 1984), 1–42.

3 *A Guide to Lithuania's Baroque Monuments* (Vilnius, Lithuania: baltos lankos, 1996); Jonas Minkevičius, *Lietuvos bažnyčių menas* [The Art of Lithuanian Churches] (Vilnius, Lithuania: R. Paknys, 1993);

Algė Jankevičienė, *Lietuvos medinė sakralinė architektūra: bažnycios, koplyčios ir varpinės* [Sacred Wooden Architecture of Lithuania: Churches, Chapels, and Bell Towers] (Kaunas, Lithuania: Vilniaus dailės akademija, 2000).

4 Zita Žemaitytė, *Paulius Galaunė* (Vilnius, Lithuania: Vaga, 1988), 120–149; *Adomas Varnas* (Vilnius, Lithuania: baltos lankos, 1998), 128–140.

5 Milda B. Richardson, "Iconoclasm and Resistance. Wayside Shrines in the Struggle for Lithuanian Independence." In J. M. Mancini and Keith Bresnahan, eds. *Architecture and Armed Conflict. The Politics of Destruction* (London and New York, NY: Routledge, 2015), 103–115.

6 Žemaitytė, *Galaunė*, 120–140.

7 Marija Gimbutas, *Ancient Symbolism in Lithuanian Folk Art* (Philadelphia, PA: American Folklore Society, 1958), 5–99. Jonas Grinius maintains a purely Christian source, "Lietuvos kryžiai ir koplytėlės" [Crosses and Shrines of Lithuania]. In A. Livina, ed. *Yearbook of the Lithuanian Roman Catholic Academy of Science*, vol. V, (Rome, 1970), 1–77. See Milda B. Richardson, "The Metamorphosis of the Lithuanian Wayside Shrines 1850–1990," Ph.D. diss., Boston University, 2003.

8 Ibid., 25.

9 Colleen McDannell, *Material Christianity. Religion and Popular Culture in America* (New Haven, CT: Yale University Press, 1995), 18–24, 25–38.

10 Leonardas Sauka, *Lietuvių Tautosaka* [Lithuanian Folklore] (Kaunas, Lithuania: Šviesa, 1999), 288. Milda B. Richardson, "The Heritage of Community Art in Lithuania." In Kristin G. Congdon and Doug Boughton, eds. *Advances in Program Evaluation*, vol. 4 (Stamford, CT and London: JAI Press Inc., 1998), 55–71.

11 Jonas Basanavičius, *Lietuvos kryžiai* [Crosses of Lithuania] (Vilnius, Lithuania: Lietuvių Dailės Draugijos Leidinys, 1912). Dr. Basanavičius was the first signer of the Lithuanian 1918 Declaration of Independence and an important ethnographer: Alfred E. Senn, *Jonas Basanavičius: The Patriarch of the Lithuanian National Renaissance* (Newtonville, MA: Oriental Reseach Partners, 1980).

12 Žemaitytė, *Adomas Varnas*, 130–131.

13 Vacys Milius, "Žemės ūkio rūmai—etninės kultūros puoselėtojas" [Hall of Agriculture—The Fostering of Ethnic Culture]. In Regina Merkienė, ed. *Etninė kultūra ir tautinis atgimimas* [Ethnic Culture and National Rebirth] (Vilnius, Lithuania: Lietuvos istorijos institutas, 1994), 106–117.

14 Ibid., 106.

15 Antanas Tamošaitis, *Sodžiaus pramonė, Sodžiaus menas* [Cottage Industry, Village Art] (Kaunas, Lithuania: Žemės ūkio namai, 1931–1939).

16 Milius, "Žemės ūkio rūmai," 113.

17 Antanas Tamošaitis, "Kultūriškai apvogtas sodžius" [The Village Robbed of Culture], *Naujoji romuva*, no. 10–11 (1935): 266–267. Reprinted in Lijana Šatavičiūtė-Natalevičienė, *Antanas Tamošaitis* (Vilnius, Lithuania: Vilniaus dailės akademijos leidykla, 2003), 91–93.

18 Gerutis, *Lithuania 700 Years*, 165–176.

19 Antanas Rūkštelė, *Vilniaus Kryžiai* [Crosses of Vilnius] (Vilnius, Lithuania: VVS Leidinys, 1937).

20 Vacys Milius, "Lietuvių kryžių ir koplytėlių statymo priežastys" [The Reasons for Erecting Lithuanian Crosses and Shrines], in *Proceedings of the Lithuanian Catholic Academy of Science*, vol. XV (Vilnius, Lithuania: Katalikų Akademija, 1995), 294–302.

21 *Kaunas 1918–2015. Architektūros gidas* [Kaunas 1918–2015. Architectural Guide] (Vilnius, Lithuania: Architektūros fondas, 2015), *passim*.

22 Jolita Kančienė and Jonas Minkevičius, *Architektas Vytautas Landsbergis-Žemkalnis* (Vilnius, Lithuania: Mokslo ir enciklopedijų leidykla, 1993). Built at a time of agricultural modernization, Pienocentras, 1935, won Žemkalnis a medal at the 1937 International Exposition of Art and Technology in Paris.

23 *Kaunas 1918–2015*, passim.

24 Jolanta Bernotaitytė, comp., *Kazys Varnelis* (Vilnius, Lithuania: Lietuvos nacionalinis muziejus, 2009), 10.

25 "Augsburg," *Lithuanian Encyclopedia*. Vaclovas Biržiška, ed. (Boston, MA: Juozas Kapočius, 1953), 403–405.

26 Oral interviews with Rimas Mulokas, Mulokas's eldest son, conducted between 2013 and 2016.

27 Viktorija Matranga, ed., *Freiburg 1946. Art Exhibit Celebrating 50th Anniversary of the Freiburg School of Arts and Crafts—École des Arts et Métiers* (Chicago: Balzekas Museum of Lithuanian Culture, January 26–April 3, 1997). Rasa Andriušytė-Žukienė, *Akistatos. Dailininkas Vytautas Kazimieras Jonynas pasaulio meno keliuose* [Artist Vytautas Kazimieras Jonynas in the World of Art] (Vilnius, Lithuania: Lietuvos dailės muziejus, 2007), 67–68, 80–90.

28 Andriušytė-Žukienė, *Jonynas*, 29.

29 Ibid., 86.
30 Ernest Benjamin Koenker, *The Liturgical Renaissance of the Roman Catholic Church* (Chicago, IL: University of Chicago Press, 1954), vi, 10–11, 18, 195–197.
31 H. A. Reinhold, *H.A.R.: The Autobiography of Father Reinhold* (New York, NY: Herder & Herder, 1968), 38.
32 Jeremy Bonner, Christopher D. Denny and Mary Beth Fraser Connolly, eds., *Empowering the People of God: Catholic Action Before and After Vatican II* (New York, NY: Fordham University Press, 2014), 1–20. Hans A. Reinhold, "A Revolution in Church Architecture," *Liturgical Arts* (1938) 63: 123–133.
33 Rudolf Schwarz, *The Church Incarnate: The Sacred Function of Christian Architecture*, trans. Cynthia Harris (Chicago, IL: H. Regnery Co., 1958); Hugo Schnell, *Twentieth Century Church Architecture in Germany* (Munich, Germany and Zurich, Switzerland: Verlag Schnell & Steiner, 1974).
34 Hans A. Reinhold, "The Architecture of Rudolf Schwarz," *The Architectural Forum* (1939) 70: 22–27.
35 Randall B. Smith, "Don't Blame Vatican II. Modernism and Modern Catholic Church Architecture," *Sacred Architecture Journal* (South Bend, IN: The Institute for Sacred Architecture, 2016) 13: 1–15.
36 Marine Perret, *Inventory of the Archives of the Architect Maurice Novarina. Documents from His Paris Studio 1957–1996* (Paris, France: Archives of Haute Savoie, 2014).
37 Site visit June 2015. Ministry of Culture, Paris, France. Accessed February 10, 2018. www.culture. gouv.fr/public/mistral/merimee_fr?ACTION=CHERCHER&FIELD_1=REF&VALUE_1= PA00118416
38 Ibid.
39 Marcel Billot, ed., *The Vence Chapel, The Archive of a Creation* (Milan, Italy: Skira and Menil Foundation, 1999); Sister Jacques-Marie, *Henri Matisse, The Vence Chapel* (Nice, France: Grégoire Gardette, 1992); *Chapelle du rosaire de Dominicaines de Vence par Henri Matisse* (Paris, France: Mourlot Freres, 1963).
40 Andriušytė-Žukienė, *Jonynas*, 125.
41 Quoted in William Barnaby Faherty, S.J., *The Great Saint Louis Cathedral* (St. Louis, MO: Friends of the Cathedral, 2008), 14.
42 *Encyclopedia Lituanica*, eds. Simas Sužiedėlis and Vincas Rastenis, vol. III (Boston, MA: Juozas Kapočius, 1973), 221–222.
43 William Wolkovich-Valkavičius, *Lithuanian Religious Life in America*, vol. 3 (Norwood, MA: Lithuanian Religious Life in America, 1998), 123.
44 Richardson, *Metamorphosis*, 9–12.
45 Wolkovich-Valkavičius, *Lithuanian Religious Life in America*, vol. 2, 87. The Gothic Revival stone building was built in 1915 and demolished in 2009.
46 Tamošaitis, *Sodžiaus pramonė*; Antanas Kučas, *St. George's Parish Shenandoah, Pennsylvania*, parish publication, Brooklyn, NY, 1968, 254–264.
47 Suziedelis, *The Sword*, 235–250; Antanas J. Van Reenan, *Lithuanian Diaspora Königsberg to Chicago* (Lanham, MD, University Press of America, Inc., 1990), 113–146, 212–230; Algirdas Budreckis, "Liberation Attempts from Abroad." In Albertas Gerutis, ed. *Lithuania 700 Years*, (New York, NY: Manyland Books, 1984), 388–426; "National Lithuanian Church," *Encyclopedia Lituanica*, vol. IV (Boston, MA: Juozas Kapočius, 1975), 31–33; "Lithuanian Roman Catholic Federation of America," Ibid., vol. III, 402–404. On the occasion of the hundredth birthday of my great uncle Bishop Vincentas Padolskis (1904–60), a conference was held in Vilnius on April 30, 2004. The proceedings included papers on his collaboration with Msgr. Ladas Tulaba (1912–2002) in establishing the Lithuanian College of St. Casimir in Rome. Aldona Vasiliauskienė, "Bishop Vincentas Padolskis: Activities in the Lithuanian Catholic Academy of Sciences," in *LKMA Yearbook XXV* (Vilnius, Lithuania: Catholic Academy, 2004), 527–560; Kęstutis Žemaitis, "Bishop Vincentas Padolskis—The Shepherd of an Occupied Diocese," ibid., 501–507.
48 K. Paul Žygas, "The Lithuanian Chapel in St. Peter's Basilica," *Draugas News*, July 15, 2010, 7–10; V. Stanley Vardys, *The Catholic Church, Dissent and Nationality in Soviet Lithuania* (New York, NY: East European Quarterly, 1978). Mulokas designed a wayside shrine used in the advertising campaign for the 1965 New York World's Fair. Jonynas designed the sculpture on the exterior wall of the Vatican pavilion. The sculpture visualizes the Trilogy of the Church Militant, the Church Penitent, and the Church Triumphant: Julie Nicoletta, "Selling Spirituality and Spectacle," *Journal of the Vernacular Architecture Forum* (Fall 2015) 22: 62–88.
49 *Our Lady of Perpetual Help Church, 50th Golden Anniversary*, parish publication, Cleveland, Ohio, 1979.

50 Kathleen Curran, *The Romanesque Revival* (University Park, PA: The Pennsylvania State University Press, 2003.

51 Jonas Mulokas earned a civil engineering degree at Vytautas Magnus University in Kaunas in 1935. After his son, Rimvydas Eugene Mulokas (a.k.a. Ray, 1942–), graduated from the University of Illinois, Urbana-Champaign in 1964, and was licensed as an architect in New York in 1972, Mulokas moved his family to California. Ray became the President and CEO of Mulokas & Mulokas Construction, Inc., listed as a general contractor in Ventura, California. The family archive is not available, and it is not clear when the Mulokas & Mulokas firm was dissolved.

52 Jonynas & Shepherd Art Studio, Inc. File 612883, NY Domestic Business Corporation, founded 1955, dissolved March 5, 1980.

53 Andriušytė-Žukienė, *Jonynas*, 109, 206.

54 Wolkovich-Valkavičius, *Lithuanian Religious Life in America*, vol. 3, 114–116. Unskilled and blue-collar jobs attracted immigrants to St. Louis from the coal mines of Pennsylvania.

55 Connie Evans, "Immaculate Conception Parish Celebrates 110 Years," *Bridges* January–February 2006, 8–9.

56 John F. Knoll, "Resurrection Church: Msgr. George Dreher's Gift," *Society of Architectural Historians Missouri Valley Chapter Newsletter* XVI, no. 2 (Summer 2010): 2–3; Steven J. Schloeder, "Rudolf Schwarz and his Reception in America" *Das Munster. Zeitschrift für christliche Kunst und Kunstwissenschaft* (Regensburg: Schnell & Steiner, January 2011): 47–52; Susan Behofy, "The Day the Mass Changed," *Adoremus Bulletin* (Society for the Renewal of the Sacred Liturgy) XVI, no. 1 (March 2010).

57 "Work Starts on Nativity B.V.N. Church," *Chicago Tribune*, November 5, 1953, 82. Gregory W. Tucker, *America's Church* (Washington, DC: The Basilica of the National Shrine of the Immaculate Conception, 2000). Designed by Charles D. Maginnis in 1919, the Basilica of the National Shrine of the Immaculate Conception in Washington, DC, was blessed in 1954, following the Marian Year of 1953.

58 Ernst H. J. Gombrich, *The Sense of Order. A Study in the Psychology of Decorative Art* (Ithaca, NY: Cornell University Press, 1979, 1984), 155.

59 Michael Snodin and Maurice Howard, *Ornament. A Social History since 1450* (New Haven, CT: Yale University Press, 1996), 71–72.

60 Gombrich, *The Sense of Order*, 179.

61 Steven J. Schloeder, "The Recovery of the Symbolic." In Douglas A. Ollivant, ed. *Jacques Maritain and the Many Ways of Knowing* (Washington, DC: The Catholic University of America Press, 2002), 311.

62 Ibid., 311.

63 Ibid.

64 Margaret B. W. Graham and Alec T. Shuldiner, *Corning and the Craft of Innovation* (Oxford, UK: Oxford University Press, 2001), 79–123.

65 Milda B. Richardson, "The Ipswich Provincial House as a Sacred Modern Place," *A Bridging of Art and Faith. Sister Vincent de Paul Curran, SND de Namur* (Boston, MA: Emmanuel College, 2012), 27–37.

66 Wolkovich-Valkavičius, *Lithuanian Religious Life in America*, vol. 3, 149–150; Algis Lukas, *Lithuanian Cultural Legacy in America* (Silver Spring, MD: Lithuanian-American Community Inc., 2009), 122–123.

67 The three ethnic regions represented are the Highlands, the Lowlands and Suvalkija.

68 Site visit, August 2011. *Holy Cross 100 Years*, parish publication, Dayton, Ohio, 2014.

69 Vincent J. Scully, Jr., *The Shingle Style and the Stick Style* (New Haven, CT and London: Yale University Press, 1955, rev. 1971).

70 Gretchen Buggeln, *The Suburban Church. Modernism and Community in Post-war America* (Minneapolis, MN: University of Minnesota Press, 2015); Chad Randl, *A-frame* (New York, NY: Princeton Architectural Press, 2004); Jay M. Price, *Temples for a Modern God: Religious Architecture in Post-war America* (Oxford, UK: Oxford University Press, 2013).

71 Alfredas Kulpa-Kulpavičius (1923–2007) earned his Ph.D. in architecture from Darmstadt Technical University in 1951. A year later, he immigrated to Canada where he established an architectural firm in Toronto. In 1953, he set a precedent for Lithuanian parishes with the use of glazed facades for Our Lady of the Gates of Dawn in Hamilton and Montreal and a wood A-frame church for St. Casimir, 1959 (closed 1999), in Winnipeg, Manitoba.

72 An English summary of Baltic vernacular architecture appears in *Encyclopedia of Vernacular Architecture of the World*. Paul Oliver, ed. (Cambridge, UK: Cambridge University Press, 1997), 2: 1255–1267.

73 Richard M. Dorson, "Heart Disease and Folklore." In Jan Harold Brunvand, ed. *Readings in American Folklore* (New York, NY: W. W. Norton, 1979), 137.

74 Richardson, *Metamorphosis*, 255–285.

75 *Dedication of the Church of the Transfiguration*, parish publication, Maspeth, NY, 1962.

76 Andriušytė-Žukienė, *Jonynas*, 81.

77 Algimantas Kezys, "Sculptures by Aleksandras Marčiulionis," *Lituanus*, vol. 45, no. 4 (Winter 1999): 48–54.

78 Gabija Surdokaitė-Vitienė, *Susimąstęs Kristus* [Pensive Christ], exhibition catalog, October 8, 2015–January 30, 2016 (Vilnius, Lithuania: Bažnytinio paveldo muziejus), 107–126, 129.

79 Ibid., 110–111.

80 Wayne Franklin and Michael Steiner, eds., *Mapping American Culture* (Iowa City, IA: University of Iowa Press, 1992), 41.

81 Yi-Fu Tuan, *Space and Place: The Perspective of Experience* (Minneapolis, MN: University of Minnesota Press, 1977).

82 Amy Corning and Howard Schuman, *Generations and Collective Memory* (Chicago, IL: University of Chicago Press, 2015), 1.

83 Michael Owen Jones, *Craftsman of the Cumberlands. Tradition and Creativity* (Lexington, KY: The University Press of Kentucky, 1989), 192.

84 Andriušytė-Žukienė, *Jonynas*, 28–32, 67.

85 Cited in *Architectural Theory*. Harry Francis Mallgrove, ed. (Oxford, UK: Blackwell Publishing, 2007) 1: 211.

86 Francesco Passanti, "The Vernacular, Modernism and Le Corbusier," *Journal of the Society of Architectural Historians* (December 1997) 56: 438–451.

87 Sigfried Giedion, *Space, Time and Architecture. The Growth of a New Tradition* (Cambridge, MA: Harvard University Press, 1967), 520.

88 Fred W. Peterson, *Building Community, Keeping the Faith: German Catholic Vernacular Architecture in a Rural Minnesota Parish* (St. Paul, MN: Minnesota Historical Society Press, 1998); Christopher Martin, "Skeleton of Settlement: Ukrainian Folk Building in Western North Dakota." In Thomas Carter and Bernard L. Herman, eds. *Perspectives in Vernacular Architecture, III* (Columbia, MO: University of Missouri Press, 1989), 86–98; Joseph Sciorra, "Yard Shrines and Sidewalk Altars of New York's Italian-Americans." In Thomas Carter and Bernard L. Herman, eds. *Perspectives in Vernacular Architecture, III* (Columbia, MO: University of Missouri Press, 1989), 185–198; Thomas A. Tweed, *Our Lady of the Exile. Diasporic Religion at a Cuban Catholic Shrine in Miami* (New York, NY: Oxford University Press, 1997).

References

Andriušytė-Žukienė, Rasa. *Akistatos. Dailininkas Vytautas Kazimieras Jonynas pasaulio meno keliuose* [Artist Vytautas Kazimieras Jonynas in the World of Art] (Vilnius: Lietuvos dailės muziejus, 2007) (in Lithuanian).

"Augsburg," *Lithuanian Encyclopedia*, ed. Vaclovas Biržiška (Boston, MA: Juozas Kapočius, 1953), 403–405.

Basanavičius, Jonas. *Lietuvos kryžiai* [Crosses of Lithuania] (Vilnius: Lietuvių Dailės Draugijos Leidinys, 1912) (in Lithuanian).

Behofy, Susan. "The Day the Mass Changed," *Adoremus Bulletin* (Society for the Renewal of the Sacred Liturgy, XVI, no. 1 (March 2010).

Bernotaitytė, Jolanta, comp. *Kazys Varnelis* (Vilnius: Lietuvos nacionalinis muziejus, 2009) (in Lithuanian).

Billot, Marcel, ed. *The Vence Chapel, The Archive of a Creation* (Milan, Italy: Skira and Menil Foundation, 1999).

Bonner, Jeremy, et al., eds. *Empowering the People of God: Catholic Action Before and After Vatican II* (New York, NY: Fordham University Press, 2014).

Budreckis, Algirdas. "Liberation Attempts from Abroad." In Albertas Gerutis, ed. *Lithuania 700 Years*, 388–426 (New York, NY: Manyland Books, 1984).

Buggeln, Gretchen. *The Suburban Church. Modernism and Community in Post-war America* (Minneapolis: University of Minnesota Press, 2015).

Corning, Amy and Howard Schuman. *Generations and Collective Memory* (Chicago, IL: University of Chicago Press, 2015).

Curran, Kathleen. *The Romanesque Revival* (University Park, PA: Pennsylvania State University Press, 2003).

Dedication of the Church of the Transfiguration (parish publication, Maspeth, NY, 1962).

Dorson, Richard M. "Heart Disease and Folklore." In Jan Harold Brunvand, ed. *Readings in American Folklore*, 137–151 (New York, NY: W. W. Norton, 1979).

Evans, Connie. "Immaculate Conception Parish Celebrates 110 Years," *Bridges* (January–February 2006): 8–9.

Faherty, William Barnaby, S.J. *The Great Saint Louis Cathedral* (St. Louis, MO: Friends of the Cathedral, 2008).

Franklin, Wayne and Michael Steiner, eds. *Mapping American Culture* (Iowa City: University of Iowa Press, 1992).

Gerutis, Albertas, ed. *Lithuania 700 Years* (New York, NY: Manyland Books, 1984).

Giedion, Sigfried. *Space, Time and Architecutre: The Growth of a New Tradition* (Cambridge, MA: Harvard University Press, 1967).

Gimbutas, Marija. *Ancient Symbolism in Lithuanian Folk Art* (Philadelphia, PA: American Folklore Society, 1958).

Gombrich, Ernst H. J. *The Sense of Order: A Study in the Psychology of Decorative Art* (Ithaca, NY: Cornell University Press, 1984).

Graham, Margaret B. W. and Alec T. Shuldiner. *Corning and the Craft of Innovation* (Oxford: Oxford University Press, 2001).

Grinius, Jonas. "Lietuvos kryžiai ir koplytėlės" [Crosses and Shrines of Lithuania]. In A Livina, ed. *Metraštis Lietuvių Katalikų Mokslo Akademija*, 1–77 (Rome: Lithuanian Catholic Academy, 1970) (in Lithuanian).

A Guide to Lithuania's Baroque Monuments (Vilnius: baltos lankos, 1996).

Holy Cross 100 Years, parish publication, Dayton, Ohio, 2014.

Jankevičienė, Algė. *Lietuvos medinė sakralinė architektūra: bažnycios, koplyčios ir varpinės* [Sacred Wooden Architecture of Lithuania: Churches, Chapels, and Bell Towers] (Kaunas: Vilniaus dailės akademija, 2000) (in Lithuanian).

Jones, Michael Owen. *Craftsman of the Cumberlands. Tradition and Creativity* (Lexington: University Press of Kentucky, 1989).

Kančienė, Jolita and Jonas Minkevičius. *Architektas Vytautas Landsbergis-Žemkalnis* (Vilnius: Mokslo ir enciklopedijų leidykla, 1993) (in Lithuanian).

Kaunas 1918–2015. Architektūros gidas (Vilnius: Architektūros fondas, 2015) (in Lithuanian).

Kezys, Algimantas. "Sculptures by Aleksandras Marčiulionis," *Lituanus* 45, no. 4 (Winter 1999): 48–54.

Knoll, John F. "Resurrection Church: Msgr. George Dreher's Gift," *SAH Missouri Valley Chapter Newsletter* XVI, no. 2 (Summer 2010): 2–3.

Koenker, Ernest Benjamin. *The Liturgical Renaissance of the Roman Catholic Church* (Chicago, IL: University of Chicago Press, 1954).

Kučas, Antanas. *St. George's Parish Shenandoah, Pennsylvania*, parish publication, Brooklyn, NY, 1968.

Lukas, Algis, ed. *Lithuanian Cultural Legacy in America* (Silver Spring, MD: Lithuanian American Community, Inc., 2009).

Mallgrove, Harry Francis, ed. *Architectural Theory*, vol. 1 (Oxford: Blackwell Publishing, 2007).

Martin, Christopher. "Skeleton of Settlement: Ukrainian Folk Building in Western North Dakota." In Thomas Carter and Bernard L. Herman, eds. *Perspectives in Vernacular Architecture III*, 86–98 (Columbia, MO: University of Missouri Press, 1989).

Matranga, Viktorija, ed. *Freiburg 1946. Art Exhibit Celebrating 50th Anniversary of the Freiburg School of Arts and Crafts* (Chicago, IL: Balzekas Museum, January 26–April 3, 1997).

McDannell, Colleen. *Material Christianity. Religion and Popular Culture in America* (New Haven, CT: Yale University Press, 1995).

Milius, Vacys. "Lietuvių kryžių ir koplytėlių statymo priežastys" [The Reasons for Erecting Lithuanian Crosses and Shrines]. In *Proceedings of the Lithuanian Catholic Academy of Science XV*, 294–302 (Vilnius: Katalikų Akademija, 1995) (in Lithuanian).

———. "Žemės ūkio rūmai—etninės kultūros puoselėtojas" [Hall of Agriculture—The Fostering of Ethnic Culture]. In Regina Merkienė, ed. *Etninė kultūra ir tautinis atgimimas*, 106–117 (Vilnius: Lietuvos istorijos institutas, 1994) (in Lithuanian).

Minkevičius, Jonas. *Lietuvos bažnyčių menas* [The Art of Lithuanian Churches] (Vilnius: R. Paknys, 1993) (in Lithuanian).

Nicoletta, Julie. "Selling Spirituality and Spectacle," *Journal of the Vernacular Architecture Forum* 22 (Fall 2015): 62–88.

Oliver, Paul, ed. *Encyclopedia of Vernacular Architecture of the World*, vol. 2 (Cambridge: Cambridge University Press, 1997).

Our Lady of Perpetual Help Church, 50th Golden Anniversary, parish publication, Cleveland, OH, 1979.

Passanti, Francesco. "The Vernacular, Modernism and Le Corbusier," *Journal of the Society of Architectural Historians* 56 (December 1997): 438–451.

Perret, Marine. *Inventory of the Archives of the Architect Maurice Novarina. Documents from His Paris Studio 1957–1996* (Paris: Archives of Haute Savoie, 2014).

Peterson, Fred W. *Building Community, Keeping the Faith: German Catholic Vernacular Architecture in a Rural Minnesota Parish* (St. Paul, MN: Minnesota Historical Society Press, 1998).

Price, Jay J. *Temples for a Modern God. Religious Architecture in Post-war America* (Oxford: Oxford University Press, 2013).

Puzinas, Jonas. "The Origins of the Lithuanian Nation." In Albertas Gerutis, ed. *Lithuania 700 Years*, 1–42 (New York, NY: Manyland Books, 1984).

Randl, Chad. *A-frame* (New York, NY: Princeton Architectural Press, 2004).

Reinhold, Hans A. "The Architecture of Rudolf Schwarz," *The Architectural Forum* 70 (1939): 22–27.

———. *H.A.R.: The Autobiography of Father Reinhold* (New York, NY: Herder & Herder, 1968).

———. "A Revolution in Church Architecture," *Liturgical Arts* 63 (1938): 123–133.

Richardson, Milda B. "The Heritage of Community Art in Lithuania." In Kristin G. Congdon and Doug Boughton, eds. *Advances in Program Evaluation*, vol. 4, 55–71 (Stamford, CT, and London: JAI Press Inc., 1998).

———. "Iconoclasm and Resistance. Wayside Shrines in the Struggle for Lithuanian Independence." In J. M. Mancini and Keith Bresnahan, eds. *Architecture and Armed Conflict: The Politics of Destruction*, 103–115 (London: Routledge, 2015).

———. "The Ipswich Provincial House as a Sacred Modern Place." In *A Bridging of Art and Faith. Sister Vincent de Paul Curran, SND de Namur*, 27–37 (Boston, MA: Emmanuel College, 2012).

———. "The Metamorphosis of the Lithuanian Wayside Shrines 1850–1990," Ph.D. diss., Boston University, 2003.

———. "Remembrance and Reflection on Sacred Fragments," *Draugas News* (August 2015): 6–9.

Rūkštelė, Antanas. *Vilniaus Kryžiai* [Crosses of Vilnius] (Vilnius: VVS Leidinys, 1937) (in Lithuanian).

Sauka, Leonardas. *Lietuvių Tautosaka* [Lithuanian Folklore] (Kaunas: Šviesa, 1999) (in Lithuanian).

Schloeder, Steven J. "The Recovery of the Symbolic." In Douglas A. Ollivant, ed. *Jacques Maritain and the Many Ways of Knowing*, 303–314 (Washington, DC: Catholic University Press, 2002).

———. "Rudolf Schwarz and His Reception in America." In *Das Munster. Zeitschrift für christliche Kunst und Kunstwissenschaf*, 47–52 (Regensburg, Germany: Schnell & Steiner, January 2011).

Schnell, Hugo. *Twentieth Century Church Architecture in Germany* (Munich and Zurich: Verlag Schnell & Steiner, 1974).

Schwarz, Rudolf. *The Church Incarnate: The Sacred Function of Christian Architecture*. Translated by Cynthia Harris (Chicago, IL: H. Regnery Co., 1958).

Sciorra, Joseph. "Yard Shrines and Sidewalk Altars of New York's Italian-Americans." In Thomas Carter and Bernard L. Herman, eds. *Perspectives in Vernacular Architecture III*, 185–198 (Columbia, MO: University of Missouri Press,1989).

Scully, Vincent J., Jr. *The Shingle Style and the Stick Style* (New Haven, CT: Yale University Press, 1971).

Senn, Alfred E. *Jonas Basanavičius: The Patriarch of the Lithuanian National Renaissance* (Newtonville, MA: Oriental Reseach Partners, 1980).

Sister Jacques-Marie. *Henri Matisse, The Vence Chapel* (Nice, France: Grégoire Gardette, 1992).

Smith, Randall B. "Don't Blame Vatican II. Modernism and Modern Catholic Church Architecture," *Sacred Architecture Journal* (South Bend, IN: The Institute for Sacred Architecture) 13 (2016): 1–15.

Snodin, Michael and Maurice Howard. *Ornament. A Social History since 1450* (New Haven, CT: Yale University Press, 1996).

Surdokaitė-Vitienė,Gabija. *Susimąstęs Kristus* [Pensive Christ], exhibition catalog (Vilnius: Bažnytinio paveldo muziejus, October 8, 2015–January 30, 2016) (in Lithuanian).

Suziedelis, Saulius. *The Sword and the Cross. A History of the Church in Lithuania* (Huntington, IN: Our Sunday Visitor, Inc., 1988)

———, and Vincas Rastenis, eds. *Encyclopedia Lituanica*, vol. III (Boston, MA: Juozas Kapočius, 1973).

Tamošaitis, Antanas. "Kultūriškai apvogtas sodžius" [The Village Robbed of Culture]. *Naujoji romuva*, No. 10–11 (1935): 266–267. Reprinted in Lijana Šatavičiūtė-Natalevičienė. *Antanas Tamošaitis*, 91–93 (Vilnius: Vilniaus dailės akademijos leidykla, 2003) (in Lithuanian).

———. *Sodžiaus pramonė, Sodžiaus menas* [Cottage Industry, Village Art] (Kaunas: Žemės ūkio namai, 1931–1939) (in Lithuanian).

Tuan, Yi-Fu. *Space and Place: The Perspective of Experience* (Minneapolis, MN: University of Minnesota Press, 1977).

Tucker, Gregory W. *America's Church* (Washington, DC: The Basilica of the National Shrine of the Immaculate Conception, 2000).

Tweed, Thomas A. *Our Lady of the Exile. Diasporic Religion at a Cuban Catholic Shrine in Miami* (New York, NY: Oxford University Press, 1997).

Van Reenan Antanas J. *Lithuanian Diaspora Königsberg to Chicago* (Lanham, MD: University Press of America, Inc., 1990).

Vardys, V. Stanley. *The Catholic Church, Dissent and Nationality in Soviet Lithuania* (New York, NY: East European Quarterly, 1978).

Vasiliauskienė, Aldona. "Bishop Vincentas Padolskis: Activities in the Lithuanian Catholic Academy of Science." In *LKMA Yearbook XXV*, 527–560 (Vilnius: Lithuanian Roman Catholic Academy of Sciences, 2004) (in Lithuanian).

Wolkovich-Valkavičius, William. *Lithuanian Religious Life in America*, 3 vols. (Norwood, MA: Lithuanian Religious Life in America, 1991–98).

"Work Starts on Nativity B.V.N. Church," *Chicago Tribune*, November 5, 1953, 82.

Žemaitis, Kęstutis. "Bishop Vincentas Padolskis—The Shepherd of an Occupied Diocese." In *LKMA Yearbook XXV*, 501–507 (Vilnius: Lithuanian Roman Catholic Academy of Sciences, 2004) (in Lithuanian).

Žemaitytė, Zita. *Adomas Varnas* (Vilnius: baltos lankos, 1998) (in Lithuanian).

———. *Paulius Galaunė* (Vilnius: Vaga, 1988) (in Lithuanian).

Žygas, K. Paul. "The Lithuanian Chapel in St. Peter's Basilica." *Draugas News*, July 15, 2010, 7–10.

PART IV

Modern interiors and liturgical fittings

12

SEEING, NOT KNOWING

Symbolism, art, and "opticalism" in mid-century American religious architecture

Jeremy Kargon

> Architectural artifices are obviously optical. But since visual impressions are judged by the mind according to the mental and psychological stimulus they provide, [they] are, in essence, logical and psychological means of suggestion which influence our inner being.[1]

Among the innovations of American sacred architecture after World War II was an interrogation of the decorative arts' role both in religious life and in architecture itself. Earlier modernists' ostensible rejection of ornament was reinterpreted by some architects as a call to rebuild the relationship between art and community;[2] others called instead for the reintroduction of art which would conform to modernist principles.[3] Consequently, religious art's literal place within architectural spaces received renewed attention from architects, who had often to reconcile spiritual atavism with new and even unsettling norms of behavior, geography, and social stratification – as well as changing materials, construction practices, and methods of finance.[4]

One strategy that was used by American architects can be defined as "opticalism," a neologism that denotes the deployment of aggressive and large-scale visual effects within spaces of worship. By this definition, opticalism included the following characteristics:

- An emphasis upon visible technical innovation to signify prestige;
- The spatial *centrality* of decorative installations of an unusually stimulating nature;
- The spatial *dissociation* of religious symbol from primary visual effect.

Like other modernizing trends, opticalism reflected a process of innovation. However, that innovation was not fundamentally technological. Instead, it was *semiotic*, having to do with attenuating the relationship between sign and symbol. Mirroring broader discussions about American culture and society, religious architecture incorporated new methods with which to express religious meaning.[5] In certain cases, religious imagery was literally displaced within worship spaces not only by the tendency towards abstraction – an aesthetic shift already long under way – but also by the use of exaggerated optical effect. Opticalism could invert, therefore, the traditional hierarchy of art's relationship to architecture. No longer (merely) situated *within* architecture, artwork instead determined the spatial precinct of the sacred experience.

Three religious buildings constructed in Baltimore, Maryland between 1954 and 1963 illustrate opticalism's characteristics and its manifestation in the relationship between art and architecture: Church of the Redeemer, designed by nationally famous architect Pietro Belluschi (1899–1994); Har Sinai Congregation, designed by local firm Buckler, Fenhagen, Meyer, and Ayers (founded in 1912 and still active today as Ayers Saint Gross), and St. Paul's Evangelical Lutheran Church, designed by Chicago-based church architect Charles Stade (1924–93).These three buildings reflected in microcosm a national conversation about religion and visual culture.[6] On the surface, that conversation engaged contemporary, fast-changing social mores and their challenge to traditional religious practices.[7] At its root, however, were questions about religious values and—perhaps even more fundamentally— about whether or not those values could even be expressed by contemporary architecture.[8] Such questions lay at the conceptual center of opticalism and, quite literally, at the physical center of each of the three buildings to be considered.

Visual strategies for "a place to worship"

In 1958, the American Institute of Architects (AIA) created a series of promotional films aimed to educate the public about the role architects play in the built environment.[9] The film *A Place to Worship* presented current trends in religious architecture throughout the United States. At the start of this film, a voice-over echoed clearly the unmistakably modernist credo that, "mere imitation of past periods is out of place . . . A religion which is firmly anchored in the life of our day is best expressed by the architecture of the day."[10] The narrator went on to explain that "building technologies" and the "needs of family" were two significant influences upon architecture, but that both resulted from a more basic concern: "Today, we live in a period of accelerated change, in the whirl of a technological revolution with all its untold human consequences."[11]

This familiar trope has a historical pedigree of more than a century in Europe and the United States.[12] Its connection with religion and spirituality has been contentious and var-ied, sometimes pitting traditional religion in opposition to technological development and sometimes calling for their reconciliation.[13] The AIA's *A Place to Worship*, however, joined its words to a unique visual counterpart: the image of a superhighway in which the headlights of the cars form a luminous constellation. This image cross-faded to a view of a church win-dow and what seemed like stained glass set within a frame with a pointed arch. The frame then pulled away, like a curtain in a theater, to reveal lights of a large city's evening skyline, as the narrator intoned the words "untold human consequences." Among other things, this sequence linked a kind of perceptual gestalt with mid-century America's technology-driven culture. That gestalt was framed, however, within an architectural setting that clearly denoted "religion." The constellation of light represented the incoherent nature of a constantly chang-ing world. The film's challenge to its audience was, therefore, to find within that period's heterogeneous visual field (with an architect's help) "a place to worship."

Architects' responses to that challenge included engagement with the decorative arts, among other innovations in American religious architecture after World War II. Conventionally, three different approaches characterized architects' work.[14] Placing traditional religious artwork in new, modernistic designs was a common approach during the earliest phases of suburban expansion.[15] A small Catholic church like Baltimore's Immaculate Heart of Mary (1949, Gaudreau & Gaudreau)[16] demonstrates how architects often proposed a simple structural device, such as the wooden A-frame, to provide a visual link to older, steeped-roof religious buildings[17] (Fig. 12.1). Into this context, traditionally styled decorative artwork would be placed in obvious juxtaposition with the new architectural style.[18]

In contrast to this approach, religious art and architecture might together be "updated" through adoption of new styles such as Art Deco. Baltimore's Cathedral of Mary Our Queen (1959, Maginnis, Walsh, and Kennedy)[19] reflects the persistence of the Gothic style in religious architecture throughout the post-World War II period[20] (Fig. 12.2). Nevertheless, the late use of Art Deco in both figurative and non-figurative ornament nods towards modernism's mid-century ascendency.

FIGURE 12.1 Immaculate Heart of Mary, Baltimore, Maryland, 1949, Gaudreau & Gaudreau, architects; northwest façade (inset: detail of figurative sculpture above entry).

Photograph by the author.

FIGURE 12.2 Cathedral of Mary Our Queen, Baltimore, Maryland, 1959, Maginnis, Walsh, and Kennedy, architects; interior detail.

Photograph by the author.

FIGURE 12.3 Baltimore Hebrew Congregation, Baltimore, Maryland, 1948–51, Percival Goodman, architect; sanctuary stage, ark, and ark cover.

Ark cover © Estate of Amalie Rothschild. Photograph by the author.

Otherwise, new architecture could be planned as an armature for the display of modernist religious art. In this approach, architects sought to improve the collaborative relationship between their discipline and the decorative arts. Among the most articulate was Percival Goodman, the New York-based architect, planner, and educator. For Goodman, bringing modern art into architecture was a moral imperative.[21] As he explained to the Baltimore Artists' Union in a 1952 speech, contemporary "robot man . . . is a beast . . . One of the weapons for fighting this beast is art."[22] With his brother, sociologist Paul Goodman, Percival Goodman argued for art's support of community identity and "the state of the soul."[23] In the years after World War II, Goodman's particular focus was religious communities. Goodman's message evoked a process by which a religious community would be "suddenly brought to a new awareness of itself . . . and expressing or about to express a large part of this sentiment as a plastic action, [a] building."[24] As an architect, Goodman tried to support this expression through his synagogue designs, including Baltimore Hebrew Congregation (1948–51). In this, his first synagogue commission,[25] he actively commissioned local and national artists' art work (Fig. 12.3). The result was a process of accommodation between artist and community that was sometimes contentious.[26] Nevertheless, Goodman's Baltimore Hebrew provided many congregants their first contact with modern art outside of a gallery space.

In contrast to these approaches, opticalism as defined here emphasized the spatial characteristics of otherwise decorative elements and transformed art into architectural form. A vocal advocate for this more integrative approach was MIT-based artist György Kepes[27] (1906–2001), who shared Goodman's concern about social alienation and the role of the visual arts to address it. Known among artists for his 1944 publication *The Language of Vision*,[28] Kepes placed art's power to communicate at the center of its social (and even spiritual) agency. From this perspective, the distinction between art and architecture—or, more generally, the built environment—could no longer be meaningful in a world where signs, symbols, and diverse media competed for a diverse audience's attention.[29] A comprehensive statement of this point of view was Kepes' edited volume "The Visual Arts

Today" in *Dædalus*, the quarterly journal of the American Academy of Arts and Sciences.[30] The issue included contributions by the English-speaking world's foremost intellectuals concerned with the role of art in society, including anthropologist Margaret Mead; historians Sigfried Giedion, Rudolf Wittkower, and Ernest Gombrich; philosopher Suzanne Langer; artists Paul and Ann Rand, Edward Steichen, and Maya Deren, and many others. Kepes solicited an essay also by Le Corbusier, who echoed Kepes' worry about coherence in a visual world overwhelmed by its fecundity.[31] In this world, architecture had a special role among the other visual arts, for a synthesis was possible only within architecture:

> I believe that we are entering upon an epoch . . . in which we no longer have the right to "stick something on something," . . . where the work of art will radiate in all its power in exact concordance with the potential forces in the architectural work . . . architecture has edified an authentic symphony through light and the manner in which this light clarifies walls; its lyricism is made of intensely real psycho-physiological events.[32]

Other architects and artists commissioned by Kepes for "The Visual Arts Today" shared Le Corbusier's sentiment that modern art must be integrated within architecture, not applied to its surfaces.[33] English sculptor Reg Butler explained that "The arts may be either harmonious or complementary," but acknowledged the primacy of architectural goals in architectural spaces.[34] Walter Gropius approvingly cited a letter from French artist Jean Gorin, who wrote, "the true synthesis of the arts is to be found in the architectural work itself."[35] Likewise, painter Irene Rice Pereira wrote that contemporary art needed architecture to complete its expressive purpose: "contemporary art, in most cases, fragments the object and negates space . . . Architecture is a dynamic of relationships which involve space, give objective reality to structural form; and, within the form, is content and meaning."[36] Yet architecture itself, as a profession, might resist integration. Pietro Belluschi, then Dean of MIT's School of Architecture, wrote in the same article that architects believed "the way to give transcendent quality to a building is to emphasize its structure and to manipulate its space sequences rather than to introduce sensuous externals as it was done in the past."[37] For Belluschi, the emphasis on structure "made integration between the so-called Visual Arts and Architecture a most difficult task."[38] Belluschi's words may have been meant ironically, since Belluschi and Kepes—who commissioned Belluschi's article—had just recently completed at Baltimore's Church of the Redeemer the first of their several collaborations. Indeed, this project demonstrates the extent to which integration of "sensuous externals" could in fact find itself at the core of the architectural experience.

Opticalism in three regional examples in Baltimore, Maryland

Along with Church of the Redeemer, two other modern religious buildings in Baltimore illustrate well the innovations which underlay opticalism's effects. Designed for different sects and conceived by architects with alternatively local and national reputations, these buildings are especially well-designed examples of the architecture prescribed by *A Place to Worship*.[39] All three buildings demonstrate how prominent optical effect could, as an integral part of modern architectural space, define the locus of religious experience within it.

Church of the Redeemer (1954–58)

Pietro Belluschi with Rogers, Taliaferro, and Lamb, architects

Church of the Redeemer has been well documented in the critical literature, most comprehensively by Meredith Clausen in her books on Pietro Belluschi's life and religious architecture.[40] The architect's signature timber arches create a warm and sober character for Redeemer's sanctuary space. In a complementary fashion, the space is enlivened by a stained glass altar screen designed by György Kepes and executed by ecclesiastical glass artisan George L. Payne.[41] The scale of the altar screen is immense, filling entirely a structural bay and extending the full width of the nave opposite (Fig. 12.4). Consistent with opticalism's definition, the illuminated screen's spatial centrality is obvious, as is its exceptionally stimulating nature. The screen consists of multiple 2-foot-square concrete panels, each an inch thick, into which have been set thick shards of glass chipped to refract light with additional brilliance (Fig. 12.5). Assembled together, the illuminated color field reaches more than 30 feet high, immediately commanding worshipers' visual attention. And although the screen's colors appear to be randomly composed, from within the composition the faint figure of a cross may be seen to emerge. What was referred to earlier in this chapter as a "*dissociation* of religious symbol from primary visual effect" is here already visible, if incomplete. The luminous ensemble appears to float, the cross itself barely rising to one's attention.

FIGURE 12.4 Church of the Redeemer, Baltimore, Maryland, 1954–58, Pietro Belluschi with Rogers, Taliaferro, and Lamb, architects; nave, chancel, and altar screen.

Altar screen © Estate of György Kepes. Photograph by the author.

FIGURE 12.5 Church of the Redeemer: altar screen detail.

Altar screen © Estate of György Kepes. Photograph by the author.

György Kepes had been invited by Belluschi when an early scheme for the church's altar was rejected by the church's vestry as too austere.[42] Kepes' design, of course, was anything but austere. Nevertheless, the substance of its visual effect was not immediately apparent to the congregation. Rev. Bennett Sims, rector of Church of the Redeemer at the time of its construction, recalled his original reaction to Kepes' stained glass:

> When the screen was installed the designer, Professor [Kepes] came to see the finished work . . . I . . . walked with him down the center aisle . . . I said to him, trying to be polite but definite, "Why did you design the cross in the window as an apology? It is so muted and indistinct that no one will see it without direction and straining." He turned to me and scoffed, "You Americans! You don't know the difference between a sign and a symbol. All you seem to want are signs like Coca Cola and Mobil Gas. They are so shallow that you grasp them in an instant and they never endure in your inner life. They are tin-pan alley stuff, or pop-art. But a symbol is radically different. You don't grasp it. It grasps you. It asks for your deep attention and once that attention has been given the symbol will take hold of your soul and feed you in new ways each time you encounter it. It's the mystical character of all true art. It speaks to the soul . . . That altar screen is designed to nourish your soul and lure you over and over again to its presence"[43]

Kepes' distinction between sign and symbol and the tactical consequences of that distinction is fundamental to the artist's influential theoretical writing, starting with *Language of Vision*.[44] In that book, Kepes outlined trends in modernist art, but he did so in order to promote his particular program of "dynamic iconography," defined as the reconciliation between "the image in its original role as a dynamic experience based upon . . . the senses" and "the meaningful signs of . . . visual relationships."[45] Accordingly, symbol and sign have both to coexist, subject to the artist and architect's effective choreography.

Kepes' explanation to Rev. Sims also recalls philosopher Susanne Langer's distinction between discursive and presentational symbols. Langer (1895–1985) had contributed to Kepes' edition of *Dædalus* after having built a sophisticated theoretical framework for understanding how art is experienced and understood by its audience.[46] Discursive symbols—usually words or the visual "signs" to which Kepes referred—are stable, direct, and clear in any context, including experiential ones. On the other hand, presentational symbols convey their meaning only within the context of a complete (and complex) experience. In her popular book *Philosophy in a New Key*,[47] Langer wrote:

> Their very functioning as symbols depends on the fact that they are involved in a simultaneous, integral presentation . . . The recognition of presentational symbolism as a normal and prevalent vehicle of meaning widens our conception of rationality far beyond the traditional boundaries.[48]

In the context of a space for worship, a theory of presentational symbolism could reciprocally extend artists' conception of sacredness beyond its source in religious ritual. Doing so lay at the heart of opticalism. Within Belluschi's design for Church of the Redeemer, one's encounter with Kepes' altar screen evokes the powerful (and ineffable) gestalt experience to which Langer refers in her book.

Har Sinai Synagogue (1953–59)

Buckler, Fenhagen, Meyer, and Ayers, architects

The possibility of imbuing architectural form with meaning in this manner was especially compelling among religious sects for which no canonical iconography existed. Unlike Catholics or Episcopalians, for instance, American Jews inherited a self-contradictory tradition of material culture.[49] Art and craft in traditional synagogues were typically limited to liturgical objects.[50] Synagogue design might be more or less sophisticated depending upon the wealth and legal status of a particular community.[51] On the other hand, Jewish ritual art provided a vocabulary of obvious, discursive symbolism for designers' use. One example, Baltimore's Har Sinai Congregation illustrates how, during the design process, a "functional"

FIGURE 12.6 Har Sinai Synagogue, Baltimore, Maryland, 1953–59, Meyer and Ayers, architects; tessellated dome above sanctuary.

Photograph by the author.

architectural form was superseded by a symbolically charged one. It was then itself transformed into something *without* obvious symbolic meaning. The result was a stunning interior sanctuary space recalling what architect Erich Mendelsohn once called "tellurian and planetary things."[52] (Fig. 12.6)

The Har Sinai congregation was founded in 1844 and led early on by Rabbi David Einhorn, an intellectual leader of Reform Judaism in the United States.[53] Despite its progressive roots, Har Sinai joined other Jewish congregations by moving a century later to Baltimore's second-tier suburbs, still within city limits but well past the historical core of the city.[54] By 1953, the congregation had commissioned a "contemporary, multi-purpose building of flexible design," visibly simple, functional, and unremarkable.[55] At this time, two prominent examples of modernist architecture had already been realized for Baltimore's Jewish community: Percival Goodman's Baltimore Hebrew Congregation, completed the previous year; and Erich Mendelsohn's Beth El synagogue, of which only the religious school was completed.[56]

In mid-century America, Erich Mendelsohn was especially prominent in the Jewish discourse about religion, art, and architecture.[57] His essay "In the Spirit of Our Age," which appeared in *Commentary* in 1947, established generally the parameters by which architects justified their designs for Jewish congregations.[58] He wrote, "our temples should reject the anachronistic representation of God as a feudal lord, should apply contemporary building styles and architectural conceptions to make God's house a part of the democratic community in which he dwells."[59] Nevertheless, even Mendelsohn's modernist synagogues incorporated elements derived from buildings of the pre-modern era. In the unrealized Baltimore Beth El sanctuary, a series of vaults evokes the shape of curved tablets, a common motif in Jewish ritual art.[60] More directly relevant for Har Sinai Synagogue is the influence of Mendelsohn's design of a prominent dome for Cleveland's Park Synagogue (1945–50).[61] The hemispherical dome sits with unease upon an otherwise sophisticated, asymmetrical building plan.[62]

At the end of 1953, the Har Sinai congregation commissioned Baltimore firm Buckler, Fenhagen, Meyer, and Ayers[63] to produce alternative designs. Mendelsohn had died earlier that year, before Har Sinai could begin in earnest to plan their new synagogue, but the architects' first scheme reflected clearly the influence of Mendelsohn's first, widely published

FIGURE 12.7 Har Sinai Synagogue, rendering of schematic design, 1955. © Buckler, Fenhagen, Meyer, and Ayers (later Meyer and Ayers), architects.

Collection of Peggy and Brennan Harrington.

design of an American synagogue, Bnai Amoona in St. Louis, Missouri.[64] Yet, by July 1954, the design had completely changed (Fig. 12.7). A round sanctuary, surrounded by classrooms and flanked by a social hall, established the direction for subsequent design development. The reference to Mendelsohn's Park Synagogue is obvious.

Like the Park Synagogue, the new design for Har Sinai featured a domed sanctuary, into which a wedge-shaped building element has been inserted. At the interior, however, the two projects could hardly have been more different. Whereas the interior of Mendelsohn's dome is a smooth, quasi-platonic form, Har Sinai's interior is aggressively tessellated (Fig. 12.8). As a promotional pamphlet explained, "the great dome . . . has a many-faceted interior ceiling to aid in acoustics, light distribution, and striking appearance."[65] At the building's consecration, a newspaper report told that the "suspended plaster ceiling was hung from the underside of the dome. It is a geometric formation of inverted pyramidal shapes. The various surface planes are designed to distribute sound evenly to all points in the temple."[66] Here was the functional rationale for the architects' design, but acoustical considerations alone can hardly account for the faceted dome's startling impact. From any point within the congregation's seating area, the effect's totality is hard to grasp. The dome's contours resist measure, and the visual field appears to pulsate like a moiré pattern, alternating light and dark. Although hardly traditional in any sense, the dome's soffit evokes unambiguously a biblical notion: an energetic and dynamic firmament.

The soffit's folds are continued by mullions of the clerestory glass at the dome's base, recalling Buckminster Fuller's geodesic domes (1949 onwards). Patented in 1954,[67] Fuller's light structures become a popular symbol of technology's utopian promise.[68] At Har Sinai, however, steel mullions are obviously non-structural and are akin rather to the caming[69] of traditional stained glass. In this example, therefore, opticalism is realized by the profound spatial centrality of the building's most stimulating visual effect, which resists any additional interpretation. A nine-pointed star figure relates to no obvious symbol, and any residual "orientalism"

FIGURE 12.8 Har Sinai Synagogue, illustration of the proposed sanctuary, 1958.

© Meyer and Ayers, architects. Source: Jewish Museum of Maryland Archives.

of the rotational tiling is hard to credit. Instead, Har Sinai's soffit anticipates the op art of the succeeding decade, sharing "the effect of dazzle . . . reversible perspective . . . and the super-position of elements in space."[70]

St. Paul's Evangelical Lutheran (1960–63)

Charles Stade, architect

Such optical effects—including the "dazzle"—often defied expectations established by a building's exterior. St. Paul's Evangelical Lutheran Church of Glen Burnie, located southwest of Baltimore's municipal boundary, is an especially compelling example. Its design aligns closely with the AIA's promotional sloganeering in *A Place to Worship*. As described at the time of its dedication, the building was "designed to be used; to be lived with in the contemporary society, and to be lived in by its family . . . The use of modern materials and contemporary form relate the building to twentieth century time and space."[71] Steeped in the sophisticated visual culture of the Lutheran artistic community, St. Paul's designers nevertheless adopted that visual strategy implicitly endorsed by *A Place to Worship*: to use optical means by which to define clearly a sacred precinct within the diverse architectural forms of suburban place-making.[72]

A member of the Missouri Synod since its founding in 1908, St. Paul's Evangelical saw a five-fold increase in membership after World War II, rising from 150 in 1940 to 730 by the end of the 1950s.[73] A new pastor, the Rev. Paul T. Dannenfeldt, assumed his post in 1959 following the congregation's purchase of a large property approximately a mile from the existing church. To plan the new facility, St. Paul's leadership commissioned the architectural office of Charles E. Stade, a Chicago firm (1951–81) with strong connections to the Lutheran Missouri Synod.[74] Partner Harry F. Anderson, later the CEO of Perkins and Will, was the principal in charge. Design for the new church began in 1960, and the facility was dedicated at the end of March, 1963.[75] A preliminary sketch at the start of the process is typical of Stade's work for other Lutheran communities throughout the Midwest. The design

FIGURE 12.9 St. Paul's Evangelical Lutheran Church, Baltimore, Maryland, drawing of the exterior, 1962.

© Estate of Charles Stade, architect. Source: St. Paul's Evangelical Lutheran Church Archives.

included an A-frame structural system, a long nave, and a tall, vertical glass element on the façade behind which was located the chancel. By the start of construction in 1962, however, the exterior design had been revised to include a pitched roof above the sacristy, an extended narthex, and a free-standing tower design signifying—according to Stade's office—"the great mountains of Holy Scripture"[76] (Fig. 12.9). The façade had been simplified, and the large glass window removed.

Even with these changes, the church was typical of Stade's many other A-frame designs.[77] One interior feature, however, was exceptional: an architect-designed translucent marble screen, back-lit to provide a luminous and ethereal effect throughout the chancel (Fig. 12.10). Called a reredos[78] throughout the written record of the church's planning, the screen transformed St. Paul's interior in a manner unprecedented in Stade's œuvre. Few visual innovations in that period's church architecture had such a visual impact.

St. Paul's reredos predates by several months the well-known architectural application of translucent marble at Yale's Beinecke Library (1963, Skidmore, Owings & Merrill). Other possible precedents include non-luminous examples such as the walls in the Barcelona Pavilion (1929, Ludwig Mies van der Rohe) or the matched-vein marble walls of funerary monuments. At St. Paul's, the marble patterns draw attention towards the reredos' line of symmetry, and the marble's back-lit glow places chancel fittings in sharp relief. As a purely visual experience, St. Paul's reredos is a striking example of opticalism: an obvious innovation, the reredos occupies the focus of the architectural space (immediately behind the chancel itself). Yet, it supports no obvious religious interpretation.

FIGURE 12.10 St. Paul's Evangelical Lutheran Church, chancel and reredos, 1960–63.
Photograph by the author.

Its effect has partly to do with the reredos' size. Like Kepes' altar screen at Church of the Redeemer, St. Paul's reredos extends from floor to underside of the roof structure. The decision to fill the space in this way was, evidently, the congregation's own. A letter from Principle in Charge Harry Anderson to a member of the Building Committee reveals that the original design was lower, with a level top.[79] The architect argued that raising the marble surface "to conform to the angle of the roof deck . . . will entail extra cost," and added that he "personally [did] not feel that the premium would be worth the effect."[80] Nevertheless, the change was made, and the resulting installation reaches from floor to roof deck.

Extensive discussions concerning other elements of the chancel were held among Church leadership, architect, artisans, and an "ecclesiologist," the prominent religious artist Ernst Schwidder.[81] Their conversations covered a carved wood pulpit, lectern, altar carvings, and a figure of Christ "in the moment of victory on the cross."[82] Echoing György Kepes' words at the Church of the Redeemer, Anderson wrote to Rev. Dannenfeldt:

> It should be remembered however, that it is a symbol not a furnishing. The difference, as I see it, is that a symbol points to an idea or incident while a furnishing serves some specific function although it will also be symbolic in its ideal form.[83]

This explanation recalls philosopher Susanne Langer's definition of presentational symbolism, discussed earlier in this chapter. But the reredos—a "furnishing"—defied simple integration thematically with the rest of the chancel. Rev. Dannenfeldt used repeatedly the word "symbology" to describe the ensemble of ritual objects with explicit religious content. The reredos was obviously part of the church's symbology, but it was difficult for Dannenfeldt to find words appropriate for explaining the reredos' role. Its visible patterns teased at associations, none of which could have been intended by him, by the ecclesiologist, or by the architect. Years after the church's construction, Dannenfeldt offered the following explanation:

> many people have seen different faces or different symbology here but there was nothing intentional. And so whether you see the Trinity or you see the face of Jesus, it's simply accidental. But one thing certainly is that it is very interesting and creates a soft background for the crucifix.[84]

Dannenfeldt attributed the concept to the architect, and added:

> This was a totally new idea at that time and he was waiting for the right church to start it and we stuck our necks way out in order to subscribe to this . . . in our new sanctuary. . . [We] are so glad we did because it is truly beautiful.[85]

At the ceremony of St. Paul's dedication, in March 1963, Charles Stade's design team explained, "the white marble reredos reaching from floor to ceiling, identifies the chancel space. In bold relief against its whiteness, stands the altar."[86] That contrast contributed to the church's unique impact. Local Baltimore architects acknowledged the result and awarded St. Paul's a merit award from the local chapter of the AIA that same year.[87] The jurors stated: "Through the use of a transparent marble reredos a sense of opaque openness is effected around the altar. This boundary of light establishes the visual climax and the focal point of worship in the Lutheran rite."[88] In other words, the reredos served primarily to define visually a precinct not just of space, but of *sacred* space. The reredos was an installation integral to, yet obviously different from, the surrounding architectural design. It was not an art object as such; the reredos had no autonomous "symbology" that would allow it to operate as religious art in the conventional sense. It operated purely as an agent of opticalism: connoting prestige in its obvious innovation; stimulating worshippers' vision at the focal point of the nave, yet remaining dissociated from obvious symbolism. It continues to do so today, defining clearly the spatial boundaries of sacred experience within St. Paul's Evangelical Lutheran Church.

Conclusion: "opticalism" and faith

Assessed together, these three buildings share obvious similarities. Located in Baltimore City or its close suburbs, Church of the Redeemer and Har Sinai are almost exact contemporaries, from commission to consecration. St. Paul's was designed and built less than five years later. Their functional programming was similar, serving congregants only recently relocated to the city's second-tier suburbs. Different, of course, were the religious practices and beliefs of each congregation. Common also to all three projects, however, was the role of art in architecture and the conceptual influence of György Kepes. His works at Redeemer and other local projects over the next decade were closely followed models for installations in other Baltimore religious buildings, public sculpture, art exhibits, and even road graphics.[89] We can discern Kepes' influence in the public's reception of projects like the Redeemer's chancel screen and, subsequently, in Har Sinai's and St. Paul's openness to its vivid optical effects in their main religious spaces.

That three different religions could share such an approach suggests at least some common theological basis. For many architects in mid-century America, theologian Paul Tillich (1886–1965) provided a feasible conceptual template for engaging religious faith across denominations. As architectural historian Meredith Clausen has explained, Tillich was among the public intellectuals most visible to American church architects in the mid-to-late 1950s.[90] His talk "Theology and Architecture" was published in *Architectural Forum* in 1955,[91] and his later involvement with the Boston-based Society for the Arts, Religion, and Contemporary Culture gave him a national platform from which to discuss architects' role in all three. Renewed spirituality in modern times needed its reflection in contemporary art, and as Tillich told his audience directly: "Probably the way modern religious art will be reborn is through architecture."[92]

Tillich's position lay at the core of opticalism in religious architecture. He asked his readers (which included architects like Pietro Belluschi and artists like György Kepes) the questions "What is faith?" and "What is faith *not*?"[93] Like Susanne Langer before him, Tillich related these questions to sense perception and to the certainty afforded by seeing, as opposed to knowing. In particular, Tillich likened seeing to religious faith. "He who sees a green color sees a green color and is certain about it. He cannot be certain whether the thing which seems to him green is really green . . . But he cannot doubt that he sees green."[94] Likewise, "The certitude of faith is 'existential,' . . . its certitude is not the uncertain certitude of a theoretical judgment."[95] The semiotic innovation of opticalism was based on just this operation. *Seeing*, not *knowing*: opticalism's large-scale installations were conceived to provoke a leap of faith, founded most essentially in sensation.

Not long after Tillich addressed Architectural Forum, Kepes shared his similar perspective with an audience at New York University.[96] He evoked for them the same themes made visible in the film *A Place to Worship:*

> Industrial civilization has torn us apart from the relatedness that people knew in a smaller world . . . We are incapable of absorbing the new landscape with its wealth of new sensations . . . We have, then, two interdependent tasks in front of us: we have to span the gap between man and his newly won possessions . . . and we have to build bridges within ourselves and reach an inner oneness, a union of our sensory, emotional, and symbolic aspects of our life.[97]

For Kepes, the religious sensibility and love offered one model for doing so: "Love in a person or in a deep religious sense translates every experience to embrace so that we project our basic sense of belonging to everything and everybody we encounter."[98] But another shared experience served better our society—art:

> Artistic, creative experience in making or in reliving an artistic form can also serve as an inner guide or guardian . . . the artistic form is a dynamic organizer of life, enabling us to deal with environment and directing and controlling our own development . . . But there is another, still deeper role of the artistic experience . . . [Others have described] religion as a world loyalty. In a certain sense, artistic experience leads us to such a world loyalty . . . Sensations, the emotional, and the rational illumination are spun in a living, unbroken, complete spectrum. By experiencing it, we are bound with deep loyalties to our total horizon.[99]

For Kepes, and for those mid-century worshippers who would experience directly the effect of opticalism in the architecture of their churches or synagogues, that total horizon would define their "place" to worship.

Notes

1 P. A. Michelis, "Refinements in Architecture," *Journal of Aesthetics and Art Criticism* 14, no. 1 (1955): 21.
2 Advocates for the relationship between art and community included Percival Goodman (1904–89), architect of many synagogues after 1945. See Kimberly Elman and Angela Giral, eds., *Percival Goodman: Architect, Planner, Teacher, Painter* (New York, NY: Columbia University Press, 2000): 53–61. Among American church architects, Pietro Belluschi espoused similar values. See Meredith Clausen, *Spiritual Space: The Religious Architecture of Pietro Belluschi* (Seattle, WA: University of Washington Press, 1992): 31–32.
3 Such architects included Gordon Bunshaft, Eero Saarinen, and Marcel Breuer. See John Burchard, "Alienated Affections in the Arts," in György Kepes, ed., "The Visual Arts Today," *Dædalus* 89, no. 1 (Winter 1960): 54.
4 Eleanor Bittermann, *Art in Modern Architecture* (New York, NY: Reinhold Publishing Corporation, 1952), 3–4.
5 Gretchen Buggeln, *The Suburban Church: Modernism and Community in Post-war America* (Minneapolis, MN: University of Minnesota Press, 2015), xxiv.
6 Bruce Forbes and Jeffrey Mahan, eds., *Religion and Popular Culture in America* (Berkeley, CA: University of California Press, 2000): 9–18. Concerning the relationship between American religious practice and built environment studies (including architecture) see Kathleen Conzen et al., "The Place of Religion in Urban and Community Studies," *Religion and American Culture: A Journal of Interpretation* (Summer, 1996): 107–129.

7 Charles Lippy, *Being Religious, American Style* (Westport, CT: Greenwood Press, 1994), 195ff.

8 Paul Goldberger, "On the Relevance of Sacred Architecture Today." In Karla Britton, ed. *Constructing the Ineffable: Contemporary Sacred Architecture* (New Haven, CT: Yale University Press, 2010), 229. As explained later in this chapter, these questions were of particular interest to theologian Paul Tillich, influential among American architects in the 1950s. See Tillich, "Theology and Architecture," in *Architectural Forum* 103, no. 6 (1955): 131–134. Reprinted in John and Jane Dillenberger, *On Art and Architecture* (New York, NY: Crossroad Publishing Company, 1987).

9 "P/R Tools Available for Chapter Use from the AIA," *Florida Architect*, June 1959, 25. Thanks to Gretchen Buggeln, Valparaiso University, for bringing to my attention *A Place to Worship*. She discusses the film in the context of Charles Stade's design for Valparaiso Chapel in "The Shape of a New Era: Valparaiso's Chapel of the Resurrection in Historical Context," *The Cresset* 73, no. 3: 6–14.

10 The American Institute of Architects, *A Place to Worship* (1958), film; time mark approximately 2'30".

11 Ibid., time mark approximately 1'47"–1'57".

12 Lewis Mumford, *Technics and Civilization* (New York, NY: Harcourt Brace Jovanovich, 1963), 9–12.

13 One example is Frank Lloyd Wright, "The Art and Craft of the Machine," in *Writings and Buildings* (New York, NY: Meridian Books, 1967), 55–73. Originally published in 1901, this essay contrasts Wright's embrace of technology with William Morris' and John Ruskin's religion-inspired critique of industrialization. See also Jay Newman, *Religion and Technology: A Study in the Philosophy of Culture* (Westport, CT: Praeger, 1997), 3.

14 Bittermann, *Art in Modern Architecture*, 4–5.

15 This was particularly true in Catholic churches and Protestant sects with well-established traditions in the visual arts. See Jeffery Howe, *Houses of Worship* (San Diego, CA: Thunder Bay Press, 2003), 321–323.

16 Baltimore-based Gaudreau and Gaudreau Architects (now known as Gaudreau Inc.) was founded in 1927 by Boston native Lucien E. D Gaudreau. Their work included buildings for institutions and higher education as well as for the Catholic Church. Source: www.gaudreauinc.com/history, accessed July 18, 2017.

17 Buggeln, *The Suburban Church*, 85ff.

18 "Work Started on New Church: Catholic Edifice to Arise in Baltimore County," *Baltimore Sun*, September 19, 1949, 20.

19 Maginnis, Walsh & Kennedy, founded in 1905, was a Boston-based firm known for its designs for the Catholic Church. See Rev. J. Joseph Gallagher, *The Guide Book* (Baltimore, MD: Cathedral of Mary Our Queen, 1960), 8.

20 Kathryn Geraghty, "5 Years, 1000 Men, $8,500,000 Fulfill a Dream," *Baltimore Sun*, November 15, 1950.

21 Kimberly Elman, "The Quest for Community: Percival Goodman and the Design of the Modern American Synagogue," in Elman and Giral, *Percival Goodman: Architect, Planner, Teacher, Painter*, 58–59.

22 "Art-Architect Link Stressed," *Baltimore Sun*, March 19, 1952, 13.

23 Paul and Percival Goodman, "Public Faces in Private Places," manuscript dated July 1947, 1. Percival Goodman Papers.

24 Percival and Paul Goodman, "Modern Artist as Synagogue Builder: Satisfying the Needs of Today's Congregations," *Commentary* 7, no. 1 (January 1949): 55.

25 Elman and Giral, *Percival Goodman: Architect, Planner, Teacher, Painter*, 186.

26 Carol Wharton, "Artists Shower Talent On A New Synagogue," *Baltimore Sun*, May 4, 1952, A3.

27 Kepes was a Hungarian-born artist, educator, and inventor. He came to the United States in 1937, where he taught at the New Bauhaus in Chicago before moving to MIT in 1947.

28 György Kepes, *The Language of Vision* (Chicago, IL: Paul Theobald and Company, 1961), 200ff.

29 Ibid.

30 Kepes, "The Visual Arts Today," *Dædalus* 89 (1960).

31 Le Corbusier, "Architecture and the Arts," in Kepes, "The Visual Arts Today," 46.

32 Ibid., 49.

33 Ibid.

34 Reg. Butler in "Views on Art and Architecture: A Conversation," in Kepes, "The Visual Arts Today," 64.

35 Walter Gropius in "Views on Art and Architecture: A Conversation," 72.

36 Irene Rice Pereira in "Views on Art and Architecture: A Conversation," 69.

37 Pietro Belluschi in "Views on Art and Architecture: A Conversation," 67.

38 Ibid.

39 American Institute of Architects, *A Place to Worship*.

40 Clausen, *Spiritual Space,* and *Pietro Belluschi: Modern American Architect* (Cambridge, MA: The MIT Press, 1994).

41 The studios of George L. Payne in Paterson, New Jersey, were founded in 1896 and became a nationally-prominent manufacturer of ecclesiastical stained-glass windows. The glass itself was manufactured in Chartres, France, by the *dalle de verre* technique. See Sherrie Eatman, "Dalles de Verre," *Glass News*, no. 16 (2004): 12.

42 Bennett J. Simms, *The Time of My Life* (Hendersonville, NC: Bennett J. Sims Institute for Servant Leadership, 2006), 14.

43 Bennett J. Sims, "Reminiscence and Prophecy," address delivered at *Beyond Preservation: A Week-end Symposium to Honor the Architectural Heritage of Pietro Belluschi*, 31 October 1998. Archives of Church of the Redeemer. Baltimore, Maryland.

44 Kepes, *Language of Vision*.

45 Ibid., 200.

46 Susanne Langer, *Feeling and Form: A Theory of Art* (New York, NY: Charles Scribner's Sons, 1953).

47 Susanne Langer, *Philosophy in a New Key* (New York, NY: The New American Library, 1954).

48 Ibid., 78–79.

49 Samantha Baskind and Larry Silver, *Jewish Art: A Modern History* (London: Reaktion Books, 2011), 115–162.

50 Janay Jadine Wong, "Synagogue Art of 1950s: A New Context for Abstraction," *Art Journal* 53, no. 4 (1994): 37.

51 Rachel Wischnitzer, *Synagogue Architecture in the United States* (Philadelphia, PA: The Jewish Publication Society of America, 1955), 3. See also the survey of historical examples in "The Synagogue and its Decoration," in Vivian Mann, ed., *Jewish Texts on the Visual Arts* (New York, NY: Cambridge University Press, 2000), 69–99.

52 Letter to Louise Mendelsohn, June 24, 1917. In Oskar Beyer, ed., *Eric Mendelsohn: Letters of an Architect* (New York, NY: Abelard-Schuman, 1967), 40.

53 Jonathan Sarna, "The Debate over Mixed Seating in the American Synagogue." In Jack Wertheimer, ed., *The American Synagogue: A Sanctuary Transformed* (Hanover, NH: University Press of New England, 1995), 370.

54 Jeremy Kargon, "A Symbolic Landscape for Suburbia: Baltimore Chizuk Amuno's 'Hebrew Culture Garden,'" *Journal of Urban History* 40, no. 4 (2014): 767.

55 Allan R. Wexler, quoted in "Har Sinai Plans New Temple, School on Park Heights Site," *Baltimore Sun*, September 6, 1953.

56 Bruno Zevi, *Erich Mendelsohn: The Complete Works* (Boston, MA: Birkhauser Publishers, 1999), 328–330.

57 Samuel Gruber, *American Synagogues: A Century of Architecture and Jewish Community* (New York, NY: Rizzoli, 2003), 85.

58 Erich Mendelsohn, "In the Spirit of Our Age," *Commentary* 3, no. 6 (1947): 541–542.

59 Ibid., 541.

60 Zevi, *Erich Mendelsohn*, 328.

61 Walter Leedy, Jr. *Eric Mendelsohn's Park Synagogue* (Kent, OH: Kent State University Press, 2012).

62 Ibid., 92–93.

63 Founded in Baltimore in 1912, Buckler, Fenhagen, Meyer and Ayers specialized in commercial and institutional architecture, especially schools and university buildings. The firm's name became "Meyer and Ayers" in 1955 and is known today as Ayers Saint Gross.

64 Kathleen James-Chakraborty, *In the Spirit of Our Age: Eric Mendelsohn's B'nai Amoona Synagogue* (St. Louis, MO: Missouri Historical Society Press, 2000), 49ff.

65 Har Sinai Building Committee, "A Look Inside Our New Building: Altar and Ark," *Building Progress Report*, no. 2, March 1958, 1.

66 "Har Sinai Temple is Consecrated," *Baltimore Sun*, September 20, 1959.

67 Buckminster Fuller, *Inventions: The Patented Works of R. Buckminster Fuller* (New York, NY: St. Martin's Press, 1983), 127–144.

68 Vivien Greene, "Utopia/Dystopia," in *American Art* 25, no. 2 (2011): 6–7.

69 "Caming" refers to the metal bands which are placed between pieces of glass in stained glass windows.

70 Frank Popper, "Op-Art," *Grove Art Online* (2006), www.groveart.com/.

71 Charles Edward Stade and Associates, with Ernest C. Schwidder and David Elder, "Architectural Concept," in dedication, St. Paul's Evangelical Lutheran Church, March 31, 1963, 12.

72 American Institute of Architects, *A Place to Worship*.
73 "Glen Burnie Church Okays Building Plan," *Evening Sun*, September 21, 1960.
74 Buggeln, *The Suburban Church*, 41.
75 Arthur Janushek, "St. Paul's Ev. Lutheran Church: An Historical Perspective," in *10th Anniversary of the Church Dedication*, March 25, 1973: 8 (Baltimore, MD: Archives of St. Paul's Evangelical Lutheran Church).
76 Stade et al., "Architectural Concept," 12.
77 Buggeln, *The Suburban Church*, 114.
78 A "reredos" is a decorative altarpiece or screen located behind the altar.
79 Harry F. Anderson, letter to Arne Rasmussen (member of St. Paul's Building Committee), April 13, 1962. Archives of St. Paul's Evangelical Lutheran Church.
80 Ibid.
81 Ernest Schwidder (1931–98) was a specialist in wood carving known for highly mannered, yet representational, liturgical art.
82 Arne Rasmussen, letter to Ernest C. Schwidder, January 9, 1963. Archives of St. Paul's Evangelical Lutheran Church.
83 Ernest C. Schwidder, letter to Rev. Paul Dannenfeldt, May 28, 1962. (This letter was typed on Stade, Dolan, and Anderson Architects letterhead; at this time, Schwidder had joined Stade's office.) Archives of St. Paul's Evangelical Lutheran Church.
84 Page One Video "The Symbology of St. Paul's Lutheran Church Chancel Architecture," Paul Dannenfeldt, narrator (no date), Archives of St. Paul's Evangelical Lutheran Church.
85 Ibid.
86 Stade et al., "Architectural Concept," 12.
87 "Merit Award: St. Paul's Evangelical Lutheran Church," *Baltimore: Business Magazine of Metropolitan Baltimore* 56, no. 12 (1963): 22.
88 Ibid.
89 Jean-Marie Bolay, "De la ville perçue à la ville qui perçoit: György Kepes et la Smart City," *Scienza & Filosofia* 13 (2015): 207, www.scienzaefilosofia.it/res/site70201/res692081_S-F_13.pdf.
90 Clausen, *Spiritual Space*, 24–26.
91 Tillich, "Theology and Architecture."
92 Ibid., 193.
93 Belluschi and Tillich were participants at the 1955 *Architectural Forum* session; Kepes participated with Tillich in 1957 at a conference at MIT.
94 Paul Tillich, *Dynamics of Faith* (New York, NY: Harper & Row, 1957), 33.
95 Ibid., 34–35.
96 György Kepes, talk to the Art-Industrial Arts Conference, NYU (22 March 1958). Smithsonian Archives of American Art, Reel 5303, #41.922.
97 Ibid.
98 Ibid.
99 Ibid.

References

American Institute of Architects. *A Place to Worship*. Film, 1958.
"Art-Architect Link Stressed," *Baltimore Sun*, March 19, 1952, 13.
Baskind, Samantha and Larry Silver. *Jewish Art: A Modern History* (London: Reaktion Books, 2011).
Beyer, Oskar, ed. *Eric Mendelsohn: Letters of an Architect* (New York: Abelard-Schuman, 1967).
Bittermann, Eleanor. *Art in Modern Architecture* (New York: Reinhold Publishing Corporation, 1952).
Bolay, Jean-Marie. "De la ville perçue à la ville qui perçoit: György Kepes et la Smart City." *Scienza & Filosofia* 13 (2015): 284–214, www.scienzaefilosofia.it/res/site70201/res692081_S-F_13.pdf.
Buggeln, Gretchen. "The Shape of a New Era: Valparaiso's Chapel of the Resurrection in Historical Context." *The Cresset* 73, no. 3: 6–14.
———. *The Suburban Church: Modernism and Community in Post-war America* (Minneapolis, MN: University of Minnesota Press, 2015).
Burchard, John. "Alienated Affections in the Arts." *Dædalus* 89, no. 1 (Winter 1960): 52–61.

Clausen, Meredith. *Pietro Belluschi: Modern American Architect* (Cambridge, MA: The MIT Press, 1994).

———. *Spiritual Space: The Religious Architecture of Pietro Belluschi* (Seattle, WA: University of Washington Press, 1992).

Conzen, Kathleen et al. "The Place of Religion in Urban and Community Studies." *Religion and American Culture: A Journal of Interpretation* 6, no. 2 (Summer 1996): 107–129.

Eatman, Sherrie. "Dalles de Verre." *Glass News* 16 (November 2004): 11–14.

Elman, Kimberly. "The Quest for Community: Percival Goodman and the Design of the Modern American Synagogue." In *idem* and Angela Giral, eds. *Percival Goodman: Architect, Planner, Teacher, Painter*, 58–59 (New York, NY: Columbia University Press, 2000).

——— and Angela Giral, eds. *Percival Goodman: Architect, Planner, Teacher, Painter* (New York, NY: Columbia University Press, 2000).

Forbes, Bruce and Jeffrey Mahan, eds. *Religion and Popular Culture in America* (Berkeley, CA: University of California Press, 2000).

Fuller, Buckminster. *Inventions: The Patented Works of R. Buckminster Fuller* (New York: St. Martin's Press, 1983).

Gallagher, J. Joseph. *The Guide Book* (Baltimore, MD: Cathedral of Mary Our Queen, 1960).

Geraghty, Kathryn. "5 Years, 1000 Men, $8,500,000 Fulfill a Dream," *Baltimore Sun*, November 15, 1950.

Goldberger, Paul. "On the Relevance of Sacred Architecture Today." In Karla Britton, ed. *Constructing the Ineffable: Contemporary Sacred Architecture*, 222–231 (New Haven, CT: Yale University Press, 2010).

Goodman, Percival and Paul Goodman. "Modern Artist as Synagogue Builder: Satisfying the Needs of Today's Congregations," *Commentary* 7, no. 1 (January 1949): 51–55.

———. "Public Faces in Private Places," manuscript dated July 1947, 1. Percival Goodman Papers.

Greene, Vivien. "Utopia/Dystopia." *American Art* 25, no. 2 (Summer 2011): 2–7.

Gruber, Samuel. *American Synagogues: A Century of Architecture and Jewish Community* (New York: Rizzoli, 2003).

Har Sinai Building Committee, "A Look Inside Our New Building: Altar and Ark," *Building Progress Report*, March, 1958.

"Har Sinai Plans New Temple, School on Park Heights Site," *Baltimore Sun*, September 6, 1953.

"Har Sinai Temple is Consecrated," *Baltimore Sun*, September 20, 1959.

Howe, Jeffery. *Houses of Worship* (San Diego, CA: Thunder Bay Press, 2003).

James-Chakraborty, Kathleen. *In the Spirit of Our Age: Eric Mendelsohn's B'nai Amoona Synagogue* (St. Louis, MO: Missouri Historical Society Press, 2000).

Janushek, Arthur. "St. Paul's Ev. Lutheran Church: An Historical Perspective." *10th Anniversary of the Church Dedication* (Baltimore, MD: Archives of St. Paul's Evangelical Lutheran Church, 1973).

Kargon, Jeremy. "A Symbolic Landscape for Suburbia: Baltimore Chizuk Amuno's 'Hebrew Culture Garden.'" *Journal of Urban History* 40, no. 4 (2014): 762–791.

Kepes, György. *Language of Vision* (Chicago, IL: Paul Theobald and Company, 1961).

———. Presentation to the Art-Industrial Arts Conference, New York University (March 22, 1958).

———. "The Visual Arts Today." *Dædalus* 89 (1960).

Langer, Susanne. *Feeling and Form: A Theory of Art* (New York, NY: Charles Scribner's Sons, 1953).

———. *Philosophy in a New Key* (New York: The New American Library, 1954).

Leedy, Walter. *Eric Mendelsohn's Park Synagogue* (Kent, OH: Kent State University Press, 2012).

Lippy, Charles. *Being Religious, American Style* (Westport, CT: Greenwood Press, 1994).

Mann, Vivian, ed. *Jewish Texts on the Visual Arts* (New York, NY: Cambridge University Press, 2000).

Mendelsohn, Erich. "In the Spirit of Our Age." *Commentary* 3, no. 6 (June 1947): 541–542.

"Merit Award: St. Paul's Evangelical Lutheran Church," *Baltimore: Business Magazine of Metropolitan Baltimore* 56, no. 12 (1963): 22.

Michelis, P. A. "Refinements in Architecture." *Journal of Aesthetics and Art Criticism* 14, no. 1 (1955): 19–43.

Mumford, Lewis. *Technics and Civilization* (New York: Harcourt Brace Jovanovich, 1963).

Newman, Jay. *Religion and Technology: A Study in the Philosophy of Culture* (Westport, CT: Praeger, 1997).

Popper, Frank. "Op-Art," *Grove Art Online* (2006), www.groveart.com/.

"P/R Tools Available for Chapter Use from the AIA," *Florida Architect*, June 1959, 25.

Sarna, Jonathan. "The Debate Over Mixed Seating in the American Synagogue." In Jack Wertheimer, ed. *The American Synagogue*, 363–394 (Hanover, NH: University Press of New England, 1995).

Sims, Bennett J. "Reminiscence and Prophecy," address delivered at *Beyond Preservation: A Week-end Symposium to Honor the Architectural Heritage of Pietro Belluschi*, 31 October 1998. Archives of Church of the Redeemer. Baltimore, Maryland.

———. *The Time of My Life* (Hendersonville, NC: The Bennett J. Sims Institute for Servant Leadership, 2006).

Stade and Associates, with Ernest C. Schwidder and David Elder. "Architectural Concept," dedication (Baltimore, MD: St. Paul's Evangelical Lutheran Church, 1963).

Tillich, Paul. *Dynamics of Faith* (New York: Harper & Row, Publishers, Inc., 1987).

———. "Theology and Architecture." In Jane and John Dillenberger, eds. *On Art and Architecture*, 188–198 (New York: Crossroad Publishing Company, 1987).

Wharton, Carol. "Artists Shower Talent On A New Synagogue," *Baltimore Sun*, May 4, 1952, A3.

Wischnitzer, Rachel. *Synagogue Architecture in the United States* (Philadelphia, PA: The Jewish Publication Society of America, 1955).

Wong, Janay Jadine. "Synagogue Art of 1950s: A New Context for Abstraction." *Art Journal* 53, no. 4 (Winter 1994): 37–43.

"Work Started on New Church: Catholic Edifice to Arise in Baltimore County," *Baltimore Sun*, September 19, 1949, 20.

Wright, Frank Lloyd. *Writings and Buildings* (New York: Meridian Books, 1967).

Zevi, Bruno. *Erich Mendelsohn: The Complete Works* (Boston, MA: Birkhauser Publishers, 1999).

13

THE SANCTUARY WALL

Unitarian rationalism illuminated

Ann Marie Borys

American Unitarians grew more unified in their desire to use modern architecture to make their modern religion visible in the decades following World War II.[1] As a "fellowship of seekers," Unitarians felt some obligation to "provide the opportunity of expression for the best in creative thought in whatever form our most advanced knowledge may cast it."[2] Many of modernism's spatial and aesthetic characteristics were highly suited to Unitarian sensibilities. Still, an over-arching question remained for Unitarian church architecture: how to shape an appropriate worship space for a denomination that has no ritual, no theology, and no creed.

One of modernism's central themes that, for the most part, would not suit other denominations experimenting with modern forms was in fact highly desirable to Unitarians and could potentially guide design: continuity between indoor and outdoor spaces.[3] Traditionally, sacred space and services aim to establish an alternate sense of space and time, and the architecture generally supports that by creating a strong sense of interiority.[4] Unitarian churches, however, are not sacred space in the fullest sense of the word—there is no shared belief that divinity resides in the space nor that being in the space puts one in closer touch with divinity.[5] Though not regarded as sacred, the Unitarian sanctuary is intended to be a spiritual place for believers and non-believers alike; its spirituality arises from an awareness of the interconnectedness of all things.[6] Nature, both the proof and the symbol of cosmic unity, provides a vital source of spiritual meaning for Unitarians.[7] This spiritual sense is often captured in the architecture by a visible connection to nature, a reminder of the unity of all things. It is therefore common for mid-century Unitarian churches to have entire walls of glass to unite the sanctuary with its natural surroundings, allowing an inspiring view of gardens, fields, or woods. Frank Lloyd Wright advocated for this in his organic architecture theory and some of his sacred architecture design, especially in his 1948 design for the Unitarian church in Madison, Wisconsin.[8] However, the church-building boom of the 1950s included some suburban sites where conditions did not readily allow a high degree of openness for celebrating nature. This chapter argues that in some cases a highly articulated sanctuary wall, though appearing as a barrier between exterior and interior realms, provides the vital connection to nature's spirituality. Thus the wall enhances the sacredness of the sanctuary.

Three case studies were investigated: the Unitarian Church of Arlington, Virginia (UCA,[9] 1960–64), University Unitarian Church in Seattle, Washington (1956–59), and St. John's Unitarian Church in Cincinnati, Ohio (1958–60). The three churches were designed within a five-year span, and all include expressive walls that display modernism's interest in making the structural system visible. They were selected for their variety of geographic conditions (thus, various light conditions), and different primary materials. Yet they share a dramatic sanctuary wall assembly that allows worship to take place within a space enhanced by nature. Detailed spatial and experiential analysis and digital daylighting simulations reveal the unique qualities of innovative designs that were tailored to the site conditions and to the congregations' characters.

Design without precedents

Unitarian church design has no established architectural tradition that may direct architects in designing a new church. Although historical roots in the New England meetinghouse are sometimes referenced, American Unitarianism only became distinctly defined about the same time that the meetinghouse form fell out of use.[10] Nineteenth-century Unitarian churches exhibited variety in their forms, many of which followed the changing styles of the times along with other Protestant denominations.[11] The denomination continued to develop its liberal conscience, and by the mid-twentieth century, Unitarians had embraced diverse beliefs and predominantly humanistic values.[12] Since members were welcome to determine their own beliefs, there was no standard liturgy that could guide the design of an appropriate church building and no religious symbols to incorporate. There was a progressive interest in the aesthetics of the modern movement, understood to resonate with their optimistic view of human nature, human creativity, social issues, and relation to nature. Within this general denominational outlook, each congregation worked with an architect to articulate their own ethos and identity.[13]

A well-known example of this process resulted in the distinctive masonry walls that envelope the sanctuary of Louis I. Kahn's First Unitarian Church of Rochester, New York (1962, addition 1969), one of the icons of twentieth-century American church architecture (Fig. 13.1).

FIGURE 13.1 First Unitarian Church, Rochester, New York, 1962; Louis I. Kahn, architect. Photograph by the author.

Kahn's encounter with the congregation is amply documented: apparently his natural, intuitive sympathy for Unitarian ideas and values contributed to his selection from a field of nationally recognized modern architects under consideration.[14] His ongoing inquiry and reflection on the congregation's ethical and spiritual orientations fueled his design process.

The most important Unitarian values are individual freedom, democracy as the basis for all relations, reason, tolerance, and fellowship.[15] An Enlightenment-based rationalism rejects miracles as explanations for worldly phenomena and faith in anything that cannot be seen or known. They place their faith in the human capacity for knowledge and creativity. Congregations are democratic and non-hierarchical in their organization; the sanctuary is not a room for predictable social patterns, but "a setting for the exploration of new ideas and for stimulus to creative thinking . . . a church of reason, of common-sense, of practical usefulness . . . a laboratory of the human spirit."[16] Modern architecture's fundamental characteristics—exposed structure, asymmetry, lack of ornament, and the use of ordinary or industrial materials—all suited their views. This concept is demonstrated through the chapter case studies. Each one is analyzed first in terms of site conditions and the overall design response. Then a detailed look at the sanctuary walls is presented with special attention to the quality of light in each sanctuary.

Site and structure at UCA, Arlington, Virginia

The Unitarian Church of Arlington (design 1960–61; construction 1962–64)[17] was designed with the explicit intention to express Unitarian beliefs[18] (Fig. 13.2). This suburban congregation was founded in 1948 when members of Washington's All Souls Church, the only Unitarian church in the metropolitan area, began meeting closer to home in a series of rented spaces. They soon purchased a site on the edge of a residential neighborhood just west of Arlington National Cemetery and erected a modest brick church facing First Place South.[19] It was expanded in 1953, and then continued growth led to the need for further expansion by 1956.[20] Members quickly understood that parking was a limitation, so their first step was the purchase of adjacent lots to the north and east, bringing their property to about four acres. They intended to expand their existing building and use the newly acquired land for parking.[21]

FIGURE 13.2 Unitarian Church of Arlington, Arlington, Virginia, 1960–64; Charles M. Goodman, architect.

Photograph by the author.

Architect Charles Goodman (1906–92) was commissioned in 1959 based on his established reputation for innovative design—in fact, he was the foremost modernist in the Washington area at the time.[22] Goodman used a spare language of exposed structure and large areas of glass, and his work was known for sensitive integration with the site.[23] The congregation wanted a design that would express the UCA's "leadership within the denomination . . . [at a time when] Unitarian congregations across the country hired modernist architects to design . . . a church for the modern era."[24]

Goodman persuaded the building committee that the grove of trees and the topography of the eastern point would be more advantageous for the sanctuary than for parking.[25] Placing the new church on that part of the site would allow the building to be set in an appealing landscape rather than relating to an uninspiring residential streetscape. Also, the geometry of the bounding roadways insured that a building in that location would remain free from any future neighboring construction. Their existing building could be used for most religious education and administrative functions, so the program for the new building consisted of a worship space, a social hall, and a few additional classrooms.[26] Owing to cost overruns, only the sanctuary and its basement classrooms were completed to Goodman's design in the early 1960s. By the time the congregation could afford to add the social hall in the 1990s, a new design was commissioned.[27]

This project is unique among Goodman's work for the interest he took in the beliefs and values of his client.[28] Goodman had completed two churches prior to UCA, but he was inspired by this commission to research church architecture in general, and to visit two recently completed Unitarian churches in New York and New Jersey.[29] Most importantly, he read sermons of the minister and documents assembled by the building committee with congregational input; he also met with members of the congregation to ask questions:

> Goodman's thoughtful consideration of the congregation's specific needs and his careful study of the history and beliefs of the Unitarian faith, resulted in a Sanctuary building that was specifically suited to the UCA congregation and was a physical reflection of its beliefs and aspirations.[30]

Goodman wrote a full explication of his design and its derivation from those beliefs. Interestingly, he made no mention of Wright's Unity Temple (1906) though his design clearly shares some of its formal characteristics (e.g. a cubic volume, a flat roof cantilevered over a continuous clerestory, and exposed concrete structure and enclosure).

Goodman asserted that the square plan and the prominent flat roof were chosen because they are generic characteristics of temple, rather than church, form,[31] which he defined as a place for a "doctrine of free and open discourse . . . directed toward the principle of unity through diversity of beliefs, in which reason displaces dogma and simplicity and warmth enhances the fellowship of men."[32] He wanted to make a building that would inspire not only the members of the congregation, but the community in which it was located. While the exterior of the building is striking, the interior space was the more superior aspect of the architecture, as noted by an awards jury in 1965.[33]

Though the sanctuary was set into a grove of trees, the church space could not be opened to nature in a grand way because adjacent roads on this part of the site were relatively close, and they were busy arteries. Traffic activity and noise would need to be screened out, and in turn, the sanctuary would need some visual privacy. Using precast concrete, Goodman designed a wall that alternated between solid and void (Fig. 13.3). At ground level, the solid is more dominant, but the effect still feels somewhat porous. Above, a strong connection to the grove was established by a continuous clerestory tucked under a hovering roof plane. The views out into the trees are more than a reminder of nature; they actually create a secondary spatial realm for the sanctuary in the grove. As Goodman explained:

> The upper ribbon of glass completely surrounding the Auditorium will seem to extend the interior in all directions and frame views of the upper fingering of trees as their branches reach for the sky. The suggestion of serenity and quiet urbanity. . .should be conducive to the thoughtful repose for which you have suggested a desire."[34]

Today, the design of the walls does not seem particularly innovative because the basic strategy was widely adopted in commercial and institutional buildings of the 1960s and into the '70s. But at the time, the bold scale of the exposed pre-cast concrete columns and the simple infill panels flanked by vertical glazed voids was a novel approach. Goodman described the building envelope as a "system of walls and transparent planes which are discontinuous and whose surfaces act as an instrument on which ever changing light will perform with a virtuosity enchanting to the human eye."[35] He attributed the relatively unusual choice of pre-cast concrete for a church building simply to his desire for a 60-foot clear span roof, but his disposition towards trying new materials was well established.[36] The novel use of pre-cast concrete for the church resulted in an extended construction schedule because the methods were still experimental in the Washington, D.C. area. But the material was suited to his concept of a wall, which he defined as "a series of parts joined together,"[37] meaning that opaque and transparent surfaces were composed in consideration of privacy and openness.

On the exterior, the somewhat heavy and repetitive grid of columns and beams is enlivened by the dynamism of the roof plane extending surprisingly far out over the wall in all directions. The dramatic overhang was necessary to shade the tall clerestory, and even then, it proved inadequate against solar heat gain.[38] Though this floating roof plane dominates our perception of the building, the design of the wall as a screen was the true challenge.

FIGURE 13.3 Unitarian Church of Arlington, interior.

Photograph by the author.

To counter the heaviness of the precast concrete, the ground floor was recessed to suggest that the sanctuary hovers lightly on its site. The lyricism of Goodman's rendering was not completely captured by the physical forms, but a play between heavy and light was nonetheless achieved on the exterior. On the interior, the apparent weight of the concrete is further reduced by the lively action of direct sunlight and the softening of all surfaces as light diffuses across the space.

Site and structure at University Unitarian, Seattle, Washington

The first church that University Unitarian built in 1915–16 was located near the University of Washington campus and designed by noted local architect Ellsworth Storey. Growth after World War II prompted the construction of a new building in the mid-1950s. Having determined that an addition was not feasible, a vacant site was purchased in a predominantly residential area a few miles to the north and east.[39] This long thin site stretches along a north–south arterial, and is bounded to the north by a side street. While all four corners of the intersection would eventually have institutional buildings, the steeply sloping site is otherwise surrounded by modest single-family homes built after the war on relatively small lots.

The new home of the University Unitarian congregation (design 1956–58; construction 1958–59) was straightforward in terms of planning and execution (Fig. 13.4). The program included worship space, social hall (with kitchen), religious education classrooms, and administrative offices. A building committee solicited congregational input on identity and values, and also created a detailed space program.[40] The congregation adopted a lengthy statement submitted in response to the building committee's survey by industrial designer and congregational member Gideon Kramer, which he characterized as a set of "performance specifications."[41] In his words, the design of the new church "should result not in a monument but in a 'Symbol', a symbol of the summation of man's knowledge, of his attitude and relationship towards his fellowman and the universe;" adding "this requires new methods. This requires that the designer be inspired and dedicated. . . appreciative of the subtleties necessary to achieve such an environment."[42] At one point, the committee was in contact with Charles Eames, but they finally decided on a local architect, thinking that the project would get more consistent attention.[43] They selected Paul Kirk (1914–95), whose reputation for originality was based on his regionally inflected modernism in residential design.[44] University Unitarian was his first church commission.[45] Kirk first explored a sculptural form with innovative translucent walls, but rejected it after material testing reports from the University of Washington left uncertainties regarding its performance over time.[46] He then settled on a more modest orthogonal composition to fit the long rectangular site. Following principles of functionalist modernism, he split the building according to two major program elements, tailoring each to its own needs. The formal energy of the abandoned scheme was condensed into a single memorable façade[47] (Fig. 13.4).

The sanctuary and the social hall were each formally articulated and visible from the main artery, while religious education spaces were distributed across both components in the lower level, which had an eastern exposure. The social hall adheres to modernist conventions— low and planar, with a flat roof and a spatial articulation based on exposed wood structure and walls arranged in a play of solid and void. His more unorthodox sanctuary is "boxy" by comparison, vertically proportioned, and marked by two opposing and offset pitched roofs. Modern elements include the asymmetry of the two roof planes and in the regularity of the

FIGURE 13.4 University Unitarian Church, Seattle, Washington, 1956–59; Paul H. Kirk, architect. Photograph by the author.

exposed wood structural frames. These two divergent forms are connected physically by a bridge, and aesthetically by materials and a similar spatial clarity.

The values and identity of the congregation allowed Kirk to infuse his design with elements of Pacific Northwest regionalism, such as the use of wood, and attention to light in a region known for gray skies and dark winters.[48] Glulam structural members were no longer innovative for churches, but Kirk made the unusual choice of a long-spanning beam over the typical three-hinged arch[49] (Fig. 13.5). His diagonally pitched beams pierce the exterior wall with a cantilever and develop an external expression of the space of the sanctuary. Screening elements of vertical wood slats give additional texture and warmth to interior spaces.

The congregation, however, also inspired some departures from the norms typically associated with Pacific Northwest regionalism. Principal among these departures is the strongly vertical nature of the sanctuary. This verticality is a striking contrast from a perfect example of the usual low-pitched roof forms of the region just across the street: the Northeast Branch of the Seattle Public Library (1954) designed by Paul Thiry. Kirk's form,

FIGURE 13.5 University Unitarian Church, interior. Photograph by the author.

though vertical, could have been more integrated to its site had it been placed lower on the steeply sloped site—another hallmark of the Pacific Northwest.[50] But Kirk chose to allow the bold form to stand out and communicate. Further departures include roof planes that do not extend to create eaves with deep shadows. Corners of the elements that capture the interior space are tightly turned, expressing a more solid sense of mass than the usual modernist assembly of planar elements.

On the façade, the eleven structural wood frames that form the interior space are dramatically exposed (Fig. 13.4). The columns supporting the approximately 50-foot-long clear span of glulam beams are visible between white stucco panels that fill each bay on the upper half of the west-facing wall. Each beam continues outward from the wall a full 6 feet, where a post then drops down to the similarly extended floor beams. These posts support vertical screening elements of wood and colored glass that shade the glazing on the lower half of the wall. Below that, the floor beams project past the post to rest on an areaway retaining wall and support a bench that runs the entire length of the building. The areaway contains a sunken garden and admits light to the classrooms located beneath the sanctuary. This structural expression enlivens the façade with pattern and shadow and creates an exchange between interior and exterior spaces. Because the site offered little in the way of natural features, a limited view of nature for worshipers inside the sanctuary is provided by the garden in the areaway.

The interior space of the sanctuary is inflected dramatically toward the street façade by the pitch of the wider part of the roof toward it (Fig. 13.5). However, only the glulam beams stretch in a single gesture upward for the full width of the space. The roof plane is interrupted abruptly as the last third is lifted up and pitched in the opposite direction. The resulting east-facing vertical plane is filled with clerestory windows that light the solid upper portion of the west wall. Unfortunately, appreciation of this complex spatial arrangement is somewhat delayed as one enters the sanctuary. An organ loft hanging from the roof beams of the first four bays blocks a full view of the western wall. However, by the time a visitor is halfway inside, the full excitement of the wall captures all attention. The glazed lower half allows the space to expand out into the zone of the areaway and the depth of the projecting structure on the exterior. There the space finds another bounding layer in the wood screening elements that span between the outer posts. The wall is playful; it invites closer exploration. Standing near the windows, looking up and down, looking in and out, one is occupying a unique space that shares equally in the interior and exterior conditions. This zone is also the line along which east light from above meets the ambient light from the sky to the west and merges in the sanctuary space.

Site and structure at St. John's Unitarian, Cincinnati, Ohio

St. John's Unitarian Church (design 1958–59, construction 1960)[51] illustrates a different, but not uncommon, story of 1950s suburban church construction (Fig. 13.6). This well-established congregation was not forced to consider moving due to growth; in fact the congregation was shrinking. It chose to move from its central location in the urban core of an aging American city to a suburban context in 1948 in order to provide greater convenience for a majority of its members. In addition, the move released the congregation from the financial burden of maintaining and repairing a large 75-year old Gothic revival structure.[52]

Their new site, near the University of Cincinnati in the Clifton neighborhood, was technically still within city limits, but Clifton had been settled as a streetcar suburb and it still consisted primarily of single-family houses on individual lots. Their Resor Avenue site is a mid-block single-house lot on the north side of an east–west street amid comfortably sized middle-class homes built in the early twentieth century. This site was quieter than those of the Arlington and Seattle churches, but it was also more constrained in terms of positioning the new church building within it.

The St. John's congregation undertook a phased approach to meeting their needs.[53] A social hall and a small administrative area were built first in an unremarkable utilitarian fashion. The social hall served as a worship space during a decade-long fundraising campaign. A basement under a portion of this building was used for meetings and for religious education. The sanctuary, religious education classrooms, and a library were finally initiated as a more conscientiously designed addition. It remained the only architecturally expressive element of the completed whole, and the only part of the complex visible from the street.

Architect John Garber (1916–88), of the local firm Garber, Twedell & Wheeler, re-oriented the existing entry lobby and circulation space in the original block structure to form a narthex. Garber then fronted it along its entire south edge with a taller sanctuary structure. Three of its walls are relatively plain muted gray masonry; the two end walls are sharply raked on the top edge to match the single pitch of a corrugated metal roof above, and each is terminated by a fin wall. On the exterior, these masonry fin walls form the backdrop for a contrasting expressive façade (Fig. 13.6). Its blazing white metal panels are held in place by closely spaced spiky white steel columns that project past the roofline for a full 8 feet. Dark glazing at the floor level and roof-line creates a strong impression of solid and void. The partly exposed basement level is set back, so the sanctuary's precise height within is visible and appears to float. While the placement of windows and the illusory lightness are similar to the Arlington church, the materials' actual lightness and thinness are completely different. The whole wall is bowed slightly to accentuate its quality as a thin diaphragm that has been stretched across one side of the masonry box. These material qualities are still dramatic today; it was a decidedly avant-garde choice for its context and time.

FIGURE 13.6 St. John's Unitarian Church, Cincinnati, Ohio, 1958–60; John Garber, architect. Photograph by A. Harfmann.

FIGURE 13.7 St. John's Unitarian Church, interior.

Photograph by A. Harfmann.

The church's façade forms a backdrop to an expanse of lawn, where the original plan called for a sculpture to be placed. The wall stretches across most of the 120-foot-wide site, with room left on the margins for driveways in and out of the rear parking lot. Garber employed a relatively new material vocabulary in a novel way, producing an intentionally provocative design. Steel tended to be chosen for its spanning strength, allowing the columns to be placed at wide intervals. Here, the steel supports are closely spaced along a single plane, not part of a frame. The external column supports only the roof; a paired interior column supports the floor. The spacing on 4-foot intervals helps establish the effect of a screen rather than a wall. The character of this unapologetically modern expression is startling (Fig. 13.6). The designer may not have had a particular association in mind, but if he did, it may have been the "good neighbor" gesture of a picket fence.

The impact of this wall on the experience of the interior space is equally dramatic (Fig. 13.7). The pitch of the metal roof orients the space toward this single largest surface within. The material and color differences, as well as the light pouring in along the top and bottom, add a quality of radiance to the entire space. A glazed slot between the wall and the masonry fin wall creates a spatial zone intended for circulation along the wall, and allows a sense of spatial extension to the exterior as the wall plane continues past the glass. This slot frames the view of an evergreen tree, drawing nature into the assembly of symbolic elements at the front of the sanctuary. Everyone can view the sky through the upper rank of windows, and those seated closer to the south edge can also look down and out onto green lawn. Exposed simple structure, the independence of each prominent architectural element coupled with the use of non-traditional materials and an asymmetrical composition all contribute to the unapologetic modernism, announced on the exterior by a sense of floating above the ground plane (Figs. 13.6, 13.7). The clarity of independent elements is underscored on the interior by lines of daylight along their edges that lend luminance to the whole space.

"Clarity and reason"—an articulate light

The Unitarian Church of Arlington, University Unitarian, and St. John's Unitarian each make a bold statement with a striking façade, and in each case the interior space is even more compelling. The somewhat aggressive nature of their exteriors belies the allure of these remarkable walls in the context of rooms with other elements, materials, and orders. They are a bounding condition of spaces that each have their own character. Inside, two other functions of these façades are revealed: the careful curation of views of natural elements of the site and, most importantly, the distinctive effects of natural light that each creates. Photographs of the three interiors convey some of the qualities of sunlight in the spaces (Figs. 13.3, 13.5, 13.7), but they are inadequate for understanding the range of movement of light through the space over time. Consideration of every season of the year allows a much more complete understanding and appreciation of the role of natural light in enhancing the sacredness of the sanctuary.

To analyze this crucial aspect, digital daylighting simulations were utilized to approximate the conditions of a Sunday morning service throughout the year.[54] Three-dimensional digital models of the interior spaces were created to simulate and evaluate luminance distribution characteristics under daylighting conditions at midmorning on the 21st day of each month of the year (Figs. 13.8, 13.9, 13.10). The models incorporated material properties with reflectance values, location and orientation, and site context adjacent to the building. Simulations assumed clear skies, but an additional simulation was run for cloudy skies in Seattle.[55] The analysis attempted to capture two primary properties: the range of daylighting conditions throughout the year, and the impact of the design of the sanctuary wall on the quality of light. Hourly simulations were used to obtain accurate luminance distributions across key times and sky conditions specific to the patterns of use and the geographic location. These daylighting simulations were performed using physically accurate geometric lighting models constructed from the architects' original construction documents and contemporary photographs.

Goodman had little constraint in orienting the Arlington sanctuary on its site. However, once he had envisioned a continuous clerestory under a floating roof plane, he had to place the speaker's platform to the north in order to avoid direct light and glare in the faces of the congregation during services. The orientation is therefore close to the cardinal points, and coincidentally also in alignment with the original church building on the other side of the site. The two lateral walls therefore face east and west, their textures animated by the changing position of the sun throughout the day.

Despite its square dimensions, the sanctuary space of UCA is directional. Like a basilican hall church,[56] UCA's major supports line the lateral edges, and the beams spanning between them create a diminishing sequence in space. Although the vocabulary of basic wall elements was uniform on all edges, the side walls are far more rhythmic due to the supports. The deep concrete columns punctuate the wall vividly, and give their full thickness to the perceptual experience. The accented rhythm is visible throughout the year, as seen in the daylighting simulations (Fig. 13.8).

On sunny days, church-goers might enter from full daylight reflecting from the east-facing concrete surfaces, and step briefly into a small vestibule where more limited daylight would allow eyes to adjust. Upon entry into the sanctuary from the southeast corner, the "extraordinary natural lighting"[57] of the spatial volume would be softer, with an even quality to balance the strong contrasts of the east wall receiving the morning sunlight. Along the east edge, the visitor could proceed past the brightly lit chambers created by the slot openings at each column or could take refuge on a bench in the shadowy depth of the wall.

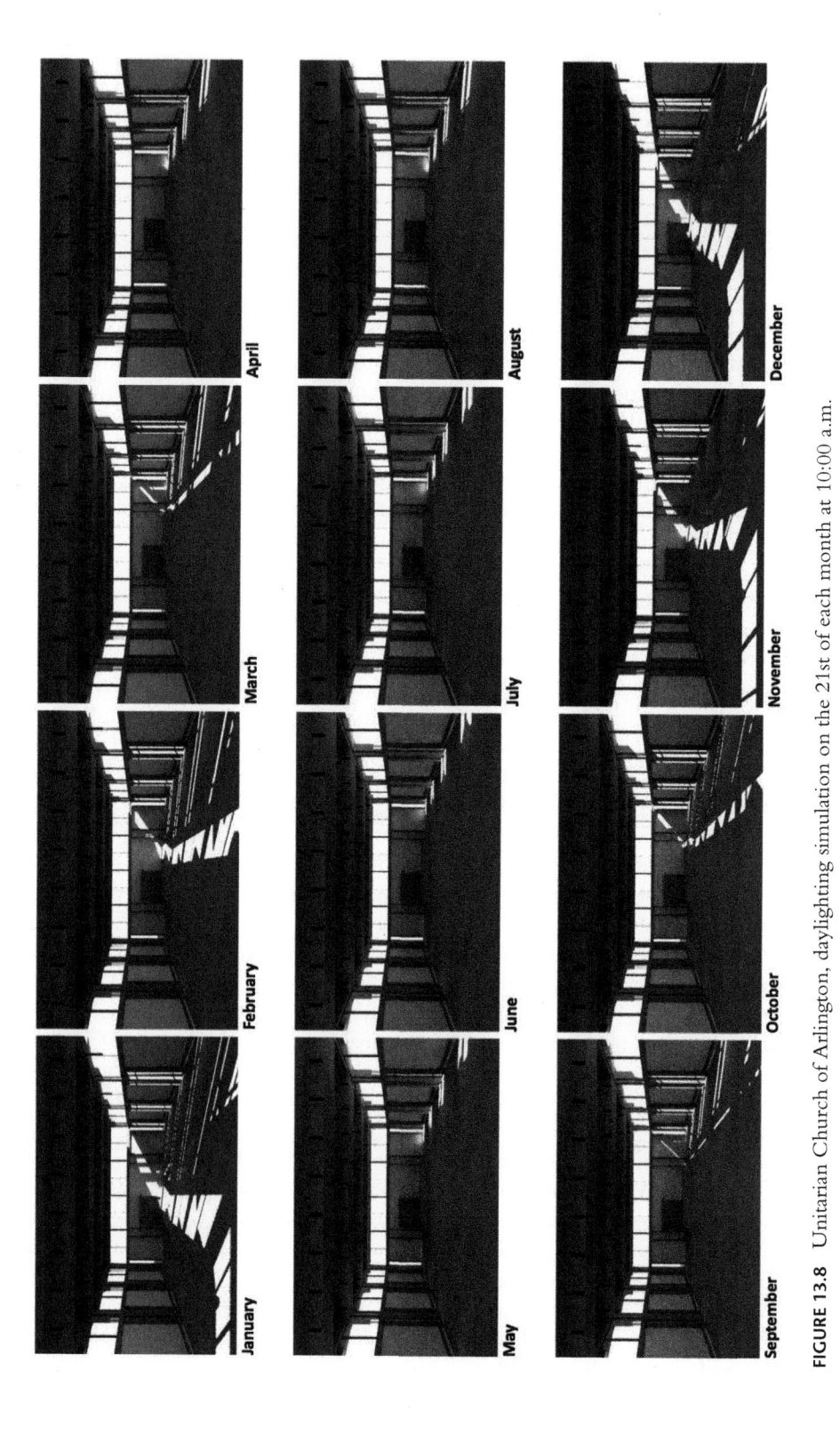

FIGURE 13.8 Unitarian Church of Arlington, daylighting simulation on the 21st of each month at 10:00 a.m.
Digital model and simulation: University of Washington Integrated Design Lab.

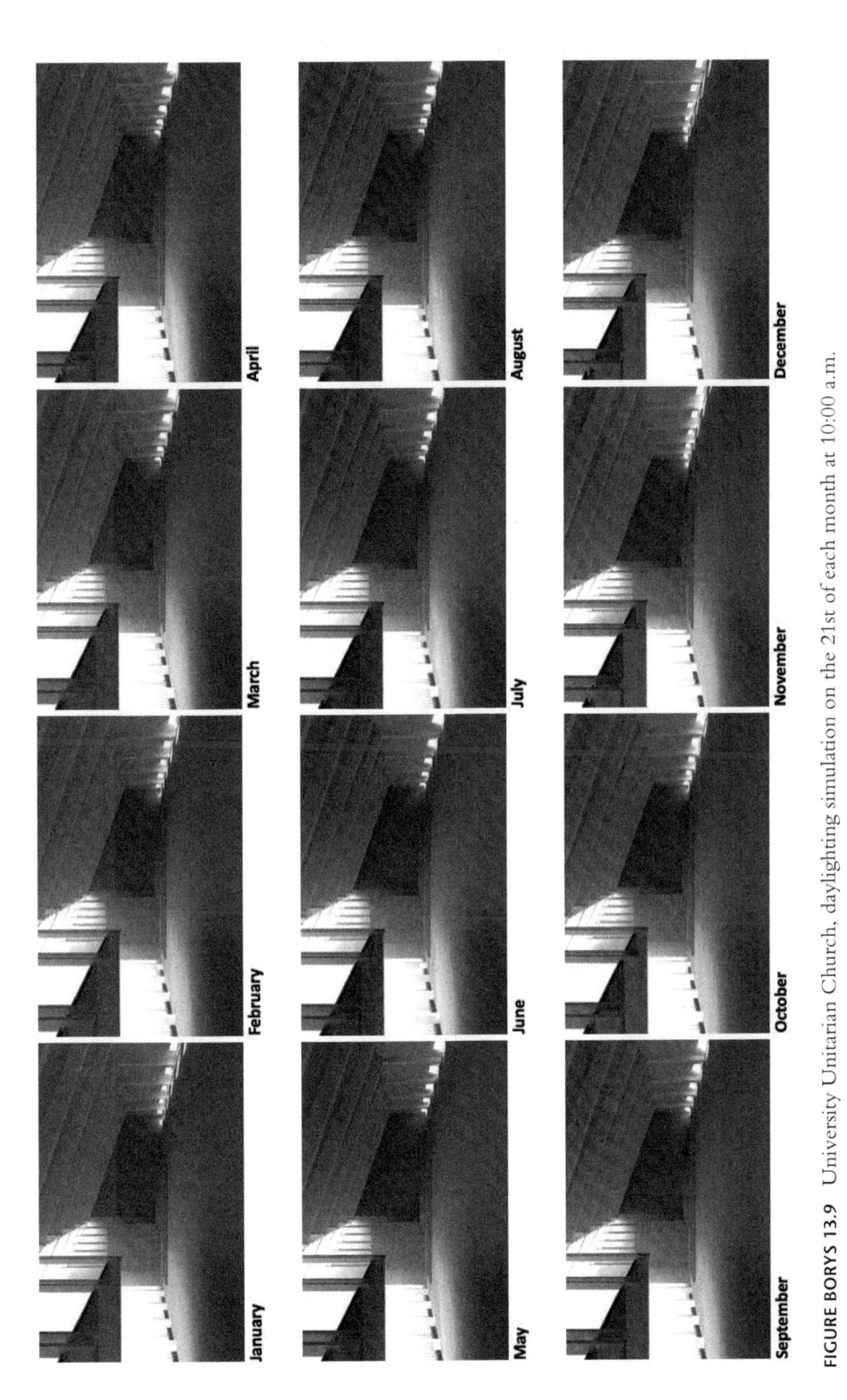

FIGURE BORYS 13.9 University Unitarian Church, daylighting simulation on the 21st of each month at 10:00 a.m.

Digital model and simulation: University of Washington Integrated Design Lab.

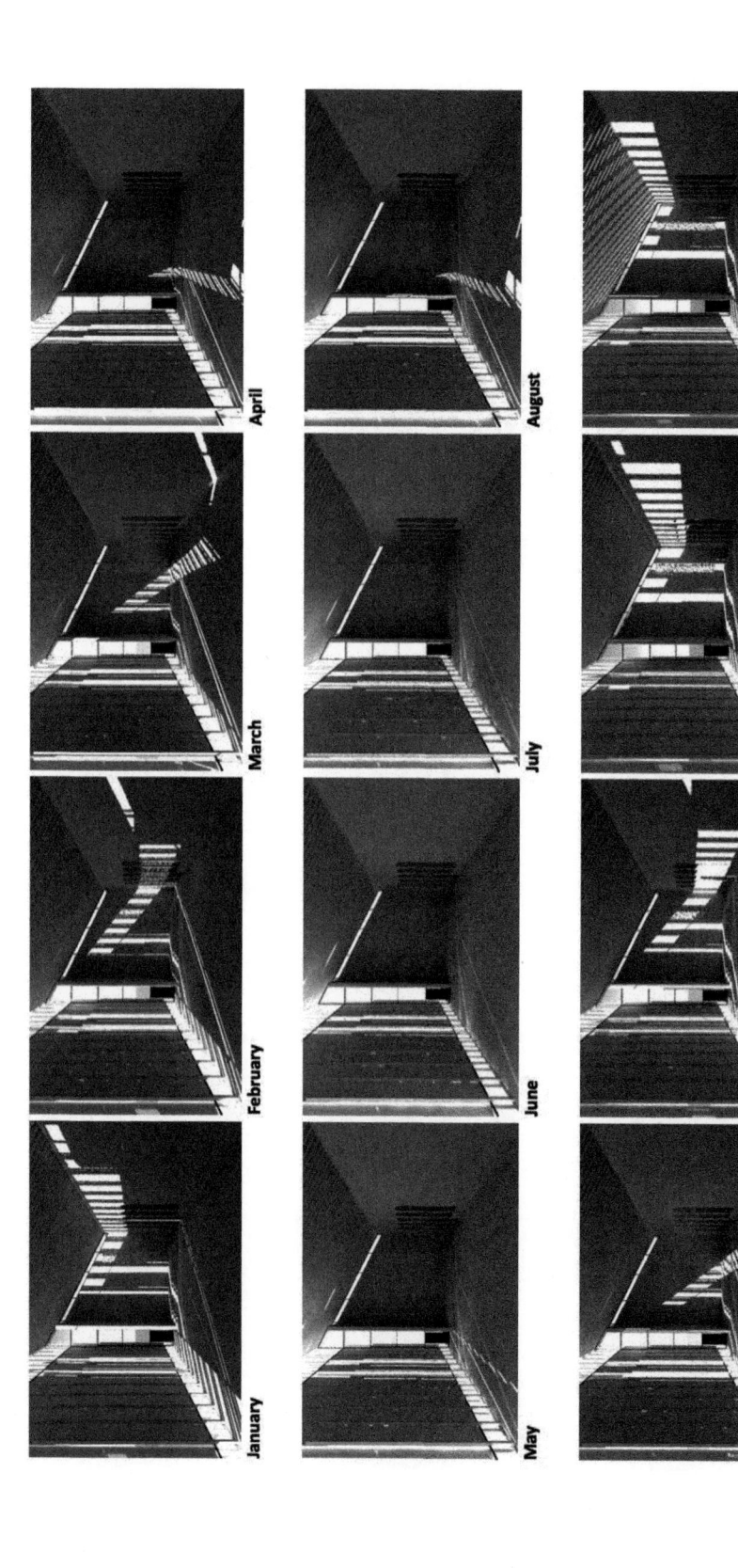

FIGURE 13.10 St. John's Unitarian Church; daylighting simulation on the 21st of each month at 10:00 a.m.

Digital model and simulation: University of Washington Integrated Design Lab.

The views into the tree canopy motivated Goodman's design of the clerestory. Though the character and pattern of light that enters was secondary, it was certainly anticipated. A broad swath of direct sunlight enters the space during services for several months of the year, reaching fully halfway into the space when the winter sun is at its lowest angle. Goodman's intention to have seating arranged in a pinwheel fashion may have been a way to allow worshippers to turn their backs on uncomfortable glare in winter months. The light that perforates the perimeter at the lower story of the walls illuminates the columns, lightening the visual weight of the concrete. The streaks of sunlight from the paired slots at each column reveal a diurnal time visible in the length of a service. Just as worshipers can take delight in seeing the movement of the leaves and branches of the trees, they can mark the season and the hour by the changing condition and position of sunlight in the space.

Light is never a secondary consideration for designers in the Pacific Northwest. The latitude and climate demand efforts to maximize natural light, even when the sun is not shining. The Seattle street grid and lot lines gave Paul Kirk the same general orientation that Goodman chose in Arlington. Kirk could have opened up toward the east, where topography assured that later construction would not interfere. But he did not design University Unitarian for lively and animated direct sunlight that was unreliable. The prevailing weather condition he designed for was an overcast sky.

The entry vestibule of University Unitarian extends into a circulation space—a narthex—that opens generously on the right to the social hall, while entry to the sanctuary is located further along. The sequence in terms of light goes from the brightness of the outdoors to a sheltered and shadowy entrance. From there, the narthex has windows along its northern edge, but its lower ceiling creates a muted effect compared to the adjacent social hall—well-lit with south-facing and clerestory windows. Entry into the sanctuary requires a deliberate left turn to cross a bridge with four translucent skylights and no windows. From the unmodulated whiteness of the bridge, one enters the complex lightscape of the sanctuary—low and dark towards the east, and lofty and glowing towards the west. The degree of contrast is visible in the daylighting simulations (Fig. 13.9).

The light of the University Unitarian sanctuary can be viewed in two ways: it is oppositional across the width of the space, but uniform along its length. Along the east wall, small windows are set right at floor level. They light the outer aisle and visually mark the edge of the room. In contrast, the entire west wall is opened to a height of 15 feet for its full length. This large area of glazing is necessary to make use of ambient skylight as a source on overcast days. Panels of vertical wood slats and colored glass outside the wall screen views of the neighborhood and could provide solar protection when the space was occupied in the afternoon. To boost the morning light, Kirk introduced the east-facing clerestory just 20 feet away from the upper, opaque portion of the west wall. The large clerestory (also about 15 feet tall) is filled with milk white and light yellow opaque colored glass in a rectangular grid. As such, the light entering is always diffused. This creates a lofty chamber of light, and illuminates the wood beams that cut through it. It highlights the warmth of the materials and the clarity of the structure.

By eschewing direct and lively light, Kirk created a warm glowing chamber that is inviting even on gloomy winter days. Kirk embraced the expected norm of the grey Seattle climate by admitting a large amount of diffuse light. He was sympathetic to his Unitarian clients who valued light for light's sake—light as a reminder of the sun's importance to life, rather than light as a symbol of the divine.[58] It follows a similar intention as Frank Furness's design for the light of First Unitarian Church in Philadelphia (1883). Furness, son of a Unitarian minister, used a continuous overhead skylight to produce a uniform wash of non-directional light that stressed "clarity and reason over mystical obfuscation."[59] The simulations show that Kirk succeeded in creating a glowing chamber without any direct sunlight, one that provides a steady warmth and presence of light that varies little throughout the year, despite the swings of daylight conditions that Seattle's latitude creates. In contrast with Goodman's classical symmetry and casual attitude towards the play of direct sunlight across the space, "light gave University Unitarian Church its form,"[60] that is, an asymmetrical section that creates a container of glowing ambient light.

Garber's design for St. John's goes even further in crafting the admittance of light, displaying a calendrical symbolism as well as animating the structure and creating space: "The syncopation of sun and earth have given the structure its shape."[61] Like Kirk, Garber was constrained by the site orientation. His main exposure was to the south, so he clearly needed to control the impact of any direct light in the space. A low and somewhat dark vestibule leads into the bright interior. From the threshold, the opposite bright wall appears mostly opaque, although the glazed void between the top of the wall and the roof brings lightness. Continuous glazing is also used at the floor level, where light enters and marks a circulation path along the spatial slot between the masonry structure and the south façade.[62]

Garber used the sunlight to increase the contrast between the gray masonry box that forms three sides of the space and the two metal planes that complete its enclosure: the south-facing façade and the roof. Daylighting simulations show the brilliance of the wall throughout the year (Fig. 13.10). Light entering the upper register of windows was calculated to strike the opposite wall right at its juncture with the roof in December, when the sun is at its lowest angle of the year. This design lights up the underside of the roof, so that it appears to float. Because the sanctuary is only 30 feet wide, the sunlight strikes lower down the wall for another four months of the year. There are four months when direct sunlight falls onto the congregation rather than the wall, but it comes from behind in the morning. For another three months, the sun's angle is high enough that it does not enter at all in mid-morning. Looking at the simulations across the year, the overall effect of this design was to successfully animate the plain masonry wall.

Garber's careful choreography of direct sunlight is most evident in three interruptions to the south wall's uniform treatment. At three of the twenty bays, the solid portion of the wall is 'peeled' outward to a calculated angle, and glazing extends for the full height of the wall. These slots are positioned and configured to bring a shaft of direct light to the front of the sanctuary space on the solstices and equinoxes. At those times, sun also lights something special—either the "Joy" sculpture by Bertoia on the front wall or, in midwinter, the front wall of an adjacent chapel. The intended path for each is inscribed on the concrete floor so that throughout the year the most special conditions can be anticipated (Fig. 13.10). These constructed patterns are visible in the summer months of the simulation. As the streaks of actual sunlight appear in the other months, the simulations show that there is also visual interest in how time can be measured by the distance between them and the inscribed paths.

Conclusion: "natural order revealed over time"

Unitarianism is a religion based on ethics rather than on faith or creed; it "does not require a belief in the supernatural . . . the moral order of the universe is not a reflection of God's character; it is a natural order revealed over time, and one in which we participate."[63] When faced with the need to build, Unitarian congregations work collaboratively with their architects by expressing their beliefs and values rather than proposing architectural precedents or particular formal features. They value innovation as a celebration of human creativity, and they allow for originality in design. Connecting the sanctuary to nature is perhaps the most consistent means of making it a spiritual place.[64] Since the 1950s, Unitarian congregations have encouraged modern architects to freshly reinterpret the spiritual connection of sanctuary and nature.

The major problem each architect confronted in designing these three mid-century churches was how to connect the sanctuary to natural elements on a suburban site, while also providing a sense of retreat and the possibility of transcendent moments. The site conditions required that the worship spaces be given some degree of visual privacy and acoustic isolation. In each case, the response was a sanctuary wall designed as a carefully woven screen, more like a fence than a wall. They express abstract Unitarian values of reason and tolerance by the provocation of a bold and extraordinary presence; yet at the same time each startles, it also reveals. They harness modernism's clarity of structure to engage our intellect and our senses with the elements of the wall and the qualities of their materials. These wall assemblies, together with situated attention to views and distinctive qualities of light, give each one a unique congregational identity.

They share an enclosure system that creates both spatial and visual drama, experienced internally as a shadow box of nature. Each one comes to life with its own condition of sunlight, which makes it a part of nature and cosmos, expressive of freedom and democracy.[65] This same intention was shared by Kahn at Rochester, of which Vincent Scully said, "the whole massing and profiling of the exterior and the marvelous plasticity of its walls derive from the lighting of the interior."[66] This clear light of everyday experience provides the individual an orientation in this world, reminding worshipers of their place and "fostering a sense of confidence and legitimacy" in gathering to recall "the privileges and responsibilities"[67] that are inherent to the Unitarian sense of world order.

Notes

1 Albert Christ-Janer and Mary Mix Foley, *Modern Church Architecture: A Guide to the Form and Spirit of 20th Century Religious Buildings* (New York, NY: McGraw-Hill, 1962), 265.
2 Gideon Kramer, "Response to Building Committee Survey," April 15, 1954, Box 48, University Unitarian Church Archives.
3 Sigfried Giedeon, *Space, Time and Architecture* (Cambridge, MA: Harvard University Press, 1967), lvi.
4 Mircea Eliade, *The Sacred and the Profane: The Nature of Religion* (New York, NY: Harcourt, Brace, Jovanovich, 1959), 20–113; see also Paul Tillich, "Contemporary Protestant Architecture" in Christ-Janer and Foley, *Modern Church Architecture*, 124.
5 Andrea Greenwood and Mark W. Harris, *An Introduction to the Unitarian and Universalist Traditions* (Cambridge: Cambridge University Press, 2011), 201.
6 Christ-Janer and Foley, *Modern Church Architecture*, 272.
7 David Robinson, *The Unitarians and the Universalists* (Westport, CT: Greenwood Press, 1985), 71–83.
8 Anat Geva, *Frank Lloyd Wright's Sacred Architecture* (London and New York, NY: Routledge, 2012); Joseph Siry, *Beth Sholom Synagogue: Frank Lloyd Wright and Modern Religious Architecture* (Chicago, IL: University of Chicago Press, 2012), 256.
9 Many Unitarian congregations changed their name to reflect the 1961 merger with Universalism. The congregation in Arlington, VA is now UUCA; however, I am using the name at the time of design and construction.

10 Peter Benes, *Meetinghouses of Early New England* (Amherst, MA: University of Massachusetts Press, 2012), 204–17.

11 "Postcards of Unitarian and Universalist Churches, 1890–1930," BMS 349, Special Collections, Andover-Harvard Theological Library, Harvard Divinity School.

12 Conrad Wright, *Stream of Light: a Sesquicentennial History of American Unitarianism* (Boston, MA: Unitarian Universalist Association, 1975), 110–114.

13 Archival materials of the three cases presented here and of more than a dozen other mid-century churches I have documented followed this approach.

14 Sarah Williams Goldhagen, *Louis Kahn's Situated Modernism* (New Haven, CT: Yale University Press, 2001), 138.

15 Greenwood and Harris, *An Introduction to the Unitarian and Universalist Traditions*, 8–9.

16 Charles M. Goodman, "'The Unitarian Church of Arlington—The New Building,' The Envelope," 1964, Unitarian Universalist Church of Arlington, 1–2; Goodman is quoting from sermons of the UCA minister Ross Weston.

17 Kathryn Ritson, "Unitarian Universalist Church of Arlington," National Register of Historic Places Registration Form (Virginia Department of Historic Resources, 2014), 5–6.

18 Goodman, "'Unitarian Church of Arlington,' Envelope," 1–5.

19 Ritson, "Unitarian Universalist Church of Arlington," 17.

20 Ibid.

21 Ibid., 19.

22 Ibid., 15.

23 Elizabeth Lampl, "Charles M. Goodman and 'Tomorrow's Vernacular.'" In Richard W. Longstreth, ed. *Housing Washington: Two Centuries of Residential Development and Planning in the National Capitol Area* (Chicago, IL: Columbia College, 2010), 230.

24 Ritson, "Unitarian Universalist Church of Arlington," 14.

25 Goodman, "'Unitarian Church of Arlington,' Site," 4–5.

26 Ritson, "Unitarian Universalist Church of Arlington," 29.

27 Ibid., 21.

28 Ibid., 15.

29 Ibid., 34 n. 46.

30 Ibid., 31.

31 Goodman, "'Unitarian Church of Arlington,' Envelope," 3.

32 Ibid., 3.

33 Ritson, "Unitarian Universalist Church of Arlington," 32.

34 Goodman, "'Unitarian Church of Arlington,' Envelope," 5.

35 Ibid., 4.

36 Ronald W. Marshall and Barbara A. Boyd, "Charles Goodman: Production, Recognition, and Reflections," *The Modernism Magazine* vol. 2, no. 3 (1999): 41–42.

37 Ibid., 45.

38 A staff member noted that there are times of year that the sanctuary is too warm to schedule afternoon weddings; shades have been installed on the south-facing clerestory.

39 Board minutes 1953, Box 7, University Unitarian Church Archives; see also "UUC History," YouTube video, 5:40. Posted by "f v," November 10, 2017. https://youtu.be/90_yqoSWdyk.

40 Memo to the Board, July, 1954, Box 48, University Unitarian Church Archives.

41 Kramer, "Response to Building Committee Survey."

42 Ibid.

43 "Space Requirements," September 24, 1956, Box 48, University Unitarian Church Archives.

44 David A. Rash, "Paul Hayden Kirk." In Jeffrey Karl Ochsner, ed. *Shaping Seattle Architecture* (Seattle, WA: University of Washington Press, 1994), 253.

45 "Paul Kirk Turns to Church Design," *Western Architect & Engineer* vol. 221 (April 1961): 21

46 Paul Hayden Kirk, "Paul Hayden Kirk Papers, 1958–1967," University of Washington Libraries.

47 Architectural drawings of Kirk, Wallace, and McKinley, HA15-HA29 Tube 8, Special Collections, University Libraries, University of Washington.

48 Rash, "Paul Hayden Kirk," 253.

49 Andreas Jordahl Rhude, "Structural Glued Laminated Timber: History and Early Development in the United States" *APT Bulletin* vol. 29 no. 1 (1998): 11–17.

50 David E. Miller, *Toward a New Regionalism* (Seattle, WA: University of Washington Press, 2005), 7–8.

51 Architectural drawings of Garber, Tweddell, and Wheeler, dated February 1959, St. John's Unitarian Church files; and "Our History" on St. John's website: http://stjohnsuu.org/about-us/our-history/, accessed March 29, 2017.
52 St. John's Unitarian Universalist Church Records 1817–2001, Mss 1060, "Series 1-Council Minutes," Cincinnati History Library and Archives.
53 Ibid., "Series 2-Buildings."
54 The daylighting simulations conducted in this study were developed by the Integrated Design Lab, University of Washington. The architects' original construction documents and numerous photographs of the three case studies were used to create physically accurate geometric lighting models. Radiance synthetic imaging system developed by Greg Ward at the Lawrence Berkeley National Laboratory and Rhino 3D modeling software were used in creating those models. Then, daylight luminance simulations were generated using DIVA for Rhino and the Grasshopper visual programming tool.
55 The data is converted to luminance maps with per-pixel lighting data using a standard luminance scale (10–2500 cd/m2). The maps are digital renderings that allow an evaluation of the visual character of the daylighting throughout the year. See also: http://radsite.lbl.gov/radiance/refer/ray.html.
56 Goodman, "'Unitarian Church of Arlington,' Plan," 1. The only church precedent Goodman cited was a medieval hall church, St. Maria Zur Wiese, Soest, Germany.
57 Ritson, "Unitarian Universalist Church of Arlington," 8.
58 Michael J. Lewis, *Frank Furness: Architecture and the Violent Mind* (New York, NY: W.W. Norton, 2001), 161–162.
59 Kirk, "Paul Hayden Kirk Papers, 1958–1967," University of Washington Libraries.
60 "Paul Kirk Turns to Church Design," 22.
61 John Garber, "Architecture," in the church dedication program, 1960.
62 Unfortunately, the current arrangement of seating does not maintain this clear intention.
63 Greenwood and Harris, *An Introduction to the Unitarian and Universalist Traditions*, 4.
64 Ibid., 208.
65 Geva, *Wright's Sacred Architecture*, 191. Wright connected light in church buildings to freedom and democracy; his ideas about sacred space were deeply rooted in his Unitarian values and his family history.
66 Vincent Scully, *American Architecture and Urbanism* (New York, NY: Henry Holt and Co., 1969), 216.
67 Lindsay Jones, *The Hermeneutics of Sacred Architecture: Experience, Interpretation, Comparison*, vol. 2 (Cambridge, MA: Harvard University Press, 2000), 31.

References

Benes, Peter. *Meetinghouses of Early New England* (Amherst, MA: University of Massachusetts Press, 2012).
Christ-Janer, Albert and Mary Mix Foley. *Modern Church Architecture: A Guide to the Form and Spirit of 20th Century Religious Buildings* (New York, NY: McGraw-Hill, 1962).
Eliade, Mircea. *The Sacred and the Profane: The Nature of Religion* (New York, NY: Harcourt, Brace, Jovanovich, 1959).
Geva, Anat. *Frank Lloyd Wright's Sacred Architecture: Faith, Form and Building Technology* (New York, NY: Routledge, 2012).
Giedion, Sigfried. *Space, Time and Architecture: The Growth of a New Tradition*, 5th edn. (Cambridge, MA: Harvard University Press, 1967).
Goldhagen, Sarah Williams. *Louis Kahn's Situated Modernism* (New Haven, CT: Yale University Press, 2001).
Goodman, Charles M. "'The Unitarian Church of Arlington—The New Building' Report of Charles M. Goodman, FAIA," 1964. Unitarian Universalist Church of Arlington.
Greenwood, Andrea, and Mark W. Harris. *An Introduction to the Unitarian and Universalist Traditions* (Cambridge: Cambridge University Press, 2011).
Jones, Lindsay. *The Hermeneutics of Sacred Architecture: Experience, Interpretation, Comparison*. vol. 2 (Cambridge, MA: Harvard University Press, 2000).

Kirk, Paul Hayden. "Paul Hayden Kirk Papers, 1958–1967," University of Washington Libraries Special Collections.

Lampl, Elizabeth. "Charles M. Goodman and 'Tomorrow's Vernacular.'" In Richard W. Longstreth, ed. *Housing Washington: Two Centuries of Residential Development and Planning in the National Capitol [Sic] Area* (Chicago, IL: Center for American Places at Columbia College, 2010).

Lewis, Michael J. *Frank Furness: Architecture and the Violent Mind* (New York, NY: W. W. Norton, 2001).

Marshall, Ronald W., and Barbara A. Boyd. "Charles Goodman: Production, Recognition, and Reflections." *The Modernism Magazine* 2, no. 3 (1999): 40–47.

Miller, David E. *Toward a New Regionalism: Environmental Architecture in the Pacific Northwest* (Seattle, WA: University of Washington Press, 2005).

"Paul Kirk Turns to Church Design." *Western Architect & Engineer* 221 (April 1961): 20–29.

"Precast Concrete: A Survey of Current US Practice." *Architectural Record* 119, no. 7 (June 1956): 215–220.

Rash, David A. "Paul Hayden Kirk." In Jeffrey Karl Ochsner, ed. *Shaping Seattle Architecture: A Historical Guide to the Architects*, 252–257 (Seattle, WA: University of Washington Press, 1994).

Rhude, Andreas Jordahl. "Structural Glued Laminated Timber: History and Early Development in the United States." *APT Bulletin* 29, no. 1 (1998): 11–17.

Ritson, Kathryn. "Unitarian Universalist Church of Arlington." National Register of Historic Places Registration Form. Virginia Department of Historic Resources, 2014.

Robinson, David. *The Unitarians and the Universalists* (Westport, CT: Greenwood Press, 1985).

Scully, Vincent. *American Architecture and Urbanism* (New York, NY: Henry Holt and Co., 1969).

Siry, Joseph. *Beth Shalom Synagogue: Frank Lloyd Wright and Modern Religious Architecture* (Chicago, IL: University of Chicago Press, 2012).

Tillich, Paul. "Contemporary Protestant Architecture" in Albert Christ-Janer and Mary Mix Foley, eds. *Modern Church Architecture: A Guide to the Form and Spirit of 20th Century Religious Buildings* (New York, NY: McGraw-Hill, 1962).

Wright, Conrad. *A Stream of Light: a Sesquicentennial History of American Unitarianism* (Boston, MA: Unitarian Universalist Association, 1975).

14

TRADITION AND TRANSCENDENCE

Eero Saarinen's MIT Chapel and the nondenominational ideal

Joseph M. Siry

Among mid-century sacred interiors, Eero Saarinen's Kresge Chapel at the Massachusetts Institute of Technology (MIT), dedicated in June 1955, is exceptional. It exemplifies the retention of liturgical spatial conventions while serving a nondenominational ideal. It shares the modernist emphasis on space, light, and material surfaces, but its interior evokes tradition and a transcendent spiritual experience (Fig. 14.1). This chapter focuses on how Saarinen, committed as he was to the modern movement, responded to the concerns of an institutional client who sought a symbolic familiarity and accessibility in a chapel for all faiths.

At the project's inception, MIT's president, James Rhyne Killian, Jr., and its Dean of Students, the Rev. Everett Moore Baker, were both Unitarians.[1] They brought the perspective of their liberal denominational culture, with its historic sensitivity to and valuation of the diversity of religions, to the new problem of a nondenominational college chapel. In addition, one may argue that Saarinen brought his background in a Finnish Lutheran tradition to a design that partly invoked the conventions of Christian churches, but also alluded to more archaic and universal themes in religious architecture. As such, the chapel interior is rooted in Christian tradition and yet bridges to a nondenominational ideal. This raises a broader question of how mid-century American modernism understood its relationship to earlier sacred spaces, and how an architect like Saarinen acknowledged and resolved paradoxical priorities.

Imagining a chapel for MIT

MIT committed to build a chapel in the wake of World War II, after the institution's deep involvement in military research that included the development of the atomic bomb.[2] Underlying MIT's initiative for a chapel was a broader concern for the moral education of future scientists in the wake of the horrific war.[3] This concern became the keynote for the 1949 inauguration of President Killian. In his address at the "Mid-Century Convocation on the Social Implications of Scientific Progress," he stressed that the scientist "must be politically and morally responsible; he must test his actions by their human impact."[4] Not having a chapel on campus, students attended services held in classrooms or local churches, of which there were few close by, as the institute was then in a mainly industrial district.[5]

FIGURE 14.1 Kresge Chapel, Massachusetts Institute of Technology, Cambridge, Massachusetts, 1950–55, Eero Saarinen and Associates, with Anderson and Beckwith, architects; interior looking west toward altar with metal screen by Harry Bertoia, and pulpit (left) and lectern (right).

Photograph © Ezra Stoller/Esto, id no. 109Q.006, 1955.

In February 1948, Baker heard the concerns of the Institute's Protestant and Catholic student associations about the lack of a worship space on campus. He sent a memorandum to Killian, proposing a small chapel, where an individual could "go for a moment of silent meditation." Baker wrote:

> The same room could be used by small discussion groups or meetings of students of different denominations . . . It must symbolize the religious interests and aspirations of the whole community, rather than those of a particular traditional religious group within it. It could prove to be a very interesting educational experiment . . . for the whole social organization of our community.[6]

In a subsequent memorandum of December 1949 to Killian on "The Need for a Chapel Auditorium," Baker asserted: "The lack of a chapel and the facilities it would afford to the enrichment of the spiritual in the life of our students and Faculty is immediately evident within and without the community."[7] He held that "It is difficult to think of America without the village church and the meeting house. It is equally difficult to imagine M.I.T. of tomorrow fulfilling its many responsibilities to our nation and our world without its chapel and its meeting house."[8] New Englanders had borrowed the term "meetinghouse" from the Quakers to designate compact buildings for both worship and civic gathering. Meetinghouses avoided extravagance for both financial and symbolic reasons.[9] In Anglican usage, strictly speaking, a church was a consecrated structure, distinct from both colonial Puritan meetinghouses and other buildings created for Nonconformist groups in England, such as the Unitarians, who often called their houses of worship "chapels."[10] In earlier modern architecture, this cultural memory informed such Unitarian Universalist churches as Frank Lloyd Wright's Unity Temple in Oak Park, Illinois, of 1905–09.[11]

In his address at the dedication of Saarinen's auditorium and chapel in May 1955, Killian invoked the meetinghouse as central for its civic and religious role on its town common—an historic image that represented his concern for the moral education of scientists.[12] In the minds of Killian and Baker, the historic meetinghouse was an apt precedent for the institutional ideal of a chapel that would not privilege any one religion, but would offer a place for meditation and services to students of different faiths.[13] Earlier Baker voiced a similar idea in his baccalaureate address at Dartmouth College in 1949, when he suggested that students be religious:

> By that I do not mean that you must belong to any special ecclesiastical organization or that you be committed to a particular creed or dogma.
>
> Some of you either by volition or inheritance are—some are not. I do mean, however, that you shall, because of the privilege that you have enjoyed and the responsibility that is yours, live in accord with a concept of religion which is not particular, but, for the commonweal of tomorrow's world, is essential.[14]

Killian and Baker echoed traditional Unitarian views on the distinction between humanity's multiple religions and the unifying ideal of religion. American Unitarians had committed to the study and valuation of world religions, especially Asian faiths, since the early nineteenth century.[15] The chapel was to serve individual and group worship for all faiths. However, at its origins, only Protestants, Catholics, and Jews were mentioned, even though MIT in 1945 had over three hundred foreign students among its undergraduate and graduate enrollment of nearly two thousand, including contingents from India, China, and the Near East, in addition to Europe and Latin America.[16] In his report of 1954 Killian wrote further: "The small devotional chapel which we are building at MIT . . . will be in the completest sense nonsectarian, equally available to individuals and groups of all faiths."[17] Its purpose was two-fold:

> *First,* to stand as a symbol of the place of the spirit in the life of the mind and as a physical statement of the fact that MIT has a right and a responsibility to deal with ideals as well as ideas . . . *Second,* to provide ready opportunity for students and other members of our community to worship as they choose, to have on campus a building, beautiful and evocative of reverence and meditation, where those who wish may enter and worship in their fashion.[18]

MIT's approach of creating a single building for worship for the three different major US religions contrasted with that of Brandeis University in Waltham, Massachusetts, where three free-standing structures arranged around a pond amid a grove of trees represented the Catholic, Protestant, and Jewish traditions.[19] MIT, although a much larger institution, built a single chapel, thus seeking an architectural solution that was more challenging in terms of expressing a transcendent religious ideal without using specific denominational symbols.

Baker's proposal of December 1949 informed MIT's application of April 1950 to the Kresge Foundation "in support of a program in Development of Citizenship and Christian Character."[20] Given the foundation's support for religious institutions and education in the humanities, the proposal was for a "Kresge School of Human Relations, which would enrich MIT's technological education by increased emphasis on humanities, social sciences, character building activities, and religion."[21] The proposal included an "Auditorium-Chapel building" seating approximately twelve hundred.[22] It also mentioned "a small, but dignified chapel seating around 100," although it was not then clear that this would be a separate building.[23] The application noted Dean Baker's mandate to supplement interest in the sciences with an "environment and activities which would develop civic responsibility and moral character."[24] As such, the auditorium, "though less distinctively religious in atmosphere, could be used for larger religious gatherings."[25]

On 1 July 1950, MIT announced that the Kresge Foundation had awarded the institute $1.5 million to construct a "meeting house" dedicated to public gatherings and religious convocations.[26] The president's "Specifications for Auditorium-Chapel for MIT," dated July 17, did not clarify that the chapel seating 75–100 would be a distinct building, but that "there should be a separate entrance to the chapel as well as access to and from the chapel from the auditorium."[27] The building committee sought the best possible architect and selected Saarinen on the recommendation of William Wurster, outgoing Dean of the School of Architecture.[28] His successor from January 1951, Pietro Belluschi, who had designed a number of modernist post-war American churches, supported Saarinen's experimental, creative, yet functional approach to both the auditorium and the chapel.[29] On October 3, Killian described the "auditorium-chapel" as still a single building, but he also imagined that the "devotional" chapel might be "connected with the auditorium by an ambulatory or some similar architectural device."[30] The chapel should be "a place small, reverential in feeling, definitely spiritual in intent." He hoped "that it might have a quality of romantic beauty and that the chapel particularly could avoid too much austerity and coldness."[31] As *Architectural Forum*'s editor later wrote, "it would be a structure without time or place, and therefore of all times and places."[32] Killian favored innovation, even if

> it is accompanied by controversy and reveals deep divergencies in taste—and here I speak knowingly. This is the price of creativity in the arts, and we should be willing to risk the controversy in order to achieve a mutation in taste or to afford the searching, creative minds of our time an opportunity to try new solutions.[33]

Saarinen, working with Boston architects Anderson and Beckwith, developed his design over 1951 and 1952 before its early publication in January 1953 (Fig. 14.2).[34] By then he imagined the auditorium and chapel as separate buildings set in an open space as a new campus common on the west side of Massachusetts Avenue across from MIT's main entrance. This was marked by the domed Rogers Building and its columnar portico (Fig. 14.3). MIT's neoclassical buildings, six stories high, generously windowed, and clad in Indiana limestone, were the work of Welles Bosworth, a Beaux-Arts trained architect, and built between 1916 and 1930.[35] Separated from the main campus by the avenue, the auditorium and chapel were among dormitories and athletic facilities. Saarinen envisioned that existing buildings on the west side of Massachusetts Avenue, including the residential neo-Tudor Bexley Hall, would be demolished, and that the avenue would be depressed to enable a pedestrian bridge leading from the Rogers Building over the avenue to the new campus common, with a parking garage below (not built).[36] The model also shows a one-story linear building and covered walkway along the site's south side that would link the chapel to the auditorium like a cloister walk or outdoor ambulatory (not built) (Fig. 14.2).[37] The chapel's narthex extended to its south rather than to the east as later built. The chapel and auditorium were to be built on an elevated podium-like lawn that had the aura of a sacred space (Fig. 14.3).

In February and March 1953, the MIT community's comments on the auditorium were generally favorable, while those on the chapel were more critical, although the building committee ultimately commended Saarinen's cylindrical solution to Killian in June 1953.[38] Given MIT's linked agenda for the two buildings, their formal symbiosis was a key problem. The auditorium was clear in its modernist emphasis on structural innovation as a reinforced concrete shell, with its roof as one-eighth of a sphere supported at three points on heavy abutments. A white marble slab in the lobby bears the inscription: "The Kresge Auditorium—The Meeting House of the Massachusetts Institute of Technology." By contrast, the chapel, offset south of the auditorium's main east–west axis, was a cylinder with load-bearing brick walls. Although different in size and form, the pair of structures had a carefully calculated geometrical, material, and spatial relation to each other. The chapel was characteristic of smaller post-war chapels at American universities built for a multi-faith, less dogmatic view of religion. They were distinct from the large chapels designed for Protestant worship and seating two thousand or more at schools like Princeton University and the University of Chicago earlier in the twentieth century.[39]

Eero Saarinen's father Eliel, whose father had been a Finnish Lutheran minister, had long been involved with the design of modernist churches.[40] Father and son had collaborated on

FIGURE 14.2 Kresge Chapel and Kresge Auditorium, MIT, model of original site plan, looking southwest. From *Architectural Forum* 98, no. 1 (January 1953): 127.

Photograph by Richard Shirk. Courtesy of Kevin Roche John Dinkeloo and Associates LLC.

the First Christian Church (formerly Tabernacle Church of Christ), in Columbus, Indiana (1939–42), and on Christ Evangelical Lutheran Church in Minneapolis (1949). In 1956, the National Council of Churches Commission on Architecture selected the latter as the best of 72 Protestant churches of modern design in the United States since 1930.[41] These buildings featured a dual scheme of natural light analogous to that which Eero adapted in the MIT Chapel: a diffused light from low translucent windows along the nave, and a tall vertical window to one side of the altar (Fig. 14.4).[42] It aimed to evoke spiritual feelings in a space "where the problem is to bring light in so that it moves and plays dramatically."[43]

Among the most outstanding 18 of these 72 Protestant structures, the council cited the MIT Chapel, even though it was officially nondenominational.[44] In addition to designing the MIT Chapel (1950–55), Saarinen also worked on three other nondenominational campus chapels: the Prayer Chapel at Drake University, Des Moines, Iowa (1952–56); Stephens College Chapel, Columbia, Missouri (1953–56); and Concordia Senior College Chapel, Fort Wayne, Indiana (1953–58). All their designs related to the MIT Chapel's, seeking appropriate expression of contemporary spiritual sensibilities. As Eero Saarinen said, "Civilizations of the past seem to have placed a greater, almost spiritual value on architecture . . . Is it not possible that architecture may, some day, play this higher role again?"[45]

Saarinen began his design of the chapel with Killian's premise that the large urban MIT campus was full of activity, traffic, bustle, and noise, so the chapel should be a place to "escape from the madding crowd and find peace and solitude."[46] Killian hoped that the architect "could give it some of the aspiring quality of some of the other traditional religious styles without necessarily using any one of these traditional styles."[47]

FIGURE 14.3 Kresge Chapel and Kresge Auditorium, MIT, aerial view of site as first built looking southeast, with Bexley Hall to east and the Rogers Building across Massachusetts Avenue. Stratton Student Center was later built to the north of the green.

From *Architectural Forum* 104, no. 3 (March 1956): 156. Photograph by Laurence Lowry.

FIGURE 14.4   Christ Evangelical Lutheran Church, Minneapolis, Minnesota, 1949–50, Eliel and
Eero Saarinen, architects; looking west.

© Massachusetts Institute of Technology, photograph by G. E. Kidder Smith, id. no. 116464, 1974.

Saarinen's schemes included a rectangular steel-and-glass chapel, like the shape of MIT's
academic buildings, and following Mies van der Rohe's Robert F. Carr Memorial Chapel
of St. Savior at the Illinois Institute of Technology in Chicago, published in 1949 and completed in 1952.[48] Although sponsored by the Episcopal Diocese of Chicago, the chapel had
a nondenominational focus and hosted a range of Christian and Jewish religious services and
clubs.[49] A rectangular chapel recalled larger basilican churches historically associated with
collective Christian worship. But Saarinen ultimately decided on a circular plan (Fig. 14.5).
He "believed it most important to make the chapel ideal for the meditation of the single
individual."[50] He said: "A circular chapel seemed preferable because it permitted a more
direct relationship between the person meditating and the altar."[51] The idea of a circular
chapel with undulating walls and an offset circular oculus owes much to Matthew Nowicki's
sketches for an unrealized Brandeis University chapel, done in collaboration with Eero
Saarinen in 1949–50.[52] Eliel Saarinen also developed a circular plan for the chapel at Stephens
College before his death on July 1, 1950. In 1947, Harrison and Abramovitz had designed a
small cylindrical chapel with a circular light clerestory for Evanston Congregation Hillel at
Northwestern University.[53] Published in 1948 and built in 1952, it antedated Saarinen's MIT
design, first published in January 1953, with working drawings in March and May 1954.[54]

The MIT Chapel as built

The built MIT Chapel was seen as "a complete break with traditionalism in an attempt to
provide a retreat for religious services and contemplation in a community bristling with
activity."[55] It is set in a grove of London plane trees planted in a grid to its north and south
(Fig. 14.3). Originally, Saarinen had intended to seclude the chapel in trees extending to its

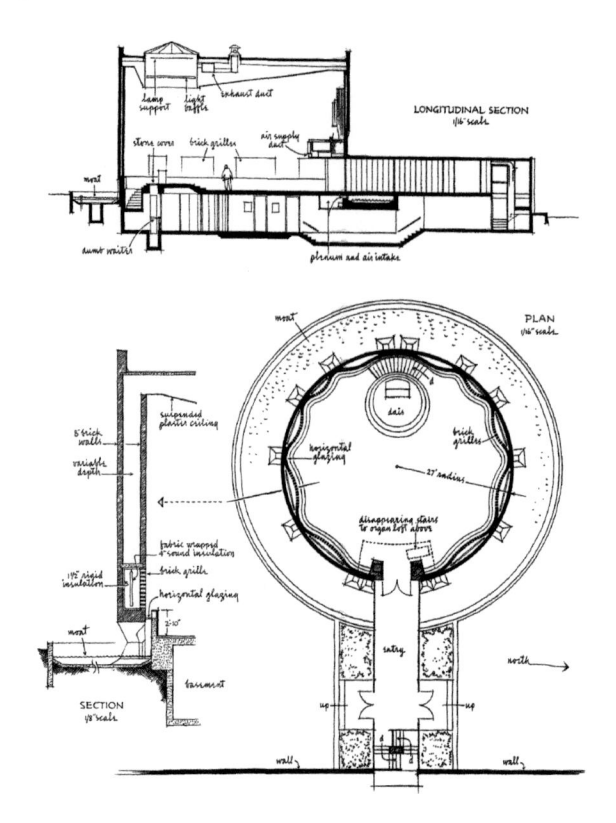

FIGURE 14.5 Kresge Chapel, MIT, main floor plan, wall section, and longitudinal section.

From *Progressive Architecture* 37, no. 1 (January 1956): 67. Courtesy of Kevin Roche John Dinkeloo and Associates LLC.

west side as well, but as built the chapel is treeless on that side facing Kresge Auditorium.[56] One must enter the narthex up steps on its north or south side at a distance from the circular interior, so that the experience of entering the main dimmed space is attenuated relative to the daylit campus. It creates a passage from the mundane to the sacred (Fig. 14.5). The rectangular corridor-like narthex is 34 ft. 5 in. long (less than the chapel's 54 ft. 4 in. diameter), and lined with bluish-gray variably translucent stained glass. Saarinen designed different glass patterns on the south and north sides (Fig. 14.6). He saw the connection between the narthex and chapel as clumsy, yet the narthex is effective as an intermediate space.[57]

The chapel's brick exterior and interior walls recalled Aalto's Baker House, MIT's first post-war dormitory, named for Rev. Baker, who died in 1950. For the chapel, Saarinen chose a richly varied pattern of New England water-struck brick with a smooth, dense surface (Fig. 14.7). Every fourth course is a header course, as a variation on an American or common bond. This brick's high firing temperature gave it great strength and durability but also irregular shapes and colors ranging from black through shades of red, which are mixed in the wall above the 13 arches around the base. The faceted bricks are laid at irregular and varied angles with deeply recessed mortar joints, and some bricks project to enrich the wall's relief and play of light and shadow (Fig. 14.7). The chapel's inner undulating and outer cylindrical 8-inch-thick brick walls are a load-bearing, steel-reinforced structure just over 32 feet high. Aalto had also used brick for curved load-bearing structural walls outside Baker House's reinforced concrete frame.[58] The curvatures of the chapel's brick inner walls gave

FIGURE 14.6 Kresge Chapel, MIT, narthex looking west into chapel.

Photograph © Ezra Stoller/Esto, id no. 109Q.005, 1955.

FIGURE 14.7 Kresge Chapel, MIT, exterior looking east, showing brick arches set in moat around base and spire and bell tower by Alexander Roszak.

Photograph © Ezra Stoller/Esto, id no. 109Q.010, 1955.

lateral structural support to the tall outer walls, and the double wall presumably assisted with the interior's acoustic and thermal isolation. For Saarinen "It seemed right to use a traditional material, such as brick, for the chapel—for brick would be a contrast to the auditorium and yet the same material as the surrounding dormitories."[59]

The interior wall curves so that its surface turns from convex to concave relative to the central space (Fig. 14.5). The undulations decrease in width from the rear entrance toward the frontal altar, where they increase again to either side behind the altar. The spacing of the piers and arches supporting the walls follows the same dimensions. The arches on the outside occur where the exterior wall and the undulating interior wall meet (Fig. 14.5). Saarinen observed: "the concept of the windowless cylinder . . . implied the self-contained, inward-feeling which was desirable for a chapel of this kind."[60] The 13 arches have spans and shapes that vary from broadly segmental to narrowly stilted (Fig. 14.7). Saarinen regretted that they were as not as sculpturally three-dimensional as the archivolts of Romanesque churches.[61] The arches rest on polished red granite bases set in a circular moat of water some 2 feet deep and 12 feet wide, so the moat's overall diameter is about 75 feet. The water's glittering reflections are one source of natural light inside the chapel, brought in through horizontal glass plates between the inner curved brick walls and the wainscoting of oak-groove paneling (Figs. 14.8, 14.9). Reinhold Martin observed: "The effect is a double pulsation: The undulating walls rhythmically blocking and revealing the indirect lighting, and the gentle movement of the water itself."[62] The only other source of natural light is the circular oculus set in the depth of the trussed roof above the frontal altar. The effect of the two sources of changing natural light in the dim space is mystical and evocative, following traditional religious architecture.

FIGURE 14.8 Kresge Chapel, MIT, interior showing horizontal glass between inner wainscoting and inner undulating brick wall.

Photograph © Ezra Stoller/Esto, id no. 109Q.009, 1955.

The altar and its sculpture

A richly veined white marble altar stands 3 feet high atop the rear of a three-stepped circular base of white travertine about 15 feet in diameter (Fig. 14.1). The marble altar alludes to the immovable altars of Roman Catholic churches as well as some Protestant churches.

A rendering of the chapel published in MIT's alumni journal, *Technology Review*, in June 1952 showed the altar topped by a tall cross as in Protestant churches. However, there is no crucifix or other fixed specific religious icon atop the table. Liturgical objects appropriate to Protestant, Roman Catholic, and Jewish services were (and still are) kept in a "sacristy" or "robing room" on a lower floor beneath the altar and lifted by a small elevator to be placed on the altar for services. Vestments were stored in this lower room.[63] There is also a curving staircase from this lower level behind the altar's base. As in a Protestant church, an angled lectern stands to the right as one faces the altar, and a curved pulpit on the left, both designed by Saarinen. The altar-like block, lectern, and pulpit lacked specific liturgical symbols, which was consistent with MIT's original guidelines for the chapel developed in July 1950, before Saarinen was hired.[64] In this way, Saarinen's architecture captured the conceptual paradox inherent in the program for a chapel envisioned by Unitarian administrators who aspired to a nondenominational ideal.

The three circular travertine steps toward the altar are not concentric; rather, they step back so that the step treads are widest toward the front facing the seating, making the ascent to the table more inviting from that direction (Figs. 14.1, 14.5). The dark gray-green ceiling descends from the room's periphery to the oculus's 12-foot-diameter circular steel frame. The oculus's deep honeycomb funnels the natural light directly down on the altar. Downward-directed lamps above the honeycomb also shine on the whitish altar and its stepped base, giving them a reflective glow. Saarinen wrote, "the atmosphere of spiritual otherworldliness would also be conveyed by the light."[65] One observer wrote:

> With only a minimal amount of artificial lighting, the interior of the chapel is quite dimly lit even on the brightest day. This heightens the effect of the shimmering reflections on the walls and focuses attention on the altar lit from above.[66]

Behind the altar, sculptor Harry Bertoia, who had worked with the Saarinens at Cranbrook from 1939, designed a screen made of small highly reflective brass plates suspended on vertical steel wires. Bertoia worked on interior sculptures as screens of small glittering pieces of sheet metal fastened to wires both in Saarinen's General Motors Technical Center in Warren, Michigan, in 1953, and in Skidmore Owings and Merrill's Manufacturers Hanover Trust Company's headquarters in New York City, in 1954.[67] Espousing a modernist aesthetic, he said of his work: "In the sculpture I am concerned primarily with space, form, and the characteristics of metal." Like his chair designs of the same period, the sculptures "are mostly made of air . . . Space passes right through them."[68] He valued this concept:

> In the sculpture you have one kind of metal rod, or nails welded and braised together, and that is the horizontal support. It is very clear, there is no confusion. The sheet metal pieces act only vertically—they are held in place by the [horizontal] rods.[69]

The opposite relationship obtains in the reredos-like screen that Bertoia created for the MIT Chapel. The sculpture is made of 24 vertical metal cords spaced equidistantly in an arc that follows the curvature of the second travertine step behind the altar. The cords stretch down from within the circular reveal of the oculus, where their points of attachment are obscured against the honeycomb's glare, suggesting the transition from the earthly to the celestial. During the installation, Bertoia could tell when the cords were tight enough by the sounds they made if plucked.[70] Along the cords are small, textured, flat, rectangular brass cross-plates, as well as a number of open rectangles and triangles made of wire. They are welded to the taut vertical cords at different angles to variably reflect the descending light. Also, they are fastened to the cords near their centers, not along their outer edges, so that the plates appear to float freely in space on either side of each cord (Fig. 14.1). Bertoia had sought to realize "the floating-in-space idea" in his sculpture and furniture.[71] The reflections off his screen change during the day and the seasons.[72] The observer in the chapel does not see the source of either the constantly varying reflected light from below around the walls or the continuously changing light from above, due to the depth of the oculus relative to the chapel's roof. Although the oculus can be found in historic structures at least as far as back as Rome from the first century C.E., Saarinen sought a transcendent effect from above through reference to phenomena in nature:

> I have always remembered one night on my travels as a student when I sat in a mountain village in Sparta. There was bright moonlight over head and there was a soft, hushed secondary light around the horizon. That sort of bilateral lighting seemed best to achieve this other-worldly sense. Thus, the central light would come from above the altar—dramatized by the shimmering golden screen by Harry Bertoia—and the secondary light would be reflected up from the surrounding moat through the arches.[73]

The 768-pipe organ designed by Walter Holtkamp is also lit from above. Its wood and metal piping, carefully scaled to the room, complements Bertoia's screen opposite (Fig. 14.10). Organ pipes and altar screen reflect daylight from above, connoting the transcendent beyond the walls.

The MIT Chapel's building systems

In addition to lighting, Saarinen incorporated a scientific approach to acoustics. He observed: "The interior wall was curved, both for acoustical reasons, and to give the space a lack of sharp definition and an increased sense of turning inward."[74] MIT Professor Robert Newman, of the acoustic consulting firm of Bolt, Beranek and Newman, explained: "there should be audible reverberation [for both speech and music] consistent with brick as a hard and therefore sound-reflecting material."[75] On the other hand, "it should not be so reverberant that speech and music could not be heard clearly and distinctly."[76] Newman wrote:

> Had the walls been built to conform with the circular shape of the exterior, there would have been serious concentrations of sound in various parts of the room. The walls were "broken up" with undulations of varying size to minimize these focusing effects.[77]

The interior became a "rotunda for the eye, but not for the ear."[78] The other major factor was that

> The audience itself is the chief contributor to the sound-absorbing treatment of the Chapel but, in order to give some control of reverberation even when no audience is present and to bring the reverberation time down to a reasonable value for all types of

services, we introduced sound absorbing material into certain of the lower wall areas [behind the perforated brick].[79]

As shown in the section, this consisted of 4-inch-thick insulating vertical sheets hung in the cavities behind the perforated brick, which partly absorb and partly disperse sound reflecting off these curving walls (Fig. 14.9). Above this level, the non-perforated brick allows desirable reverberation for organ music.

Below the undulating brick walls all around the room is a wainscoting or dado of ¾-inch-thick vertical oak boards that screens the horizontal glass where reflected light enters from the moat (Figs. 14.8, 14.9). This dado around the chapel's periphery also serves to partly absorb and partly reflect sound, like the hard plaster ceiling, which also "gives no trouble, since it is an inverted cone which spreads rather than concentrates the sound."[80] The ceiling and upper brick walls were not acoustically treated, so that the organ, whose loft is at the chapel's rear above the entrance door, emits sounds well supported by reverberation in the upper half of the room.[81] The overall acoustic effect is one of isolation from the outdoors, consistent with the overall sense of visual enclosure created by the cylindrical brick walls.

Another element designed not to distract from the chapel's contemplative emphasis and traditional aura is the heating and ventilating equipment. The air-supply duct is located at the

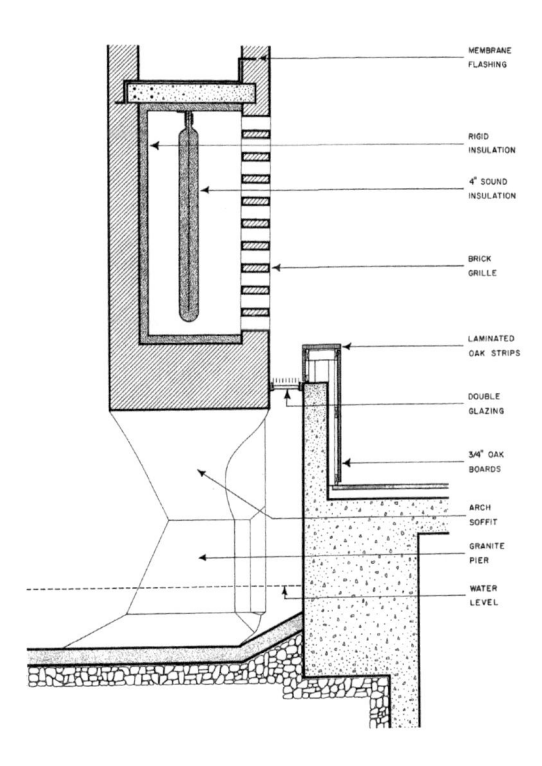

FIGURE 14.9 Kresge Chapel, MIT, wall section showing sound insulation behind brick grilles, above horizontal double glass and moat.

From *Architectural Record* 119, no. 1 (January 1956): 157. Courtesy of Kevin Roche John Dinkeloo and Associates LLC.

base of the organ loft over the chapel's entrance, and the exhaust duct is through the circular oculus, so it is not separately visible. Thus a worshipper sees no modern heating or ventilating elements, nor did they originally hear built-in electronic sound amplification.

A symbol of a chapel

Saarinen said:

> Since this is, uniquely, a nondenominational chapel, it is essential to create an atmosphere which was not derived from a particular religion, but from basic spiritual feelings. A dark interior seemed right—an interior completely separated from the outside world (to which the narthex passage would serve as a sort of decompression chamber).[82]

He also wrote: "I think we managed to make it a place where an individual can contemplate things larger than himself."[83] Still, some claim that the chapel's circular form and skylit interior evoke associations with ancient temples at least as far back as the Roman temple of Vesta at Tivoli (c. 80 B.C.E.), and with even more archaic sources.[84] Consistent with the emphasis on the individual and the inclusion of all faiths, the chapel does not have pews but rather six rows of ladder-backed, rush-seated wood chairs, called "cathedral chairs," angled toward the frontal altar on either side of a central aisle from the rear door (Fig. 14.10).[85] Even though Saarinen was a major designer of modernist chairs, here he designed the chairs as variations on traditional ones. The chairs remind some observers of Shaker furniture, but they were of a type created in sets for the naves of cathedrals, such as those in England during the Victorian period.[86] Thus, although they are not specifically religious symbols, the chairs derive from those in traditional Christian churches.

FIGURE 14.10 Kresge Chapel, MIT, interior looking back toward entrance, showing cathedral chairs, and organ loft, with travertine steps, altar, and screen in foreground.

Photograph © Ezra Stoller/Esto, id no. 109Q.008, 1955.

The floor has cream-colored Roman travertine plates set on a diamond pattern relative to the axis of entrance and altar. The travertine of the floor merges visually with that of the circular steps leading up to the ceremonial altar table. As a type of stone, the travertine carries classical, and specifically Roman, associations.

While the interior is bare of religious icons, the exterior element that signifies the chapel's religious purpose is the spired cast aluminum bell tower, which like the interior alludes to an historic Christian motif, but is sufficiently abstract as to be open to interpretation. Saarinen designed its general form, but the final version was the work of the sculptor Theodore Roszak, his first major architectural commission (Fig. 14.7).[87] The 1,300-pound bell was cast in MIT's own foundry.[88] The raising of this "spire" and its bell in December 1955 marked the chapel's completion. At 45 feet high, this sculpture is much taller than the chapel rotunda itself, and significantly increases its scale. Saarinen's collaboration with the artist was similar to his relationship to Bertoia. The architect produced an idea for a sculptural element that was consistent with his overall vision for the building, and the sculptor had freedom of interpretation.[89] Roszak made at least forty preparatory drawings of variations on the final motif.[90] In November 1955, as it was being completed, he wrote that the bell tower and spire were "basically 'gothic'" and were "a simplified version of the gargoyle" as an exterior sculptural convention of medieval cathedrals.[91] The spire's three vertical lines represented the three religious traditions that shared the chapel. He explained that its form referred both to "the symbol of the trinity as well as the recurrent forms of the two superimposed triangles in the 'Star of David.'"[92] Of such collaborations, Saarinen said: "the artist . . . brings to the building the special sensitivity that he has."[93] Like other elements of the chapel's architecture, the bell tower alludes to traditional symbols without reproducing them.

Conclusion

The MIT Chapel was widely acclaimed as one of the most extraordinary American religious buildings of its period, due to its interior that evokes a special spiritual experience for all. Though Saarinen was critical of some details, he was pleased with the interior: "It has captured just the right spirit that we intended it to."[94]

Like his older contemporaries such as Pietro Belluschi, Saarinen was acutely sensitive to the historical and cultural challenges of modern religious buildings. He said

> religion today does not have the expanding optimism of the past and is sustained during this nonreligious period by the force of its traditions. In such a soil, new forms don't grow. Therefore, religious architecture as we find it today depends either on traditional forms—or else, on forms developed in residential and other architecture.[95]

Though a modernist architect, he was convinced that a religious building had to be timeless. In this spirit, the dancing light reflected into the chapel's walls from the surrounding moat brought to mind grottoes accessed by water, such as those on the Island of Capri in Italy.[96] The interior effects thus managed to bridge between the romantically naturalistic and the religiously conventional, with the space's central image of an elevated altar lit from above. As such, its details and furnishings alluded to older worship spaces.

However, the sanctuary was designed as nondenominational, and its aim was to evoke a spiritual response without invoking historical forms tied to specific religions. One editor commented after the chapel opened the architect, in effect, was asked to resolve differences historically unresolvable in terms of architectural space and form. The resolution has been made in terms of the least common denominator, and in this moated, windowless structure of simple shape, the high sense of removal and calm necessary to meditation has been achieved.[97]

Later in the 1980s, one observer wrote: "With no specific iconography to interfere, one is left to contemplate one's own beliefs."[98] Saarinen balanced collective memory of tradition and non-historical spirituality, which was the chapel's core purpose. He said: "A building has to have an overall concept which is, in a sense, a design philosophy, a design religion, we might call it, which filters down to every little detail."[99] Sitting in the chapel, one feels that every detail—from the marble steps to the skylight's honeycomb—was considered for its contribution to the overall architectural effect. The central issue that Saarinen explored—the appropriate expressive use of new building methods for devotional space—is one that transcended denominational and national cultures. Most important was the elemental spiritual effect created by the architecture.

He was clearly proud of the chapel's overall effect as having met the extraordinary challenge that MIT had tried to articulate. At his death in 1961 at age 51, the Saarinen family conducted the memorial service for the architect in this chapel, which, along with the auditorium, had been Saarinen's first completed building when it was dedicated in June 1955.[100]

Acknowledgments

I thank Professor Anat Geva, Texas A&M University, for her astute editing of this chapter, and my wife, Professor Susanne Fusso, Wesleyan University, for her meticulous reading.

Notes

1 Killian chaired the Standing Committee of Wellesley's Unitarian Church and served on the Board of Directors and as Moderator of the American Unitarian Association, where Baker was Vice President (1937–42). See www.harvardsquarelibrary.org/biographies/james-r-killian-jr-2/ (accessed February 15, 2018), and *Everett Moore Baker* (New York, NY: privately printed, 1951).

2 Margaret M. Grubiak, "Educating the Moral Scientist: The Chapels at I.I.T. and M.I.T.," *Arris: Journal of the Southeast Chapter of the Society of Architectural Historians* 18 (2007): 1–24; Reinhold Martin, "The MIT Chapel: An Interdiscursive History." In Arindam Dutta, ed., *A Second Modernism: MIT, Architecture, and the 'Techno-Social' Moment* (Cambridge, MA: SA+P Press and MIT Press, 2013), 72–105.

3 Grubiak, "Educating the Moral Scientist," *passim*; and Martin, "MIT Chapel," 76–77. See also Killian, "The Scientist in the Community, the Classroom, the Chapel," *Christian Register* 135 (January 1956): 10–11, 29–30.

4 James R. Killian, Jr., quoted in John Ely Burchard, ed., *Mid-Century: The Social Implications of Scientific Progress* (Cambridge, MA: MIT Press; New York, NY: John Wiley and Sons, 1949), 455. Quoted in Grubiak, "Educating the Moral Scientist," 7.

5 Grubiak, *White Elephants on Campus: The Decline of the University Chapel in America, 1920–1960* (Notre Dame, IN: University of Notre Dame Press, 2014), 99.

6 E. M. Baker, letter to James R. Killian (then Vice President of MIT), February 9, 1948, AC.0004 MIT Office of the President, 1930–1958 [hereafter AC.0004], box 131, folder 5, MIT Archives. Quoted in Chiara Baglione, "Eero Saarinen: Kresge Chapel, MIT, Cambridge, Massachusetts," *Domus* 74, no. 791 (July 2010): 5.

7 Baker, memorandum "Re: The Need for a Chapel Auditorium" to Killian, December 12, 1949, 1. AC.0004, box 131, folder 5, MIT Archives. Quoted in Grubiak, "White Elephants on Campus," 106, and Martin, "MIT Chapel," 91.

8 Ibid., 3.

9 Marian C. Donnelly, *The New England Meeting Houses of the Seventeenth Century* (Middletown, CT: Wesleyan University Press, 1968); and Peter Benes, *Meetinghouses of Early New England* (Amherst, MA: University of Massachusetts Press, 2012).

10 Gretchen Buggeln, "New England Orthodoxy and the Language of the Sacred." In Louis P. Nelson, ed., *American Sanctuary: Understanding Sacred Spaces* (Bloomington, IN: Indiana University Press, 2006), 17–36.

11 Joseph M. Siry, *Unity Temple: Frank Lloyd Wright and Architecture for Liberal Religion* (New York, NY: Cambridge University Press, 1996), esp. 51–59.

12 Massachusetts Institute of Technology News Service, "Full text of an address prepared by Dr. James R. Killian, Jr., President of the Massachusetts Institute of Technology, for delivery at the Dedication of the Kresge Auditorium and the MIT Chapel at 3:30 o'clock on Sunday afternoon, May 8," with annotations, AC.0004, box 131, folder 8, MIT Archives. Quoted in Grubiak, "Educating the Moral Scientist," 7.

13 Killian, "Our Religious Program, from President Killian's Report to members of the Corporation for the year ending October, 1954," in "President's Report Issue," *Massachusetts Institute of Technology Bulletin* 90, no. 2 (November 1954): 29–32, quoted in "The Trend of Affairs," *Technology Review* 57, no. 8 (June 1955): 426. Partly quoted in Grubiak, "Educating the Moral Scientist," 8.

14 Baker, "Baccalaureate Address, Dartmouth College, June 12, 1949," in *Everett Moore Baker* (New York, NY: privately printed, 1951), 103–104.

15 William R. Hutchison, *The Modernist Impulse in American Protestantism* (Cambridge, MA: Harvard University Press, 1976), 24–29; and Siry, *Unity Temple*, 202–203.

16 John Burchard, *Q.E.D.: M.I.T. in World War II* (New York, NY: John Wiley and Sons, 1948), 287, 289.

17 Killian, "Our Religious Program," quoted in "Trend of Affairs," 428. The inscription outside the door reads: "This building gives embodiment to the responsibility of the Massachusetts Institute of Technology to maintain an atmosphere of religious freedom wherein students may deepen their understanding of their own spiritual heritage, freely pursue their own religious interests, and worship God in their own way."

18 Ibid.

19 Max Abramovitz designed the chapels as built in 1955. See his account "An Unusual Design for Collegiate Religion," *Architectural Record* 119, no. 1 (January 1956): 151, 152.

20 "Application to the Kresge Foundation from the Massachusetts Institute of Technology ...," April 11, 1950, AC.0004, box 131, folder 12, MIT Archives. Quoted in Martin, "The MIT Chapel," 89.

21 Karl T. Compton to The Trustees, Kresge Foundation, April 11, 1950, 1, in "Application to the Kresge Foundation from the Massachusetts Institute of Technology ...," AC.0004, box 131, folder 12, MIT Archives. Quoted in Grubiak, *White Elephants on Campus*, 108.

22 "Enclosure to Application to the Kresge Foundation from the Massachusetts Institute of Technology (Statement of Background and Details)," April 11, 1950, 20. AC.0004, box 131, folder 12, MIT Archives.

23 Ibid.

24 "Application to the Kresge Foundation from the Massachusetts Institute of Technology," 1, AC.0004, box 131, folder 12, MIT Archives. Quoted in Martin, "MIT Chapel," 90.

25 "Enclosure to Application to the Kresge Foundation from the Massachusetts Institute of Technology (Statement of Background and Details)," April 11, 1950, 21. AC.0004, box 131, folder 12, MIT Archives.

26 News Service, Massachusetts Institute of Technology, "For Release in the Morning Papers of July 1, 1950," AC.0004, box 131, folder 12, MIT Archives. Quoted in Martin, "MIT Chapel," 91.

27 "Specifications for Auditorium-Chapel for MIT," July 17, 1950, AC 4, box 131, folder 5, MIT Archives.

28 Meredith L. Clausen, *Pietro Belluschi: Modern American Architect* (Cambridge, MA: MIT Press, 1994), 205.

29 Meredith L. Clausen, *Spiritual Space: The Religious Architecture of Pietro Belluschi* (Seattle, WA: University of Washington Press, 1992).

30 Killian to Robert M. Kimball, October 3, 1950, AC.0004, box 131, folder 5, MIT Archives. Quoted in Martin, "MIT Chapel," 93.

31 Ibid.

32 "Saarinen Challenges the Rectangle," *Architectural Forum* 98, no. 1 (January 1953): 127.

33 Killian, "The Acceptance Address," *Technology Review* 57, no. 8 (June 1955): 402.

34 "Saarinen Challenges the Rectangle," 126–133.

35 In 1938 Bosworth proposed a neoclassical chapel. Mark Jarzombek, *Designing MIT: Bosworth's New Tech* (Boston, MA: Northeastern University Press, 2004), 112; and Grubiak, *White Elephants on Campus*, 100–102.

36 "Saarinen Challenges the Rectangle," 127; and Grubiak, *White Elephants on Campus*, 108.

37 Ibid.

38 Baglione, "Eero Saarinen," 11, and 15, n29.

39 Grubiak, "Educating the Moral Scientist," 1–2.

40 Albert Christ-Janer, *Eliel Saarinen: Finnish-American Architect and Educator* (Chicago, IL: University of Chicago Press, 1979).

41 "National Council Selects Outstanding Modern Churches," *Architectural Record* 120, no. 1 (July 1956): 10–12.

42 "Christ Church," *Architectural Forum* 93, no. 1 (July 1950): 80–85; and Ozayr Saloojee, "The Next Largest Thing: The Spatial Dimensions of Liturgy in Eliel and Eero Saarinen's Christ Church Lutheran, Minneapolis," *Nexus Network Journal* 12 (2010): 213–237.

43 Undated typescript of remarks by Eero Saarinen on the work of Ludwig Mies van der Rohe, 3–4, box 28, folder 117, Eero Saarinen Collection, MS 593, Yale University, Manuscripts and Archives. Quoted in Martin, "MIT Chapel," 103.

44 "National Council Selects Outstanding Modern Churches," 10–12.

45 Eero Saarinen, quoted in "Saarinen Challenges the Rectangle," 127. See Jennifer Komar Olivarez, "Churches and Chapels." In Eeva-Liisa Pelkonen and Donald Albrecht, eds. *Eero Saarinen: Shaping the Future* (New Haven, CT: Yale University Press, 2006), 266–275; and Baglione, "Eero Saarinen," 13.

46 Killian, letter to R. M. Kimball, October 3, 1950, as in note 30. Quoted in Grubiak, "Educating the Moral Scientist," 8; and Grubiak, *White Elephants on Campus*, 111.

47 Ibid.

48 Baglione, "Eero Saarinen," 11, 14. On Mies' IIT chapel, see Grubiak, "Educating the Moral Scientist," 3–6; "Churches," *Architectural Forum* 91, no. 6 (December 1949): 61; "Ludwig Mies van der Rohe Designs a Chapel," *Architectural Record* 112, no. 6 (December 1952): 26; and "A Chapel: Robert F. Carr Memorial Chapel of St. Saviour, Illinois Institute of Technology," *Arts and Architecture* 70, no. 1 (January 1953): 18–19.

49 Grubiak, "Educating the Moral Scientist," 3–4.

50 Saarinen, quoted in "Buildings in the Round," *Architectural Forum* 104, no. 1 (January 1956): 119.

51 Ibid.

52 On Saarinen and Nowicki, see Olivarez, "Churches and Chapels," in Pelkonen and Albrecht, eds., *Eero Saarinen*, 269–270; and Baglione, "Eero Saarinen," 13.

53 "Student Religious Center Based on Synagogue," *Architectural Record* 103, no. 6 (June 1948): 138–140; and "Building Types Study No. 199: College Buildings," *Architectural Record* 113, no. 6 (June 1953): 140–142.

54 The earliest publication was "Saarinen Challenges the Rectangle." Dated working drawings for the MIT Chapel (Job 5303) are in the Eero Saarinen Collection, MS 593, box 214, Yale University, Manuscripts and Archives.

55 Saarinen, quoted in Technology Review Staff, "Structures—Spherical and Cylindrical," *Technology Review* 57, no. 8 (June 1955): 399.

56 Ibid., 392; and Olivarez, "Churches and Chapels," 270.

57 Saarinen, "M.I.T. Auditorium and Chapel, Cambridge, Massachusetts, 1950–1955." In Aline B. Saarinen, ed., *Eero Saarinen on His Work* (New Haven, CT and London: Yale University Press, 1962), 36.

58 Lawrence W. Speck, "Baker House and the Modern Notion of Functionalism." In Stanford Anderson, Gail Fenske, and David Fixler, eds., *Aalto and America* (New Haven, CT and London: Yale University Press, 2012), 196.

59 Saarinen, "M.I.T. Auditorium and Chapel," 36.

60 Saarinen, quoted in "Trend of Affairs," 387.

61 Saarinen, "M.I.T. Auditorium and Chapel," 36.

62 Martin, "MIT Chapel," 101.

63 Georges Benoit-Levy, "Églises modernes aux États-unis; The MIT Chapel à Cambridge (Massachusetts)," *La Construction Moderne* 73 (January 1957): 35.

64 "Specifications for Auditorium-Chapel for MIT," as in note 27.

65 Saarinen, quoted in "Trend of Affairs," 387–388.

66 Thompson S. Lingel, "Eero Saarinen at the MIT, Cambridge," *Ottagono* 89 (June 1988): 83.

67 "Metal Sculpture—Harry Bertoia," *Arts and Architecture* 72, no. 1 (January 1955): 18–19.

68 Bertoia, quoted in "Pure Design Research," *Architectural Forum* 97, no. 1 (January 1952): 145.

69 Ibid., 146.

70 Celia Bertoia, *The Life and Work of Harry Bertoia: The Man, The Artist, the Visionary* (Atglen, PA: Schiffer Publishing, 2015), 105.

71 Bertoia, quoted in "Pure Design Research," 146.

72 June Kompass Nelson, *Harry Bertoia: Sculptor* (Detroit, MI: Wayne State University Press, 1970), 33.

73 Saarinen, "MIT Auditorium and Chapel," 36.

74 Ibid.

75 Robert Newman, quoted in "New Chapel at MIT," *Progressive Architecture* 37, no. 1 (January 1956): 66.

76 Ibid.

77 Ibid.

78 R. H. Bolt, "Designing the Acoustics of the MIT Chapel," *Robert Bradford Newman Student Award Funds Newsletter* 89, 2. Quoted in Baglione, "Eero Saarinen," 13.

79 Newman, quoted in "New Chapel at M.I.T.," 66.

80 Ibid.

81 "Buildings in the Round," 119.

82 Saarinen, "MIT Auditorium and Chapel," 36.

83 Ibid.

84 "Saarinen Challenges the Rectangle," 130. See Pia Panella, "Eero Saarinen's Massachusetts Institute of Technology Chapel: The Architectural Interpretation of Non-Denominational Space," M.A. thesis, University of Virginia, 2005, passim.

85 "Buildings in the Round," 119.

86 John Brandler, "Cathedral Chairs," *Furniture History* 15 (1979): 68.

87 H. H. Arnason, *Theodore Roszak* (Minneapolis, MN: Walker Art Center, 1956), 16–17.

88 Sarah H. Wright, "Architectural Wonders, Chapel, Kresge, Turn 50," *MIT Tech Talk* 50, no. 5 (19 October 2005), 9.

89 Saarinen, "M.I.T. Auditorium and Chapel, Cambridge, Massachusetts, 1950–1955," 36.

90 Theodore Roszak: Working Drawings for MIT Bell Tower, MIT List Visual Arts Center, August 15, 2005–December 16, 2005. https://listart.mit.edu/exhibitions/theodore-roszak-working-drawings-mit-bell-tower (accessed November 22, 2017).

91 Theodore Roszak, letter to Francis E. Wylie, November 24, 1955, folder "MIT—Cambridge Campus, Building W15—Chapel—Written Material," General Collection, MIT Museum. Quoted in Grubiak, "Educating the Moral Scientist," 8; and Grubiak, "White Elephants on Campus," 115.

92 Ibid.

93 "Eero Saarinen," in John Peter, ed. *The Oral History of Modern Architecture; Interviews with the Greatest Architects of the Twentieth Century* (New York, NY: Harry N. Abrams, 1994), 194.

94 Saarinen, quoted in "Buildings in the Round," 119.

95 Saarinen, quoted in "Saarinen Challenges the Rectangle," 130.

96 Ibid.

97 "An Unusual Design for Collegiate Religion; Chapel: Interdenominational," *Architectural Record* 119, no. 1 (January 1956): 154–156.

98 Lingel, "Eero Saarinen at the MIT," 84. I felt this atmosphere when I went to the chapel for individual meditation while a graduate student at MIT (1980–84). Since then, when I seek a meditative focus, I still imagine myself in that space, as if the memory of it alone is enough to calm the spirit. In 2014–15, EYP Architects, Boston, directed an extensive rehabilitation of the Kresge Auditorium and MIT Chapel.

99 "Eero Saarinen," in Peter, ed., *Oral History of Modern Architecture*, 208.

100 Lingel, "Eero Saarinen at the MIT," 84.

References

Abramovitz, Max. "An Unusual Design for Collegiate Religion," *Architectural Record* 119, no. 1 (January 1956): 147–153.

Arnason, H. H. *Theodore Roszak* (Minneapolis, MN: Walker Art Center, 1956).

Baglione, Chiara. "Eero Saarinen: Kresge Chapel, MIT, Cambridge, Massachusetts," *Domus* 74, no. 791 (July 2010): 4–25.

Baker, Everett Moore. "Baccalaureate Address, Dartmouth College, June 12, 1949." In *Everett Moore Baker* (New York, NY: privately printed, 1951, 99–106).

Benes, Peter. *Meetinghouses of Early New England* (Amherst, MA: University of Massachusetts Press, 2012).

Benoit-Levy, Georges. "Églises modernes aux États-unis; The MIT Chapel à Cambridge (Massachusetts)," *La Construction Moderne* 73 (January 1957): 34–35.

Bertoia, Celia. *The Life and Work of Harry Bertoia: The Man, The Artist, the Visionary* (Atglen, PA: Schiffer Publishing, 2015).

Brandler, John. "Cathedral Chairs," *Furniture History* 15 (1979): 68.

Buggeln, Gretchen. "New England Orthodoxy and the Language of the Sacred." In Louis P. Nelson, ed., *American Sanctuary: Understanding Sacred Spaces*, 17–36 (Bloomington, IN: Indiana University Press, 2006).

"Buildings in the Round," *Architectural Forum* 104, no. 1 (January 1956): 116–121.

"Building Types Study no. 199: College Buildings, Two Campus Religious and Social Centers," *Architectural Record* 113, no. 6 (June 1953): 140–144.

Burchard, John. *Q.E.D.: M.I.T. in World War II* (New York, NY: John Wiley and Sons, 1948).

Burchard, John Ely, ed. *Mid-Century: The Social Implications of Scientific Progress* (Cambridge, MA: MIT and New York, NY: John Wiley and Sons, 1949).

"A Chapel: Robert F. Carr Memorial Chapel of St. Saviour, Illinois Institute of Technology," *Arts and Architecture* 70, no. 1 (January 1953): 18–19.

"Christ Church," *Architectural Forum* 93, no. 1 (July 1950): 80–85.

Christ-Janer, Albert. *Eliel Saarinen: Finnish-American Architect and Educator* (Chicago, IL: University of Chicago Press, 1979).

"Churches," *Architectural Forum* 91, no. 6 (December 1949): 57–73.

Clausen, Meredith L. *Pietro Belluschi: Modern American Architect* (Cambridge, MA: MIT Press, 1994).

———. *Spiritual Space: The Religious Architecture of Pietro Belluschi* (Seattle, WA: University of Washington Press, 1992).

Donnelly, Marian C. *The New England Meeting Houses of the Seventeenth Century* (Middletown, CT: Wesleyan University Press, 1968).

Grubiak, Margaret M. "Educating the Moral Scientist: The Chapels at I.I.T. and M.I.T.," *Arris: Journal of the Southeast Chapter of the Journal of the Society of Architectural Historians* 18 (2007): 1–24.

———. *White Elephants on Campus: The Decline of the University Chapel in America, 1920–1960* (Notre Dame, IN: University of Notre Dame Press, 2014).

Hutchison, William R. *The Modernist Impulse in American Protestantism* (Cambridge, MA: Harvard University Press, 1976).

Jarzombek, Mark, *Designing MIT: Bosworth's New Tech* (Boston, MA: Northeastern University Press, 2004).

Killian, James R. "The Acceptance Address," *Technology Review* 57, no. 8 (June 1955): 401–402.

———. "Our Religious Program, from President Killian's Report to members of the Corporation for the year ending October, 1954," in "President's Report Issue," *Massachusetts Institute of Technology Bulletin* 90, no. 2 (November 1954): 29–32, quoted in "The Trend of Affairs," *Technology Review* 57, no. 8 (June 1955): 385–390, 426, 428.

——— "The Scientist in the Community, the Classroom, the Chapel," *Christian Register* 135 (January 1956): 10–11, 29–30.

Lingel, Thompson S. "Eero Saarinen at the MIT, Cambridge," *Ottagono* 89 (June 1988): 80–85.

"Ludwig Mies van der Rohe Designs a Chapel," *Architectural Record* 112, no. 6 (December 1952): 26.

Martin, Reinhold. "The MIT Chapel: An Interdiscursive History." In Arindam Dutta, ed. *A Second Modernism: MIT, Architecture, and the 'Techno-Social' Moment*, 72–105 (Cambridge, MA: SA+P Press and MIT Press, 2013).

"Metal Sculpture—Harry Bertoia," *Arts and Architecture* 72, no. 1 (January 1955): 18–19.

"National Council Selects 'Outstanding' Modern Churches," *Architectural Record* 120, no. 1 (July 1956): 10–12.

Nelson, June Kompass. *Harry Bertoia: Sculptor* (Detroit, MI: Wayne State University Press, 1970).

"New Chapel at M.I.T.," *Progressive Architecture* 37, no. 1 (January 1956): 66–67.

Olivarez, Jennifer Komar. "Churches and Chapels." In Eeva-Liisa Pelkonen and Donald Albrecht, eds., *Eero Saarinen: Shaping the Future* (New Haven, CT: Yale University Press, 2006, 266–275).

Panella, Pia. "Eero Saarinen's Massachusetts Institute of Technology Chapel; The Architectural Interpretation of Non-Denominational Space," M.A. thesis, University of Virginia, 2005.

Peter, John. "Eero Saarinen." In John Peter, ed. *The Oral History of Modern Architecture; Interviews with the Greatest Architects of the Twentieth Century*, 192–211 (New York, NY: Harry N. Abrams, 1994).

"Pure Design Research," *Architectural Forum* 97, no. 1 (January 1952): 142–147.

Saarinen, Aline B., ed. *Eero Saarinen on His Work* (New Haven, CT and London: Yale University Press, 1962).

"Saarinen Challenges the Rectangle," *Architectural Forum* 98, no. 1 (January 1953): 126–133.

Saarinen, Eero. "M.I.T. Auditorium and Chapel, Cambridge, Massachusetts, 1950–1955" In Aline B. Saarinen, ed. *Eero Saarinen on His Work* (New Haven, CT and London: Yale University Press, 1962, 34–39).

Saloojee, Ozayr. "The Next Largest Thing: The Spatial Dimensions of Liturgy in Eliel and Eero Saarinen's Christ Church Lutheran, Minneapolis," *Nexus Network Journal* 12 (2010): 213–237.

Siry, Joseph M. *Unity Temple: Frank Lloyd Wright and Architecture for Liberal Religion* (New York, NY: Cambridge University Press, 1996).

Speck, Lawrence W. "Baker House and the Modern Notion of Functionalism." In Stanford Anderson, Gail Fenske, and David Fixler, eds., *Aalto and America*, 193–206 (New Haven, CT, and London: Yale University Press, 2012).

"Student Religious Center Based on Synagogue," *Architectural Record* 103, no. 6 (June 1948): 138–140.

Technology Review Staff, "Structures—Spherical and Cylindrical," *Technology Review* 57, no. 8 (June 1955): 391–400, 430, 432.

"An Unusual Design for Collegiate Religion; Chapel: Interdominational," *Architectural Record* 119, no. 1 (January 1956): 154–157.

Wright, Sarah H. "Architectural Wonders, Chapel, Kresge, Turn 50," *MIT Tech Talk*, 50, no. 5 (October 19, 2005).

EPILOGUE

Phillip James Tabb

The middle of the twentieth century marked an extraordinary moment in human history—in its wake was the devastation of World War II and the emergence of the Cold War, while in its immediate future was an era of unprecedented growth, economic security and material gain. Post-war Europe, the Soviet Union, and Japan focused on reconstruction, while in the United States there was vast prosperity, expansion, and maturation of the American Dream, which was the national ethos in which freedom included the opportunity for prosperity and success. To James Truslow Adams in 1931, the American Dream suggested that life should be better and richer and fuller for everyone, with opportunity for each according to ability or achievement regardless of social class or circumstances of birth.[1] According to the US Census Bureau, the decade of the 1950s saw an increase in population of nearly 30 million people.[2] The American Dream certainly accelerated through the cultural solidity of this time through the medium of modernism. Zygmunt Bauman referred to this phenomenon as "*solid modernity*," which is in dire contrast to our current contemporary condition of "*liquidity modernity*"[3]—the former having the characteristics of fixity, durability and predictability; and the latter with characteristics of globalization, changeability and uncertainty. For this mid-century modernity, American solidarity promoted stability, optimism, and confidence for an expanding "baby booming" culture. It was a denominational society in action solidifying normalcy, family values, and religion. And according to Gretchen Buggeln in *The Suburban Church: Modernism and Community in Post-war America*, "Thousands of churches, scattered throughout the American suburbs of the 1950s and 1960s, assert the vitality and reach of the post-war modern church movement."[4]

Architecture and city-making paralleled these trends in religion and, in fact, contributed to the modernists' agenda in significant ways. It was characterized by a break-away from historical forms and hierarchical structures of religious space, while promoting clear simplicity, abstraction, spatial openness, functionalism, serial production, new materiality, and a common language and doctrine.[5] Industrialized building methods forged a new building construction industry that was just beginning to be tapped.[6] Modern architecture was a perfect coupling with the emerging democratization of religious practices and forwarding denominational agendas, especially in America. Modern religious architecture minimized symbolism, de-emphasized liturgical programs. And according to David Ray Griffin in *Reenchantment without Supernaturalism*, the religious worldview focused on "naturalism" in lieu of metaphysical or supernatural references.[7] They sought to become authentic, optimistic, economically feasible and responsive to family values. The worship space designs shifted from the more formal axial historical forms to more centralized forms. The role of local building committees aided in creating space programs that supported these emerging faith communities. Building programs included religious spaces, fellowship halls, libraries, and Sunday schools. If the "family room" was the new addition to the American home, then the "fellowship hall" was its equal in ecclesiastical programs. The suburban churches were often sited on isolated plots of land surrounded by parking lots responding to generational mobility, and they propagated from New England to California.

Diversity, pluralism, and religious liberty had increasingly fragmented American religious life in seemingly positive ways. The suburban landscape provided a plethora of mass migration of new religious building programs across America.[8] Urban architecture was eclipsed by the constellating effect of the owner-occupied, single-family home, the introduction of car garages, all surrounded by a yard, and they were repeated in single-use neighborhoods outside the urban core.[9] This typology came to define everyday experience for most American households, and the religious culture followed with the emergence of the suburban church. Alison Smithson, in *Team 10 Primer* stated that the C.I.A.M. Congress of 1953 in Aix-en-Provence declared there was a life-style change with its symbol, the motor-car.[10] Smithson went on to say that this new lifestyle inhibited walking and that there is no longer a continuous experience of the city, but rather an interrupted series of isolated events [the suburbs]. To Delores Hayden in *A Field Guide to Sprawl*, the American landscape during the second half of the twentieth century was dominated by interstate highways and automobile-oriented buildings.[11] This shift certainly was an enabler for the proliferation of the suburban church in America, as the church and residential districts were inextricably linked by the need for easy access and convenient parking. Population increase, stabilized economy, religious diversity, suburban expansion, and the automobile created a modern systemic culture.

The Modern Movement in sacred architecture explored experiments that created different kinds of sacred experiences. At the beginning of the mid-century, two modern examples of architecture expressed quite different forms of sacred experience: an outward exhilarating and inspiring connection to the divine, and an inward, more contemplative, one focused on individual experience. The Roman Catholic chapel Notre Dame du Haut at Ronchamp, France and the Rothko Chapel in Houston, Texas exemplify these qualities.[12] The Chapel of Ronchamp is located on an isolated site outside of the small French town of Ronchamp. Designed by Le Corbusier in 1950 with construction completed in 1955, it is an abstract representation of the three Marian programs: the annunciation, the assumption, and the coronation.[13] Most often though, the chapel is described as an extraordinary expression of modernists' principles of light, plasticity of form and use of concrete. The exterior building shape soars and the interior south truncated window wall is an uplifting and inspiring composition in light. The interior is mystical and punctuated with constellations of sparkling star-like light (Fig. E.1). By contrast, Rothko Chapel is a non-denominational chapel located on an urban site in Houston, Texas, designed by Philip Johnson and Howard Barnstone, and constructed in 1971 (Fig. E.2). Its opaque orthogonal geometry houses 14 visual works of artist Mark Rothko. There are three walls with triptychs and five with single paintings. With no windows, the chapel was originally designed with a large eight-fold polygonal skylight above the main space, but since then the space has been fitted with a translucent shade protecting Rothko's paintings. Nevertheless, the experience is introverted and somber, peaceful and contemplative, yet is restoring and reflective. The centralized plan allows for either special events, meditations, or individual viewings of the Rothko paintings. The Chapel at Ronchamp is uplifting and full of light. The Rothko Chapel is inward and darker in nature. These are not differences of good and evil, but rather spiritual movement outward while the other is inward. (Figs. E.3, E.4)

Another rather unusual example was the Garden Grove Community Church in Orange County, California, founded by Robert H. Schuller in 1955. For six years thereafter, services were held in a drive-in theater.[14] Arguably, this was a radical departure from, and perhaps even an affront to mainstream sacred architecture. The efficiencies for this typology were obvious with entertainment technologies, easy access, parking for everyone, speakers for each of the car-confined congregants, and there was even a snack bar. This unusual worship experience gave way to the construction of the Crystal Cathedral, designed by

FIGURE E.1 Notre Dame du Haut Chapel at Ronchamp, France, exterior, 2007.
Photograph by the author.

FIGURE E.2 Rothko Chapel, Houston, Texas, exterior, 1971.
Photograph by Hickey-Robertson.

FIGURE E.3 Chapel at Ronchamp, interior, 2007.

Photograph by the author.

FIGURE E.4 Rothko Chapel, interior, 2015.

Photograph by Ben Doyle.

Philip Johnson and construction completed in 1980. The light-filled space was defined by 10,000 panes of glass and accommodated a congregation of 2,736 people.[15] Nevertheless, modern culture was changing. If the experience of the Chapel at Ronchamp was *inspiring*, and Rothko Chapel was *ensouling*, then Garden Grove Community Church was certainly *entertaining*, and a harbinger of the mega-churches of today.

The seminal works of sacred architecture at mid-century were primarily led with projects on university campuses where building programs were smaller in size, liturgical programs were typically generalized or even eliminated, the creation of pure space was possible, and prominent architects were the authors of these emerging designs.[16] The campus chapel was a perfect building typology through which to bring forward emerging doctrines of modernism. As illustrated by three chapters in this volume: the non-denominational Chapel of St. Saviour at the IIT campus in Chicago designed in 1952 by Mies van der Rohe was an ennobling attempt to express the purity of sacred space within a utilitarian setting.

Its virtues were proportion, simplicity, economy, and durability, as it was stripped of any ornament, symbols, or iconographic programs. In contrast was the Tuskegee University Chapel designed by Paul Rudolph and John Welch in 1958. This chapel was expressive, employing many of the modernists' design elements, influences by Frank Lloyd Wright on one hand and by Le Corbusier on the other. It includes a curved concrete roof, natural light streaming through diagonal-shaped stained glass windows, and a dynamic quality in interior space. The spiritual agenda and centrality of religious life was paramount. The third university chapel in the book is the M.I.T. Chapel, designed by Eero Saarinen. It responded to a nondenominational student community with the creation of an intimate scaled circular space.

Mid-century modernism provided signature architects with experimentation in regards to the challenges of architectonic, aesthetic, economic, and religious freedoms afforded by this modern era. The organic architectural legacy of Frank Lloyd Wright was still of influence in the early phases of the century and was evident and can be seen in the works of Herb Greene, Bruce Goff, and Fay Jones at mid-century. However, new themes emerged, and among the notable architects representing this modern era were: Mies van der Rohe and Walter Gropius with functionalism and rationalism, Philip Johnson and Edward Larrabee Barns with spatial generosity and boiled down neo-classicism, Le Corbusier and Paul Rudolf with an anti-bourgeois brutalism, and Eero Saarinen, Oscar Niemeyer, and Pietro Belluschi with plasticity of form and structural prowess. Sacred architecture was fertile ground for the experiments of this time.

Not all the modern examples of sacred architecture conformed to strictly modernist cardinal rules. Some chapters in this volume illustrate examples of a new kind of hybrid that blended modernism and historicism, including Eastern Orthodox and Byzantine congregations in particular. While Catholic churches used modernism to address changes in their faith that culminated in Vatican II, the American Lutheran church also enjoyed a progressive expression that was consistent with its tradition. This is described in the book's chapters about the Catholic Churches in suburban Los Angeles, the Lutheran churches designed by Texas architect Eugene Wukasch, and those designed by Lithuanian immigrant architects. While Wukasch integrated regional concerns with modernism, the Lithuanian community integrated vernacular architectural forms with modernist vocabulary that mixed glass and steel with iconic elements. At the center of this hybridity was an interest in forwarding religious identities while simultaneously salvaging certain roots yet maintaining a distance from an often-ambivalent past. These examples became a harbinger of the postmodern era—promoting subtlety, complexity, ambiguity, double-coding, and historicism—that followed a few decades later. Yet common to many of these divergent religious directions was the American church-goer—replete with weekly services, Sunday schools, Bible classes, vacation camps, church picnics, and potluck suppers.

Bold forms and a new palette of building materials led to imaginative expressions of modern sacred architecture. Advances in construction methods and building materials enabled new explorations in the creation of space and form. This was true for the utilization of concrete in various forms from reinforced and pre-stressed concrete to thin-shelled and waffle-type construction. The parabolic shape and conical section proved to be robust building forms, enabling expanding congregations and re-invigorating modern faith. By being both lightweight and efficient, the form was used to minimize materials and increase structural performance while also being capable of achieving impressive spans. The longer structural spans allowed for more monumental designs with unobstructed interior space accommodating either axial or centralized plans. The examples in the section about the parabola and concrete include St. Stephen's Lutheran Church in Northglenn, Colorado designed by Charles Haertlng; B'nai Amoona Synagogue designed by Eric Mendelsohn; Paul Rudolph's Christian Science Building, and St. Mary's Cathedral in San Francisco designed by Pietro Belluschi and Pier Luigi Nervi in the mid-1960s. These are all good examples of a union of concrete parabolic arches, while Paul Rudolf's Christian Science Building is an example of innovative use of concrete.

Denominational identity was occupying new territory in American religious architecture with the coexistence of pure modernism and selective historicism. The suburbs and university campuses were primary recipients of expansion and experimentation. Expansion of the suburbs provided the need for proximate connections to the re-invigoration worship and community building. The church was now within easy driving distance, with provision of ample parking for the automobile. University campuses provided student religious life. The challenge, of course, was the chapel's ability to adapt to such varying denominations and religious ministries. Modernism provided the solution with the creation of neutral spaces capable of flexibility towards interfaith settings and non-denominational functions. Common among the sacred places in other locations in the world was the idea that a sacred place was a storied place, and therefore, possessed special qualities of experience.[17] This was not so true of the American suburban churches, which were most often sited on inexpensive land nearby large residential developments with little redeeming spiritual qualities.[18] Many of the early churches were modeled after "A-frames," because of their aesthetic, economical, and symbolic form language.[19] However, as congregations grew and floor plan requirements enlarged, the architectural forms flattened and the gable roofs created awkward proportions. Churches were sitting targets for intellectual and religious criticism where they saw suburban complacency amidst post-war consumerism and convenient middle-class lifestyles as being so separated from the "ugly problems of the day."[20] Yet despite the often-uninspiring architecture, the spiritual life seemed to flourish through the function of the interiority of religious practices and the fellowship among the congregation members themselves.

Modernism provided an interrogation of the visual effects of ornament, symbolism, metaphysics, and interior expressions of liturgical programs in favor of interiority of rational family-oriented space. Some examples incorporated artifacts and artworks designed to contribute to religious services and faith rituals, and were imbued with transcendent qualities. Light and art-glass were an important source contributing to transcendent experiences. Father Marie-Alain Couturier connected liturgical matters with modern art. Together with Father Pie-Raymong Regamey, they edited *L'Art Sacré*, which influenced contemporary architects and incredible works such as Henri Matisse and the Vence Chapel of Chapelle du Rosaire; Le Corbusier and the Chapel of Notre Dame du Haut, and the Notre-Dame de Toute Grace du Plateau d'Assy.[21] They argued that a masterpiece of art would always be more effective than a religious work of lesser value. This new form of spiritual art was a break-away from literal religious representations and traditions to a new virtue of their revelatory, revitalizing and contemplative capacities.

The general idea for this revolution in liturgical art was the introduction of abstract and provocative expressions of living art into religious architecture. As discussed in the book's last section on interior and liturgical fittings, the introduction and emphasis upon visible technical innovations were among the effects. The spatially active sanctuary walls of Unitarian churches provided modern compositions with the play of light reflecting the humanist values of the denomination. Art was not only confined to a certain faith. As shown in the book, various houses of worship in Baltimore, for example, incorporated art as part of their modernist design. The non-denominations chapel at the MIT campus by Eero Saarinen demonstrates the simple exterior is contrasted by the interior mystical quality and light that were meant to awaken spirituality.

Although not specifically examined in this book, the First Unitarian Church in Rochester, New York, built from 1962 to 1969 and designed by Louis I. Kahn, followed similar modernist principles, yet it responded to traditional Unitarian values. It had a complex building program promoting community, learning, thought, questioning, and discovery. It was constructed with brick, concrete block, and cast-in-place concrete that gave the buildings a massive presence. Yet, the sanctuary, being in the center of the building, was made of concrete and directed natural light into the space through four light towers situated at each corner of the sanctuary. The towers act as filters that saturate the sanctuary throughout the day constantly changing the perceptive qualities of the space even as the seasons change.[22] Both Kresge Chapel and the First Unitarian Church are examples of the focus on the interiority of sacred experience characteristic at this time.

In retrospect, this mid-twentieth century moment framed catalytic momentum for modern architectural development and accelerated expansion of religious building. This created new interests in the relationship between architectural form and function, and the relationship between sacred space and experience. This period in history reflected an amazing confluence of cultural, religious, and architectural change. Arguably, these relationships led to a pluralistic and many-voiced discourse that informed modern sacred architecture. We must remember that with the guidance of many wonderful seminal works of architecture as discussed in this book, there was an enormous propensity and hegemony of ordinary or everyday architecture. This was never more evident than with the proliferation of suburban churches across America. Their demeanor was comfortable and affordable, accessible and genuine, and was modest and innocent.[23] And certainly for the more celebrated works of sacred architecture at this time, they were a source of inspiration and shared optimism.

Notes

1 James Truslow Adams, *The Epic of America*, 1st edn. (Bethesda, MD: Simon Publications, 2001).
2 The United States Census 1940–2000, www.census.gov/newsroom/cspan/1940census/CSPAN_1940slides.pdf (accessed March 15, 2018).
3 Zygmunt Bauman, *Liquid Modernity* (Cambridge, UK: Polity Press, 2012), 2–3.
4 Gretchen Buggeln, *The Suburban Church: Modernism and Community in Post-war America* (Minneapolis, MN: University of Minnesota Press, 2015), 29.
5 William J. R. Curtiss, *Modern Architecture Since 1900* (London: Phaidon Press Limited, 1996), 395.
6 Alison Smithson, ed. *Team 10 Primer* (Cambridge, MA, MIT Press, 1968), 6–8.
7 David Ray Griffin, *Reenchantment without Supernaturalism: A Process Philosophy of Religion* (Ithaca, NY: Cornell University Press, 2001), 21–31.
8 Buggeln, *The Suburban Church*, xxi.
9 Phillip James Tabb and Senem Deviren, *The Greening of Architecture: A Critical History and Survey of Contemporary Sustainable Architecture and Urban Design* (London: Ashgate Publishing Limited, 2013), 26–28.
10 Smithson, *Team 10 Primer*, 8.
11 Delores Hayden, *A Field Guide to Sprawl* (New York, NY: W.W. Horton & Company, Inc., 2004), 8.

12 Phillip Tabb, *Semantic Cosmologies of the Ronchamp and Rothko Chapels* (Houston, TX: Image of the Not-Seen: Search for Understanding, The Rothko Chapel Art Series, 2005), 809–899.

13 Robert Coombs, *Mystical Themes in Le Corbusier's Architecture in the Chapel Notre Dame du Haut at Ronchamp* (Lewiston, NY: Edwin Mellen Press, 2000), 150–152.

14 Garden Grove Community Church, https://en.wikipedia.org/wiki/Crystal_Cathedral (accessed March 18, 2018).

15 Tabb and Deviren *The Greening of Architecture*, 70–71.

16 Margaret M. Grubiak, "Educating the Moral Scientist: The Chapels at I.I.T. and M.I.T.," *Arris: Journal of the Southeast Chapter of the Society of Architectural Historians* 18 (2007): 1–24.

17 Belden Lane, *Landscapes of the Sacred: Geography and Narrative in American Spirituality* (Baltimore, MD: John Hopkins University Press, 2002), 16.

18 Ibid.

19 Buggeln, *The Suburban Church*, 85.

20 Jane Yong Kim, "The Quietly Dangerous Suburban Church," *The New Republic*, https://newrepublic.com/article/126778/quietly-dangerous-suburban-church (accessed March 14, 2018).

21 *L'Art Sacré*, https://en.wikipedia.org/wiki/Ateliers_d%27Art_Sacré (accessed March 6, 2018).

22 David B Brownlee and David G. De Long, *Kahn: In the Realm of Architecture* (New York, NY: Universe Publishing, 1997), 83–85.

23 Steven Harris and Deborah Berke, eds., *Architecture of the Everyday*, (New York, NY: Princeton University Press, 1997), 216–222.

References

Adams, James Truslow. *The Epic of America*, 1st edn. (Bethesda, MD: Simon Publications, 2001).

Bauman, Zygmunt. *Liquid Modernity* (Cambridge, UK: Polity Press, 2012).

Brownlee, David B. and David G. De Long. *Kahn: In the Realm of Architecture* (New York, NY: Universe Publishing, 1997).

Buggeln, Gretchen. *The Suburban Church: Modernism and Community in Post-war America* (Minneapolis, MN: University of Minnesota Press, 2015).

Coombs Robert. *Mystical Themes in Le Corbusier's Architecture in the Chapel Notre Dame du Haut at Ronchamp* (Lewiston, NY: Edwin Mellen Press, 2000).

Curtiss, William J. R., *Modern Architecture Since 1900* (London: Phaidon Press Limited, 1996).

Harris, Steven and Deborah Berke, eds. *Architecture of the Everyday* (New York, NY: Princeton University Press, 1997).

Griffin, David Ray, *Reenchantment without Supernaturalism: A Process Philosophy of Religion* (Ithaca, NY: Cornell University Press, 2001).

Grubiak, Margaret M. "Educating the Moral Scientist: The Chapels at I.I.T. and M.I.T.," *Arris: Journal of the Southeast Chapter of the Society of Architectural Historians* 18 (2007): 1–24.

Hayden, Delores. *A Field Guide to Sprawl* (New York, NY: W.W. Horton & Company, Inc., 2004).

Kim, Jane Yong. "The Quietly Dangerous Suburban Church," *New Republic* (Accessed March 14, 2018). https://newrepublic.com/article/126778/quietly-dangerous-suburban-church.

Lane, Belden. *Landscapes of the Sacred: Geography and Narrative in American Spirituality* (Baltimore, MD: John Hopkins University Press, 2002).

L'Art Sacré. (Accessed March 6, 2018). https://en.wikipedia.org/wiki/Ateliers_d%27Art_Sacré.

Smithson, Alison, ed. *Team 10 Primer* (Cambridge, MA: MIT Press, 1968).

Tabb, Phillip. *Semantic Cosmologies of the Ronchamp and Rothko Chapels* (Houston, TX: Image of the Not-Seen: Search for Understanding, The Rothko Chapel Art Series, 2005).

——— and Senem Deviren. *The Greening of Architecture: A Critical History and Survey of Contemporary Sustainable Architecture and Urban Design* (London: Ashgate Publishing Limited, 2013).

United States Census 1940–2000. (Accessed March 15, 2018). www.census.gov/newsroom/cspan/1940census/CSPAN_1940slides.pdf.

INDEX